Mission and Business Philosophy

Mission and Business Philosophy

Winning Employee Commitment

Andrew Campbell and Kiran Tawadey

Heinemann Professional Publishing

Heinemann Professional Publishing Ltd
Halley Court, Jordan Hill, Oxford OX2 8EJ

OXFORD LONDON MELBOURNE AUCKLAND SINGAPORE
IBADAN NAIROBI GABORONE KINGSTON

First published 1990

British Library Cataloguing in Publication Data
Campbell, Andrew
    Mission and business philosophy: winning employee
        commitment.
    1. Organizations. Commitment of personnel
    I. Title II. Tawadey, Kiran
    302.35

ISBN 0 434 90314 0

Printed in Great Britain by
Billings Ltd of Worcester

Contents

Preface

In November 1987, the Research Committee of the newly formed Ashridge Strategic Management Centre enthusiastically approved a research proposal on mission and mission statements. The committee consisted of the chief planners of Britain's largest companies – BP, BOC, Courtaulds, ICI, Lloyds Bank, and United Biscuits.

At BP the central planning team had been asked to draft a mission and philosophy statement for the company. Courtaulds was at the time in the middle of a major effort to develop its corporate identity and to define something that managers were calling 'Courtauldsness'. At ICI, it had been decided to work on a philosophy statement that could be included in the annual report. And managers in United Biscuits were considering how their mission and philosophy should develop as the founder and chairman, Sir Hector Laing, drew near to retirement.

The research proposal had been sparked by the raising of certain questions by the managers of these companies. What should be in a mission statement? How long should it be? How do you prevent it from being just motherhood? Why have a statement at all? Is it useful? Who should it be written for? How should it be used? How can we avoid the problems that arose the last time we tried to articulate a company philosophy?

The first part of the research was to review the literature. To begin with we found no reference to the subject. The *Business Periodicals Index* had no entries on the subject of mission. A look through the last 10 years of the *Harvard Business Review* also failed to provide a reference. A longer search through the general management literature then turned up a chapter in Peter Drucker's book *Management: Tasks, Responsibilities and Practices*, in which he states: 'that business purpose and business mission are so rarely given adequate thought is perhaps the most important single cause of business frustration and failure'. He goes on to articulate what he believes should be the contents of a mission and purpose statement.

This general management literature search turned up similar references in books like *In Search of Excellence* by Peters and Waterman, *Theory Z* by William Ouchi, *Corporate Cultures* by Deal and Kennedy, and *A Behavioural Theory of the Firm* by Cyert and March. These consultants and academics were reinforcing Drucker's view that mission is important.

The importance of mission was further underlined by reading three books by famous businessmen: *A Business and its Beliefs* by Thomas Watson Jr of IBM, *Not for Bread Alone* by Konosuke Matsushita, founder of Matsushita Electric, and *Don't Ask the Price* by Marcus Sieff of Marks and Spencer. Each of these leaders emphasizes the importance of having a clear corporate philosophy to guide a business and its people.

We began to realize that having a clear philosophy, or as we labelled it 'having a sense of mission', is important. We also began to realize that having a sense of mission is not necessarily connected to having a mission statement. While some companies with a clear sense of mission also have mission statements (Hewlett-Packard and IBM being two famous examples), other companies with an equally strong sense of mission have no mission statements (Marks and Spencer and Egon Zehnder before 1986 were two companies we spoke to). Moreover there are many companies with mission statements that have no clear sense of mission.

At this point we switched our research focus from mission statements to a sense of mission and we broadened our literature search. We began looking at related fields of literature: motivation theory, leadership theory, culture and the management of change. In these fields the literature also emphasizes the importance of mission.

We had come to conclude that mission is central to the leadership task, is essential for gaining the maximum motivation from employees (especially as society becomes more affluent and people's basic needs are catered for) and is the starting point for defining the values that should underpin an organization's culture.

With this understanding we defined our field research to cover three areas. We collected mission statements from nearly 200 companies around the world. Many were from British companies, but we made sure that at least 40 per cent of our sample was from the rest of Europe, the USA and Japan. These statements were not all called mission statements. The titles varied enormously: 'Our Mission', 'Vision, Values and Philosophy', 'A Business Philosophy', 'The Five Principles of Mars', 'The ICL Way', 'The Character of the Company'. But they all aimed to describe the major philosophies of their organization.

We analysed these statements for content and we tried to understand why some of them seemed to speak to us about their companies specifically while others read like bland sentences that could have been used by any company. We subsequently compiled a report around these statements called 'Do you need a good mission statement?', published by the *Economist Publications*, 1990.

The second part of our research involved finding companies that we felt had a sense of mission and talking to them about it. We asked naive questions such as, 'Do you have a mission and what is it?' and we got replies that reinforced and gave clarity to much of what we had read in the literature.

We learnt that values are vital to organization unity, loyalty and motivation. Most managers are more attached to the organization's values than they are to its goals. Enthusiastic loyalty appears to exist when the organization's values are similar to the individual's values. Strategy and vision and medium term goals all take second place to values in the minds of the managers we spoke to.

We began to realize that mission is important because it is the link between strategy, organization values and employee values. It is the vehicle for linking the commercial-rational side of corporate life with the emotional-moral element that fuels the energy of human endeavour. Without this link there is no emotion and even the best strategy will make little progress.

Our third area of research focused on how mission can be managed. We identified four situations where companies had tried radically to change their mission. By documenting these cases we were able to extract commonalities and identify some general points about how leaders can actively manage the mission of their organizations. The detailed results of this research are summarized in a book called *A Sense of Mission*, Andrew Campbell, Marion Devine and David Young, Economist Books/Hutchinson, 1990.

This book is an attempt to pull together all that we have learnt in our two years of research. We came to realize that a sense of mission is essentially an emotional feeling by the people in the organization. An organization with a sense of mission has captured the emotional support of its people.

Chapter 1 summarizes what we learnt through our own field research. It defines our use of the term mission and explains why we believe this is a central concept in the management of organizations.

Chapters 2–6 describe what we have learnt from reading the research and commentary of other writers. At the beginning of each chapter we explain what is important about the pieces we have included and in front of each piece we have, where necessary, given an explanation of its context.

Finally in Chapter 7 we provide some advice to managers, students or consultants faced with the problem of writing a mission statement or assessing the quality of an existing statement. We have pulled together all we have learnt in the form of a questionnaire that has proved to be of use to practitioners.

Acknowledgements

Our research into mission was paid for by the Ashridge Strategic Management Centre with special sponsorship from the Boston Consulting Group. The project was approved at the first Research Committee meeting of the Centre in November 1987 by the founding members of the Committee – BP, BOC, Courtaulds, ICI, Lloyds Bank, United Biscuits and the Strategic Planning Society. Throughout its somewhat circuitous progress it was enthusiastically encouraged and guided by the Committee and the additional members Digital, Grand Metropolitan and Shell who joined in 1988. Without the financial and emotional support given so generously by the Committee and the Boston Consulting Group none of this could have happened.

We also want to praise the generosity of the companies that gave precious management time to share their experiences with us and to send us their mission statements. Our thanks go to the authors and publishers who gave permission for us to reproduce the chapters and articles which follow. Finally we would like to acknowledge the support of Sally Yeung in collating the material and liaising with the publishers.

Chapter 1

What is mission?

Many managers use the word 'mission' to define the business that an organization is in. In one of Britain's largest diversified companies, each operating company is expected to define a mission for its business. The group planning coordinator described mission as follows: 'We have been asking operating companies to agree with the centre a mission for their businesses. We want a precise description of what business each operating company is going to focus on and where the boundary lines are. It can be a difficult process, but it is recognized as being valuable to both sides.' Used in this way, the definition of mission is an important part of the strategic planning process and, in many companies we have been involved with, it can be a highly rewarding activity. Clarity about the boundaries around a business is essential to good planning.

However, in this book we are going to use the word mission in a much broader way. We are going to explore the concept of mission in the context of a 'sense of mission'. We have noted that some companies appear to have clarity about what they are doing and enthusiasm for doing it. They have a sense of what their mission is. This sense is not universal among employees and managers, but enthusiasm and clarity is noticeable in a significant number. In companies like Bulmers, the Hereford based cider and drinks company, Egon Zehnder, one of the leading international executive search firms, Dist (disguised case), a US distributor of white goods and industrial controls, Marks and Spencer, Britain's most famous retailer, and The Body Shop, an international retailer of cosmetics, we found managers who bubbled with enthusiasm about their company and what it does. They had no problem answering the question 'Why are you proud of your company?' or 'Why are you enthusiastic about your work?'. As one manager from The Body Shop put it, 'We really do believe that the environment is important. We don't make enough of it in recruiting. After people join they are surprised at the number of things we do. They say that they didn't realize how seriously we take it.'

Talking to people like this manager in The Body Shop, we could tell that they had a sense of what their company was trying to do. It is this type of mission that we are interested in: a mission that generates emotion and enthusiasm.

What is mission?

Through interviewing managers in companies with a sense of mission, we have developed a definition of mission that is much broader than the traditional usage of the word. Our definition includes elements that we have called 'purpose', 'strategy', 'values' and 'behaviour standards'. We will provide a brief definition of these terms in this chapter. For a fuller explanation the reader should turn to Chapter 7, Do you have a good mission statement?, which is devoted to explaining our definition of mission more fully.

Figure 1.1 is a diagram of our definition of mission. We have called it the Ashridge Mission Model.

Figure 1.1   *The Ashridge Mission Model*

Purpose is the most philosophical part of the mission. It provides an explanation of why the organization exists; or to put it another way, for whose benefit is all this effort being exerted. Some chief executives dedicate their companies to the shareholders, arguing that the company exists to create wealth for shareholders. Other organizations, like partnerships, are dedicated to their working owners. Others, like consumer cooperatives, are dedicated to their customers. Each of these organizations has chosen a single group as their reason for existing.

These single constituency organizations are, however, too simplistic for many of today's large companies. Many large companies have developed a multi-constituency definition of why their organizations exist. They argue that the company is an association of stakeholders. Shareholders, employees, customers and suppliers come together through the company as a means of fulfilling their needs. The company's purpose is to fulfil these needs. To do so the company must define the relationship with each of these stakeholders so that the stakeholder is clear as to what he or she will get out of an association with the company. For example, shareholders will get high returns on their money and customers will get quality products at reasonable prices. These multi-constituency companies believe in a stakeholder definition of purpose: that the company exists to serve the needs of all its stakeholders.

Some companies, mainly those with a strong sense of mission, have rejected the stakeholder definition of purpose. They have defined purpose as some objective that is more important than any of the stakeholders; something that could be described as a higher ideal. In Marks and Spencer, one manager described the purpose as being to raise standards for the working man or woman; at The Body Shop they talk about cosmetics that don't harm animals or the environment; and at Dist, managers refer to customer service. Whether the company has a moral crusade, like Marks and Spencer or The Body Shop, or whether it just aspires to be the best, like Dist, it has a purpose that provides the basis for a cause; something that can rise above the selfish interests of stakeholders and provide the basis for a sense of mission.

Defining purpose in an inspirational way is, we believe, important to the creation of an inspirational mission. It does not mean that the stakeholders are unimportant. The company still needs to define its relationship with each stake-holder. The value of an inspirational purpose is that it can help to draw together the stakeholders, particularly the employees. By recognizing that the company has a purpose of its own, stakeholders can commit to supporting the company not only because of the commercial benefits, but also because the cause is worthwhile.

Strategy is the second element of our definition of mission. Strategy is the commercial logic of the business. It is one of the logics that link behaviour and decisions to purpose. To define strategy, management must define the business domain in which the company is going to compete. It must also provide some rationale that identifies the competitive advantage or distinctive competence that will enable the company to hold a special position in the chosen business domain.

For Dist the business domain is any distribution business where there is an opportunity to excel through customer service. Competitive advantage will be based on a service oriented culture and human relations approach. For Egon Zehnder, the business domain is worldwide executive search. Competitive advantage comes from a professional approach to search combined with a one-firm cooperative culture.

However, strategy as such has no influence on a company if it cannot be converted into decisions and behaviour standards. Strategy must define action and behaviour if it is to have any impact. Hence the third element of the mission model is behaviour standards.

Behaviour standards are instructions about how managers and employees should behave. We are talking about things like Marks and Spencer's standard of visible management. Managers must be seen in the stores and management attention to the business must be visible through communication, open meetings, or whatever mechanism makes sense.

As one director explained, 'Visibility is vital. The employees need to know that the Chairman and the Board are in touch with the business and are thinking about it. One way is through store visits. In a normal week the 12 board members will probably between them visit about 25 stores. These are not red letter days. We will just go in and talk with some of the management and supervisors. It's about getting out and listening to the organization.'

In Egon Zehnder one of the behaviour standards is cooperation. An Egon Zehnder consultant willingly helps another consultant within his or her own office or from another office. This standard is essential to the one firm concept. As a result, most client assignments have two consultants working as a team. Philip Vivian, a consultant, said,

> Collaboration and cooperation are very important and this is unusual in this industry. It is essential that we recognize each other's skills and switch assignments or work as a team. It is also critical for international work. We have one Japanese assignment that is being coordinated from Tokyo, Milan, Paris, London and Frankfurt. So we have to work as a team. It doesn't always work out perfectly because of the inevitable problems of communication. But the 'one firm' concept helps. We all know we are working for the same firm – no office is going to lose out if it helps another.

Visible management and collegiate cooperation are both broad behaviour instructions that can affect much of management behaviour. They are also clearly linked to the specific retailing and executive search strategies that these two companies follow. But behaviour standards can also be more detailed and on seemingly less relevant issues, so long as the behaviour has symbolic value.

The Body Shop's behaviour standard of having two waste paper baskets, one for recyclable paper and one for other items, is an example of this. It demonstrates to everyone every day that The Body Shop takes environmental issues seriously. Employees are even expected to attend training sessions on what type of waste to put in each bin. The symbolic value of this behaviour standard is substantial.

Behaviour standards are therefore part of the organization's way of doing business. They are things that managers have come to feel are important to the effective running of the business. They are the ten commandments of the business.

These behaviour standards are defined not only by the company's strategy; they are also defined by its values. Our definition of mission recognizes that there are two reasons for doing something in an organization. The first is a strategic or commercial reason; the second is a moral or value based reason.

Values are the beliefs that underpin the organization's management style, its relations to employees and other stakeholders, and its ethics. In organizations with a sense of mission, values provide the emotional logic for managers and employees. They are the justification for managers and employees to say that their behaviour is not only good strategically but also good in itself: the right way to behave. Employees who have personal values similar to the organization's values find a sense of fulfilment and meaning in their work and behaviour standards. It is this sense of doing something worthwhile that gives them a sense of the company's mission.

Strong missions exist when these four elements are closely knitted together: when strategy and values are supportive and reinforcing; when behaviour standards are clear and justified by both the commercial strategy and the company's values; and when all three elements are linked by a purpose that reaches towards something more elevating than stakeholder satisfaction.

Take the clothing retailing activities of Marks and Spencer. The strategy is to produce better quality, classic products through close relationships with manufacturers. By selling these products at normal prices, Marks and Spencer create such a volume of sales that fixed overhead costs are much lower than for competitors and more than compensate for lower retail margins. Linked to this strategy are values based on quality, value for money, service and people care. Behaviour standards such as the company's human relations policies or visible management style tie the strategy and values together. To sell goods in high volumes, service is critical. By looking after people well and being visibly interested in the operating issues of the business, managers create an atmosphere in which staff want to look after customers and help the business succeed. Finally, these elements of strategy, values and behaviour standards are linked together in an inspiring way by Marks and Spencer's purpose of raising the standards of the working man and woman.

Described in this way and starting with strategy, the Marks and Spencer mission may seem coldly objective, even calculating. But when operated by managers genuinely committed to raising standards, who have an overwhelming enthusiasm for quality and people care, the mission becomes exciting and enticing, infusing large numbers of staff with a sense of mission.

Why is mission important?

People are more motivated and work more intelligently if they believe in what they are doing and trust the organization they are working with. Psychologists and organization behaviourists recognize that most people are searching for meaning in their life. If an organization can provide meaning for an employee on top of pay and conditions, it will inspire the greater commitment and loyalty that we have labelled a sense of mission.

The most powerful source of this commitment is the link between behaviours, the organization's values and the employees' values. If the behaviour standards in an organization are value laden (can be justified in value terms) they can have meaning for employees. Furthermore if the values are those close to the heart of the employee, then the employee feels a sense of mission about the activity.

The meanings and values that create a sense of mission are self evident in the Boy Scouts, in some charities, in religious organizations and in the better police forces, but they are hard to imagine in commercial organizations. Nevertheless, our research shows that a sense of mission can be created in commercial organizations, such as the examples we have already given.

We have argued that this emotional commitment comes mainly from clear values. We should acknowledge that motivation and commitment can also come from clear strategy, from the excitement of achievement, from the honour of being the best and from the thrill of winning. We are avoiding the issue of whether strategy is more important than values. But we are arguing that strategy alone is not enough. We believe that organizations also need to create strong values if they seek the benefits of having a sense of mission.

The benefits of creating a sense of mission are numerous. Inevitably they overlap with the benefits of clear strategy, such as better decision making, clearer communication, greater ease in delegation with its benefit of a lower need for supervision. But a sense of mission, enhanced by clear values, gives additional benefits.

The main advantage seems to be the loyalty and commitment of the management and employees. This is well illustrated by a story told by Lord Sieff in 1982, about a Mrs Williams.

> I got a letter at the end of November from a Mrs Williams, a part-time stockroom assistant at our Chatham store, who writes to me that she knows that the Chatham area is in a bit of a depression, that the store catalogue is poor.
>
> Now she serves on the floor on a Saturday. She said last Saturday she had to refuse within five minutes three customers, for lines which she knows are overall in the catalogue, but Chatham does not have them. It cost us £100 in sales.

Now remember, this lady gets no commission, she's on a flat rate. And she wrote, 'It's not good enough. Do you know we get customers coming from the Isle of Sheppey or the Isle of Grain, and it's wrong.'

I couldn't go down, so I sent my personal assistant, who came back with a report that the range at Chatham was poor. We improved the range and the increase in sales within the space of three weeks was dramatic.

It is Mrs Williams' belief in Marks and Spencer, that the company could get it right, that shines through in this example.

The second big advantage concerns people selection and development. Organizations with clear values find it easier to select, recruit, promote and develop the right kind of people. In part it is a process of self-selection. Individuals who do not agree with the organization's values will choose to leave. Here we give another quote from a Marks and Spencer director.

I think what I have just described is not for everybody. There is a strong underlying sense of paternalism in the M&S approach. In exchange for adhering to M&S's way of doing things, you know that the company will look after you and support you. In M&S you are asked to conform in a way that is not everybody's cup of tea.

Some suddenly realize it's not for them. The number of times I have heard people say that they enjoyed working for M&S but that it's not a company that suits them.

It is also a tool for helping managers make better decisions about selection, promotion and development. Training can be slanted to underpin the values and culture that the company is trying to reinforce, and an additional selection criterion can be used: does this person embody the values we believe in? Egon Zehnder takes great care to choose new consultants who will fit their values and culture. The mechanism for doing this is to expose the candidate to 10 or 12 consultants in three or four different offices. It can be a long interviewing process, but it helps to identify people who won't fit.

Anita Roddick at The Body Shop takes the same care in choosing franchisees for new Body Shop outlets. 'We have the back-up to teach almost anyone to run a Body Shop,' she said. 'What we can't control is the soul.' To this end, the strict vetting all applicants receive is balanced by seemingly offbeat questions like: How would you like to die? What is your favourite flower? Who is your heroine in history or poetry? – all questions that give Roddick a feel for whether the applicant is someone she can work with comfortably.

The third, most important benefit comes from greater cooperation and trust. Organizations with a sense of mission find it easier to work together, to respect each other and to search for the solution that is in the best interest of the organization rather than individual departments. We have already given an example of the importance of cooperation in Egon Zehnder. There, consultants recognize that the trust between offices necessary to do good international assignments would be almost impossible to create without the bonding provided by a 'one firm' concept.

The rationale is almost tautological. If managers in different departments recognize the worthwhile qualities of the common cause, they are much more likely to cooperate. Also, if managers share some common values, they will find it much easier to trust each other and overcome the day to day setbacks that cause irritations and suspicions.

Cooperation and trust are hard to create in the most favourable environments. We are not trying to argue that a sense of mission will overcome all problems of 'not invented here', professional jealousy, personal rivalry and emotional incompatibility. But it will help.

Our research has also shown how strong values can help decision making. Frequently the biggest and most difficult decisions can only be made on judgement calls. A clear value framework, if it is a good one, can improve the judgement calls and help to keep them consistent. It is at the time of these big decisions that an organization's purpose is tested. By having strong links between both strategy and purpose, and values and purpose, the leaders are more easily able to keep on course. Sainsbury's decision in the 1960s not to follow other supermarket chains into Green Shield stamps is a good example. It was an important decision and the board discussed the alternatives. Choosing not to offer Green Shield stamps would cause a loss of market share and poor short term financial results. The long term effects were difficult to estimate.

Nevertheless, the directors believed that offering Green Shield stamps would not further their purpose of providing quality food at reasonable prices. It would cause prices to rise because the customer would ultimately have to pay for the stamps. Following their motto 'Good food costs less at Sainsbury's', the directors voted against stamps. It turned out to be an excellent decision, helping to position Sainsbury's as a champion of customer value. But it was the sense of mission held by the directors rather than the commercial analysis that caused them to make the right decision.

We came across another example more recently. At a planning meeting, the managing director and the planner of a division of a food company were discussing strategic options. The alternatives were 'run for cash', 'maintain position', and 'build on core strengths'. The planner said he had done a financial analysis showing that the run for cash option produced the best financial outcome. The MD showed no interest in the analysis. 'We are not that kind of company,' he said. 'We are builders of businesses. We wouldn't like rationalizing and we wouldn't be any good at it. I don't want to examine that option any further.' Whether the MD was right or not is unclear. But it was his sense of mission that made a difficult decision relatively easy for him.

While strong values make the decisions at the top easier, they also make the daily decisions throughout the organization easier. Employees and managers are continually faced with dilemmas and choices. Calculating the commercial impact of these alternatives is difficult and can be misleading. It is, therefore, easier for employees if the organization has strong values and behaviour standards to guide them through the choices.

However, a sense of mission is not necessarily beneficial. The strategy or the values can be inappropriate or misguided. By cementing the organization behind a sense of mission, management can make it hard to change course. We have examples of companies devoted to the wrong values and the wrong beliefs. In one of our interviews a personnel manager talked about some concern in his company that the values might be too overbearing.

> Some would say that it is our addiction to the company philosophy that is holding us back. Some wish we had more strategy. We have, for example, only just recently created an appointment and made someone responsible for the strategic development of the company. But the balance is still 65 per cent in favour of philosophy. And it was only last week that the Chairman attempted to reinforce the old values. He said that we must not lose sight of the principles that have made us successful.

Nevertheless, most organizations that have sound strategies are likely to benefit from management time devoted to creating a sense of mission.

How to create a sense of mission

There are two tasks that are needed to create a sense of mission. The first is the intellectual task of defining purpose, developing strategies and values that reinforce each other, and identifying the standards and behaviours that are the expression of the mission. The second is a communications and management task of making the sense of mission come alive in the organization.

Approaches and tools for achieving both of these tasks abound, ranging from a 'culture audit' as a first step in developing values, to a 'corporate identity programme' as one of the ways of symbolizing the mission. The particular method chosen should be tailored to the personalities of the senior management group and the particular organization's circumstances.

Companies in the research have followed many different paths. Those with the strongest and most longstanding missions, like Marks and Spencer, have developed their mission gradually, driven by the instincts of a powerful leader or founder. The sense of mission emerged because the leadership ran the business on a few, well communicated messages that had strategic as well as value connections. A manager in Marks and Spencer commented that, 'Marcus Sieff gave many presentations both in the company and outside. But he only ever gave one speech – the importance of good human relations.' In recent years, many of these missionary businesses have devoted time to documenting their missions to make them more explicit.

Others, such as Dist, have taken a more intellectual approach. The senior management group has worked out a mission statement which they have then used to help them run the business. The statement has usually been developed in consultation with managers in the company. Frequently the statement has been published and used as the centre-piece of a major communication or corporate identity programme.

One problem faced by these companies is that they have found it hard to develop a consensus in the top management team. This can lead to long delays in the development of the mission, to the creation of a compromise statement with more political content than philosophy, or to a half hearted implementation programme. It is apparent that creating a mission is more difficult than developing strategy.

Finally, there are some companies who have taken an operational approach to the problem. They have picked one or two operational issues, developed a consensus around how to tackle them, pushed for the necessary changes, and then encouraged a sense of mission to grow up around this operational theme. The British Airways theme of 'Putting People First' was a response to the operational problem of how to deliver better service to the customer. The effect appears to be an organization with a growing sense of mission.

Out of this diversity of approaches we have managed to distil some rules of thumb or guiding principles.

1 It takes years not months. Creating a sense of mission is a long term project. One company has been actively working at it for 10 years and has still not fully succeeded. On the other hand, if the sense of mission is imposed from above, often combined with sweeping management changes, a shorter period, say less than three years, seems to be reasonable.

   We believe most companies should set about creating a sense of mission slowly. First, it is unrealistic to expect to win support from managers and employees until the mission has proved to be effective. Second, it can take years for senior management to develop a mission that makes sense in both value and strategy terms. We know one company that became committed to a value of lifetime employment: no forced redundancies. However, in the face of a severe recession it proved unable to hold to the value, undermining faith in the mission throughout the organization.

2 True consensus is necessary within the top team. Normally a few people within a company, sometimes as few as two, form the power group at the centre. It is necessary for this group to have a sense of mission if the organization is going to have one. This does not mean that the top team needs to have fully defined the company strategy, values and behaviours, but it does mean that the top team should have consensus, especially about the values they are trying to communicate. In one company the discussion about

philosophy continued for more than two years before a consensus was reached, and this happened only after one member of the team left the business.

3 Action is a better communicator than words. The reason why the top team must have a true belief in the values is because it is their actions that will send out the message. Values are not easily communicated by speeches. They only live in an organization when managers act them out. In the research we came across a number of examples of organizations that developed a mission statement and circulated it to all employees, believing it would help raise morale and change attitudes and behaviours. When employees read the statement they became confused. 'Our organization is not like this,' they would say, adding, 'If management really believed this stuff they would have made a lot of changes.' Almost immediately cynicism would take over on the basis that management didn't believe it themselves. The lack of action behind the words made management seem even more impotent or two-faced than before, and the net result was a lowering of morale.

4 Top team visibility is essential. The values of the organization are its ethos, its personality. It is much easier for employees to identify with the ethos if they can associate it with a leader or leadership group. It is hard to believe in an organization if you feel out of touch with the leadership. Colin Marshall of British Airways gave 300 presentations to groups of 100 employees to get his message of 'putting people first' across to 30 000 employees. In other companies face to face meetings are rare, but the leadership is visible through myths and stories told about the personalities involved or through communication devices such as videos or circulated minutes of board meetings.

5 Top team continuity. Continuity of leadership is one of the biggest contributors to creating a sense of mission. Not only does it give the leaders time to think through the connections between values and strategies and to identify the pivotal behaviours; it helps to make the leaders more visible; it makes consensus more likely; and it promotes consistency, one of the most important parts of communicating a message. All of the companies with a strong sense of mission that we identified in the research had had long periods of top management continuity.

6 Statements of mission should have personality. The most highly regarded published statements were those that reflected the personality of the organization and the leadership. Frequently they were straight talking, using blunt terms rather than advertising copy. Documents that were written by the communications department and word-smithed by a committee were generally less powerful than a mission written by the chairman over the weekend. We say more about this in the last chapter in this book.

7 Strategy and values should be formulated together. An essential part of creating a mission is the resonance between strategy and values. So which should come first? The research suggests that the two should be developed in parallel. Some values and some parts of strategy will be clear at the start.

Creating a mission involves building around these starting positions to a more complete definition of strategy, values, purpose and behaviours. As one manager put it, 'If the senior management continuously return to the three basic values, these will be picked up and interpreted by the organization. But you can't manage by values alone. You must choose something that adds up to a successful and profitable operation.'

8 Management should focus on the link between behaviours and values. Employees feel a sense of mission when they believe in what they are doing and the way they do it. In our interviews it was the way people in the company behaved that was most frequently talked about. By helping an employee see the association between the task he or she is doing and some worthy value, the manager is creating meaning. It is this meaning that is at the core of a sense of mission. Even mundane tasks like photocopying can be infused with value. Though the task itself may have little meaning, the way in which it is performed can be infused with values such as excellence or caring for others or efficiency.

When is mission not appropriate?

The implication of our research is that managers will benefit from working on the values and philosophy of their organizations. By going beyond strategy thinking to mission thinking, managers can develop a link between purpose, strategy, values and behaviours that will help to create a sense of mission in their organizations.

But there are three circumstances in which this work is not appropriate: when strategy is changing or highly uncertain; when the top team is unlikely to be stable; and when there are strong differences between members of the top team.

In the previous section we pointed out the importance of a consensus among the top team. If there is little chance of this consensus being reached, there is little point in discussing mission until the top team has changed. Trying to communicate a mission that members of the top team are not going to follow is dangerous. It creates factions in the organization, demonstrates the lack of willpower of the chief executive, and breeds cynicism. It is better to remove the offending manager or delay any initiative until he or she has moved on.

This is an important rule that too many managers ignore. They often try to use a mission exercise to gain agreement and commitment from a board that is divided. In one example the personnel director who was leading the effort explained that, 'We thought if we could get the production and sales director to publicly commit to the mission statement, they would have to change their behaviour and start supporting the new philosophy.' It won't surprise any of you to know that they didn't change and the company is still caught between two philosophies.

We also pointed out the importance of continuity in the top team to ensure that the message is consistent. In companies where senior management changes regularly or in cases where the future leaders are not involved in the mission development process, it is unlikely to be a useful long term exercise. One exception occurs when a longstanding leader is near retirement. He or she may want to enshrine the company's mission in documents and corporate symbols as an aid to maintaining consistency after retirement. We predict that this will only be successful if the leader's successor is intimately involved in the process.

The third situation in which mission work is unlikely to be beneficial is when strategy is in flux. Since mission is the fusion of strategy and values it is hardest to formulate a mission if strategy is changing or uncertain. Management may need to retain flexibility in both strategy and values. The disadvantage of flexibility is the confusion it creates in the organization. The antidote seems to be for management to hold on to and reinforce one or two values from the past that will not hamper development in the future.

What is mission in a multi-business company?

Thus far we have talked about an organization as if it were one unit. But most companies are diversified, with headquarters, groups and business units. The issue is whether these multi-business companies should have one mission or multiple missions, and whether our mission research has any messages for how companies should compose their portfolios.

We believe that in most situations organizations with a sense of mission are likely to be able to out-perform those that don't have one. It follows, therefore, that most business units are likely to benefit from creating a mission.

The multi-business issue then becomes a question of how to link different business unit missions and whether and in what form to have a mission at headquarters. The issues are:

- How diversified can a group of companies be before it becomes impossible to have a shared sense of mission?
- Is there benefit in the headquarters having a sense of mission, or can the creation of mission be delegated entirely to the business unit level?

It is apparent from our research that it is possible to create a mission for a whole multi-business company so long as the level of diversity is low. Dist is an example. Their mission is about customer service and people care. All the subsidiaries are seeking to overcome their competitors by caring more for their employees and so being able to offer better service. As a result, many of the values and behaviours are the same across the organization, creating a sense of mission and identity.

It is also apparent from the research that diversified companies like Hanson and Tarmac have a sense of mission. For these organizations, the mission is mainly about the activities of headquarters, and the subsidiaries share in the mission in so far as the headquarters' values and behaviours are imposed on them. Lord Hanson's words illustrate this:

> We believed from the beginning – and 23 years has not led us to change this view – that the best results flow from three systems which operate simultaneously and continuously. The first is the identification of the man or woman on whose performance the business will succeed or fail – the manager. If you are in very complex or highly technical businesses, it is hard to identify the one person who carries the can for success or failure.
>
> The second is financial discipline. We work hard to get our operating companies to understand the concept that budgets are something you intend to achieve, not something you hope to achieve.
>
> The third is motivation. I believe very firmly in the combination of carrot and stick. We make it crystal clear what the manager's task is, but don't just leave it to him or allow him to get on with it. We require him to do it. This has a dramatic effect on the individual. Possibly for the first time in his career he senses the meaning of personal responsibility.

Hanson's mission is therefore more about the headquarters' strategy and style than it is about the subsidiaries' tasks. Yet it is our judgement that Hanson has a sense of mission equally as strong as Dist.

The conclusion we have drawn is that a multi-business company can have a mission across a diverse portfolio so long as the values espoused in the mission fit well with the subsidiaries. The fit of values at headquarters and subsidiary is clear in Dist. It is also true in Hanson. Lord Hanson only chooses businesses where his philosophy and his values will help them perform better.

Having reached this conclusion, we can also argue that headquarters will benefit from having a mission. The values and philosophy laid down by headquarters will, if the portfolio has been correctly chosen, help the subsidiaries perform better. The link between subsidiary and headquarters is, therefore, the values and behaviours they share.

A clear mission will also be helpful in developing an acquisition strategy. The best acquisition targets will be those with compatible values or ones where the values can be changed. It is not surprising, therefore, that Marks and Spencer chose to buy Brooks Brothers in the US because it 'has a very similar philosophy'; or that Sainsbury's were very careful to select a grocery chain in New England that had similar standards of quality and value for money; or Lex, when looking for a white goods dealer in Europe, preferred a company with similar values despite its poor profit record over a company with different values but a better financial statement.

A clear mission at headquarters can, therefore, be a powerful creation, helping to turn a directionless diversified company into a corporation with identity and purpose.

Leadership is more than strategy formulation. Successful leaders also instil values in their organizations that generate commitment and simplify the management task. The concept of mission presented in this book shows how purpose, strategy and values need to be linked to standards and behaviours. We believe most companies will benefit from devoting more attention to mission and we have given some advice on how this might best be done.

Chapter 2

Mission and motivation

In Chapter 1, we defined an organization with a 'sense of mission' as one where employees and managers feel an emotional attachment to the organization. It is no wonder then that the literature on motivation has many references that recognize the importance of mission as we have defined it. In the section that follows, we have included three extracts by theorists on the subject of motivation – Maslow, Herzberg and Schein. Then there is an extract from *In Search of Excellence* by Tom Peters and Robert Waterman Jr, and one from the sayings of Konosuke Matsushita, the founder of Matsushita Electric. Together these pieces demonstrate that people give their best when they believe in what they are doing; when they believe that their actions are worthwhile; when they have a sense of mission.

Dr Maslow's book *Motivation and Personality*, published in 1954, started a new wave of thinking about the way people in organizations behave and think. It has formed the basis for a number of subsequent investigations in organizational psychology. Maslow developed the 'hierarchy of needs' theory. This states that people have needs which they fulfil in an order of priority. The basic physiological needs, like food and shelter, are fulfilled first. The social needs, like safety, self-esteem and a sense of belonging, are fulfilled second. Finally, when all these other needs are fulfilled, people search for self-actualization. Maslow defines self-actualization as the 'desire for self-fulfilment, namely the tendency for [man] to become actualized in what he is potentially'. Maslow's self-actualizing person is one who has satisfied all the basic needs; who has none of the feelings of hunger; is not lacking in self-esteem; has a stable social life and does not feel 'the pangs of loneliness, of ostracism, of rejection, of friendlessness, of rootlessness'.

A person can partly achieve Maslow's self-actualization by becoming attached emotionally to an organization and its cause. Hence there is a close link between mission and the need for self-actualization. Whereas Maslow argues that this highest level need is only activated when the more basic needs are satisfied, we have observed that employees can gain fulfilment from an emotional attachment to their organization regardless of their other circumstances.

Frederick Herzberg also bases his theory on the needs of people. His article, 'One more time: How do you motivate employees?', has become a *Harvard Business Review* classic. Herzberg differentiates between factors that are intrinsic to the job that a person does and those that are extrinsic. The extrinsic factors are 'hygiene factors' and merely help to improve the superficial work environment, like higher pay, better lighting etc. The intrinsic factors he calls 'motivators' and they help to fulfil certain inner needs that people have. Examples of these motivators are 'responsibility, recognition for achievement and job satisfaction'. Herzberg believes that these help people to 'experience psychological growth'. This he calls 'job enrichment'.

Motivation that comes from a 'sense of mission' – from an emotional attachment to the organization – does not feature in Herzberg's article. He does not explicitly recognize the quest for meaning in life. Whereas it is possible to stretch Maslow's hierarchy to include our concept of mission, Herzberg's theory appears to stop short. We include his article for this reason: to show the gap that appears to exist even in the minds of the specialists.

Edgar Schein is a well known name in organizational psychology and he has written profusely on the subject. His book *Organisational Psychology* is a thorough analysis of the evolution of motivation theory, as well as relevant interpretations of his own. He looks at organizations, at the problems which organizations face, with the manager in mind, and draws many useful conclusions. Recognizing the incomplete nature of theories of motivation, Schein promotes a contingency theory, arguing that the ways in which a particular individual will behave are dependent on that individual's inherited traits, learned behaviour and perception of the situation.

The way in which an individual perceives an organization is, therefore, an important influence on motivation. Schein describes a number of different perceived relationships or psychological contracts between the organization and the individual. One of these psychological contracts clearly describes an organization with a sense of mission. In this contract the organization uses 'normative' authority, where 'membership, status and intrinsic value rewards' are important and authority is based on 'charisma and expertise'. This contract also requires a deep 'moral' commitment from the employee, 'which means that the person intrinsically values the mission of the organization and his or her job, and is personally involved and identified with the organization'.

Peters and Waterman, in their famous study of 62 American companies, noticed that successful companies treat their people like winners and that this need to feel like a winner is a pretty universal psychological need. People also 'seek transcendence', according to Peters and Waterman, and this search for an ultimate meaning in their work life makes people go to extraordinary lengths of commitment and dedication. Workers like to feel that they belong and share the goals and the culture of the organization. They gain a sense of meaning from such a relationship and are, as a result, more motivated, more fired up to work, and above all they feel good about it. This study appears to have identified companies that have, in our terms, a sense of mission.

Matsushita's book, *Not For Bread Alone*, explains the philosophy of one of Japan's most successful businessmen. Translated from the Japanese, it resounds with sincerity and dedication. All the way through the book Matsushita explains how important it is for employees to feel wanted and cared for in organizations. The sharing of inspiring values, he believes, also provides people with something more to work for than the pay cheque at the end of the month. Matsushita Electric is one of the world's best practical examples of a large organization that has attempted to motivate its employees by creating inspiration and a unity between the organization's values and the employees' innate beliefs.

These five articles helped us to understand the relationship between motivation and mission. Like the chapters on leadership and culture, this selection of readings underlines the importance of managing what Schein calls the psychological contract between employees and organizations.

Higher and lower needs
Abraham H. Maslow

Dr Maslow's book *Motivation and Personality* first appeared in print in 1954 and quickly became established as a classic in the field of humanistic psychology. It is an original statement of the author's own ideas and is based on his own experiences in psychology and therapy. The book establishes that most people have a hierarchy of needs which they seek to fulfil in a certain order of priority. At the lowest level there are needs which are basic to existence, like food. At the highest level, Maslow argues, there is the need for self-actualization. This is a term first used by Kurt Goldstein in 1939, and Maslow uses it to refer to a desire to 'become more and more what one idiosyncratically is, to become everything one is capable of'.

The chapter we have reproduced examines the different sorts of needs that people have, how they seek to achieve them and what the consequences are for society when these needs are satisfied. Maslow believes that the self-actualizing person reaches greater happiness, transcendence and a better quality of life. In organizations, this behaviour has a number of consequences: one of which is an improvement of its culture through enhancing the motivation of the people who work there.

Differences between higher and lower needs

This chapter will demonstrate that there are real psychological and operational differences between those needs called 'higher' and those called 'lower'. This is done in order to establish that the organism itself dictates hierarchies of values, which the scientific observer reports rather than creates. It is necessary thus to prove the obvious because so many still consider that values can never be more than the arbitrary imposition upon data of the writer's own tastes, prejudices, intuitions, or other unproved or unprovable assumptions. In the latter half of the chapter some of the consequences of this demonstration will be drawn.

The casting out of values from psychology not only weakens it, and prevents it from reaching its full growth, but also abandons mankind to supernaturalism, to ethical relativism, or to nihilistic valuelessness. But if it could be demonstrated that the organism itself chooses between a stronger and a weaker, a higher and a lower, then surely it would be impossible to maintain that one good has the same value as any other good, or that it is impossible to choose between them, or that one has no natural criterion for differentiating good from evil. One such principle of choice has already been set forth in Chapter 4. The basic needs arrange themselves in a fairly definite hierarchy on the basis of the principle of relative potency. Thus the safety need is stronger than the love need, because it dominates the organism in various demonstrable ways when both needs are frustrated. In this sense, the physiological needs (which are themselves ordered in a subhierarchy) are stronger than the safety needs, which are stronger than the love needs, which in turn are stronger than the esteem needs, which are stronger than those idiosyncratic needs we have called the need for self-actualization.

This is an order of choice or preference. But it is also an order that ranges from lower to higher in various other senses that are listed in this chapter.

1 *The higher need is a later phyletic or evolutionary development.* We share the need for food with all living things, the need for love with (perhaps) the higher apes, the need for self-actualization with nobody. The higher the need the more specifically human it is.

2 *Higher needs are later ontogenetic developments.* Any individual at birth shows physical needs, and probably also, in a very inchoate form, needs safety, e.g. it can probably be frightened or startled, and probably thrives better when its world shows enough regularity and orderliness so that it can be counted on. It is only after months of life that an infant shows the first signs of interpersonal ties and selective affection. Still later we may see fairly definitely the urges to autonomy, independence, achievement, and for respect and praise over and above safety and parental love. As for self-actualization, even a Mozart had to wait until he was three or four.

3 *The higher the need the less imperative it is for sheer survival, the longer gratification can be postponed, and the easier it is for the need to disappear permanently.* Higher needs have less ability to dominate, organize, and press into their service the autonomic reactions and other capacities of the organism, e.g. it is easier to be single-minded, monomaniac, and desperate about safety than about respect. Deprivation of higher needs does not produce so desperate a defense and emergency reaction as is produced by lower deprivations. Respect is a dispensable luxury when compared with food or safety.

4 *Living at the higher need level means greater biological efficiency, greater longevity, less disease, better sleep, appetite, etc.* The psychosomatic researchers prove again and again that anxiety, fear, lack of love, domination, etc., tend to encourage undesirable physical as well as undesirable psychological results. Higher need gratifications have survival value and growth value as well.

5 *Higher needs are less urgent subjectively.* They are less perceptible, less unmistakable, more easily confounded with other needs by suggestion, imitation, by mistaken belief or habit. To be able to recognize one's own needs, i.e. to know what one really wants, is a considerable psychological achievement. This is doubly true for the higher needs.

6 *Higher need gratifications produce more desirable subjective results, i.e. more profound happiness, serenity, and richness of the inner life.* Satisfactions of the safety needs produce at best a feeling of relief and relaxation. In any case they cannot produce, e.g. the ecstasy, peak experiences, and happy delirium of satisfied love, or such consequences as serenity, understanding, nobility, etc.

7 *Pursuit and gratification of higher needs represent a general healthward trend, a trend away from psychopathology.* The evidence for this statement is presented in Chapter 5.

8 *The higher need has more preconditions.* This is true if only because prepotent needs must be gratified before it can be. Thus it takes more quanta of satisfactions for the love need to appear in consciousness than for the safety need. In a more general sense, it may be said that life is more complex at the level of the higher needs. The search for respect and status involves more people, a larger scene, a longer run, more means, and partial goals, more subordinate and preliminary steps than does the search for love. The same may be said of this latter need when compared with the search for safety.

9 *Higher needs require better outside conditions to make them possible.* Better environmental conditions (familial, economic, political, educational, etc.) are all more necessary to allow people to love each other than merely to keep them from killing each other. *Very* good conditions are needed to make self-actualizing possible.

10 *A greater value is usually placed upon the higher need than upon the lower by those who have been gratified in both.* Such people will sacrifice more for the

higher satisfaction, and furthermore will more readily be able to withstand lower deprivation. For example, they will find it easier to live ascetic lives, to withstand danger for the sake of principle, to give up money and prestige for the sake of self-actualization. Those who have known both universally regard self-respect as a higher, more valuable subjective experience than a filled belly.

11 *The higher the need level, the wider is the circle of love identification, i.e., the greater is the number of people love-identified with, and the greater is the average degree of love identification.* We may define love identification as, in principle, a merging into a single hierarchy of prepotency of the needs of two or more people. Two people who love each other well will react to each other's needs and their own indiscriminately. Indeed the other's need *is* his own need.

12 *The pursuit and the gratification of the higher needs have desirable civic and social consequences.* To some extent, the higher the need the less selfish it must be. Hunger is highly egocentric; the only way to satisfy it is to satisfy oneself. But the search for love and respect necessarily involves other people. Moreover, it involves satisfaction for these other people. People who have enough basic satisfaction to look for love and respect (rather than just food and safety) tend to develop such qualities as loyalty, friendliness, and civic consciousness, and to become better parents, husbands, teachers, public servants, etc.

13 *Satisfaction of higher needs is closer to self-actualization than is lower-need satisfaction.* If the theory of self-actualization be accepted, this is an important difference. Among other things, it means that we may expect to find, in people living at the higher need level, a larger number and greater degree of the qualities found in self-actualizing people.

14 *The pursuit and gratification of the higher needs leads to greater, stronger, and truer individualism.* This may seem to contradict the previous statement that living at higher need levels means more love identification, i.e. more socialization. However it may sound logically, it is nevertheless an empirical reality. People living at the level of self-actualization are, in fact, found simultaneously to love mankind most and to be the most developed idiosyncratically. This completely supports Fromm's contention that self-love (or better, self-respect) is synergic with rather than antagonistic to love for others. His discussion of individuality, spontaneity, and robotization is also relevant (Fromm, 1941).

15 *The higher the need level the easier and more effective psychotherapy can be: at the lowest need levels it is of hardly any avail.* Hunger cannot be stilled by psychotherapy.

16 *The lower needs are far more localized, more tangible, and more limited than are the higher needs.* Hunger and thirst are much more obviously bodily than is love, which in turn is more so than respect. In addition, lower need satisfiers are much more tangible or observable than are higher need satisfactions. Furthermore, they are more limited in the sense that a smaller quantity of

gratifiers is needed to still the need. Only so much food can be eaten, but love, respect, and cognitive satisfactions are almost unlimited.

Some consequences of this differentiation

Such a point of view, namely, that (1) the higher needs and lower needs have different properties and (2) that these higher needs as well as the lower needs must be included in the repertory of basic and given human nature (*not* as different from and opposed to it) must have many and revolutionary consequences for psychological and philosophical theory. Most civilizations, along with their theories of politics, education, religion, etc., have been based on the exact contradictory of this belief. On the whole, they have assumed the biological animal, and instinctoid aspects of human nature to be severely limited to the physiological needs for food, sex, and the like. The higher impulses for truth, for love, for beauty were assumed to be intrinsically different in nature from these animal needs. Furthermore, these interests were assumed to be antagonistic, mutually exclusive, and in perpetual conflict with each other for mastery. All culture, with all its instruments, is seen from such a point of view as on the side of the higher and against the lower. It is therefore necessarily an inhibitor and a frustrator, and is at best an unfortunate necessity.

Recognizing the higher needs to be instinctoid and biological, precisely as biological as the need for food, has many repercussions of which we can list only a few.

1 Probably most important of all is the realization that the dichotomy between cognitive and conative is false and must be resolved. The needs for knowledge, for understanding, for a life philosophy, for a theoretical frame of reference, for a value system, these are themselves conative, a part of our primitive and animal nature (we are very special animals).

Since we know also that our needs are not completely blind, that they are modified by culture, by reality, and by possibility, it follows that cognition plays a considerable role in their development. It is John Dewey's claim that the very existence and definition of a need depends on the cognition of reality, of the possibility or impossibility of gratification.

If the conative is in its nature also cognitive, and if the cognitive is in its nature also conative, the dichotomy between them is useless and must be discarded except as a sign of pathology.

2 Many age-old philosophical problems must be seen in a new light. Some of them perhaps may even be seen to be pseudo problems resting on misconceptions about human motivational life. Here may be included, for instance, the sharp distinction between selfishness and unselfishness. If our

instinctoid impulses, for instance, to love, arrange it so that we get more personal 'selfish' pleasure from watching our children eat a goody than from eating it ourselves, then how shall we define 'selfish' and how differentiate it from 'unselfish'? Is the man who risks his life for the truth any less selfish than the man who risks his life for food, if the need for truth is as animal as the need for food?

Obviously also hedonistic theory must be recast if animal pleasure, selfish pleasure, personal pleasure can come equally from gratification of the needs for food, sex, truth, beauty, love, or respect. This implies that a higher-need hedonism might very well stand where a lower-need hedonism would fall.

The romantic–classic opposition, the Dionysian–Apollonian contrast, must certainly be modified. In at least some of its forms, it has been based on the same illegitimate dichotomy between lower needs as animal, and higher needs as non-animal or anti-animal. Along with this must go considerable revision of the concepts of rational and irrational, the contrast between rational and impulsive, and the general notion of the rational life as opposed to the instinctive life.

3 The philosopher of ethics has much to learn from a close examination of man's motivational life. If our noblest impulses are seen not as checkreins on the horses, but as themselves horses, and if our animal needs are seen to be of the same nature as our highest needs, how can a sharp dichotomy between them be sustained? How can we continue to believe that they could come from different sources?

Furthermore, if we clearly and fully recognize that these noble and good impulses come into existence and grow potent primarily as a consequence of the prior gratification of the more demanding animal needs, we should certainly speak less exclusively of self-control, inhibition, discipline, etc., and more frequently of spontaneity, gratification, and self-choice. There seems to be less opposition than we thought between the stern voice of duty and the gay call to pleasure. At the highest level of living, i.e. of Being, duty *is* pleasure, one's 'work' is loved, and there is no difference between working and vacationing.

4 Our conception of culture and of man's relation to it must change in the direction of 'synergy', as Ruth Benedict (Benedict, 1970; Maslow, 1965; Maslow 1964) called it. Culture can be basic need-gratifying (Maslow, 1967; Maslow, 1969a) rather than need-inhibiting. Furthermore it is created not only for human needs but by them. The culture–individual dichotomy needs re-examination. There should be less exclusive stress on their antagonism and more on their possible collaboration and synergy.

5 The recognition that man's best impulses are appreciably intrinsic, rather than fortuitous and relative, must have tremendous implication for value theory. It means, for one thing, that it is no longer either necessary or desirable to deduce values by logic or to try to read them off from authorities

or revelations. All we need to do, apparently, is to observe and research. Human nature carries within itself the answer to the questions: how can I be good? how can I be happy? how can I be fruitful? The organism tells us what it needs (and therefore what it values) by sickening when deprived of these values and by growing when not deprived.

6 A study of these basic needs has shown that though their nature is to an appreciable extent instinctoid, in many ways they are not like the instincts we know so well in lower animals. Most important of all these differences is the unexpected finding that in contradiction to the age-old assumption that instincts are strong, undesirable, and unchangeable, our basic needs, though instinctoid, are weak. To be impulse-aware, to know that we really want and need love, respect, knowledge, a philosophy, self-actualization, etc – this is a difficult psychological achievement. Not only this, but the higher they are, the weaker and more easily changed and suppressed they are. Finally they are not bad but are either neutral or good. We wind up with the paradox that our human instincts, what is left of them, are so weak that they need protection against culture, against education, against learning – in a word, against being overwhelmed by the environment.

7 Our understanding of the aims of psychotherapy (and of education, of child rearing, of the formation of the good character in general) must shift considerably. To many it still means the acquisition of a set of inhibitions and controls of the intrinsic impulses. Discipline, control, suppression are the watchwords of such a regime.

But if therapy means a pressure toward breaking controls and inhibitions, then our new key words must be spontaneity, release, naturalness, self-acceptance, impulse awareness, gratification, self-choice. If our intrinsic impulses are understood to be admirable rather than detestable, we shall certainly wish to free them for their fullest expression rather than to bind them into straitjackets.

8 If instincts can be weak and if higher needs are seen to be instinctoid in character, and if culture is seen as more, not less, powerful than instinctoid impulses, and if man's basic needs turn out to be good and not bad, then the improvement of man's nature may come about via fostering of instinctoid tendencies as well as through fostering social improvements. Indeed, the point of bettering the culture will be seen as giving man's inner biological tendencies a better chance to actualize themselves.

9 In the finding that living at the higher need level can sometimes become relatively independent of lower need gratification (and even of higher need gratification in a pinch), we may have a solution to an age-old dilemma of the theologians. They have always found it necessary to attempt to reconcile the flesh and the spirit, the angel and the devil – the higher and the lower in the human organism, but no one has ever found a satisfactory solution. Functional autonomy of the higher need life seems to be part of the answer. The higher develops only on the basis of the lower, but eventually, when

well established, may become *relatively* independent of the lower (Allport, 1955).

10 In addition to Darwinian survival-value, we may now also postulate 'growth-values'. Not only is it good to survive, but it is also good (preferred, chosen, good-for-the-organism) for the person to grow toward full humanness, toward actualization of his potentialities, toward greater happiness, serenity, peak experiences, toward transcendence (Maslow, 1969b) toward richer and more accurate cognition of reality, etc. No longer need we rest on sheer viability and survival as our only ultimate proof that poverty or war or domination or cruelty are bad, rather than good. We can consider them bad because they also degrade the quality of life, of personality, of consciousness, of wisdom.

References

Allport, G. (1955). 'An organization syndrome'. *Admin Sci. Quart.*, 12, 440–60.

Benedict, R. (1970). Unpublished lectures on *Synergy in Society*, Bryn mawr, c.1942. Excerpts to be published, *Amer. Anthropologist*.

Fromm, E. (1941). *Escape from Freedom*. New York: Farrar, Straus & Giroux.

Maslow, A. H. (1964). 'Some fundamental questions that face the normative social psychologist'. *J. Humanistic Psychol.*, 8, 143–53.

Maslow, A. H. (1965). *Eupsychian Management: A Journal*. Homewood, Ill: Irwin-Dorsey.

Maslow, A. H. (1967). 'A theory of metamotivation; the biological rooting of the value-life'. *J. Humanistic Psychol.*, 7, 93–127.

Maslow, A. H. (1969a). 'Theory Z'. *J. Transpers. Psychol.*, 7, 93–127.

Maslow, A. H. (1969b). 'Various meanings of transcendence'. *J. Transpers. Psychol.*, 1, 56–66.

One more time: how do you motivate employees?
*Frederick Herzberg**

Frederick Herzberg is Distinguished Professor of Management at the University of Utah. For many years he has been researching human motivation in the work environment and its effects on the individual's job satisfaction and mental health. His motivation-hygiene theory is fully described in his 1966 book, *Work and the Nature of Man*.

This article, a Harvard Business Review classic, discusses and dismisses traditional motivation techniques, such as reducing hours or increasing wages. Herzberg then outlines his motivation-hygiene theory, which is based on the idea that factors which lead to job satisfaction are separate to, rather than opposite, those that produce job dissatisfaction. Motivation factors, such as achievement or responsibility, are intrinsic to the job and primarily contribute to job satisfaction; whereas hygiene factors, those extrinsic to the job, such as working conditions or salary, primarily relate to job dissatisfaction. Accordingly Herzberg concludes that job enrichment is the central mechanism for motivating employees.

How many articles, books, speeches, and workshops have pleaded plaintively, 'How do I get an employee to do what I want him to do?'

The psychology of motivation is tremendously complex, and what has been unravelled with any degree of assurance is small indeed. But the dismal ratio of knowledge to speculation has not dampened the enthusiasm for new forms of snake oil that are constantly coming on the market, many of them with academic testimonials. Doubtless this article will have no depressing impact on the market for snake oil, but since the ideas expressed in it have been tested in many corporations and other organizations, it will help – I hope – to redress the imbalance in the aforementioned ratio.

'Motivating' with KITA

In lectures to industry on the problem, I have found that the audiences are anxious for quick and practical answers, so I will begin with a straightforward, practical formula for moving people.

Author's note: I should like to acknowledge the contributions that Robert Ford of the American Telephone and Telegraph Company has made to the ideas expressed in this paper, and in particular to the successful application of these ideas in improving work performance and the job satisfaction of employees.

What is the simplest, surest, and most direct way of getting someone to do something? Ask him? But if he responds that he does not want to do it, then that calls for a psychological consultation to determine the reason for his obstinacy. Tell him? His response shows that he does not understand you, and now an expert in communication methods has to be brought in to show you how to get through to him. Give him a monetary incentive? I do not need to remind the reader of the complexity and difficulty involved in setting up and administering an incentive system. Show him? This means a costly training program. We need a simple way.

Every audience contains the 'direct action' manager who shouts, 'Kick him!' And this type of manager is right. The surest and least circumlocuted way of getting someone to do something is to kick him in the pants – give him what might be called the KITA.

There are various forms of KITA, and here are some of them:

- *Negative physical KITA*. This is a literal application of the term and was frequently used in the past. It has, however, three major drawbacks: (1) it is inelegant; (2) it contradicts the precious image of benevolence that most organizations cherish; and (3) since it is a physical attack, it directly stimulates the autonomic nervous system, and this often results in negative feedback – the employee may just kick you in return. These factors give rise to certain taboos against negative physical KITA.

  The psychologist has come to the rescue of those who are no longer permitted to use negative physical KITA. He has uncovered infinite sources of psychological vulnerabilities and the appropriate methods to play tunes on them. 'He took my rug away'; 'I wonder what he meant by that'; 'The boss is always going around me' – these symptomatic expressions of ego sores that have been rubbed raw are the result of application of:
- *Negative Psychological KITA*. This has several advantages over negative physical KITA. First, the cruelty is not visible; the bleeding is internal and comes much later. Second, since it affects the higher cortical centers of the brain with its inhibitory powers, it reduces the possibility of physical backlash. Third, since the number of psychological pains that a person can feel is almost infinite, the direction and site possibilities of the KITA are increased many times. Fourth, the person administering the kick can manage to be above it all and let the system accomplish the dirty work. Fifth, those who practice it receive some ego satisfaction (oneupmanship), whereas they would find drawing blood abhorrent. Finally, if the employee does complain, he can always be accused of being paranoid, since there is no tangible evidence of an actual attack.

  Now, what does negative KITA accomplish? If I kick you in the rear (physically or psychologically), who is motivated? *I* am motivated; *you* move! Negative KITA does not lead to motivation, but to movement. So:
- *Positive KITA*. Let us consider motivation. If I say to you, 'Do this for me or

the company, and in return I will give you a reward, an incentive, more status, a promotion, all the quid pro quos that exist in the industrial organization,' am I motivating you? The overwhelming opinion I receive from management people is, 'Yes, this is motivation.'

I have a year-old Schnauzer. When it was a small puppy and I wanted it to move, I kicked it in the rear and it moved. Now that I have finished its obedience training, I hold up a dog biscuit when I want the Schnauzer to move. In this instance, who is motivated – I or the dog? The dog wants the biscuit, but it is I who want it to move. Again, I am the one who is motivated, and the dog is the one who moves. In this instance all I did was apply KITA frontally; I exerted a pull instead of a push. When industry wishes to use such positive KITAs, it has available an incredible number and variety of dog biscuits (jelly beans for humans) to wave in front of the employee to get him to jump.

Why is it that managerial audiences are quick to see that negative KITA is *not* motivation, while they are almost unanimous in their judgment that positive KITA *is* motivation? It is because negative KITA is rape, and positive KITA is seduction. But it is infinitely worse to be seduced than to be raped; the latter is an unfortunate occurrence, while the former signifies that you were a party to your own downfall. This is why positive KITA is so popular: it is a tradition; it is in the American way. The organization does not have to kick you; you kick yourself.

Myths about motivation

Why is KITA not motivation? If I kick my dog (from the front or the back), he will move. And when I want him to move again, what must I do? I must kick him again. Similarly, I can charge a man's battery, and then recharge it, and recharge it again. But it is only when he has his own generator that we can talk about motivation. He then needs no outside stimulation. He *wants* to do it.

With this in mind, we can review some positive KITA personnel practices that were developed as attempts to instill 'motivation':

1 *Reducing time spent at work* – This represents a marvelous way of motivating people to work – getting them off the job! We have reduced (formally and informally) the time spent on the job over the last 50 or 60 years until we are finally on the way to the 'six and a half day weekend'. An interesting variant of this approach is the development of off-hour recreation programs. The philosophy here seems to be that those who play together, work together. The fact is that motivated people seek more hours of work, not fewer.

2 *Spiraling wages* – Have these motivated people? Yes, to seek the next wage increase. Some medievalists still can be heard to say that a good depression will get employees moving. They feel that if rising wages don't or won't do the job, perhaps reducing them will.

3 *Fringe benefits* – Industry has outdone the most welfare-minded of welfare states in dispensing cradle-to-the-grave succor. One company I know of had an informal 'fringe benefit of the month club' going for a while. The cost of fringe benefits in this country has reached approximately 25 per cent of the wage dollar, and we still cry for motivation.

People spend less time working for more money and more security than ever before, and the trend cannot be reversed. These benefits are no longer rewards; they are rights. A six-day week is inhuman, a 10-hour day is exploitation, extended medical coverage is a basic decency, and stock options are the salvation of American initiative. Unless the ante is continuously raised, the psychological reaction of employees is that the company is turning back the clock.

When industry began to realize that both the economic nerve and the lazy nerve of their employees had insatiable appetites, it started to listen to the behavioral scientists who, more out of a humanist tradition than from scientific study, criticized management for not knowing how to deal with people. The next KITA easily followed.

4 *Human relations training* – Over 30 years of teaching and, in many instances, of practicing psychological approaches to handling people have resulted in costly human relations programs and, in the end, the same question: how do you motivate workers? Here, too, escalations have taken place. Thirty years ago it was necessary to request, 'Please don't spit on the floor.' Today the same admonition requires three 'pleases' before the employee feels that his superior has demonstrated the psychologically proper attitudes toward him.

The failure of human relations training to produce motivation led to the conclusion that the supervisor or manager himself was not psychologically true to himself in his practice of interpersonal decency. So an advanced form of human relations KITA, sensitivity training, was unfolded.

5 *Sensitivity training* – Do you really, really understand yourself? Do you really, really, really trust the other man? Do you really, really, really, really cooperate? The failure of sensitivity training is now being explained, by those who have become opportunistic exploiters of the technique, as a failure to really (five times) conduct proper sensitivity training courses.

With the realization that there are only temporary gains from comfort and economic and interpersonal KITA, personnel managers concluded that the fault lay not in what they were doing, but in the employee's failure to appreciate what they were doing. This opened up the field of communications, a whole new area of 'scientifically' sanctioned KITA.

6 *Communications* – The professor of communications was invited to join the faculty of management training programs and help in making employees

understand what management was doing for them. House organs, briefing sessions, supervisory instruction on the importance of communication, and all sorts of propaganda have proliferated until today there is even an International Council of Industrial Editors. But no motivation resulted, and the obvious thought occurred that perhaps management was not hearing what the employees were saying. That led to the next KITA.

7 *Two-way communication* – Management ordered morale surveys, suggestion plans, and group participation programs. Then both employees and management were communicating and listening to each other more than ever, but without much improvement in motivation.

The behavioral scientists began to take another look at their conceptions and their data, and they took human relations one step further. A glimmer of truth was beginning to show through in the writings of the so-called higher-order-need psychologists. People, so they said, want to actualize themselves. Unfortunately, the 'actualizing' psychologists got mixed up with the human relations psychologists, and a new KITA emerged.

8 *Job participation* – Though it may not have been the theoretical intention, job participation often became a 'give them the big picture' approach. For example, if a man is tightening 10 000 nuts a day on an assembly line with a torque wrench, tell him he is building a Chevrolet. Another approach had the goal of giving the employee a *feeling* that he is determining, in some measure, what he does on his job. The goal was to provide a *sense* of achievement rather than a substantive achievement in his task. Real achievement, of course, requires a task that makes it possible.

But still there was no motivation. This led to the inevitable conclusion that the employees must be sick, and therefore to the next KITA.

9 *Employee counseling* – The initial use of this form of KITA in a systematic fashion can be credited to the Hawthorne experiment of the Western Electric Company during the early 1930s. At that time, it was found that the employees harbored irrational feelings that were interfering with the rational operation of the factory. Counseling in this instance was a means of letting the employees unburden themselves by talking to someone about their problems. Although the counseling techniques were primitive, the program was large indeed.

The counseling approach suffered as a result of experiences during World War Two, when the programs themselves were found to be interfering with the operation of the organizations; the counselors had forgotten their role of benevolent listeners and were attempting to do something about the problems that they heard about. Psychological counseling, however, has managed to survive the negative impact of World War Two experiences and today is beginning to flourish with renewed sophistication. But, alas, many of these programs, like all the others, do not seem to have lessened the pressure of demands to find out how to motivate workers.

Since KITA results only in short term movement, it is safe to predict that the cost of these programs will increase steadily and new varieties will be developed as old positive KITAs reach their satiation points.

Hygiene vs. motivators

Let me rephrase the perennial question this way: how do you install a generator in an employee? A brief review of my motivation–hygiene theory of job attitudes is required before theoretical and practical suggestions can be offered. The theory was first drawn from an examination of events in the lives of engineers and accountants. At least 16 other investigations, using a wide variety of populations (including some in the Communist countries), have since been completed, making the original research one of the most replicated studies in the field of job attitudes.

The findings of these studies, along with corroboration from many other investigations using different procedures, suggest that the factors involved in producing job satisfaction (and motivation) are separate and distinct from the factors that lead to job dissatisfaction. Since separate factors need to be considered, depending on whether job satisfaction or job dissatisfaction is being examined, it follows that these two feelings are not opposites of each other. The opposite of job satisfaction is not job dissatisfaction but, rather, *no* job satisfaction; and, similarly, the opposite of job dissatisfaction is not job satisfaction, but *no* job dissatisfaction.

Stating the concept presents a problem in semantics, for we normally think of satisfaction and dissatisfaction as opposites, i.e. what is not satisfying must be dissatisfying, and vice versa. But when it comes to understanding the behavior of people in their jobs, more than a play on words is involved.

Two different needs of man are involved here. One set of needs can be thought of as stemming from his animal nature – the built-in drive to avoid pain from the environment, plus all the learned drives which become conditioned to the basic biological needs. For example, hunger, a basic biological drive, makes it necessary to earn money, and then money becomes a specific drive. The other set of needs relates to that unique human characteristic, the ability to achieve and, through achievement, to experience psychological growth. The stimuli for the growth needs are tasks that induce growth; in the industrial setting, they are the *job content*. Contrariwise, the stimuli inducing pain avoidance behavior are found in the *job environment*.

The growth or *motivator* factors that are intrinsic to the job are: achievement, recognition for achievement, the work itself, responsibility, and growth or advancement. The dissatisfaction avoidance or *hygiene* (KITA) factors that are extrinsic to the job include: company policy and administration, supervision, interpersonal relationships, working conditions, salary, status and security.

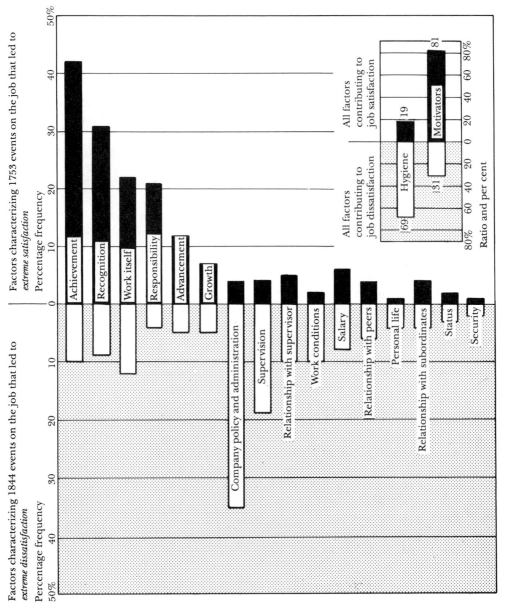

Figure 2.1 *Factors affecting job attitudes, as reported in 12 investigations*

A composite of the factors that are involved in causing job satisfaction and job dissatisfaction, drawn from samples of 1685 employees, is shown in Figure 2.1. The results indicate that motivators were the primary cause of satisfaction, and hygiene factors the primary cause of unhappiness on the job. The employees, studied in 12 different investigations, included lower level supervisors, professional women, agricultural administrators, men about to retire from management positions, hospital maintenance personnel, manufacturing supervisors, nurses, food handlers, military officers, engineers, scientists, housekeepers, teachers, technicians, female assemblers, accountants, Finnish foremen, and Hungarian engineers.

They were asked what job events had occurred in their work that had led to extreme satisfaction or extreme dissatisfaction on their part. Their responses are broken down in Figure 2.1 into percentages of total 'positive' job events and of total 'negative' job events. (The figures total more than 100 per cent on both the 'hygiene' and 'motivators' sides because often at least two factors can be attributed to a single event; advancement, for instance, often accompanies assumption of responsibility.)

To illustrate, a typical response involving achievement that had a negative effect for the employee was, 'I was unhappy because I didn't do the job successfully.' A typical response in the small number of positive job events in the Company Policy and Administration grouping was, 'I was happy because the company reorganized the section so that I didn't report any longer to the guy I didn't get along with.'

As the lower right-hand part of Figure 2.1 shows, of all the factors contributing to job satisfaction, 81 per cent were motivators. And of all the factors contributing to the employees' dissatisfaction over their work, 69 per cent involved hygiene elements.

Eternal triangle

There are three general philosophies of personnel management. The first is based on organizational theory, the second on industrial engineering, and the third on behavioral science.

The organizational theorist believes that human needs are either so irrational or so varied and adjustable to specific situations that the major function of personnel management is to be as pragmatic as the occasion demands. If jobs are organized in a proper manner, he reasons, the result will be the most efficient job structure, and the most favorable job attitudes will follow as a matter of course.

The industrial engineer holds that man is mechanistically oriented and economically motivated and his needs are best met by attuning the individual to the most efficient work process. The goal of personnel management therefore should be to concoct the most appropriate incentive system and to design the specific working conditions in a way that facilitates the most efficient use of the human machine. By structuring jobs in a manner that leads to the most efficient operation, the engineer believes that he can obtain the optimal organization of work and the proper work attitudes.

The behavioral scientist focuses on group sentiments, attitudes of individual employees, and the organization's social and psychological climate. According to his persuasion, he emphasizes one or more of the various hygiene and motivator needs. His approach to personnel management generally emphasizes some form of human relations education, in the hope of instilling healthy employee attitudes and an organizational climate which he considers to be felicitous to human values. He believes that proper attitudes will lead to efficient job and organizational structure.

There is always a lively debate as to the overall effectiveness of the approaches of the organizational theorist and the industrial engineer. Manifestly they have achieved much. But the nagging question for the behavioral scientist has been: what is the cost in human problems that eventually cause more expense to the organization – for instance, turnover, absenteeism, errors, violation of safety rules, strikes, restriction of output, higher wages, and greater fringe benefits? On the other hand, the behavioral scientist is hard put to document much manifest improvement in personnel management, using his approach.

The three philosophies can be depicted as a triangle, as is done in Figure 2.2, with each persuasion claiming the apex angle. The motivation-hygiene theory claims the same angle as industrial engineering, but for opposite goals. Rather than rationalizing the work to increase efficiency, the theory suggests that work be *enriched* to bring about effective utilization of personnel. Such a systematic attempt to motivate employees by manipulating the motivator factors is just beginning.

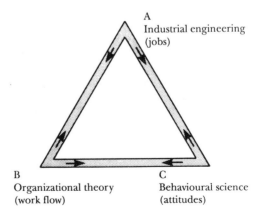

Figure 2.2   *'Triangle' of philosophies of personnel management*

The term *job enrichment* describes this embryonic movement. An older term, job enlargement, should be avoided because it is associated with past failures stemming from a misunderstanding of the problem. Job enrichment provides the opportunity for the employee's psychological growth, while job enlargement merely makes a job structurally bigger. Since scientific job enrichment is very new, this article only suggests the principles and practical steps that have recently emerged from several successful experiments in industry.

Job loading

In attempting to enrich an employee's job, management often succeeds in reducing the man's personal contribution, rather than giving him an opportunity for growth in his accustomed job. Such an endeavor, which I shall call horizontal job loading (as opposed to vertical loading, or providing motivator factors), has been the problem of earlier job enlargement programes. This activity merely enlarges the meaninglessness of the job. Some examples of this approach, and their effect, are:

- Challenging the employee by increasing the amount of production expected of him. If he tightens 10 000 bolts a day, see if he can tighten 20 000 bolts a day. The arithmetic involved shows that multiplying zero by zero still equals zero.
- Adding another meaningless task to the existing one, usually some routine clerical activity. The arithmetic here is adding zero to zero.
- Rotating the assignments of a number of jobs that need to be enriched. This means washing dishes for a while, then washing silverware. The arithmetic is substituting one zero for another zero.
- Removing the most difficult parts of the assignment in order to free the worker to accomplish more of the less challenging assignments. This traditional industrial engineering approach amounts to subtraction in the hope of accomplishing addition.

These are common forms of horizontal loading that frequently come up in preliminary brainstorming sessions on job enrichment. The principles of vertical loading have not all been worked out as yet, and they remain rather general, but I have furnished seven useful starting points for consideration in Table 2.1.

A successful application

An example from a highly successful job enrichment experiment can illustrate the distinction between horizontal and vertical loading of a job. The subjects of this study were the stockholder correspondents employed by a very large

Table 2.1   *Principles of vertical job loading*

Principle	Motivators involved
A Removing some controls while retaining accountability	Responsibility and personal achievement
B Increasing the accountability of individuals for own work	Responsibility and recognition
C Giving a person a complete natural unit of work (module, division, area, and so on)	Responsibility, achievement, and recognition
D Granting additional authority to an employee in his activity; job freedom	Responsibility, achievement, and recognition
E Making periodic reports directly available to the worker himself rather than to the supervisor	Internal recognition
F Introducing new and more difficult tasks not previously handled	Growth and learning
G Assigning individuals specific or specialized tasks, enabling them to become experts	Responsibility, growth, and advancement

corporation. Seemingly, the task required of these carefully selected and highly trained correspondents was quite complex and challenging. But almost all indexes of performance and job attitudes were low, and exit interviewing confirmed that the challenge of the job existed merely as words.

A job enrichment project was initiated in the form of an experiment with one group, designated as an achieving unit, having its job enriched by the principles described in Table 2.1. A control group continued to do its job in the traditional way. (There were also two 'uncommitted' groups of correspondents formed to measure the so-called Hawthorne Effect – that is, to gauge whether productivity and attitudes toward the job changed artificially merely because employees sensed that the company was paying more attention to them in doing something different or novel. The results for these groups were substantially the same as for the control group, and for the sake of simplicity I do not deal with them in this summary.) No changes in hygiene were introduced for either group other than those that would have been made anyway, such as normal pay increases.

The changes for the achieving unit were introduced in the first two months, averaging one per week of the seven motivators listed in Table 2.1. At the end of six months the members of the achieving unit were found to be outperforming their counterparts in the control group, and in addition indicated a marked increase in their liking for their jobs. Other results showed that the achieving group had lower absenteeism and, subsequently, a much higher rate of promotion.

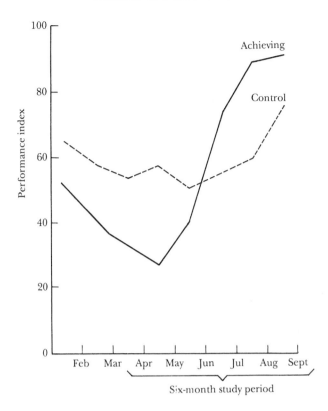

Figure 2.3 *Shareholder service index in company experiment (three-month cumulative average)*

Figure 2.3 illustrates the changes in performance, measured in February and March, before the study period began, and at the end of each month of the study period. The shareholder service index represents quality of letters, including accuracy of information, and speed of response to stockholders' letters of inquiry. The index of a current month was averaged into the average of the two prior months, which means that improvement was harder to obtain if the indexes of the previous months were low. The 'achievers' were performing less well before the six-month period started, and their performance service index continued to decline after the introduction of the motivators, evidently because of uncertainty over their newly granted responsibilities. In the third month, however, performance improved, and soon the members of this group had reached a high level of accomplishment.

Figure 2.4 shows the two groups' attitudes toward their job, measured at the end of March, just before the first motivator was introduced, and again at the end of September. The correspondents were asked 16 questions, all involving motivation. A typical one was, 'As you see it, how many opportunities do you

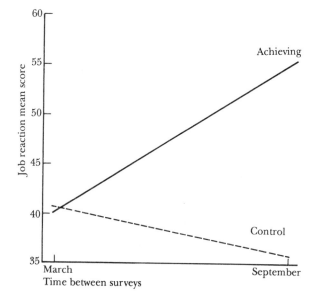

Figure 2.4   *Changes in attitudes toward tasks in company experiment (changes in mean scores over six-months period)*

feel that you have in your job for making worthwhile contributions?' The answers were scaled from one to five, with 80 as the maximum possible score. The achievers became much more positive about their job, while the attitude of the control unit remained about the same (the drop is not statistically significant).

How was the job of these correspondents restructured? Table 2.2 lists the suggestions made that were deemed to be horizontal loading, and the actual vertical loading changes that were incorporated in the job of the achieving unit. The capital letters under 'Principle' after 'Vertical loading' refer to the corresponding letters in Table 2.1. The reader will note that the rejected forms of horizontal loading correspond closely to the list of common manifestations of the phenomenon on page 35.

Steps to job enrichment

Now that the motivator idea has been described in practice, here are the steps that managers should take in instituting the principle with their employees:

1 Select those jobs in which (1) the investment in industrial engineering does

Table 2.2 Enlargement vs. enrichment of correspondents' tasks in company experiment

Horizontal loading suggestions (rejected)	Vertical loading suggestions (adopted)	Principle
Firm quotas could be set for letters to be answered each day, using a rate which would be hard to reach.	Subject matter experts were appointed within each unit for other members of the unit to consult with before seeking supervisory help. (The supervisor had been answering all specialized and difficult questions.)	G
The women could type the letters themselves, as well as compose them, or take on any other clerical functions.	Correspondents signed their own names on letters. (The supervisor had been signing all letters.)	B
All difficult or complex inquiries could be chaneled to a few women so that the remainder could achieve high rates of output. These jobs coud be exchanged from time to time.	The work of the more experienced correspondents was proof-read less frequently by supervisors and was done at the correspondents' desks, dropping verification from 100 per cent to 10 per cent. (Previously, all correspondents' letters had been checked by the supervisor.)	A
The women could be rotated through units handling different customers, and then sent back to their own units.	Production was discussed, but only in terms such as 'a full day's work is expected'. As time went on, this was no longer mentioned. (Before, the group had been constantly reminded of the number of letters that needed to be answered.)	D
	Outgoing mail went directly to the mailroom without going over supervisors' desks. (The letters had always been routed through the supervisors.)	A
	Correspondents were encouraged to answer letters in a more personalized way. (Reliance on the form-letter approach had been standard practice.)	C
	Each correspondent was held personally responsible for the quality and accuracy of letters. (This responsibility had been the province of the supervisor and the verifier.)	B,E

not make changes too costly, (2) attitudes are poor, (3) hygiene is becoming very costly, and (4) motivation will make a difference in performance.

2 Approach these jobs with the conviction that they can be changed. Years of tradition have led managers to believe that the content of the jobs is sacrosanct and the only scope of action that they have is in ways of stimulating people.

3 Brainstorm a list of changes that may enrich the jobs, without concern for their practicality.

4 Screen the list to eliminate suggestions that involve hygiene, rather than actual motivation.

5 Screen the list for generalities, such as 'give them more responsibility', that are rarely followed in practice. This might seem obvious, but the motivator words have never left industry; the substance has just been rationalized and organized out. Words like 'responsibility', 'growth', 'achievement', and 'challenge', for example, have been elevated to the lyrics of the patriotic anthem for all organizations. It is the old problem typified by the pledge of allegiance to the flag being more important than contributions to the country – of following the form, rather than the substance.

6 Screen the list to eliminate any *horizontal* loading suggestions.

7 Avoid direct participation by the employees whose jobs are to be enriched. Ideas they have expressed previously certainly constitute a valuable source for recommended changes, but their direct involvement contaminates the process with human relations *hygiene* and, more specifically, gives them only a *sense* of making a contribution. The job is to be changed, and it is the content that will produce the motivation, not attitudes about being involved or the challenge inherent in setting up a job. That process will be over shortly, and it is what the employees will be doing from then on that will determine their motivation. A sense of participation will result only in short term movement.

8 In the initial attempts at job enrichment, set up a controlled experiment. At least two equivalent groups should be chosen, one an experimental unit in which the motivators are systematically introduced over a period of time, and the other one a control group in which no changes are made. For both groups, hygiene should be allowed to follow its natural course for the duration of the experiment. Pre- and post-installation tests of performance and job attitudes are necessary to evaluate the effectiveness of the job enrichment program. The attitude test must be limited to motivator items in order to divorce the employee's view of the job he is given from all the surrounding hygiene feelings that he might have.

9 Be prepared for a drop in performance in the experimental group the first few weeks. The changeover to a new job may lead to a temporary reduction in efficiency.

10 Expect your first-line supervisors to experience some anxiety and hostility over the changes you are making. The anxiety comes from their fear that the

changes will result in poorer performance for their unit. Hostility will arise when the employees start assuming what the supervisors regard as their own responsibility for performance. The supervisor without checking duties to perform may then be left with little to do.

After a successful experiment, however, the supervisor usually discovers the supervisory and managerial functions he has neglected, or which were never his because all his time was given over to checking the work of his subordinates. For example, in the R & D division of one large chemical company I know of, the supervisors of the laboratory assistants were theoretically responsible for their training and evaluation. These functions, however, had come to be performed in a routine, unsubstantial fashion. After the job enrichment program, during which the supervisors were not merely passive observers of the assistants' performance, the supervisors actually were devoting their time to reviewing performance and administering thorough training.

What has been called an employee centered style of supervision will come about not through education of supervisors, but by changing the jobs that they do.

Concluding note

Job enrichment will not be a one-time proposition, but a continuous management function. The initial changes, however, should last for a very long period of time. There are a number of reasons for this:

- The changes should bring the job up to the level of challenge commensurate with the skill that was hired.
- Those who have still more ability eventually will be able to demonstrate it better and win promotion to higher level jobs.
- The very nature of motivators, as opposed to hygiene factors, is that they have a much longer term effect on employees' attitudes. Perhaps the job will have to be enriched again, but this will not occur as frequently as the need for hygiene.

Not all jobs can be enriched, nor do all jobs need to be enriched. If only a small percentage of the time and money that is now devoted to hygiene, however, were given to job enrichment efforts, the return in human satisfaction and economic gain would be one of the largest dividends that industry and society have ever reaped through their efforts at better personnel management.

The argument for job enrichment can be summed up quite simply: if you have someone on a job, use him. If you can't use him on the job, get rid of him, either via automation or by selecting someone with lesser ability. If you can't use him and you can't get rid of him, you will have a motivation problem.

Human nature: why is it elusive?
Edgar H. Schein

Edgar Schein (PhD) is Professor of Organizational Psychology and Management and Chairman of the Organization Studies Group, Sloan School of Management at the MIT. His impressive background in behavioural psychology gives him a knowledgeable perspective on the problems of organizational behaviour. This book, recently revised, was first published in 1965 and is one of three he has authored on the subject.

The book contains a section on motivation in which Schein reviews much of the existing literature on this subject. He goes a step further, however, and says that the experimental evidence to support these biological theories (i.e. Maslow's hierarchy of needs, Herzberg's motivators, etc.) is paltry. He goes on to describe an 'organizational perspective'. This is the relationship people have with their organizations. He identifies three types. A coercive organization is one where membership is forced and there is little or no voluntary participation. The utilitarian organization has members who are there for what they can get out of the organization. The third type is the normative organization, whose members willingly share its goals and values. However, most organizations are a mixture of two or all of the above types. In the piece we have reproduced, Schein describes how individuals relate to organizations and how this relationship affects their motivation in their work. He concludes that management, therefore, ought not to make decisions based solely on biological needs as defined by Herzberg or Maslow, but also on the relationships that may exist in each case.

One of the persistent problems of organizational psychology has been to develop a concept of human nature which would provide managers with clues on how to recruit, select, and manage people in order to obtain productivity for the organization and satisfaction for the employee. Typically we have looked toward theories of motivation to find such a concept – what makes people work, what ultimate needs or motives drive them, how important is money as a motivator, how similar are people in their motivation, what kinds of incentives will workers respond to if one wants to increase their productivity, why are some people highly motivated while others slack off or even turn their energy and creativity toward undermining the organization?

There are a great many competing theories of motivation which purport to explain the behavior of people in organizations, but there is relatively little clear research support for any of them. It is as if every theory that is proposed – such as the need for *security*, or the need to use one's *competencies*, or the need for *self-actualization* – is partially true in that it explains the behavior of *some* employees or *some* managers *some* of the time. But every time we attempt to generalize, we find that other, more important phenomena seem to be at work that vitiate the proposed theory. People sometimes work for money but then, to our surprise, fail to respond to a financial incentive system; people clearly want to use their competencies but then sometimes refuse a clearly more challenging job; people become demotivated and less interested in their work, yet the quality of what they do remains high. How are we to explain all of these inconsistencies and how is a manager to develop sensible, rational policies for dealing with people?

The biological fallacy

One major explanation for the variation we see in human behavior is that such behavior is only *partially* determined by whatever inner needs or motives we bring with us as members of a biological species. A far greater determinant of what we do is our learned motives and responses, which reflect our culture, our family situation, our socio-economic background, and the actual here-and-now forces operating within any given life situation. In other words, our motives and needs are largely determined by our *perceptions* of the situation we find our-selves in, and those perceptions are themselves largely determined by prior learning.

For example, whether or not money will motivate me may depend largely upon my perception of myself as in need of more or less money, and that perception will depend in part upon how I relate my own status and condition to that of others with whom I identify, who represent my 'reference group'. If I have come from very humble origins and have finally achieved a reasonable subsistence level and perceive myself as 'having made it' by whatever standards I assimilated in the subculture in which I grew up, I will react very differently to a monetary incentive than if I am a business school graduate starting out at the bottom of my career, aspiring to a high level in the organization and to a position of wealth which will prove to the world that I have really made it 'to the top'.

In other words, even though human beings may start with similar biological and genetic tendencies, they develop different patterns of needs, motives, talents, attitudes, and values that reflect the particular upbringing and socio-cultural situation in which they find themselves. To give another example, a manager may have learned that one way to deal with workers is to involve them participatively in certain kinds of decisions, to build a climate of mutual trust and open communication with them. That strategy may work very well with a worker whose own parents have grown up in a middle class, business oriented community, yet it may fail dismally with a third-generation political activist whose family helped initiate the development of unionism and has always operated from the initial assumption that managers can *never* be trusted.

So not only is it a fallacy to look for 'human nature' in our biological origins, but there is overwhelming evidence that some of the strongest motivational determinants of human behavior are *situational* and *role related*. For example, an otherwise unaggressive person might fly into a rage and quit a job if he or she is insulted by a boss or treated in an undignified manner; a totally honest individual might embezzle company funds if confronted by a medical crisis at home; an indolent worker might suddenly become super energetic if a co-worker is someone with whom he or she has always felt highly competitive; a person who was always unwilling to travel for the company might suddenly want to travel because the children have grown up and a new set of activities is needed to stimulate the relationship between the person and his or her spouse; a worker might really produce at a high level for a boss who treats him or her fairly but becomes a saboteur if the treatment is perceived as unfair.

Sociologists have a concept called 'the definition of the situation', by which they mean that human beings are always operating in some kind of situation the meaning of which is defined by the collective perceptions of, assumptions about, and expectations one has for that situation. We never operate in a social vacuum. We are always moving from one situation to another, and how we react, what our motives will be, will depend largely on how we define or structure that situation. When we enter new situations – as when we take a new job or join a new organization – the process of *socialization* can be defined partly as being taught or learning how to define or think about a given subset of that situation – what to do in the presence of the boss, how hard to work after hours, and so forth.

If we are to understand what a person is doing in a given situation and why, we must seek to understand the person's definition of the situation. If the organization has introduced a monetary incentive system to increase production, and yet production does not increase, the answer may well be that the workers are defining the situation as one in which working a little harder may lead to disrupted friendships, loss of pleasant social contacts, and possibly a later reduction in how much they will be paid for a given piece of work. From that perspective the monetary gains are not worth the risks, and behavior will not change, not because money is unimportant in some general motivational scheme, but because in that particular situation the workers' need for money was weighed by them against other values and motives which were operating. The same workers who fail to respond to a particular monetary incentive scheme may quit their jobs to take a higher paying one somewhere else. Does that make them inconsistent? No. It simply means that motives are tied to particular situations, and we cannot assume that the same motives apply to all people at all times in all situations.

The assumption that human nature is fixed and consists of a single set of motives that operate the same way in each of us has not received much scientific support. *Yet there are consistencies in how people behave.* These consistencies probably derive from the common perspectives we adopt through our various experiences of being socialized into a culture, a family, a socio-economic stratum, a community, and ultimately an organizational role.

The need for a sociological/situational perspective

Some of the most predictable human responses occur in face to face interactions and some of the strongest human motives derive from immediate face to face encounters. Anthropologists such as Edward Hall (1959, 1966, 1977) and sociologists such as Erving Goffman (1959, 1963, 1967) have shown us very clearly how highly regularized our social behavior is and how strongly we feel about maintaining the 'interactional order'. For example, we all know that one of the easiest ways to induce anger in someone is to insult them, and it is easy to embarrass oneself or one's associates by making a fool of oneself (by saying or doing something stupid or out of line). Learning good manners, tact, *savoir faire*, how to get along with others is given tremendous emphasis by most parents, even though the exact rules of the game (what is good manners or what is tactful) will vary from subculture to subculture.

The South African psychologist Raymond Silberbauer (1968) tells of having to make white foremen in the gold mines aware of some of the cultural rules of various tribal groups from which workers are recruited. For example, workers were being perceived as untrustworthy and 'shifty-eyed' by the foremen because they never looked directly at a foreman. The foremen were unaware that it was a mark of *disrespect* to look directly into the eyes of a superior! For males to hug each other is learned as a positive sign of friendship in Latin America, yet may arouse real anxiety and suspicion of homosexuality in an American supervisor unfamiliar with such customs. In most multinational companies horror stories abound of how managers from one culture mismanaged situations because they did not know the simple rules of interaction in another culture. But the same phenomenon occurs within our own society across socio-economic groups, geographical regions, groups of different religious origins, and so on.

Pride and dignity are powerful feelings, and the desire to maintain one's dignity or 'face' may be a far more powerful motivator than any of the ones we typically find in the lists put together by personality psychologists, for example, needs for power, achievement, security, and so on. As the industrial psychologist Norman Maier (1973) points out in his text, companies will spend a good deal of money to cover a mistake made by an officer in order to protect his or her feelings, that is, not to make the person 'lose face'. As Goffman (1967) and other sociologists have pointed out, this motive is so important because if we cannot trust others to protect our face and dignity, the whole social order becomes unsafe. If I am to feel secure in my dealings with others, I must be able to believe that they will not unduly take advantage of me, and I must show them by behaving with tact that I also can be trusted. Once we violate these norms of interaction, the very fabric of society begins to be torn down. Violators are subject to ostracism and may be viewed as emotionally unstable and in need of psychiatric treatment. Persistent violators of basic rules of conduct may be put into psychiatric hospitals until they learn to 'get along with others'.

Many severe labor-management crises can only be understood from the perspective of the threats or insults perceived by workers that often go far deeper than wages or working conditions. The 'joke' about employees' restrooms being a good deal shabbier than management's may be rather humorless if one takes this perspective. The important conclusion is that one cannot really understand what kinds of event will threaten someone's dignity without taking a situational and sociological perspective, without studying the norms and values of the particular people in the group being observed.

The developmental perspective

The developmental perspective is simply an extension of the sociological/ situational one in that it alerts us to the fact that needs, motives, values, and norms all change with the evolution of society, with the growth and development of organizations, and, most importantly, with the growth and development of the individual. What may have been a paramount need or value at one stage in a person's life may change completely at another stage (Schein, 1978; Hall, 1976). One of the great problems in studying human behavior scientifically is that one cannot easily distinguish between factors that remain stable and those amenable to change and growth. As we will see later, part of life development is a process of stabilizing one's self-image and one's values, yet there are dramatic cases of change in mid-life and old age which cannot be ignored. Managers must be alert to such changes and not predicate decisions on motivational theory assumed applicable only to those of a certain age or cultural group.

The organizational perspective

One of the major situational factors that determines patterns of motivation is the *organizational context* of behavior. How the organizations we work in or belong to treat us, the kinds of norms and values that operate in them, the kinds of authority and power exercised, all will powerfully affect our actions and the kinds of motives from which we act. This argument can best be understood in an historical context by noting that organizations do change their basic pattern of power and authority. It can also be understood if we compare a wide range of types of organizations in terms of their basic psychological contracts with their members.

Etzioni (1961) has provided a very useful typology of such individual-organization relationships by classifying organizations on the basis of (1) the kind of *power* or *authority* they use to elicit compliance and (2) the kind of *involvement* they elicit from members of the organization. On the authority dimension, Etzioni has identified three basically different types of organizations in terms of whether they use pure coercive power, economic or other material incentives combined with rational-legal authority, or 'normative' rewards or incentives. Organizations in this last group generally provide opportunities for their members to contribute to goals which are intrinsically valued and congruent with individual goals and also display either a charismatic or a rational leadership style. Table 2.3 shows examples of each of the pure types as well as examples of some mixed structures which involve combinations of authority types.

This typology is based on a different principle from the Blau and Scott typology shown in Chapter 2 and is more useful for our purposes in that it focuses on the internal 'climate' of the organization instead of the ultimate purpose or function of different kinds of organizations in society.

Etzioni also distinguishes three types of involvement of organization members, as follows: (1) *alienative*, which means that the person is not psychologically involved but is coerced to remain as a member; (2) *calculative*, which means that the person is involved to the extent of doing a 'fair day's work for a fair day's pay'; and (3) *moral*, which means that the person *intrinsically* values the mission of the organization and his or her job, and is personally involved and identified with the organization.

Table 2.4 shows the nine types of organizational relationships that could logically result from this typology. Etzioni points out, however, that the type of personal involvement possible depends to a large extent on the kind of power or authority exercised by the organization. Hence there is a tendency for organizations to cluster in certain cells of the table, primarily along the diagonal from upper left to lower right. Thus, if we look at the examples in Table 2.3, we see that the kinds of organizations listed under coercive would typically

Table 2.3 *Classification of organizations based on type of power or authority*

A   Predominantly *coercive*, non-legitimate authority
         Concentration camps
         Prisons and correctional institutions
         Prisoner of war camps
         Custodial mental hospitals
         Coercive unions

B   Predominantly *utilitarian*, rational-legal authority, use of
     economic rewards
         Business and industry (with a few exceptions)
         Business unions
         Farmers' organizations
         Peacetime military organizations

C   Predominantly *normative*, use of membership, status, intrinsic value
     rewards, authority based on charisma or expertise
         Religious organizations (churches, convents, and so on)
         Ideologically based political organizations or parties
         Hospitals
         Colleges and universities
         Social unions
         Voluntary associations and mutual-benefit associations
         Professional associations
         Business organizations when they are first founded

D   *Mixed* structures
         Normative-coercive: combat units
         Utilitarian-normative: most labor unions
         Utilitarian-coercive: some early industries, some farms,
            company towns, ships

Source: Based on Etzioni (1961).

with what they give in the way of rewards and the kind of authority they use. If a have highly alienated members. Utilitarian organizations, on the other hand, would tend to have calculative members who expect primarily economic rewards for their performance but who do not feel they have to like their jobs or their employer. The kinds of organizations listed under normative tend to have members who belong because they value the goals of the organization and like to fulfill their organizational roles. That is, they consider it morally right to belong.

We can restate this point in our terms by saying that the organizational types that fall along the diagonal have workable or 'fair' psychological contracts with their members. What the organizations get in the way of involvement is in line

Table 2.4   *Types of power-authority versus types of involvement*

	Coercive	Utilitarian	Normative
Alienative	*		
Calculative		*	
Moral			*

* Represents the predominent types.
Source: Based on Etzioni (1961).

utilitarian organization like a manufacturing concern expects its employees to like their work – that is, to be morally involved – it may be expecting workers to give more than they receive. Or if a normative organization such as a university wishes to maintain the moral involvement of its faculty, it must use a reward-and-authority system in line with such involvement. If university administrators withhold status or privileges such as academic freedom, for example, they will be violating their psychological contract with professors. The faculty will probably respond either by redefining its role and changing the nature of its involvement from moral to calculative – which might mean putting in minimum class and office hours based on the amount of pay received – or by becoming alienated, that is, doing the required amount of teaching and research, but without concern for quality and without enthusiasm.*

The above typology represents 'pure' types of organizations seldom found in real-world circumstances. Most organizations are a complex mixture of several types. Nevertheless, it is useful to describe the pure types and to consider the basic dimensions of type of authority-power and type of psychological involvement. Historically, there has been a shift away from pure coercive and normative types of organizations toward various combinations of utilitarian with either normative or coercive. Particularly in the development of business and industry, we have witnessed the movement from a coercive atmosphere in which labor was compelled to follow company dictates because of the scarcity of jobs and an overall low standard of living, to company concern for adequate economic rewards, job security, and many other kinds of employee benefit. The growth of unions and collective bargaining has promoted the utilitarian, rational-legal type of contractual relationship between management and labor (Harbison and Myers,1959).

As business and industry have become more complex and more dependent on high quality performance from both managers and workers, a trend has begun toward making the psychological contract more utilitarian-normative. By this I

* We have seen in recent years a considerable growth in faculty unionization, typically related to feelings on the part of a faculty that members were not being fairly treated on issues such as pay, opportunities to influence university policy, and the like (Baldridge, 1971; Ladd & Lipset, 1975).

mean that companies are seeking to establish new kinds of relationships with their members. These new relationships to some degree abandon purely utilitarian conceptions in favor of normative ones. Members are increasingly expected to like their work, to become personally committed to organizational goals, and to become creative in the service of these goals; in exchange, they are given more influence in decision making, thus reducing the authority of management.

One way of interpreting the events on many university campuses in the late 1960s is to note that students shifted the basis of their involvement from moral (being in college because they valued education for its own sake) or calculative (being in college because education paid off in better jobs and better future income) toward alienative (being in college only because of pressure to be there and finding the educational offerings irrelevant, hypocritical, or degrading). Professors' authority, being based on their scholarly expertise in a given area of inquiry, could function only so long as students accepted this expertise as *relevant* to their own values and goals. Once students defined professors' expertise as irrelevant, those professors no longer had any rational authority. They then had to rely on utilitarian authority (hope that students would see the need of an education for their own future economic well-being) or coercive authority (threaten to flunk students who were disrespectful or failed to do the work). Much of the anger felt by students and the anxiety expressed by professors in the late 1960s was due to the breakdown of the psychological contract between them. Such a breakdown basically denotes a fundamental questioning of the relationship (based on common values or goals) between the parties. Once this happens, one can expect a breakdown of communication, a failure of mutual understanding, and increasing frustration leading to various kinds of emotional responses on both the part of professors and students (Schein, 1970).

The 1970s have witnessed a gradual return to a more calculative and moral form of student involvement, but many of the basic values of the 1960s have remained – rejection of arbitrary authority, greater concern for the relevance of education, greater concern for nature and the environment, greater individualism, and greater concern for self-expression (Yankelovich, 1974).

Contingency theories

One of the resolutions to the problem of defining human nature has been to develop what have come to be called 'contingency theories'. Such theories emphasize that there are no simple generalizations about human behavior in organizations, but that if one can spell out enough of the prior situational conditions, enough about the human actors in the situation, and enough about the properties of the task and the environment within which the task is being carried out, one can then specify hypotheses or propositions.

Such propositions would typically be in the form of: 'If these and these conditions are true, then the manager should do such and so.' A simple version might be: 'If the manager is dealing with a group of workers from an economically disadvantaged minority with low experience and skill levels, he or she should institute a training programe, tightly structured rules, good economic incentives, and a high degree of supportive activities to help the workers gain self-confidence.' On the other hand, 'If the manager has at his or her disposal a group of sophisticated, experienced engineers, who are to design a new piece of high-technology equipment, he or she should give the group a maximum degree of freedom, provide consultative help to them as necessary, worry more about recognition than monetary incentives, and work collaboratively with the group in setting rules rather than imposing them.'

In the area of how to organize work, similar kinds of contingency theories are being developed pertaining to how to divide labour, how to integrate effort, how much to decentralize, how to control the organization, and so on. The important point to recognize about these theories is that they represent progress in understanding reality, a reality that social scientists are discovering derives from the interplay of cultural, economic, organizational, and technological forces. While it is still worthwhile to ask basic questions such as, what is human nature? or what is an organization? we must recognize that *we will not find simple answers.* We will have occasion throughout this book to refer to attempts to find such simple answers, but the thrust of my argument will be that human beings and the ways in which they interact are too complex for any 'blanket' theory to explain.

Summary

In this chapter we have taken a broad look at some of the parameters that help define 'human nature' and the psychological contract between organizations and their members. First of all, it is necessary to remind ourselves that human behavior and motivation cannot be understood except from a sociological/situational and developmental perspective. Second, it is important to recognize that different kinds of organizations depend upon different kinds of authority and power, and this in turn limits the kind of involvement their members can have – that is, leads to certain kinds of psychological contracts. Finally, we should recognize that there has been a historical evolution in the use of authority and power from more coercive forms toward more rational-legal and normative forms. In the next chapter we will examine in more detail how these historical trends have reflected themselves in managerial assumptions about human nature and the basic motivation to work.

References

Baldridge, J. V. (1971). *Power and Conflict in the University*. New York: Wiley.

Etzioni, A. (1961). *Complex Organizations*. New York: Holt, Rinehart and Winston.

Goffman, E. (1959). *The Presentation of Self in Everyday Life*. New York: Doubleday.

Goffman, E. (1963). *Behavior in Public Places*. New York: Free Press.

Goffman, E. (1967). *Interaction Ritual*. Chicago: Aldine.

Hall, D. T. (1976). *Careers in Organizations*. Pacific Palisades, Calif: Goodyear.

Hall, E. (1959). *The Silent Language*. New York: Doubleday.

Hall, E. (1966). *The Hidden Dimension*. New York: Doubleday.

Hall, E. (1977). *Beyond Culture*. New York: Anchor.

Harbison, F. and Myers, C. A. (1959). *Management in the Industrial World*. New York: McGraw-Hill.

Ladd, E. C. and Lipset, S. M. (1975). *The Divided Academy*. New York: McGraw-Hill.

Maier, N. R. F. (1973). *Psychology in Industrial Organizations*. Boston: Houghton-Mifflin.

Schein, E. H. (1970). 'The reluctant professor: Implications for university management'. *Sloan Management Review*. 12(1), 35–49.

Schein, E. H. (1978). *Career Dynamics*. Reading, Mass: Addison-Wesley.

Silberbauer, E. R. (1968). *Understanding and Motivating the Bantu Worker*. Johannesburg, South Africa: Personnel Management Advisory Service.

Yankelovich, D. (1974). 'The meaning of work', in J. M. Rosow (ed.), *The Worker and the Job*. Englewood Cliffs, NJ: Prentice-Hall.

Man waiting for motivation

Thomas J. Peters and Robert H. Waterman

Tom Peters and Robert Waterman were principals at the consulting firm McKinsey & Co. Even before their famous book was published Tom Peters set up his own consulting company called the Palo Alto Consulting Centre. He has since spawned a number of initiatives, the most famous being the Tom Peters Group. Robert Waterman stayed with McKinsey and has only recently set up his own organization.

The book was based on a sample of 62 companies including high-technology organizations, consumer goods companies, service organizations, general industrial goods companies and project management specialists. These were all excellent companies in that they had to fulfil criteria on average return on equity, return on sales, return on total capital etc. All these ratios were analysed over a period of 20 years. All the companies were found to have certain qualities in their management that enabled them to stay excellent; they had inspired leadership, motivated people and strong cultures.

In Chapter 3, 'Man Waiting for Motivation', Peters and Waterman review the research on people and motivation. They emphasize that people are irrational, that they have unrealistic self-esteem and they are 'suckers for a bit of praise'. Their conclusions are that organizations need to take advantage of these traits by providing plenty of positive reinforcement, acting in line with their beliefs and creating an elevating purpose or mission.

The central problem with the rationalist view of organizing people is that people are not very rational. To fit Taylor's old model, or today's organizational charts, man is simply designed wrong (or, of course, vice versa, according to our argument here). In fact, if our understanding of the current state of psychology is even close to correct, man is the ultimate study in conflict and paradox. It seems to us that to understand why the excellent companies are so effective in engendering both commitment and regular innovation from tens of thousands or even hundreds of thousands of people, we have to take into account the way they deal with the following contradictions that are built into human nature:

1 All of us are self-centered, suckers for a bit of praise, and generally like to think of ourselves as winners. But the fact of the matter is that our talents are distributed normally – none of us is really as good as he or she would like to think, but rubbing our noses daily in that reality doesn't do us a bit of good.
2 Our imaginative, symbolic right brain is at least as important as our rational, deductive left. We reason by stories *at least* as often as with good data. 'Does it feel right?' counts for more than 'Does it add up?' or 'Can I prove it?'

3 As information processors, we are simultaneously flawed and wonderful. On the one hand, we can hold little explicitly in mind, at most a half dozen or so facts at one time. Hence there should be an enormous pressure on managements – of complex organizations especially – to keep things very simple indeed. On the other hand, our unconscious mind is powerful, accumulating a vast storehouse of patterns, if we let it. Experience is an excellent teacher; yet most businessmen seem to undervalue it in the special sense we will describe.

4 We are creatures of our environment, very sensitive and responsive to external rewards and punishment. We are also strongly driven from within, self-motivated.

5 We act as if express beliefs are important, yet action speaks louder than words. One cannot, it turns out, fool any of the people any of the time. They watch for patterns in our most minute actions, and are wise enough to distrust words that in any way mismatch our deeds.

6 We desperately need meaning in our lives and will sacrifice a great deal to institutions that will provide meaning for us. We simultaneously need independence, to feel as though we are in charge of our destinies, and to have the ability to stick out.

Now, how do most companies deal with these conflicts? They take great pride in setting really high targets for people (productivity teams, product development teams, or division general managers), stretch targets. These are perfectly rational, but ultimately self-defeating. Why do TI and Tupperware, by contrast, insist that teams set their own objectives? Why does IBM set quotas so that almost all salespeople can make them? Surely TI has lazy workers. And no matter how intelligent IBM's hiring, screening, and training programs are for their salespeople, there is no way that this giant is going to get all superstars on its salesforce. So what's going on?

The answer is surprisingly simple, albeit ignored by most managers. In a recent psychological study (Myers, 1980) when a random sample of male adults were asked to rank themselves on 'the ability to get along with others', *all* subjects, 100 per cent, put themselves in the top half of the population. Sixty per cent rated themselves in the top 10 per cent of the population, and a full 25 per cent ever so humbly thought they were in the top one per cent of the population. In a parallel finding, 70 per cent rated themselves in the top quartile in leadership; only two per cent felt they were below average as leaders. Finally, in an area in which self-deception should be hard for most males, at least, 60 per cent said they were in the top quartile of athletic ability; only six per cent said they were below average.

We all think we're tops. We're exuberantly, wildly irrational about ourselves. And that has sweeping implications for organizing. Yet most organizations, we find, take a negative view of their people. They verbally berate participants for poor performance. (Most actually talk tougher than they act, but the tough talk nonetheless intimidates people.) They call for risk taking but punish even tiny failures. They want innovation but kill the spirit of the champion. With their rationalist hats on, they design systems that seem calculated to tear down their workers' self-image. They might not mean to be doing that, but they are.

The message that comes through so poignantly in the studies we reviewed is that we like to think of ourselves as winners. The lesson that the excellent companies have to teach is that there is no reason why we can't design systems that continually reinforce this notion; most of their people are made to feel that they are winners. Their populations are distributed around the normal curve, just like every other large population, but the difference is that their systems reinforce degrees of winning rather than degrees of losing. Their people by and large make their targets and quotas, because the targets and quotas are set (often by the people themselves) to allow that to happen.

In the not-so-excellent companies, the reverse is true. While IBM explicitly manages to ensure that 70 to 80 per cent of its salespeople meet quotas, another company (an IBM competitor in part of its product line) works it so that only 40 per cent of the salesforce meets its quotas during a typical year. With this approach, at least 60 per cent of the salespeople think of themselves as losers. They resent it and that leads to dysfunctional, unpredictable, frenetic behavior. Label a man a loser and he'll start acting like one. As one GM manager noted, 'Our control systems are designed under the apparent assumption that 90 per cent of the people are lazy ne'er-do-wells, just waiting to lie, cheat, steal, or otherwise screw us. We demoralize 95 per cent of the workforce who do act as adults by designing systems to cover our tails against the five per cent who really are bad actors.'

The systems in the excellent companies are not only designed to produce lots of winners; they are constructed to celebrate the winning once it occurs. Their systems make extraordinary use of non-monetary incentives. They are full of hoopla.

There are other opportunities for positive reinforcement. The most intriguing finding – in another major area of psychological research, called 'attribution theory' – is the so-called fundamental attribution error postulated by Stanford's Lee Ross (Ross, 1977). Attribution theory attempts to explain the way we assign cause for success or failure. Was it good luck? Was it skill? Did we goof? Were we defeated by the system? The fundamental attribution error that so intrigues the psychologists is that we typically treat any success as our own and any failure as the system's. If anything goes well, it is quite clear that 'I made it happen', 'I am talented', and so on. If anything bad happens, 'It's them', 'It's the system'. Once again, the implications for organizing are clear. People tune out if they feel they are failing, because 'the system' is to blame. They tune in when the system leads them to believe they are successful. They learn that they can get things done because of skill, and, most important, they are likely to try again.

The old adage is 'Nothing succeeds like success'. It turns out to have a sound scientific basis. Researchers studying motivation find that the prime factor is simply the self-perception among motivated subjects that they are in fact doing well. Whether they are or not by any absolute standard doesn't seem to matter much. In one experiment (Jones, 1977), adults were given 10 puzzles to solve. All 10 were exactly the same for all subjects. They worked on them, turned them in, and were given the results at the end. Now, in fact, the results they were given were fictitious. Half of the exam takers were told that they had done well, seven out of 10 correct. The other half were told they had done poorly, seven out of 10 wrong. Then all were given another 10 puzzles (the same for each person). The half who had been *told* that they had done well in the first round really did do better in the second, and the other half really did do worse. Mere association with past personal success apparently leads to more persistence, higher motivation, or something that makes us do better. Warren Bennis, in *The* half who had been *told* that they had done well in the first round really did do better in the second, and the other half really did do worse. Mere association with past personal success apparently leads to more persistence, higher motivation, or something that makes us do better. Warren Bennis, in *The Unconscious Conspiracy: Why Leaders Can't Lead*, finds ample reason to agree: 'In a study of school teachers, it turned out that when they held high expectations of their students, that alone was enough to cause an increase of 25 points in the students' IQ scores' (Bennis, 1976).

Research on the functions of the brain show that the left and right hemispheres differ substantially. The left half is the reasoning, sequential, verbal half; it is the 'logical' and rational half. The right half is the artistic half; it is the half that sees and remembers patterns, recalls melodies, waxes poetic. The utter distinctness of the two hemispheres has been shown repeatedly, when, for example, required surgery in cases of *grand mal* epilepsy has decoupled the links between the two halves. Studies show that the right half is great at visualizing things but can't verbalize any of them. The left side can't remember patterns, like people's faces. Those who say 'I'm no good at names, but never forget a face' aren't defective, simply a little right-brained.

Arthur Koestler points out the dominant role, like it or not, of our right brain. In his *Ghost in the Machine* Koestler attributes our basest emotions, our predilection for war and destruction, to 'an underdeveloped [right] half of the brain'. He asserts that '[our] behavior continues to be dominated by a relatively crude and primitive system' (Koestler, 1967). And Ernest Becker (1973) goes so far as to say that 'the psychoanalytic emphasis on creatureliness [i.e. our basic traits] is *the* lasting insight on human character'. He adds that it leads us urgently to 'seek transcendence', 'avoid isolation,' and 'above all fear helplessness'.

The organizational implications of this line of reasoning are inescapable, although with a potential dark side (e.g. we'll do almost anything to seek transcendence). The business researcher Henry Mintzberg (1976) amplifies the point:

One fact recurs repeatedly in all of this research: the key managerial processes are enormously complex and mysterious (to me as a researcher, as well as to the managers who carry them out), drawing on the vaguest of information and using the least articulated of mental processes. These processes seem to be more relational and holistic than ordered and sequential, and more intuitive than intellectual; they seem to be most characteristic of right-hemispheric activity.

The total of left- and right-brain research suggests simply that businesses are full (100 per cent) of highly 'irrational' (by left-brain standards), emotional human beings: people who want desperately to be on winning teams ('seek transcendence'); individuals who thrive on the camaraderie of an effective small group or unit setting ('avoid isolation'); creatures who want to be made to feel that they are in at least partial control of their destinies ('fear helplessness'). Now, we seriously doubt that the excellent companies have explicitly proceeded from right-brain considerations in developing their management practices. But the effect is such that it appears they have, especially in relation to their competitors. They simply allow for – and take advantage of – the emotional, more primitive side (good and bad) of human nature. They provide an opportunity to be the best, a context for the pursuit of quality and excellence. They offer support – more, celebration; they use small, intimate units (from divisions to 'skunk works' or other uses of teams); and they provide within protected settings opportunities to stand out – as part of a quality circle at TI, for example, where there are 9000 such entities.

Also note that this implicit recognition of the right-side traits by the excellent companies is directly at the expense of more traditional left-brain business practices: causes to fight for are a long way from 30 quarterly MBO objectives. The intimate team or small division ignores scale economies. Allowing freedom of expression by thousands of quality circles flies in the face of the 'one best way' of traditional production organization.

There is another aspect to our right brain's nature that isn't usually a part of conventional management wisdom but is clearly being nurtured by the excellent companies. That is the intuitive, creative side. Science and mathematics are thought by many to be the mecca of logical thought, and logical, rational thought certainly does feature prominently in the day to day progression of science. But as we pointed out in connection with scientific paradigm change, logic is not the true engine of scientific progress. Here's how James Watson, co-discoverer of the structure of DNA, described the double helix the night he finished his research: 'It's so beautiful, you see, so beautiful' (*The Economist*, 1980). In science the aesthetic, the beauty of the concept, is so important that Nobel laureate Murray Gell-Mann was moved to comment, 'When you have something simple that agrees with all the rest of the physics and really seems to explain what's going on, a few experimental data against it are no objection whatsoever' (Judson, 1980). When McDonald's former chairman Ray Kroc waxed poetic about hamburger buns, he hadn't taken leave of his senses; he simply recognized the importance of beauty as a starting point for the business logic that ensues.

We 'reason' with our intuitive side just as much as, and perhaps more than, with our logical side. Two experimental psychologists, Amos Tversky and Daniel Kahneman, are the leaders of a principal thrust of experimental psychology called 'cognitive biases', started about 15 years ago. In test after test, with sophisticated – even scientifically trained – subjects, our bias for the intuitive manifests itself. For example, a phenomenon they term 'representativeness' strongly affects our reasoning powers. Simply said, we are more influenced by stories (vignettes that are whole and make sense in themselves) than by data (which are, by definition, utterly abstract). In a typical experiment, subjects are told a story about an individual, given some relevant data, and then asked to guess the individual's career. The subjects are told, say, 'Jack is a 45-year-old man. He is married and has four children. He is generally conservative, careful, and ambitious. He shows no interest in political and social issues and spends most of his free time on his many hobbies, which include home carpentry, sailing, and mathematical puzzles.' Then the subjects are told that Jack's description was selected from a population that contains 80 per cent lawyers and 20 per cent engineers. It doesn't matter that they are told the sample is lawyer-heavy; the subjects pick the occupation on the basis of their stereotype of the occupation. In this case, most of the subjects decided that Jack was an engineer (Tversky and Kahneman, 1974).

Gregory Bateson (1980) also states the case for the primacy of representativeness:

> There's a story which I have used before and shall use again: a man wanted to know about mind, not in nature, but in his private large computer. He asked it, 'Do you compute that you will ever think like a human being?' The machine then set to work to analyze its own computational habits. Finally, the machine printed its answer on a piece of paper, as such machines do. The man ran to get the answer and found, neatly typed, the words: THAT REMINDS ME OF A STORY. A story is a little knot or complex of that species of connectedness which we call relevance. Surely the computer was right. This is indeed how people think.

Related findings include:

1 We don't pay attention to prior outcomes. History doesn't move us as much as does a good current anecdote (or, presumably, a juicy bit of gossip). We reason with data that come readily to mind (called the 'availability heuristic' by Kahneman and Tversky) even if the data have no statistical validity. When we meet three friends in the space of a week in a hotel in Tokyo, we are more apt to think 'how odd' than we are to muse on the probability that our circle of acquaintances tends to frequent the same places we do.

2 If two events even vaguely co-exist, we leap to conclusions about causality. For example, in one experiment subjects are given clinical data on people and drawings of them. Later, when asked to recall what they have found, they will greatly overestimate the correlation between the way a person looks and that person's true characteristics – people who are in fact suspicious by nature were judged typically (and erroneously) to have peculiar eyes.

3 We're hopeless about sample size. We find small samples about as convincing as large ones, sometimes more so. Consider, for example, a situation in which an individual draws two balls from an urn and finds that both are red. Another person then draws 30 balls and finds that 18 are red and 12 are white. Most people believe the first sample contains the stronger evidence that the urn contains predominantly red balls, although as a purely statistical matter, the opposite is the case.

And so it goes through a wealth of experimental data, now thousands of experiments old, showing that people reason intuitively. They reason with simple decision rules, which is a fancy way of saying that, in this complex world, they trust their gut. We need ways of sorting through the infinite minutiae out there, and we start with heuristics – associations, analogues, metaphors and ways that have worked for us before.

There is both good and bad in this, although mainly good, we think. The bad part is that, as the experiments demonstrate, our collective gut is not much use in the arcane world of probability and statistics. Here is an area in which a little more training on the rational side would help! But the good element is that it probably is only the intuitive leap that will let us solve problems in this complex world. This is a major advantage of man over computer, as we will see.

Simplicity and complexity

Most acronyms stink. Not KISS: Keep It Simple, Stupid! One of the key attributes of the excellent companies is that they have realized the importance of keeping things simple despite overwhelming genuine pressures to complicate things. There is a powerful reason for this, and we turn to the Nobel laureate Herbert Simon for the answer. Simon has been deeply involved in the field of artificial intelligence in recent years, trying to get computers to 'think' more as people do rather than conducting inefficient, exhaustive searches for solutions.

Among Simon and his colleagues' most important findings, for example, is that human beings are not good at processing large streams of new data and information. They have found that the most we can hold in short term memory, without forgetting something, is six or seven pieces of data.

Again, we're faced with an important paradox for management, for the world of big companies *is* complex. Just how complex is suggested by the fact that as the number of people in a company goes up arithmetically, the number of possible interactions among them goes up geometrically. If our company has 10 employees, we can all stay in touch with one another because the number of ways we can interact, say, in one-on-one discussions is 45. If our company has 1000 employees, on the other hand, that same number of possible one-on-one interactions goes up to about 500 000. If there are 10 000 employees then the number rises to 50 million. To cope with the complex communications needs generated by size alone, we require appropriately complex systems, or so it would seem.

We recently read a stack of business proposals, none of which was less than 50 pages long. We subsequently went through the personal programs of the senior executives of a $500 million consumer goods company; seldom did its programs contain fewer than 15 objectives for the year, and 30 objectives was not uncommon. Not unreasonable, you say, until you realize that the team at the top is trying to keep informed on the career progress of the top 500 people in the company – perhaps 15 000 objectives. Now, what's the logical response to things getting more and more complex for the top executives? What do they do when they start getting thousands of objectives they somehow are expected to process? What do they do when all these objectives are but a tiny part of the total set of information they must deal with? Well, they hire staff to simplify things for themselves.

Staff may, in fact, simplify matters – for them. But the staff makes life miserable for the people in the field. The moment that staff, in any number, leaps into action, it starts generating information requests, instructions, regulations, policies, reports and finally questionnaires on 'how staff is doing'. Somewhere along the way to bigness, information overload sets in. Short term memory can't process it all, or even a small fraction of it, and things get very confusing.

But, as is so often the case, the excellent companies seem to have found ways of coping with this problem. For one thing, they intentionally keep corporate staffs small. Then there aren't enough corporate staff around to generate too much confusion down the line. Emerson, Schlumberger, and Dana, for example, are $3 billion to $6 billion top-performing corporations; yet each is run with fewer than 100 bodies in corporate headquarters. Ford, meanwhile, has 17 layers of management, while Toyota (and the 800 million-member Roman Catholic Church) has five. As another coping device, the excellent companies focus on only a few key business values, and a few objectives. The focus on a few key values lets everyone know what's important, so there is simply less need for daily instructions (i.e. daily short term memory overload). Rene McPherson, when he took over at Dana, dramatically threw out 22½ inches of policy manuals and replaced them with a one-page statement of philosophy focusing on the 'productive people'. (His auditors were appalled. 'That means there could be 74 different procedures in 74 different plants'. McPherson replied, 'Yes and it means maybe you guys will finally have to earn your fees.')

Many of these companies eliminate paperwork through their use of quick-hit task forces, and among the paperwork fighters P&G is legendary for its insistence on one-page memos as the almost sole means of written communication. Others 'suboptimize'; they ignore apparent economies of scale, putting up with a fair amount of internal overlap, duplication, and mistakes just so they won't have to coordinate everything, which, given their size, they couldn't do anyway. As we go through the research results in later chapters, we shall find scores of devices used by the excellent companies for keeping things simple. In every instance they are ignoring the 'real world', the complex one. They are, in a real sense, being *simplistic*, not just keeping it simple. Of course, 'more than two objectives is no objectives', the TI watchword, is unrealistic; 30 objectives *is* a more realistic description of the world. But the TI rule jibes with human nature. With a little luck and a hell of a lot of persistence, one might actually get two things done in a year.

Simon (1979), in his research on artificial intelligence, finds another fascinating result that is, finally, encouraging. Looking at long term memory, he and his colleagues studied the problem of programming computers to play chess. Within this research lies an important idea that ties together the role of the rational and the role of the intuitive. Simon started by assuming that the game of chess could be played on a strictly rationalist basis, that is, one could program the computer like a decision tree. Before moving, the computer would search ahead and examine all possible moves and countermoves. Theoretically, that can be done. However, it's not practical, for the number of possibilities is something on the order of 10 to the one hundred and twentieth power (a trillion, by contrast, is only 10 to the twelfth power). The fastest of modern day computers can do something like 10 to the twentieth calculations in a century. So programming our chess-playing computer to behave rationally is just not feasible.

Struck by the notion, Simon went on to research what good chess players really do. In conducting his research, he asked chess masters – the best in the world – to look briefly (for 10 seconds) at games that were already in progress, the boards still containing around 20 or so pieces. He found that the chess masters could later recall the locations of virtually all the pieces. That doesn't fit with short term memory theory at all. When class A players (one rank below masters) were asked to do the same test, they scored much less well. Maybe chess masters have better short term memories. But here's the rub with that idea: neither the masters nor the class A players could remember where the pieces were on chessboard set-ups that were randomly generated without games in progress. Something else must be at work.

The something else, Simon believes, is that the chess masters have much more highly developed long term chess memories, and the memories take the form of subconsciously remembered patterns, or what Simon terms chess 'vocabularies'. While the class A player has a vocabulary of around 2000 patterns, the chess master has a vocabulary of around 50 000 patterns. Chess players use decision-tree thinking, it appears, only in a very limited sense. They begin with the patterns: Have I seen this one before? In what context? What worked before?

When we start to dwell on the implications of Simon's research, we are struck by its applicability elsewhere. The mark of the true professional in any field is the rich vocabulary of patterns, developed through years of formal education and especially through years of practical experience. The experienced doctor, the artist, the machinist, all have rich pattern vocabularies – Simon is now calling them 'old friends'.

This notion ought to be celebrated for, in our minds, it is the real value of experience in business. It helps to explain the importance of management by wandering around. Not only do the employees benefit from being paid attention to. The experienced boss has good instincts; his vocabulary of old-friend patterns tells him immediately whether things are going well or badly.

The vocabulary-of-patterns notion ought to do several things for us as we think about its implications for excellence in management. It should help us trust our gut more often on key business decisions. It should lead us to ask the advice of customers and workers more frequently. And finally it should encourage all of us to think hard about the value of experimenting as opposed to merely detached study.

Positive reinforcement

B. F. Skinner has a bad reputation in some circles. His techniques are seen as ultimately manipulative. He actually sets himself up for attack from all quarters. In his popular treatise *Beyond Freedom and Dignity*, for instance, he calls for nothing less than a sweeping 'technology of behavior' (Skinner, 1971). He says that we are all simply a product of the stimuli we get from the external world. Specify the environment completely enough and you can exactly predict the individual's actions. We are confronted with the same problem that the rationalists ran into with economic man. Just as economic man can never know enough (i.e. everything) to maximize his utility function, we can't ever come close to specifying the environment completely enough to predict behavior. Unfortunately, though, we tend to throw out some of Skinner's extremely powerful and practical findings because of the arrogance of his claims and the implicit ideology associated with them.

If we look further, we find that the most important lesson from Skinner is the role of positive reinforcement, of rewards for jobs well done. Skinner and others take special note of the asymmetry between positive and negative reinforcement (essentially the threat of sanctions). In short, negative reinforcement will produce behavioral change, but often in strange, unpredictable, and undesirable ways. Positive reinforcement causes behavioral change too, but usually in the intended direction.

Why spend time on this? It seems to us that central to the whole notion of managing is the superior/subordinate relationship, the idea of manager as 'boss', and the corollary that orders will be issued and followed. The threat of punishment is the principal implied power that underlies it all. To the extent that this underlying notion prevails, we are not paying attention to people's dominant need to be winners. Moreover, repeated negative reinforcement is, as Skinner says, usually a dumb tactic. It doesn't work very well. It usually results in frenetic, unguided activity. Further, punishment doesn't suppress the desire to 'do bad'. Says Skinner: 'The person who has been punished is not thereby simply less inclined to behave in a given way; at best, he learns how to avoid punishment' (Skinner, 1971).

Positive reinforcement, on the other hand, not only shapes behavior but also teaches and in the process enhances our own self-image. To give a negative example first, suppose that we get punished for 'not treating a customer well'. Not only do we not know what specifically to do in order to improve; we might well respond by 'learning' to avoid customers altogether. In Skinner's terms, 'customer' *per se*, rather than 'treating a customer badly', has become associated with punishment. On the other hand, if someone tells us via a compliment from a 'mystery shopper' that we 'just acted in the best traditions of XYZ Corporation in responding to Mrs Jones's minor complaint', well, that's quite different. Per Skinner, and our own experience, what we are now likely to get is an employee out beating the bushes to find more Mrs Joneses to treat well. He or she has learned that a specific (positive) behavior pattern leads to rewards and has at the same time satisfied the insatiable human need to enhance one's self-image.

Heinz's highly successful frozen foods subsidiary, Ore-Ida, is trying an intriguing variation on this theme in order to encourage more learning and risk taking in its research activities. It has carefully defined what it calls the 'perfect failure', and has arranged to shoot off a cannon in celebration every time one occurs. The perfect failure concept arises from simple recognition that all research and development is inherently risky, that the only way to succeed at all is through lots of tries, that management's primary objective should be to induce lots of tries, and that a good try that results in some learning is to be celebrated even when it fails. As a by-product, they legitimize and even create positive feelings around calling a quick halt to an obviously failing proposition, rather than letting it drag on with resulting higher cost in funds and eventually demoralization.

Positive reinforcement also has an intriguing Zen-like property. *It nudges good things on to the agenda instead of ripping things off the agenda.* Life in business, as otherwise, is fundamentally a matter of attention – how we spend our time.

Thus management's most significant output is getting others to shift attention in desirable directions (e.g. 'Spend more time in the field with customers'). There are only two ways to accomplish such a shift. First, we attempt through positive reinforcement to lead people gently over a period of time to pay attention to new activities. This is a subtle shaping process. Or we can 'take the bull by the horns' and simply try to wrestle undesirable traits off the agenda (e.g. 'Quit staying in the office filling in forms'). Skinner's argument is that the wrestler's approach is likely to be much less efficient, even though it may not seem that way in the very short run. That is, ripping items off an agenda leads to either overt or covert resistance: 'I'll get out of the office, if you insist, but I'll spend the time in the local pub.' The 'nudge it on the agenda' approach leads to a natural diffusion process. The positively reinforced behavior slowly comes to occupy a larger and larger share of time and attention. By definition, *something* (who cares what?) less desirable begins to drop off the agenda. But it drops off the agenda on the basis of our sorting process. The stuff that falls off is what we want to push off in order to make room for the positively reinforced items. The difference in approach is substantial. If, by force of time alone (a non-aversive force), *we* choose to push a low priority item off, then it is highly unlikely that we will cheat on ourselves and try to do more of the less attractive (just pushed off the agenda) behavior. So, back to Zen; the use of positive reinforcement goes with the flow rather than against it.

Our general observation is that most managers know very little about the value of positive reinforcement. Many either appear not to value it at all, or consider it beneath them, undignified, or not very macho. The evidence from the excellent companies strongly suggests that managers who feel this way are doing themselves a great disservice. The excellent companies seem not only to know the value of positive reinforcement but how to manage it as well.

As Skinner (1971) notes, the way the reinforcement is carried out is more important than the amount. First, it ought to be *specific*, incorporating as much information content as possible. We note, for instance, that activity based MBO systems ('Get the Rockville plant on line by 17 July') are more common in the excellent companies than are financially based MBOs.

Second, the reinforcement should have *immediacy*. Thomas Watson, Sr, is said to have made a practice of writing out a check on the spot for achievements he observed in his own peripatetic management role. Other examples of on-the-spot bonuses were mentioned frequently in our research. At Foxboro, a technical advance was desperately needed for survival in the company's early days (Kennedy). Late one evening, a scientist rushed into the president's office with a working prototype. Dumbfounded at the elegance of the solution and bemused about how to reward it, the president bent forward in his chair, rummaged through most of the drawers in his desk, found something, leaned over the desk to the scientist, and said, 'Here!' In his hand was a banana, the only reward he could immediately put his hands on. From that point on, the small 'gold banana' pin has been the highest accolade for scientific achievement at Foxboro. Lest that seem too mundane, at HP we unearthed a tale of marketers anonymously sending pound bags of pistachios to a salesman who sold a new machine.

Third, the system of feedback mechanisms should take account of *achievability*. Major gold banana events are not common, so the system should reward small wins. Good news swapping is common in the excellent companies.

The fourth characteristic is that a fair amount of the feedback comes in the form of *intangible* but ever-so-meaningful attention from top management. When you think about it, with management's time being as scarce as it is, that form of reinforcement may be the most powerful of all.

Finally, Skinner asserts that regular reinforcement loses impact because it comes to be expected. Thus *unpredictable* and *intermittent* reinforcements work better – the power of walking the shop floor again. Moreover, small rewards are frequently more effective than large ones. Big bonuses often become political, and they discourage legions of workers who don't get them but think they deserve them. Remember, we all think we're winners. Have you ever been around a member of a product launch team who didn't think that it was really his personal contribution that turned the tide in getting the new widget out the door? The small reward, the symbolic one, becomes a cause for positive celebration rather than the focus of a negative political battle.

Skinner's reinforcement notions have many offshoots. Arguably the most important is Leon Festinger's now widely held 'social comparison theory' (Festinger, 1954). His hypothesis, presented in 1951, was simply that people most strenuously seek to evaluate their performance by comparing themselves to others, not by using absolute standards. (Actually, this line of inquiry has origins going back to 1897, when Norman Triplett observed in a controlled experiment that bicyclists 'race faster against each other than against a clock'). We see many evidences of the use of social comparison by the excellent companies. Among them are regular peer reviews (the mainstay of the TI, Intel, and Dana management systems); information made widely available on comparative performance (sales groups, tiny productivity teams, and the like); and the purposefully induced internal competition (for example, among P&G brand managers). All are practices that stand in marked contrast to the conventional management techniques. As a young man, Rene McPherson was nearly fired in 1955 for telling people in his plant what their sales and profits were and how they stacked up against other plants. In 1972, as Dana's chairman, he visited a Toledo plant, open since 1929, where managers and employees had never been exposed to performance information. This tale is sadly not exceptional. We expect people to be motivated in a vacuum.

To put things into proper perspective, however, we should stress that we are *not* advocating reinforcement as the starting point for theory on what makes excellent companies tick. Skinner's work is important, and, as we said, underutilized in most management theory and practice. But the larger context of high performance, we believe, is *intrinsic motivation*. On the surface, self-motivation is opposed in many ways to the beliefs of reinforcement theory; but in our minds the two contexts fit together nicely. In experiment after experiment, Edward Deci of the University of Rochester (1972) has shown that lasting commitment to a task is engendered only by fostering conditions that build intrinsic motivations. In plain talk, Deci finds that people must believe that a task is inherently worthwhile if they really are to be committed to it. (In addition, he also finds that if we too regularly reward a task, we often vitiate commitment to it.)

It may not be surprising that managers have not taken a shine to the use of positive reinforcement. It smacks of the Brave New World, on the one hand (too tough), and of arbitrary back patting on the other (too soft). However, we are surprised at the degree to which intrinsic motivation has been under-utilized in most companies. The excellent companies, by contrast, tap the inherent worth of the task as a source of intrinsic motivation for their employees. TI and Dana insist that teams and divisions set their own goals. Virtually all of the excellent companies are driven by just a few key values, and then give lots of space to employees to take initiatives in support of those values – finding their own paths, and so making the task and its outcome their own.

Action, meaning and self-control

Probably few of us would disagree that actions speak louder than words, but we behave as if we don't believe it. We behave as if the proclamation of policy and its execution were synonymous. 'But I made quality our number one goal years ago,' goes the lament. Managers can't drive forklifts any more. Yet they do still act. They do *something*. In short, they pay attention to some things and not to others. Their action expresses their priorities, and it speaks much louder than words. In the quality case alluded to above, a president's subordinate clarified the message, 'Of course, he's for quality. That is, he's never said, "I don't care about quality." It's just that he's for everything. He says, "I'm for quality," twice a year and he acts, "I'm for shipping product," twice a day.' In another case, a high technology company president pinned his company's revitalization hopes on new products, publicly proclaiming (e.g. to the securities analysts) that they were on the way. A look at his calendar and phone log revealed that only three per cent of his time was actually spent on new products. Yet he kept asking us in all sincerity why even his closest allies weren't getting the message.

Intriguingly, this ambiguous area is a subject of heated long term debate in psychology. There are two schools of thought. One says that attitudes (beliefs, policies, proclamations) precede actions – the 'Tell, then do' model. The other, clearly more dominant, reverses the logic. The Harvard psychologist Jerome Bruner (1973) captures the spirit when he says, 'You more likely act yourself into feeling than feel yourself into action.' A landmark experiment, carried out in 1934, (Freedman et al, 1978) spurred the controversy. It demonstrated unequivocally that there is often little relationship between explicitly stated belief and mundane action:

> LaPiere, a white professor, toured the United States in 1934 with a young Chinese student and his wife. They stopped at 66 hotels or motels and at 184 restaurants. All but one of the hotels or motels gave them space, and they were never refused service at a restaurant. Sometime later a letter was sent to these establishments asking whether they would accept Chinese as guests. [There was a strong anti-Chinese bias in the United States at the time.] Ninety-two per cent said they would not. LaPiere, and many after him, interpreted these findings as reflecting a major inconsistency between behavior and attitudes. Almost all the proprietors *behaved* in a tolerant fashion, but they expressed an intolerant *attitude* when questioned by letter.

Analogously, what's called 'foot-in-the-door research' (Freedman and Fraser, 1966) demonstrates the importance of incrementally acting our way into major commitment. For instance, in one experiment, in Palo Alto, California, most subjects who initially agreed to put a *tiny* sign in their front window supporting a cause (traffic safety) subsequently agreed to display a billboard in their front yard, which required letting outsiders dig sizable holes in the lawn. On the other hand, those not asked to take the first small step turned down the larger one in 95 cases out of 100.

The implications of this line of reasoning are clear: only if you get people *acting*, even in small ways, the way you want them to, will they come to believe in what they're doing. Moreover, the process of enlistment is enhanced by explicit *management* of the after-the-act labeling process – in other words, publicly and ceaselessly lauding the small wins along the way. 'Doing things' (lots of experiments, tries) leads to rapid and effective learning, adaptation, diffusion, and commitment; it is the hallmark of the well-run company.

Moreover, our excellent companies appear to do their way into strategies, not vice versa. A leading researcher of the strategic process, James Brian Quinn (1981), talks about the role of leadership in strategy building. It doesn't sound much like a by-the-numbers, analysis-first process. He lists major leadership tasks, and the litany includes amplifying understanding, building awareness, changing symbols, legitimizing new viewpoints, making tactical shifts and testing partial solutions, broadening political support, overcoming opposition, inducing and structuring flexibility, launching trial balloons and engaging in systematic waiting, creating pockets of commitment, crystallizing focus, managing coalitions, and formalizing commitment (e.g. empowering 'champions'). The role of the leader, then, is one of orchestrator and labeler: taking what can be gotten in the way of action and shaping it – generally after the fact –

into lasting commitment to a new strategic direction. In short, he makes meanings.

The leading mathematician Roger Penrose says, 'The world is an illusion created by a conspiracy of our senses' (Forward, 1980). Yet we poor mortals try valiantly, at times desperately, to inscribe meaning on the *tabula rasa* given to us at birth. As Bruno Bettelheim (1976) has observed in *On the Uses of Enchantment*, 'If we hope to live not just from moment to moment, but in true consciousness of our existence, then our greatest need and most difficult achievement is to find meaning in our lives.' Bettelheim emphasizes the historically powerful role of fairy tales and myths in shaping meaning in our lives.

As we worked on research of our excellent companies, we were struck by the dominant use of story, slogan, and legend as people tried to explain the characteristics of their own great institutions. All the companies we interviewed, from Boeing to McDonald's, were quite simply rich tapestries of anecdote, myth, and fairy tale. And we do mean fairy tale. The vast majority of people who tell stories today about T. J. Watson of IBM have never met the man or had direct experience of the original more mundane reality. Two HP engineers in their mid-twenties recently regaled us with an hour's worth of 'Bill and Dave' (Hewlett and Packard) stories. We were subsequently astonished to find that neither had seen, let alone talked to, the founders. These days, people like Watson and A. P. Giannini at Bank of America take on roles of mythic proportions that the real persons would have been hard pressed to fill. Nevertheless, in an organizational sense, these stories, myths, and legends appear to be very important, because they convey the organization's shared values, or culture.

Without exception, the dominance and coherence of culture proved to be an essential quality of the excellent companies. Moreover, the stronger the culture and the more it was directed toward the marketplace, the less need was there for policy manuals, organization charts, or detailed procedures and rules. In these companies, people way down the line know what they are supposed to do in most situations because the handful of guiding values is crystal clear. One of our colleagues is working with a big company recently thrown together out of a series of mergers. He says: 'You know, the problem is *every* decision is being made for the first time. The top people are inundated with trivia because there are no cultural norms.'

By contrast, the shared values in the excellent companies are clear, in large measure, because the mythology is rich. Everyone at Hewlett-Packard knows that he or she is supposed to be innovative. Everyone at Procter & Gamble knows that product quality is the *sine qua non*. In his book on P&G, *Eyes on Tomorrow*, Oscar Schisgall (1981) observes: 'They speak of things that have very little to do with price of product . . . They speak of business integrity, of fair treatment of employees. "Right from the start," said the late Richard R. Deupree when he was chief executive officer, "William Procter and James

Gamble realized that the interests of the organization and its employees were inseparable. That has never been forgotten." '

Poorer-performing companies often have strong cultures, too, but dysfunctional ones. They are usually focused on internal politics rather than on the customer, or they focus on 'the numbers' rather than on the product and the people who make and sell it. The top companies, on the other hand, always seem to recognize what the companies that set only financial targets don't know or don't deem important. The excellent companies seem to understand that *every* man seeks meaning (not just the top 50 who are 'in the bonus pool').

Perhaps transcendence is too grand a term for the business world, but the love of product at Cat, Bechtel, and J&J comes very close to meriting it. Whatever the case, we find it compelling that so many thinkers from so many fields agree on the dominating need of human beings to find meaning and transcend mundane things. Nietzsche believed that 'he who has a *why* to live for can bear almost any *how*' (Frankl, 1963). John Gardner (1978) observes in *Morale*, 'Man is a stubborn seeker of meaning'.

Some of the riskiest work we do is concerned with altering organization structures. Emotions run wild and almost everyone feels threatened. Why should that be? The answer is that if companies do not have strong notions of themselves, as reflected in their values, stories, myths, and legends, people's only security comes from where they live on the organization chart. Threaten that, and in the absence of some grander corporate purpose, you have threatened the closest thing they have to meaning in their business lives.★

So strong is the need for meaning, in fact, that most people will yield a fair degree of latitude or freedom to institutions that give it to them. The excellent companies are marked by very strong cultures, so strong that you either buy into their norms or get out. There's no half-way house for most people in the excellent companies. One very able consumer marketing executive told us, 'You know, I deeply admire Procter & Gamble. They are the best in the business. But I don't think I could ever work there.' She was making the same point that Adam Myerson at *The Wall Street Journal* had in mind when he urged us to write an editorial around the theme: 'Why we wouldn't want to work for one of our excellent companies.' The cultures that make meanings for so many repel others.

★ The converse, apparently, is also true. When we were working for our first client in Japan on a problem that had nothing to do with organization, we happened to witness a major reorganization in process at the same time as our study. We were startled by the dramatic nature of the change and the speed with which it took place. Within a week, nearly all the top 500 executives had changed jobs, many had moved from Tokyo to Osaka or vice versa, the dust had settled, and business was proceeding as usual. We concluded that the Japanese were able to reorganize as seemingly ruthlessly as they did because security was always present; not security of position, for many were demoted or transferred to subsidiary companies, but security that had its roots in solid cultural ground and shared meanings.

Some who have commented on our research wonder if there is not a trap or two in the very strength of the structures and cultures of the well-run companies. There probably is. First, the conventions are so strong that the companies might be blindsided by dramatic environmental change. This is a fair point. But we would argue that in general the excellent company values almost always stress being close to the customer or are otherwise externally focused. Intense customer focus leads the prototypical excellent company to be unusually sensitive to the environment and thus *more* able to adapt than its competitors.

For us, the more worrisome part of a strong culture is the ever present possibility of abuse. One of the needs filled by the strong excellent company cultures is the need most of us have for security. We will surrender a great deal to institutions that give us a sense of meaning and, through it, a sense of security. Unfortunately, in seeking security, most people seem all too willing to yield to authority, and in providing meaning through rigidly held beliefs, others are all too willing to exert power. Two frightening experiments, those of Stanley Milgram at Yale and Philip Zimbardo at Stanford, warn us of the danger that lurks in the darker side of our nature.

The first, familiar to many, are Stanley Milgram's experiments on obedience (Milgram, 1974). Milgram brought adult subjects off the street into a Yale lab and asked them to participate in experiments in which they were to administer electric shocks to victims. (In fact, they were not doing so. The victims were Milgram conspirators and the electric shock devices were bogus. Moreover, the experimental protocol made it appear that the choice of both the victim and the shocker was random.) Initially, Milgram had the victims placed in one room and the shock givers in another. Following instructions given to them by a white-coated experimenter (the authority figure), the shock givers turned the dial, which went from 'mild' to 'extremely dangerous'. On instruction, they administered the electricity, and to Milgram's surprise and disappointment, the experiment 'failed'. All went 'all the way' in administering shock. One hundred per cent followed orders, although in earlier written tests over 90 per cent predicted they would not administer any shock whatsoever.

Milgram added embellishments. He connected the rooms with a window, so the shock givers could see the 'victims' writhe in pain. He added victim 'screams'. Still, 80 per cent went to 'intense' on the dial, and 65 per cent went to 'extremely dangerous'. Next he made the victims appear to be 'homely, 40-year-old female accountants'. He took the experiments out of the university and conducted them in a dreary downtown loft. He had the shock giver hold the victim's hand on the electric charge plate. All these steps were aimed at breaking down the subject's acceptance of the white-coated experimenter's authority. None worked very well. People still by and large accepted authority.

Milgram postulated numerous reasons for the outcome. Was it genetic? That is, is there species-survival value in hierarchy and authority that leads us all to submit? Are people simply sadistic? He concluded, most generally, that our culture 'has failed almost entirely in inculcating internal controls on actions that have their origin in authority'.

In the other case, Zimbardo advertised in a newspaper in Palo Alto, California (a prototypical upper class community), soliciting volunteers for a 'prison' experiment (Zimbardo and White, 1971). At dawn one Saturday morning he went out, picked the volunteers up, booked them, and took them to a wallboard 'prison' in the basement of the Stanford University psychology building. Within hours of their arrival, the randomly assigned 'guards' started acting like guards and the randomly assigned 'prisoners' started acting like prisoners. Well within the first 24 hours, the guards were behaving brutally – both physically and psychologically. By the end of the second day, a couple of the prisoners were on the verge of psychotic breakdown and had to be released from the experiment. 'Warden' Zimbardo, afraid of his own behavior as well as that of the others, stopped the experiment four days into a 10-day protocol.

The lessons are applicable to the cultures of the excellent companies, but the apparent saving grace of the latter is that theirs are not inwardly focused. The world of the excellent company is especially open to customers, who in turn inject a sense of balance and proportion into an otherwise possibly claustrophobic environment.*

On the whole, we stand in awe of the cultures that the excellent companies have built. Despite their inherent dangers, these cultures have made their companies unique contributors to society. Grand old Ma Bell, beleaguered though she currently may be by deregulation, gave America a telephone system that by almost any measure is the best in the world. Theodore Vail's 75-year-old insistence that the company was not a telephone company but a 'service' company had everything to do with that achievement.

Finally, and paradoxically, the excellent companies appear to take advantage of yet another very human need – the need one has to control one's destiny. At the same time that we are almost too willing to yield to institutions that give us meaning and thus a sense of security, we also want self-determination. With equal vehemence, *we simultaneously seek self-determination and security*. This is certainly irrational. Yet those who don't somehow learn to manage the tension are, in fact, technically insane. In *Denial of Death*, Ernest Becker (1973) stated the paradox: 'Man thus has the absolute tension of the dualism. Individuation means that the human creature has to oppose itself to the rest of nature [stick out]. Yet it creates precisely the isolation that one can't stand – and yet needs in

---

* Another worrisome aspect of the strong corporate culture is how well those who have spent most of their lives in it will fare on the outside should they ever leave, which some do. Our observation, though not backed by research, is that they do less well than might be expected, given their often stellar records in the top companies. It's a bit like a baseball pitcher traded away from the Yankees. These people often are totally unaware of the enormous support system they had going for them in the excellent company, and are at the very least initially lost and bewildered without it.

order to develop distinctively. It creates the difference that becomes such a burden; it accents the smallness of oneself and the sticking-outness at the same time.'

Psychologists study the need for self-determination in a field called 'illusion of control'. Stated simply, its findings indicate that if people think they have even modest personal control over their destinies, they will persist at tasks. They will do better at them. They will become more committed to them. Now, one of the most active areas of this experimentation is the study of cognitive biases. The typical experiment here (Jones, 1977) has subjects estimate their probability of success at future tasks after they have had some experience doing the same sort of activity. The results are pretty consistent: whether the subjects are adults or college sophomores, they overestimate the odds of succeeding at an easy task and underestimate the odds of succeeding at a hard one. In short, they regularly distort estimates of the possibilities of events. If their proven past record is, say, 60 per cent success at the easy task, the subjects will likely estimate their future odds of success at 90 per cent. If past demonstrated ability at the hard task is 30 per cent, the subject will put 10 per cent odds on success in the future. We need to succeed and stick out – desperately – so we overestimate the possibility of doing the easy task. And to preserve face and ensure security, we underestimate the possibility of getting the difficult task done.

A set of experiments that really highlights our need for self-determination and at the same time our desire for control is the 'shut off the noise button' variety mentioned in the Introduction. Even though we never use the button, the fact that we could if we wanted to improves our performance by quantum steps. Other similar experiments produce similar results. A subject allowed to dip his own hand into a lottery bowl will believe the odds of drawing the winning ticket to be substantially higher than if someone else does the drawing (Salancik, 1977). If a subject is given four cans of unmarked soft drinks to taste and then asked to choose his favorite, he will like his first choice much better than if the choice had been restricted to only two cans. (The drinks are the same beverage in all cases.) The fact, again, that we *think* we have a *bit* more discretion leads to *much* greater commitment.

And here, too, the excellent companies seem to understand these important, if paradoxical, human needs. Even in situations in which industry economics seem strongly to favor consolidation, we see the excellent companies dividing things up and pushing authority far down the line. These companies provide the opportunity to stick out, yet combine it with a philosophy and system of beliefs (e.g. Dana's overriding belief in 'the productive people') that provide the transcending meaning – a wonderful combination.

Transforming leadership

We often argue that the excellent companies are the way they are because they are organized to obtain extraordinary effort from ordinary human beings. It is hard to imagine that billion-dollar companies are populated with people much different from the norm for the population as a whole. But there is one area in which the excellent companies have been truly blessed with unusual leadership, especially in the early days of the company.

Leadership is many things. It is patient, usually boring coalition building. It is the purposeful seeding of cabals that one hopes will result in the appropriate ferment in the bowels of the organization. It is meticulously shifting the attention of the institution through the mundane language of management systems. It is altering agendas so that new priorities get enough attention. It is being visible when things are going awry, and invisible when they are working well. It's building a loyal team at the top that speaks more or less with one voice. It's listening carefully much of the time, frequently speaking with encouragement, and reinforcing words with believable action. It's being tough when necessary, and it's the occasional naked use of power – or the 'subtle accumulation of nuances, a hundred things done a little better,' as Henry Kissinger once put it. Most of these actions are what the political scientist James MacGregor Burns (1978) in his book *Leadership* calls 'transactional leadership'. They are the necessary activities of the leader that take up most of his or her day.

But Burns has posited another, less frequently occurring form of leadership, something which he calls 'transforming leadership' – leadership that builds on man's need for meaning, leadership that creates institutional purpose. We are fairly sure that the culture of almost every excellent company that seems now to be meeting the needs of 'irrational man', as described in this chapter, can be traced to transforming leadership somewhere in its history. While the cultures of these companies seem today to be so robust that the need for transforming leadership is not a continuing one, we doubt such cultures ever would have developed as they did without that kind of leadership somewhere in the past, most often when they were relatively small.

The transforming leader is concerned with minutiae, as well. But he is concerned with a different kind of minutiae; he is concerned with the tricks of the pedagogue, the mentor, the linguist – the more successfully to become the value shaper, the exemplar, the maker of meanings. His job is much tougher than that of the transactional leader, for he is the true artist, the true pathfinder. After all, he is both calling forth and exemplifying the urge for transcendence that unites us all. At the same time, he exhibits almost boorish consistency over long periods of time in support of his one or two transcending values. No opportunity is too small, no forum too insignificant, no audience too junior.

Burns speaks most convincingly of the leader's need to enable his followers to transcend daily affairs. He begins by faulting earlier students of leadership for their preoccupation with power, suggesting that such attention blinded them to the far more important task of instilling purpose. 'This absolutely central value [purpose] has been inadequately recognized in most theories,' he maintains (Burns, 1978). 'Leadership over human beings is exercised when persons with certain motives and purposes mobilize, in competition or conflict with others, institutional, political, psychological and other resources so as to arouse, engage and satisfy the motives of followers.' In essence, Burns says, 'Leadership, unlike naked power wielding, is thus inseparable from followers' needs and goals.' He thereby sets the stage for a concise definition of transforming leadership (Burns, 1978).

> [Transforming leadership] occurs when one or more persons *engage* with others in such a way that leaders and followers raise one another to higher levels of motivation and morality. Their purposes, which might have started out separate but related, in the case of transactional leadership, become fused. Power bases are linked not as counterweights but as mutual support for common purpose. Various names are used for such leadership: elevating, mobilizing, inspiring, exalting, uplifting, exhorting, evangelizing. The relationship can be moralistic, of course. But transforming leadership ultimately becomes *moral* in that it raises the level of human conduct and ethical aspiration of both the leader and the led, and thus has a transforming effect on both . . . Transforming leadership is dynamic leadership in the sense that the leaders throw themselves into a relationship with followers who will feel 'elevated' by it and often become more active themselves, thereby creating new cadres of leaders.

Burns, like others, believes that leaders are appealing to certain unconscious needs: 'The fundamental process is an elusive one; it is, in large part, *to make conscious what lies unconscious among followers*' (Burns, 1978). Taking Chairman Mao Tse-tung as exemplar, he comments, 'His true genius was in understanding the emotions of others' (Burns, 1978). The business psychologist Abraham Zaleznick (1977) makes much the same point in contrasting leaders and managers: 'Managers prefer working with people; leaders stir emotion.' The work of the psychologist David McClelland, notably in *Power: The Inner Experience* (1975), provides an experimentally based description of the process:

> [We] set out to find exactly, by experiment what kinds of thoughts the members of an audience had when exposed to a charismatic leader . . . They were apparently strengthened and uplifted by the experience; they felt more powerful, rather than less powerful or submissive. This suggests that the traditional way of explaining the influence of a leader on his followers has not been entirely correct. He does not force them to submit

and follow him by the sheer overwhelming magic of his personality and persuasive powers . . . In fact, he is influential by strengthening and inspiriting his audience . . . The leader arouses confidence in his followers. The followers feel better able to accomplish whatever goals he and they share.

Picking up on one of Burns's main points, leader-followers symbiosis, we find two attributes of that symbiosis especially striking: believability and excitement. On the first count, believability, we find that our value-infused top-performing companies are led by those who grew up with the core of the business – electric engineering at HP or Maytag, mechanical engineering at Fluor or Bechtel. The star performers are seldom led by accountants or lawyers. On the second count, excitement, Howard Head, inventor and entrepreneur, father of the Head ski and the Prince tennis racket, exhorts: 'You have to believe in the impossible' (Kennedy, 1980). At Hewlett-Packard, top management's explicit criterion for picking managers is their ability to engender excitement.

A simple description of the process of finding excitement is provided by James Brian Quinn (1977), who is, among other things, a long term student of the real, sloppy process of finding and achieving overarching strategic values and objectives. Quinn quotes a consumer goods chief executive officer:

We have slowly discovered that our most effective goal is *to be best* at certain things. We now try to get our people to help us work out what these things should be, how to define *best* objectively, and how to *become* best in our selected spheres. You would be surprised at how motivating that can be.

Warren Bennis (1976) has a good metaphor for the transforming leader – the leader as 'social architect'. But, to give credit where credit is due, Bennis, Burns, and we, in our comments on the excellent companies, were anticipated decades ago by both Chester Barnard and Philip Selznick, who published in 1957 an often-overlooked thin blue volume entitled *Leadership and Administration*, in which he says:

The inbuilding of purpose is a challenge to creativity because it involves transforming men and groups from neutral, technical units into participants who have a particular stamp, sensitivity, and commitment. This is ultimately an educational process. It has been well said that the effective leader must know the meaning and master the technique of the educator . . . The art of the creative leader is the art of institution building, the reworking of human and technological materials to fashion an organism that embodies new and enduring values . . . To institutionalize is to *infuse with value* beyond the technical requirements of the task at hand. The prizing of social machinery beyond its technical role is largely a reflection of the unique way it fulfills personal or group needs. Whenever individuals become attached to an organization or a way of doing things as persons rather than as technicians, the result is a prizing of the device for its own sake. From the standpoint of the committed person, the organization is changed from an expendable tool into a valued source of personal satisfaction . . . The institutional leader, then, *is primarily an expert in the promotion and protection of values*.

We should pause briefly here, as we exalt values, to ask what values? Maybe, for one, we might suggest simply 'to be best' in any area, as James Brian Quinn says, or to 'be true to our own aesthetic', as Walter Hoving said of himself and Tiffany's (Gerston, 1981). Perhaps it's Ray Kroc (1977) of McDonald's seeing 'beauty in a hamburger bun', or Watson's 'respect for the individual' at IBM, or Dana's belief in 'the productive people' or 'Forty-eight-hour parts service anywhere in the world' at Caterpillar. Corny? Only if we are cynical. Such values are transforming for the companies that live them.

Much of our discussion has verged on the high-sounding, for example, the talk of creating a transforming purpose. It *is* high-sounding, but at the same time it is simply practical. We have argued that man is quite strikingly irrational. He reasons by stories, assumes himself to be in the top 10 per cent judged by any good trait, needs to stick out and find meaning simultaneously, and so on. Yet management practice seldom takes these foibles and limitations into account.

The excellent company managements, however, do take these things into account – either consciously or unconsciously. The result is better relative performance, a higher level of contribution from the 'average' man. More significant, both for society and for the companies, these institutions create environments in which people can blossom, develop self-esteem, and otherwise be excited participants in the business and society as a whole. Meanwhile, the much larger group of non-excellent performers seems to act, almost perversely, at odds with every variable we have described here. Losing instead of winning is the norm, as are negative rather than positive reinforcement, guidance by the rule book rather than tapestries of myths, constraint and control rather than soaring meaning and a chance to sally forth, and political rather than moral leadership.

References

Bateson, G. (1980). *Mind and Nature: A Necessary Unity*. New York: Bantam Books, p. 14.

Becker, E. (1973). *The Denial of Death*. New York: Free Press, pp. 94, 153–4.

Bennis, W. (1976). *The Unconscious Conspiracy: Why Leaders Can't Lead*. New York: AMACOM, p. 174.

Bettelheim, B. (1976). *On the Uses of Enchantment: The Meaning and Importance of Fairy Tales*. New York: Knopf, p. 3.

Bruner, J. S. (1973). *On Knowing: Essays for the Left Hand*. New York: Atheneum, p. 24.

Burns, J. MacGregor (1978). *Leadership*. New York: Harper & Row pp. 13, 18–19, 20, 40, 254.

Deci, E. L. (1972). 'The Effects of Contingent and Non-contingent Rewards and Controls on Intrinsic Motivations'. *Organizational Behavior and Human Performance*, vol. 8, pp. 217–29.

The Economist (1980). 'How to Get a Bright Idea', 27 December, p. 61.

Festinger, L. (1954). 'A Theory of Social Comparison Processes'. *Human Relations*, vol. 7, pp. 117–40.

Foward, R. L. (1980). 'Spinning New Realities'. *Science 80*, December, p. 40.

Frankl, V. E. (1963). *Man's Search for Meaning*. New York: Pocket Books, p. 164.

Freedman, J. L. and Fraser, S. C. (1966). 'Compliance Without Pressure: The Foot-in-the-Door Technique'. *Journal of Personality and Social Psychology*, vol. 4, pp. 195–202.

Freedman, J. L., Sears, D. O. and Carlsmith, J. M. (1978). *Social Psychology*, 3rd edn. Englewood Cliffs, NJ: Prentice Hall, p. 299.

Gardner, J. W. (1978). *Morale*. New York: Norton, p. 15.

Gerston, J. (1981). 'Tiffany's Unabashed Guardian of Good Taste Relinquishes Helm'. *San Francisco Examiner*, 5 January, p. C2.

Jones, R. A. (1977). *Self-fulfilling Prophecies: Social, Psychological and Physiological Effects of Expectancies*. Hillsdale, NJ: Lawrence Erlbaum Associates, pp. 133, 167.

Judson, H. F. (1980). *Search for Solutions*. New York: Holt, Rinehart and Winston, p. 22.

Kennedy, A. A. Personal communication.

Kennedy, R. (1980). 'Howard Head Says, "I'm giving Up the Thing World" '. *Sports Illustrated*, 29 September, p. 72.

Koestler, A. (1967). *The Ghost in the Machine*. Now York: Macmillan, p. 274.

Kroc, R. (1977). *Grinding It Out: The Making of McDonald's*. New York: Berkley, p. 98.

McClelland, D. C. (1975). *Power: The Inner Experience*. New York: Irvington, pp. 259–60.

Milgram, S. (1974). *Obedience to Authority: An Experimental View*. New York: Harper & Row.

Mintzberg, H. (1976). 'Planning on the Left Side and Managing on the Right'. *Harvard Business Review*, July–August, p. 53.

Myers, D. G. (1980). 'The Inflated Self'. Mentioned in 'How do I Love Me? Let Me Count the Ways'. *Psychology Today*, p. 16.

Quinn, J. B. (1977). 'Strategic Goals: Process and Politics'. *Sloan Management Review*, Fall, p. 26.

Quinn, J. B. (1981). 'Formulating Strategy One Step at a Time'. *Journal of Business Strategy*, Winter, pp. 57–9.

Ross, L. (1977). 'The Intuitive Psychologist and His Shortcomings. In Berkowitz, L. (ed). *Advances in Experimental Social Psychology*, vol. 10, pp. 173–220.

Salancik, G. R. (1977). 'Commitment and the Control of Organizational Behavior and Belief'. in Staw, B. M. and Salancik, G. R. (eds) *New Directions in Organizational Behavior*. Chicago: St Clair Press, pp. 20ff.

Selznick, P. (1957). *Leadership in Administration: A Sociological Interpretation*. New York: Harper & Row, pp. 17, 28, 149–50, 152–3.

Shisgall, O. (1981). *Eyes on Tomorrow: The Evolution of Procter & Gamble*. Chicago: J. G. Ferguson, p. xi.

Simon, H. A. (1979). 'Information Processing Models of Cognition'. *Annual Review of Psychology*. Palo Alto, California: Annual Reviews, vol. 30, p. 363.

Skinner, B. F. (1971). *Beyond Freedom and Dignity*. New York: Knopf, pp. 5, 81, 34ff.

Tversky, A. and Kahneman, D. (1974). 'Judgement Under Uncertainty: Heuristics and Biases'. *Science*, 27 September, p. 1124.

Zaleznick, A. (1977). 'Managers and Leaders: Are They Different?'. *Harvard Business Review*, May–June, p. 72.

Zimbardo, P. and White, G. (1971). The Stanford Prison Experiment: A Simulation of the Study of the Psychology of Imprisonment conducted August 1971 at Stanford University (script for slide show).

Human resources and philosophy
Konosuke Matsushita

Konosuke Matsushita founded Matsushita Electric Company in 1918. Inspired by innovations in the field of technology, he left his job as an apprentice in a bicycle shop where he was earning 25 cents a day. He developed his first product in his living room, which was a double outlet adapter permitting the one outlet Japanese home to double its capacity. Today Matsushita Electric is a leader in electrical goods, not only in Japan but in the world.

Much of the success of the company can be attributed to the foresight and sagacity of the founder. As a result of a religious experience early in his career, Matsushita realized that people need spiritual support as well as financial support. He reasoned that if he could provide this through a company philosophy he would enhance the loyalty and commitment of his employees. *Not for Bread Alone* also describes this philosophy. In the extract we have reproduced, we see some of the dedication with which Matsushita seeks to help the employees' inner selves.

1 An objective sense of self

When you think about it, a private enterprise is really a public institution, in so far as it is expected to contribute some benefit to society as a whole. Given the public nature of its *raison d'être*, a private firm, large or small, must help its members grow as people and become responsible citizens. The young men and women who join a company that has a personnel policy designed to enrich their human potential are fortunate indeed.

A sense of self and the ability to be objective are qualities that I believe corporate management should try to cultivate in employees. Sound sense and good judgement are important for anyone, but especially for businessmen. A businessman must face all kinds of situations that can change from one moment to the next. He must perceive the situation accurately and respond – often quickly – with the most appropriate decision. One cannot assess a situation correctly, however, unless he knows his own strengths and weaknesses. A company, or any group for that matter, composed of people who know themselves and who can deal adequately with any given situation will be successful. That kind of group, furthermore, will work together well, free of internal schisms.

An organization whose members lack perspective and an objective sense of self, on the other hand, will probably not last very long. Its individual members may be competent and have all the right information, but they will not be able to pass sound, unified judgement on the problems that confront them.

Still, we are all human; only God can know the truth about everything. We have no way of knowing what is absolutely correct or of judging the truth. It is impossible to teach your employees how to assess a situation correctly. But you can tell them always to remember the importance of sound judgement, and they can learn by experience. The person with a sense of self is aware of his own imperfections and, at the same time he is determined to be accurate in his evaluation of a situation. Without those qualities, including the willingness to keep trying, he will not go far in business.

Managers and workers alike must never cease the effort to develop the ability to make sound judgements. A company composed of such individuals will be strong and prosperous, and will be able to multiply its contribution to society.

2 Trust your employees

People often compliment me on the way I handle personnel management. 'What is your secret?' they ask. That is hard to answer, since I do not have any special conscious techniques. All I can do is explain my basic attitude toward the people who work for me.

There are several ways of managing one's employees. One, apparently, is to use extraordinary wisdom and exert charismatic leadership in order to inspire workers to do their best. I have never approached my job that way since, lacking both those qualities, I do not belong to this category of manager. I am the type who consults his staff and asks for *their* wisdom. I have found that people are generally more willing to cooperate when you solicit their advice than when you try to tell them how to do everything. If I have any 'secret', it is a natural inclination to trust my staff and seek their cooperation.

I do not claim that my approach is always workable or widely applicable. An exceptionally competent manager who is capable of arriving at the right decisions without consulting his subordinates will get the job done the most efficiently by issuing orders. Such streamlined management often brings great benefits to the company and everyone concerned.

If a manager does not have that sort of capability, then my style of personnel managament is perhaps more desirable. I often have the feeling that any one of my employees is more competent and more knowledgeable than I am. Perhaps because I had very little formal education, I am prone to admire others for their achievements and skills. I trust my employees for what they know and what they have. So when I want to get something done, I tell one of them, 'I can't do it but I know you can.' Someone who knows he is trusted tries to do his best and eventually succeeds.

All this should not be taken to mean that I never give orders and never scold my employees. In my capacity as president or board chairman, I have had to use strong words on occasion in reprimanding people on my staff for their failures or blunders. But I have never thought myself superior to them in intelligence or knowledge.

An observation I have made over the years is that companies whose top management trusts and praises their employees are by and large successful. In contrast, when the president is the type who complains frequently about staff incompetence, the company itself is usually in trouble. I have no statistics to prove this, but I believe there is some truth in it. The 'I am better than you' attitude on the part of the top person can cost him his entire business. A genuine sense of humility, on the other hand, will give him huge dividends, both tangible and intangible.

3 A priceless opportunity

Once a junior executive in my company made an error serious enough that I could not overlook it. I wrote him a letter containing an official reprimand, but before giving him the letter I called him into my office to tell him what I was about to do. I then asked him how he would react to getting a letter from me regarding his misconduct. 'If you don't think you deserve it, then there is no point in giving it to you,' I told him. 'But if you acknowledge your wrongdoing and are sorry for it, then it is worth the trouble, as it might help you improve your performance in the future. If you think the letter of reprimand is too late to change anything and, therefore, useless, I won't give it to you.'

The young man said he would be happy to receive the letter. Just as I was about to hand it over, his immediate supervisor and one of his colleagues walked into the room.

'You have come at an opportune moment,' I said to them. 'I was just about to give your associate a letter of reprimand, which he says he is happy to receive. I am very pleased at his attitude.' I told them that I would like to read the letter to them so they could be witnesses to it.

After reading the letter, I told them that I thought they were all lucky to have someone to tell them off. 'If I made such a mistake,' I said, 'there is no one who would say anything right to me, but you can bet there would be a lot of criticism behind my back. And it doesn't help at all. I would go on making the same error. It is good that you have me and others to point out your mistakes and tell you to shape up. Once you are promoted to top positions, no one is going to protest, no matter what you do. That is why you should consider this a priceless opportunity.'

My approach in this case was probably not altogether orthodox, to say the least, and I know it would not necessarily work in another situation. But the person in question took me seriously, and later he became an outstanding manager.

4 Everyone is an asset

High calibre skills in executing a job and working with others are in great demand today, but they are hard to find in the same person. In every corporation, top management is constantly trying to raise the quality of their personnel through recruitment and training programs, but it takes a great deal of perseverance as well as wisdom and resourcefulness on the part of the manager to improve the caliber of his staff.

How do we go about educating our employees, and what can managers do to help each worker grow? There are as many answers to these age old questions as there are managers, but for me, one method seems to have worked over the years quite well. Basically, that is to deliberately seek out the positive qualities in each person, and never try to find fault with him. This has been easy for me, partly because of my own propensity to notice the merits in people before I see their demerits, and partly because I have more peace of mind if I approach people that way.

If I tended to see only the negative side of an employee, I could never assign him to a responsible job without feeling qualms. I would be constantly worried about him making some very damaging error. To be so preoccupied would affect my performance as manager; I would not be able to concentrate on the more important policy matters of the company. What is worse is when a manager's lack of trust and confidence in the workers inhibits him from any bold moves or radical measures. If he does not dare to act boldly when circumstances demand it, his company as a whole is going to suffer.

All said and done, however, I must confess that at times I overestimate people, putting them into positions they are not ready for. But I would rather overrate the abilities of my employees than underestimate them. It often turns out that if you put a person in a post and give him your full confidence, he does his best to live up to your expectations. Whether the person is appointed department manager or director of a subsidiary, he usually 'grows into the job', gaining abilities commensurate with his new responsibility.

A person makes a position; if he is incompetent, his position will suffer, and if he is competent, the prestige and authority of his position will grow. Despite all the talk about the 'level of incompetence', I believe that most people are perfectly capable of learning to do the job they are assigned to, and doing it well.

But they must work harder than ever before. Their supervisor must constantly encourage them, helping them to overcome their shortcomings and weaknesses. I would say that a manager ought to give at least 70 per cent of his attention to the positive qualities of his subordinates; 30 per cent is enough for those points that need improvement or changing. Employees, for their part, should try to see the strong points in their managers as much as possible. Positive attitudes on both sides will augment the productivity of the team, and contribute to the personal growth of all concerned.

5 For bread *and* values

I know the analogy probably sounds outrageous, but I wonder if there is not a certain parallel between childrearing and employee education. I am talking about the crucial importance in both of conviction. If we want to bring up our children properly, we need to have clear ideas of the basic goals in a life of integrity and humanity, and how to be a good member of the family and community. Everyone has a different world view and outlook on life; one is not necessarily right and the others wrong. The important thing, whatever our outlook, is never to vacillate in our attitudes towards the basic issues. When parents have firm convictions, they will be consistent in what they say and do and in the way they treat their children. That approach will have only a positive influence, and will be of great help in guiding them in the right direction as they grow up.

People in top management also need firm, well-formed views on society, business, and life if they are to exert a solid influence on those under their supervision. When senior executives are consistent in their thinking and behaviour, their subordinates will trust them and follow their examples with a sense of security. But corporate management requires a little more than conviction and consistent attitudes. It needs what I call a sense of purpose.

Every company, no matter how small, ought to have clear cut goals apart from the pursuit of profit, purposes that justify its existence among us. To me, such goals are an avocation, a secular mission to the world. If the chief executive officer has this sense of mission, he can tell his employees what it is that the company seeks to accomplish, and explain its *raison d'être* and ideals. And if his employees understand that they are not working for bread alone, they will be motivated to work harder together toward the realization of their common goals. In the process, they will learn a great deal more than if their objectives were limited to pay scales. They will begin to grow as people, as citizens, and as businessmen.

One can gain the required knowledge and experience over the years simply working with a company, even if its management has no sense of mission to share with the employees. But knowledge and experience alone will not help one develop into a person of wisdom, with maturity and depth to his personality. What he needs is a philosophy that gives a frame to his thoughts and guides his behaviour. Top management can assist in the employee's personal growth by spelling out the company's philosophy.

6 On the job experience

Each spring, young people fresh out of college join our company; they all undergo a period of orientation and training at factories or sales outlets. When the company was still small, there was no need for this kind of program, because on the job training alone was enough to give the employee an overall perspective of our operations. Even white collar workers were closely involved in day to day production and sales activities. Engineers responsible for research and development and those engaged in design work actually tightened screws and assembled parts on the shop floor in the course of their daily routine. Men in charge of marketing and sales planning were in direct contact with the dealers. They were aware of exactly what was going on in the front line of the market.

As the company grew larger, however, work became more specialized and more compartmentalized. On the job training in the area of one's specialty is still useful and necessary, but it can no longer prepare the employee adequately for a long career with the firm. That is why we try to send all our new employees to factories and sales outlets for broad, practical experience before assigning them to a particular slot in the corporate apparatus.

In a way, a businessman is like a practicing physician; he must have broad 'clinical' knowledge and experience, in addition to theoretical knowledge in his special field. No matter how conversant with medical theory, a doctor cannot treat a patient with confidence or conscience unless he also has a certain amount of clinical practice behind him. Likewise, a business school graduate cannot be called a businessman until he gains some practical experience.

Suppose a man who never actually has been a salesman become a sales manager. He sits down at his desk and tries to draw up a marketing plan. He may be bright and competent, but his plan will be based on ideas and second-hand knowledge. Chances are that it will be of little practical use and will ultimately fail. If, on the other hand, the sales manager has undergone two or three years of apprenticeship at a retail store or a wholesale company and has mastered the basics of sales that way, any plan he conceives later will reflect his first-hand knowledge of the business.

Similarly, college educated engineers with no production line experience would have difficulty designing or developing a good product with a high degree of manufacturing feasibility. A few years of workshop experience at a young age gives them a clear notion of how their designs and ideas are incorporated into the finished products. That knowledge can only have a positive influence on their research and development work.

A period of apprenticeship for young college educated workers is just one of many approaches to personnel training. What is most important to remember is that businessmen and engineers are more like clinical practitioners than academicians or theoreticians.

Reproduced from Matsushita, Konosuke (1984). *Not For Bread Alone: A Business Ethos, A Management Ethic*, PHP Institute Inc. by permission of Panasonic Europe (Headquarters) Ltd.

Chapter 3

Mission and culture

Culture is a subject that has recently become central to the management of organizations. This chapter helps to connect culture and mission. We see mission as the fusion between strategy and values that creates strong behaviour standards for the organization.

Writers on culture describe organizations with strong cultures in much the same terms. They are organizations where there is a strong link between values and behaviour. The link between mission and culture is the organization's values. As a result, much of the literature that describes companies with strong cultures is also describing companies with strong missions.

William G. Ouchi, in his management bestseller *Theory Z*, conceptualizes a theoretical framework applicable to both the Japanese and American systems. Ouchi explains how Japanese companies have increased their productivity three times as fast as their American counterparts. He does this with some unusual insights into the workings of Japanese companies. For example, he was in close contact with Akio Morita of Sony Corp and spent a long time observing Sony. Ouchi defines a Z organization as one where trust and egalitarianism are central values and he explains why these values lead to better performance. His work demonstrates the importance of values. His naïvety is in the implied assumption that Theory Z values are in some way superior to the alternatives.

In *Corporate Cultures*, Deal and Kennedy explain the importance of managing the soft side of organizations – the 'rites and rituals of corporate life'. 'Culture' defines the day to day actions that belong in an organization. By managing the rites and rituals, companies can help to create a strong philosophy in the organization that will control the day to day actions. Deal and Kennedy are underlining the importance of values both as a management tool for controlling behaviour and as a motivator that gives meaning to work activities.

In 'Minerva's Owl', William Weiss focuses on the importance of choosing values with which employees can identify. It is only when people can easily identify with the organizational values and guidelines that they begin to create meaning for employees. At the time of writing 'Minerva's Owl' Weiss, the chairman and CEO of Ameritech, was developing a value system for his organization and voices all the hope and enthusiasm one would expect from someone in such a situation. He believes that corporate values are related to the corporate conscience as well as to the purpose of the organization. The corporate conscience is a 'practical judgment about the morality of a concrete action or decision'. In other words, the management needs to have determined its value system and encourage behaviour that conforms to it. The value system cannot be widely divergent from the employee's own ethical guidelines, otherwise the employee would be living a Jekyll and Hyde existence.

Tom Watson Jr was in a very different role when he wrote *A Business and its Beliefs*. He was describing a company that had already developed a strong value system. Watson Sr, his father, had been the founder of IBM and had joined the company when it was a demoralized organization. He set about building an organization that would prosper and set an example to others. IBM as we know it today was born. Tom Watson Jr has documented his father's thoughts, beliefs and methods in clear and simple text. The three IBM beliefs – respect for the individual, dedication to customer service, and excellence in everything we do – are supported by numerous examples of behaviour within the organization to illustrate the importance of these beliefs. Watson Jr believes that values are much more important and much longer lasting than strategy.

Anthony G. Athos and Richard Tanner Pascale provide a more holistic view of organizations in *The Art of Japanese Management*. They see values as a critical ingredient, but one of a number of important ingredients. They use the McKinsey 7S model to explain how organizations work. The model defines seven important characteristics of organizations. There are hard characteristics – structure, systems and strategy; and there are the softer characteristics – style, skills, staff (people) and superordinate goals. This latter 'S' was subsequently changed to shared values. The art of great management is to mould all seven 'S's to create a high performing organization.

The role of shared values has a central position in Athos and Pascale's diagram of the McKinsey model, suggesting that they see values as the unifying element that gives meaning to the whole. They refer to values as the 'spiritual fabric' of the organization. The additional interest of the Athos and Pascale work is their analysis of IBM which contrasts with the thoughts of Watson.

All of these pieces on organization culture focus on values and how they can be developed. Strong values exist when they are acted out daily in the company. For this to happen, employees must believe in the values, for it is this commonly held belief that is the organization's culture. What we have tried to show is that a sense of mission and a strong culture are overlapping concepts.

The Z organization
William Ouchi

William Ouchi is professor in the Graduate School of Management at the University of California at Los Angeles. His famous book, *Theory Z*, argues that some American corporations have successfully adapted Japanese management methods to their own cultures. These 'Type Z' organizations promote managerial ability and corporate prestige, and value individual responsibility and consensus decision making.

This chapter explores the features of such organizations that closely resemble Japanese companies, and their adaptation to western cultural constraints. What emerges as important is that Type Z companies promote actions and decisions that 'fit' with the company's style and its values. This sort of organization is founded on commitment and trust, and is 'a constant culture, a community of equals who cooperate with one another to reach common goals'. However, Ouchi also makes the point that since the organization is so firmly grounded in its values, it will find it difficult to adapt itself to a different environment which requires a change in those values.

Each Type Z company has its own distinctiveness – the United States military has a flavor quite different from IBM or Eastman Kodak. Yet all display features that strongly resemble Japanese firms. Like their Japanese counterparts, Type Z companies tend to have long term employment, often for a lifetime, although the lifetime relationship is not formally stated. The long term relationship often stems from the intricate nature of the business; commonly, it requires lots of learning-by-doing. Companies, therefore, want to retain employees, having invested in their training to perform well in that one unique setting. Employees tend to stay with the company, since many of their skills are specific to that one firm with the result that they could not readily find equally remunerative nor challenging work elsewhere. These task characteristics that produce the lifelong employment relationship also produce a relatively slow process of evaluation and promotion. Here we observe one important adaptation of the Japanese form. Type Z companies do not wait 10 years to evaluate and promote: any western firm that did so would not retain many of its talented employees. Thus such firms frequently provide the sorts of explicit performance interviews that are commonplace. However, promotions are slower in coming than at Type A companies.

Career paths in Type Z companies display much of the 'wandering around' across functions and offices that typifies the Japanese firm. This effectively produces more company-specific skills that work toward intimate coordination between steps in the design, manufacturing and distribution process. An employee who engages in such 'non-professional' development takes the risk that the end skills will be largely non-marketable to other companies. Therefore, long term employment ties into career development in a critical way.

Typically Type Z companies are replete with the paraphernalia of modern information and accounting systems, formal planning, management by objectives, and all of the other formal, explicit mechanisms of control characterizing the Type A. Yet in Z companies these mechanisms are tended to carefully for their information, but rarely dominate in major decisions. By contrast, managers in big companies, hospitals, and government agencies often complain about feeling powerless to exercise their judgement in the face of quantitative analysis, computer models, and numbers, numbers, numbers. Western management seems to be characterized for the most part by an ethos which roughly runs as follows: rational is better than non-rational, objective is more nearly rational than subjective, quantitative is more objective than non-quantitative, and thus quantitative analysis is preferred over judgements based on wisdom, experience and subtlety. Some observers, such as Professor Harold Leavitt of Stanford University, have written that the penchant for the explicit and the measurable has gone well beyond reasonable limits, and that a return to the subtle and the subjective is in order (see Leavitt, 1978).

In a Type Z company, the explicit and the implicit seem to exist in a state of balance. While decisions weigh the complete analysis of facts, they are also shaped by serious attention to questions of whether or not this decision is 'suitable', whether it 'fits' the company. A company that isolates sub-specialities is hardly capable of achieving such fine-grained forms of understanding. Perhaps the underlying cause is the loss of the ability for disparate departments within a single organization to communicate effectively with one another. They communicate in the sparse, inadequate language of numbers, because numbers are the only language all can understand in a reasonably symmetrical fashion. Let us consider one example.

A matter of company style

One of the more dramatic new businesses to develop during the decade of the 1970s was the digital watch industry. At the outset, the digital or electronic watch presented a mystery to everyone in the business. The old, mainline watch firms such as Timex and Bulova were suspicious of the new semi-conductor technology which replaced the mainspring and the tuning fork. The semi-conductor firms that knew this technology supplied parts to other companies and did not know the business of selling goods to the individual consumer. I watched the reaction of two of these semi-conductor firms to a new business opportunity: one of these firms previously identified as a quite pure example of Type A, and the other a relatively pure example of Type Z. I was busily studying these two companies for reasons unrelated to the watch business as the story unfolded before me.

The digital watch seemed from the first to hold out the promise of a huge new industry. This new watch, which was more accurate, more reliable, and cheaper than the conventional timepiece, held the promise of replacing almost all timepieces in the western world. Company A performed a careful analysis of the potential market, estimating the number of digital watches that could be sold at various prices, the cost of manufacturing and distributing these watches to retail outlets, and thus the potential profits to be earned by the firm. Company A, already a supplier of the central electronic component, possessed the necessary technical skill. The executives of the company knew that the business of selling consumer goods was unfamiliar to them, but they felt that they could develop the necessary knowledge. Following their analysis of the situation, they proceeded to go out and buy a company that manufactured watch cases, another that manufactured wrist bands for watches, and within weeks after their go-ahead decision, were in the watch business. Starting from zero, Company A rapidly gained a major share of the watch business and, 18 months after the decision, was a major factor in the new industry and earned large profits on digital watches.

The executives of Company Z also recognized the opportunities in digital watches; they too manufactured the key electronic component that is the heart of the digital watch. Their analyses of the market promised very great rewards should they enter the business. But at Company Z, the numbers never dominate. The top executives at the firm asked whether this business really fit their 'style'. They saw the anticipated profits but wondered whether this would be a one-shot success or whether the company could continue to be an innovator and a leader in the watch business in the years to come. Most importantly, entering the watch business seemed to conflict with the company's philosophy. In Company Z, talking about the company philosophy is not considered soft-headed, wishful or unrealistic. Rather, the company consists of a set of managers who see clearly that their capacity to achieve close cooperation depends in part on their agreeing on a central set of objectives and ways of doing business. These agreements comprise their philosophy of business, a broad statement that contemplates the proper relationship of the business to its employees, its owners, its customers and to the public at large. This general statement must be interpreted to have meaning for any specific situation, and it is therefore important that managers be sufficiently familiar with the underlying corporate culture so that they can interpret the philosophy in ways which produce cooperation rather than conflict. One element of the philosophy concerns the kinds of products the company should manufacture, and that statement seemed clearly to exclude a product like the digital watch. On that basis, it seemed, the philosophy outweighed the financial analysis, and the watch project should have ended there.

But it didn't. A second major element of this corporation's philosophy had to do with preserving the freedom of employees to pursue projects they felt would be fruitful. In particular, the freedom of a unit manager to set goals and pursue them to their conclusion is cherished. In this case, a young general manager with a proven record of success wanted to take the company into the watch business. The top executives of the company disagreed with his judgement but were unwilling to sacrifice the manager's freedom. Two very central values conflicted in their implications for action. What was striking about this case was that values, not market share or profitability, lay at the heart of the conflict in Company Z.

Let me not seem to imply that Company Z is unconcerned with profitability. The record is clear. Company Z is among the fastest growing, most profitable of major American firms. Every manager knows that projects survive only as long as they produce profits well above what other companies demand. But at Company Z, profits are regarded not as an end in itself nor as the method of 'keeping score' in the competitive process. Rather, profits are the reward to the firm if it continues to provide true value to its customers, to help its employees to grow, and to behave responsibly as a corporate citizen. Many of us have heard these words and are by now cynical about that kind of a public face which frequently shields a far less attractive internal reality. One of the distinctive features of Company Z is that these values are not a sham, not cosmetic, but they are practiced as the standard by which decisions are made. Again, the process is not faultless. Some managers within the firm are skeptical about the wisdom of these values and about the firm's true commitment to them, but by and large, the culture is intact and operating effectively.

Why a philosophy of management when firms in a free enterprise economy are supposed to seek profits only? In a large organization, it is impossible to determine over the period of a few months or a year whether a business segment is profitable or not. Suppose that you become the manager in charge of a new division created to enter the digital watch market. You buy the electronics from another division, you share salespersons with other divisions, you draw on a central engineering staff to design and maintain both your product and your manufacturing process, you rely heavily on the good name of the company to promote your product, and you staff your new operation with skilled managers and technicians who are products of the company's training programs. How much should you be charged for each of these inputs to your business? No one can know. Someone, inevitably, will come up with some numbers, sometimes referred to as 'transfer prices' and other times referred to as 'magic numbers', and these numbers will be used to calculate your costs in order to subtract those from your sales revenues so that a profit can be measured. Everyone, however, knows that the stated profits are a very inexact measure of your true profits, and that your true profits are unknowable.

Suppose that your company is in fact run by a strict profitability standard. If you are being undercharged for the central engineering services, then you will use as much engineering as you can, thereby taking that service away from some other use in the company. If another divison manager asks to borrow three of your experienced staff, you may deny this request or send three not very skilled persons instead, since another's success is not reflected in your profits. In many ways, large and small, the inexact measurement of value will result in an explicit, formal mechanism that yields low coordination, low productivity and high frustration.

Organizational life is a life of interdependence, of relying upon others. It is also a life of ambiguity. Armen Alchian and Harold Demsetz, two distinguished economists at UCLA, have argued that where teamwork is involved the measurement of individual performance will inevitably be ambiguous. Knowing this, and understanding the extreme complexity of interdependence in their business, the top management of Company Z has determined that explicit measures not be the final arbiter of decision making. They feel that if most of the top managers agree on what the company ought to be trying to do and how, in general, it ought to go about that set of tasks, then they will be able to rely on their mutual trust and goodwill to reach decisions far superior to anything that a formal system of control could provide.

They furthermore understand that the informal, implicit mechanisms of control cannot succeed alone. They can develop only under the conditions of stable employment, slow evaluation and promotion, and low career specialization. Even with those aids, however, the subtle and the implicit must be supported with the crutch of formal control and analysis in a large, multi-product, multi-national, multi-technology organization in which a complete agreement on values and beliefs can never be fully realized.

In the end, Company Z authorized the general manager to enter a relatively small and specialized segment of the digital watch market. He had the opportunity to 'grow' his new venture if it succeeded, but the initial venture was small enough that its failure would not jeopardize the health of the company overall. Three years after the initial decisions by both companies, the picture was quite different. Following a dramatic surge in sales and profits, Company A had encountered stiff competition from other firms who were more experienced than they in this industry. Eighteen months after their initial success, they had taken severe losses and had sold their watch business to a competitor. They were, once again, back to zero in watches. Company Z also experienced an early success with its more limited digital watch venture, and after the initial success they, too, experienced stiff competition and a decline in profits. Rather than sell off the business, however, they slowly de-emphasized it, continuing to service the watches that they already had sold and, perhaps, maintaining the skeletal business as a valuable lesson from which future managers could learn.

A matter of company substance

In Type Z organizations, as we have seen, the decision making process is typically a consensual, participative one. Social scientists have described this as a democratic (as opposed to autocratic or apathetic) process in which many people are drawn into the shaping of important decisions. This participative process is one of the mechanisms that provides for the broad dissemination of information and of values within the organization, and it also serves the symbolic role of signaling in an unmistakable way the cooperative intent of the firm. Many of the values central to a corporate culture are difficult to test or to display. Some do not come into play more than once every few years, when a crisis appears (for example, the commitment to long term employment, which is tested only during a recession), while others, such as the commitment to behave unselfishly, are difficult to observe. These values and beliefs must be expressed in concrete ways if they are to be understood and believed by new employees, particularly since new employees arrive with the expectation that all companies are basically the same: they are not to be trusted, not to be believed. Consensual decision making both provides the direct values of information and value sharing and at the same time openly signals the commitment of the organization to those values. When people get together in one room to discuss a problem or to make a decision, that meeting is often noticed and even talked about: it is a highly visible form of commitment to working together. Typically, Type Z organizations devote a great deal of energy to developing the interpersonal skills necessary to effective group decision making, perhaps in part for this symbolic reason.

In Type Z companies, the decision making may be collective, but the ultimate responsibility for decision still resides in one individual. It is doubtful that westerners could ever tolerate the collective form of responsibility that characterizes Japanese organizations. This maintenance of the sense of individual responsibility remains critical to western society but it also creates much tension in the Type Z organization. When a group engages in consensual decision making, members are effectively being asked to place their fate to some extent in the hands of others. Not a common fate but a set of individual fates is being dealt with. Each person will come from the meeting with the responsibility for some individual targets set collectively by the group. The consensual process, as defined by Professor Edgar Schein of MIT, is one in which members of the group may be asked to accept responsibility for a decision that they do not prefer, but that the group, in an open and complete discussion, has settled upon (see Schein, 1969). This combination of collective decision making with individual responsibility demands an atmosphere of trust. Only under a strong assumption that all hold basically compatible goals and that no one is engaged in self-serving behavior will individuals accept personal responsibility for a group decision and make enthusiastic attempts to get the job done.

The holistic orientation of Type Z companies is in many ways similar to that found in the Japanese form but with some important differences. The similarity has to do with orientation of superior to subordinates and of employees at all levels to their co-workers. Type Z companies generally show broad concern for the welfare of subordinates and of co-workers as a natural part of a working relationship. Relationships between people tend to be informal and to emphasize that whole people deal with one another at work, rather than just managers with workers and clerks with machinists. This holistic orientation, a central feature of the organization, inevitably maintains a strong egalitarian atmosphere that is a feature of all Type Z organizations.

If people deal with one another in segmented ways, as one role to another rather than as one human being to another, then these dehumanized relationships easily become authoritarian. Feelings of superiority and inferiority prevail in relationships narrowly defined and constrained to 'my' duties as department head and 'your' duties as worker. That attitude, out of step in a democratic society, implies class distinctions. The subordinate will inevitably be alienated both from the superior who takes such an attitude and from the company that he or she represents. The superior is often relieved of some of the anxiety and stress that come with having to respond to the needs of others, whether those are superiors, subordinates or peers. Most of us cannot block off the requests or complaints of superiors and peers, but if we become impersonal and formal and thus distant from the needs of subordinates, that gives one less thing to worry about. Of course we recognize that feeling as being improper, unfair and unproductive, but short term pressures will often beckon in that direction.

An organization that maintains a holistic orientation and forces employees at all levels to deal with one another as complete human beings creates a condition in which de-personalization is impossible, autocracy is unlikely, and open communication, trust, and commitment are common. In one Type Z company with which I am familiar, each plant in the company holds a monthly 'beer bust' at the end of a working day. Beer and snacks are consumed, neither in large quantities, and informal games and skits are frequently offered. Any manager who regularly fails to take part in the beer bust will fail to achieve success and continued promotion. Is this an example of 'politics at work', of 'it's who you know, not what you know', or is it simply a holdover from earlier days?

The beer bust, as I interpret it, is similar to the cocktails after work shared by bosses and subordinates in Japan. Both have the same group of people who work together each day now cast in different roles. The hierarchy of work, somewhat relaxed in this setting, gives people the opportunity to interact more as equals, or at least without the familiar hierarchical roles. Technicians can express their willingness to regard foremen as regular people rather than as superiors to be suspected. Managers show subordinates their acceptance of them as equals, as whole human beings. In this particular company with the beer bust, managers must be willing to engage in frivolous games and skits in which their obvious lack of skill and their embarrassment bring them down to earth both in their own eyes and in the eyes of their subordinates.

Very few of us are superior to our fellow workers in every way. As long as we cling to our organizational roles, we can maintain the fiction that we are indeed superior in every way. But if we engage these people in social intercourse, the fiction is dispelled. The natural force of organizational hierarchy promotes a segmented relationship and a hierarchical attitude. A holistic relationship provides a counterbalance that encourages a more egalitarian attitude.

Egalitarianism is a central feature of Type Z organizations. Egalitarianism implies that each person can apply discretion and can work autonomously without close supervision, because they are to be trusted. Again, trust underscores the belief that goals correspond, that neither person is out to harm the other. This feature, perhaps more than any other, accounts for the high levels of commitment, of loyalty, and of productivity in Japanese firms and in Type Z organizations.

Let us return briefly to Douglas McGregor's 'Theory X' and 'Theory Y' assumptions about human nature. McGregor's work drew heavily on that of former student Chris Argyris of Harvard University (Argyris, 1964). Argyris argued that motivation in work will be maximal when each worker pursues individual goals and experiences psychological growth and independence. Close supervision diminishes motivation, retards psychological growth and hampers personal independence and freedom. However, supervision can be supportive in 'Theory Y' only when the supervisor trusts workers to use their discretion in a manner consistent with the goals of the organization. Thus the connection between an egalitarian style of management and mutual trust.

The central importance of trust is revealed in a study of utopian societies by Rosabeth Moss Kanter (Kanter, 1972). Kanter described the Amana (refrigerators), the Oneida (tableware), and other utopian communities that succeeded as commercial enterprises. In these communities one of the key values was egalitarianism – equality of influence and of power. Consistent with this value, all explicit forms of supervision and of direction were foregone. Now the problem was how to ensure a high level of discipline and hard work without hierarchical supervision and monitoring of production. The chief danger was of self-interest in the form of laziness, shirking and selfishness at work. Such behavior could not readily be corrected without hierarchy, and other means had to be found to limit such tendencies. The answer was to develop a complete unity of goals between individuals and the community such that an autonomous individual would naturally seek to work hard, cooperate and benefit the community. In order to accomplish this complete socialization, utopian communities engaged in a variety of practices that had the objective of developing common goals. Open sex or complete celibacy, the most dramatic of these, both have characterized all successful utopian communes in the United

States. From Kanter's pont of view, open sex and complete celibacy are functionally equivalent: each prevents the formation of loyalties to another individual and so preserves the loyalty of all to the community. Open sex allows no free choice of partners but rather a strict assignment of older men to younger women and older women to younger men. As soon as partners begin to show preference for one another in this system, they are reassigned. The example illustrates both the great difficulty of achieving complete goal integration in a western society and the central importance of selfless goals in non-hierarchical organizations.

Type Z organizations, unlike utopian communities, do employ hierarchical modes of control, and thus do not rely entirely upon goal congruence among employees for order. Nevertheless, they do rely extensively upon symbolic means to promote an attitude of egalitarianism and of mutual trust, and they do so in part by encouraging a holistic relation between employees. Self-direction replaces hierarchical direction to a great extent which enhances commitment, loyalty, and motivation.

Argyris challenged managers to integrate individuals into organizations, not to create alienating, hostile and impersonally bureaucratic places of work. In a real sense, the Type Z organization comes close to realizing that ideal. It is a consent culture, a community of equals who cooperate with one another to reach common goals. Rather than relying exclusively upon hierarchy and monitoring to direct behavior, it relies also upon commitment and trust.

The theory behind the Theory Z organization

The difference between a hierarchy – or bureaucracy – and Type Z is that Z organizations have achieved a high state of consistency in their internal culture. They are most aptly described as clans in that they are intimate associations of people engaged in economic activity but tied together through a variety of bonds.* *Clans* are distinct from *hierarchies*, and from *markets*, which are the other two fundamental social mechanisms through which transactions between individuals can be governed. In a market, there will be competitive bidding for, say, an engineer's services as well as for a weaver's baskets. Each will know the true value of their products according to the terms the market sets. In a

---

* Here and elsewhere in the book I refer to industrial clans. The meaning of *clan* I derive from the use by the sociologist Emile Durkheim. In this usage, a disorganized aggregation of individuals is a *horde*, the smallest organized unit is a *band*, and a clan is a group of bands. A clan is an intimate association of individuals who are connected to each other through a variety of ties. The members of a clan may or may not share blood relations. Here I refer to an intimate group of industrial workers who know one another well but who typically do not share blood relations.

bureaucracy, however, workers lack any clear sense of the value of their services. No competitive bidding sets the yearly wage for an engineering vice-president, for example. Since each job is unique, companies instead rely upon the hierarchy to evaluate performance and to estimate the amount that an employee is worth. The hierarchy succeeds only to the extent that we trust it to yield equitable outcomes, just as the marketplace succeeds only because we grant legitimacy to it. As long as the vice-president regards the president as a fair and well-informed person who will arrive at a fair appraisal of his performance, the contented employee will let the hierarchy operate unobstructed. However, mistrust will bring about pre-specified contractual protections such as those written when selling some service to an outside firm. The writing and enforcement of that contract will vastly increase the costs of managing the vice-president.

More common is the example of the hourly employee who learns, over time, that the corporate hierarchy cannot be trusted to provide equitable treatment and insists upon union representation and contractual specification of rights. The employee pays additional costs in the form of union dues, the company pays additional costs in the form of more industrial relations staff, and everyone pays more costs in the form of less cooperation, less productivity and less wealth to be shared. Thus the success of a hierarchy, or bureaucracy, can be costly. But whatever the financial cost, these protective mechanisms take over when individual contribution can be equitably assessed only through the somewhat more subtle form of bureaucratic surveillance.

By comparison clans succeed when teamwork and change render individual performance almost totally ambiguous. At these times long term commitment, supported by agreement on goals and operating methods, is necessary to achieve an equitable balance. Individual performance and reward can be judged equitably only over a period of several years, thus relationships must be long term and trust must be great.

In a market each individual is in effect asked to pursue selfish interests. Because the market mechanism will exactly measure the contribution of each person to the common good, each person can be compensated exactly for personal contributions. If one chooses not to contribute anything, then one is not compensated and equity is achieved.

In a clan, each individual is also effectively told to do just what that person wants. In this case, however, the socialization of all to a common goal is so complete and the capacity of the system to measure the subleties of contributions over the long run is so exact that individuals will naturally seek to do that which is in the common good. Thus the monk, the marine or the Japanese auto worker who appears to have arrived at a selfless state is, in fact, achieving selfish ends quite thoroughly. Both of these governance mechanisms realize human potential and maximize human freedom because they do not constrain behaviour.

Only the bureaucratic mechanism explictly says to individuals, 'Do not do what you want, do what we tell you to do because we pay you for it.' The bureaucratic mechanism alone produces alienation, anomie and a lowered sense of autonomy. This is the reason that the employees of Z companies report a higher sense of personal autonomy and freedom than do the employees of Type A companies. Feelings of autonomy and freedom make the employees in Japanese firms work with so much more enthusiasm than their counterparts in many western firms.

In the sense that Z organizations are more like clans than markets or bureaucracies, they foster close interchange between work and social life. Consider this example: Chinese-American entrepreneurs appear in greater numbers than would be expected, based on their fraction of the population as a whole. For many years, the explanation offered by social scientists was that by contrast black Americans were systematically denied access to banks and other sources of capital necessary to start a small business, whereas Asian-Americans had better access to these capital markets. As a number of studies have shown, however, both blacks and Asians find the same difficulties in raising capital for businesses (see Light, 1972). Yet Asian-Americans brought with them from their homelands the tradition of informal, revolving credit societies, the *Tanomoshi* for the Japanese-Americans and the *Hui* for the Chinese-Americans. A *Tanomoshi* or *Hui* typically consists of about one dozen individuals, each one wanting to own his own service station, a one-truck hauling service, or other such small businesses. Once each month, the group gathers at one member's home for dinner, and each person brings with him a prespecified sum of money, perhaps $1000. The host of the evening keeps the whole sum – say, $12 000 – which he then uses to buy a second truck or open his service station. The group meets in this fashion for 12 successive months until each person has put in $12 000 and has taken out $12 000. In this manner, people who would have great difficulty saving the whole sum of $12 000 are able to raise capital.

The process on closer scrutiny has some unusual properties. First, the earlier recipients of the pot effectively pay a lower interest than do the later recipients. The first host has the use of $11 000 of other people's money for one month without interest, then $10 000 (as he adds his $1000 to the second dinner), and so on. By comparison the last host has to put $11 000 dollars into the pot, money that he could have left in the bank to draw interest, before he receives his pot. Surely this is an inequitable process, yet it persists. The second interesting property is that no contracts are signed, no collateral is offered, even though the late borrowers willingly turn over large sums of money to others with no assurance that they will be paid. They have no evidence of even having made a loan that would stand up in a court of law, should there be a default.

Japanese-Americans' membership in a *Tanomoshi* is limited strictly by the geographical regions of birth in Japan, and by the region in Japan from which one's ancestors came. Among the Chinese-Americans, membership in a *Hui* is limited to those within the kinship network. Thus one can only be born into a *Tanomoshi* or a *Hui*, and one can never escape from the network of familiar, communal, social, religious and economic ties that bind those groups together. If a member should fail to make good on his obligations, members of his family would certainly take up his obligation or else pay the very high price of having all branches of the family shut out of the economic and social network of the community. This ethnically bound community thus obviates the need for contracts or collateral to protect a loan. But what about the unfair difference in the implicit interest rates paid by the early versus late borrowers? We can understand this phenomenon in two ways. First, we note that these short run inequities are made up in the long run. Because each adult in these ethnic communities typically participates in a large number of *Huis* or *Tanomoshis* over his lifetime, at times simultaneously participating in two or more. Many opportunities arise to repay past debts by taking a later position in the chain. In addition, a debt incurred to one person may be repaid to that person's son or brother, who in turn has the capacity to repay the initial creditor through one of a thousand favors. What is critical is that there be a communal memory – much like that of the corporate memory in Theory Z – and that the community have a stable membership. The effects of this memory mechanism are far-reaching. Depending on his behavior as a borrower and lender, an individual may or may not be invited to participate in various other groups and may be included in or left out of religious and social activities that could affect the marital prospects of his children, the economic prospects of his business, and so on. In fact the more valuable his *Tanomoshi* membership, the higher the price he can command in the form of sought-after affiliations. Although the individuals in a *Hui* or *Tanomoshi* do not share complete goal congruence, they are at once largely committed to a congruent set of goals which have to do with maintaining the social structure of the community, and they are also subject to the long run evaluation of an ethnically bound marketplace.

These clans also work largely on the basis of trust. Marcel Mauss, a French anthropologist, has noted that the willingness to be in someone's debt is an important signal of trust (Mauss, 1967). For instance, in most societies it is considered rude to rush over to repay a neighbor for a favor just received. To do so implies lack of trust in that neighbor and a fear that the neighbor may abuse your obligation by asking in return something you find particularly difficult or distasteful. Thus, the leaving of many debts between people amounts to evidence of their trust of one another, and the evidence of trust in turn serves as the oil that lubricates future social transactions.

The point is that organizations are social organisms and, like any other social creations, are profoundly shaped by the social environment in which they exist. As we shall see, the Type Z organization succeeds only under social conditions that support lifetime employment. The *Hui* and the *Tanomoshi* succeed in the United States only because the Chinese and Japanese immigrants found themselves living together in ethnic ghettoes.

Difficulties in translation

Despite its remarkable properties, the clan form in industry possesses a few potentially disabling weaknesses. A clan always tends to develop xenophobia, a fear of outsiders. In the words of the president of one major Type Z company: 'We simply can't bring in an outsider at top levels. We've tried it, but the others won't accept him. I consider that to be one of our biggest problems.' In other ways, too, the Type Z resists deviance in all forms. Because the glue that holds it together is consistency of belief rather than application of hierarchy, it tends indiscriminately to reject all inconsistency. The trouble is that it is difficult, perhaps impossible, to discriminate in advance between a deviant idea that is useful and adaptive and one that is simply stupid and immoral. Companies such as IBM, General Motors and Xerox, in which innovation is critical, typically segregate their researchers and those who come up with new product ideas, sometimes locating them on the opposite end of the continent from headquarters in order to shield them from the sometimes oppressive corporate culture. What happens, of course, is that those scientists indeed become deviant from the mainline culture, develop lots of different ideas, and then discover that the headquarters decision makers reject their ideas as being too deviant.

In a Type Z organization, changing people's behavior by changing a measure of performance or by changing the profit calculation is an impossibility: the only way to influence behavior is to change the culture. A culture changes slowly because its values reach deeply and integrate into a consistent network of beliefs that tends to maintain the status quo. Therefore, a Type Z organization runs the risk of becoming an industrial dinosaur, unable to react quickly enough to a major shift in the environment. Where operating changes are involved, Type Z organizations tend to be unusually adaptive. A better way to accomplish some task can be adopted without having to rewrite a book of rules specifying job descriptions and without worrying about whether this change will hurt the current way of measuring our performance. This is one of the greatest strengths of the Japanese firm. Japanese companies in the United States are fast becoming legendary for their capacity to quickly adopt changes in procedure, unencumbered by bureaucratic paraphernalia. However, the coordination in this system is provided by adherence to an underlying set of values that are deeply held and closely followed. If adaptation required a change in those values, then Type Z organizations would be at a severe disadvantage. Consider one example.

I had the opportunity to work with a large retail company that had succeeded for many years in running profitable stores of medium size in small towns. The company had thoroughly cultivated the underlying value that each store manager was an independent entrepreneur who took orders from no one, including the company president. They were encouraged to take an aggressive, 'can do' attitude towards their individual businesses, and their compensation was based entirely on the profitability of their one store. Each manager ordered goods from local distributors and ran his business quite successfully. Then the company one day determined that future growth would have to be not in small towns but in major metropolitan areas. They felt that their same discipline and entrepreneurial attitude would succeed as well in Boston as it had in Ely, Minnesota. The difference was that, in order to succeed in the highly competitive metropolitan markets, the company had to develop its own distribution network of warehouses, delivery trucks, and in some cases its own manufacturing plants in order to achieve low costs that could be passed along to potential customers. Now each store manager had to take a cooperative attitude above all else to coordinate this intricate system with the other managers on whom personal success depended. Everyone saw clearly the need for this change, but no one was able to make it. The old independent attitude, so deeply held and so widely supported by payment methods, training methods, corporate structure, and other values, was carried into the new integrated enterprise. The company has consistently lost money in these metropolitan markets, although it continues to succeed in the small towns, and the old culture survives.

Every Type Z organization that I know experiences some loss of professionalism.* Whether it is a financial analyst, a salesperson, a personnel specialist, or an engineer, a Type Z company manifests a lower level of professionalism. I systematically interviewed everyone at the level of vice-president and above at two high-technology companies, one a pure Type A and one a pure Type Z (or as nearly pure as possible). I also interviewed a random selection of employees in each company. At Company A, each person was introduced to me with pride as being, '. . . the top public relations man in the industry,' or '. . . the most innovative electrical engineer, the holder of 20 patents on circuit design', or '. . . the personnel manager who set the pattern for industry in performance appraisal'. At Company Z, by comparison, the emphasis was on how the individuals comprised a working team, with little mention of specialized skills, although great emphasis was placed on the company's practice of hiring only the most skilled and able young people and then developing them. The offices of Company A managers were typically filled with shelves of books and journals, and people would often offer me an article that they had written on their speciality. At Company Z people read fewer journals, wrote fewer articles, and attended fewer professional meetings. At the extreme, Type Z companies will express the 'not-invented-here' mentality: 'We have most of the top people in the field right here, so why should I go talk to anyone else?' The trouble, of course, comes if the company starts to slip. They will not know it, since they have no external point of comparison.

---

* I have developed this work in collaboration with Jerry B. Johnson. For a complete description of the initial study, see Ouchi, W. G. and Johnson, Jerry B. (1978). 'Types of Organizational Control and Their Relationship to Emotional Well-Being'. *Administrative Science Quarterly*, vol. 23, June. We were assisted in this work by Alan Wilkins, David Gibson, Alice Kaplan and Raymond Price, to whom I am grateful.

With respect to sex and race, Type Z companies have a tendency to be sexist and racist. This is another paradox, because while Type Z companies typically work much harder and care much more about offering equality of opportunity to minorities, in some ways they have much greater obstacles to overcome than do Type A companies. As I visited the managers in the high-technology Type A, I was struck by the ethnic diversity among the upper levels of management: Spanish-Americans, Asian-Americans, Hungarian-Americans, and Anglo-Saxon-Americans. At Company A, new promotion opportunity is simply awarded to that candidate who has had the best 'bottom line' for the past few periods. Whether that manager is obnoxious or strange, succeeds by abusing his employees or by encouraging them, doesn't matter. The only thing that counts is the bottom line, and thus a diverse group of people make it to the top. How well they are able to work with one another once at the top is another question.

At Company Z the cast of top managers is so homogeneous that one member of my research team characterized the dominant culture as 'Boy Scout Macho'. That is, the top management is wholesome, disciplined, hard-working and honest, but unremittingly white, male, and middle class. Company Z has affirmative action goals at the top of its list and devotes great time and expense to recruiting, training and developing women and ethnic minorities. Why is it nonetheless typical of 'Boy Scout Macho'? Imagine that you are a general manager at Company Z. In your division you have an opening for a new manager in charge of marketing. Both a white male engineer and a female Mexican-American are completely qualified for the promotion. The difference between them is past experience. You have evaluated 40 or 50 white male engineers in the past, you have worked with them day in and day out for 20 years, and you know how to calibrate them, how to read their subtle instincts, values and beliefs. You are quite certain that you have correctly evaluated this white male engineer as being fully qualified for the job of marketing manager. But how about the female Mexican-American? How many of them have you evaluated or worked with at this level? She is probably the first. You cannot be sure that what you regard as initiative is truly that; you cannot be sure that the signs you see of ambition, of maturity or of integrity are what they seem to be. It takes time and experience to learn to read subtleties in one who is culturally different, and because subtleties are everything in the Type Z organization, you cannot be confident that you have correctly appraised this candidate, and she is therefore at a considerable disadvantage, since no one in his right mind will choose an uncertainty over a certainty.

Probably no form of organization is more sexist or racist than the Japanese corporation. They do not intentionally shut out those who are different nor do they consider male Japanese to be superior. Their organizations simply operate as culturally homogeneous social systems that have very weak explicit or hierarchical monitoring properties and thus can withstand no internal cultural diversity. To the extent that women or ethnic minorities (Caucasians or

Koreans, for example) are culturally different, they cannot succeed in Japan. The Japanese firm in the United States has a considerably greater tolerance for heterogeneity and thus can operate successfully with white people and women in high positions, but the tendency toward sameness is still present. The Type Z organization is still more open to heterogeneity, but it too requires a high level of homogeneity. Perhaps the other extreme, the cultural opposite of the Japanese firm in Japan, is the United States federal bureaucracy.

In a sense the federal bureaucracy is a microcosm of our society. Here our values of equality of opportunity for all people are crystallized, if not always realized. Much the same is true of state and local government agencies, but let us consider the federal agencies for a moment. Equality of opportunity and of treatment is taken far more seriously in the federal agencies than in almost any private sector organizations. What this means is that the government must promulgate a series of bureaucratic rules that should ordinarily prevent, in so far as humanly possible, the application of capricious or unfair standards that will harm women and ethnic minorities. Unfortunately, this set of bureaucratic rules must be geared to catch the lowest common denominator. That is, they cannot leave any rule ambiguous, to be decided on the discretion of an individual manager, since that leaves open the possibility of the manager arriving at a discriminatory interpretation. Thus the bureaucratic rules are not only explicit and inflexible but also constraining and impersonal. This thoroughgoing bureaucratization rests on the assumption that bureaucrats cannot be trusted to share the society's egalitarian goals nor to enact an egalitarian form of organization. Thus they are directed not to use their discretion and judgement. If we place a priceless value on equality in our public institutions, then we will pay any price to keep them democratic.

The price that we pay, of course, is in inefficiency, inflexibility, indolence and impersonality. All too often a federal bureau will fail to do that which makes sense because common sense does not fit the rules. All too often bureaucrats, trained not to allow personal values to intrude on decisions, will treat us, their customers, in an unfeeling manner. All too often the machinery of government will respond slowly and inefficiently with poor coordination between agencies, because they have learned not to trust one another, not to rely on subtlety, not to develop intimacy.

Social organizations are incompatible with formality, distance and contractualism. They proceed smoothly only with intimacy, subtlety, and trust. But these conditions can develop only over a long period of cultural homogenization during which the people of a nation become accustomed to one another and come to espouse a common body of values and beliefs. In a nation as young and as heterogeneous as ours, that level of cultural agreement is yet some distance away. The United States is not Japan. We are not a homogeneous body of people. Our institutions cannot operate in a wholly synchronized manner. On the other hand, we cannot allow our institutions to become so thoroughly unfeeling and unthinking that they make work and social intercourse unbearable for all of us most of the time. We must find those organizational innovations which can permit a balance between freedom and integration, which go beyond our current interpretation of individualism.

References

Argyris, C. (1964). *Integrating the Individual and the Organization*. New York: John Wiley & Sons, Inc. Chris Argyris's work has been among the most influential within the field of organizational research as well as within my own thinking. Although he is prolific, I refer here specifically to this landmark book.

Kanter, R. M. (1972). *Commitment and Community*. Cambridge: Harvard University Press.

Leavitt, H. J. (1978). *Managerial Psychology*, 4th edn. Chicago: University of Chicago Press.

Light, I. H. (1972). *Ethnic Enterprise in America*. Berkeley: University of California Press.

Mauss, M. (1967). *The Gift*. New York: W. W. Norton.

Schein, E. (1969). *Process Consultation*. Reading, Mass: Addison-Wesley.

Reproduced from Ouchi, William (1981). *Theory Z*, Chapter 6 by permission of Addison-Wesley Publishing Co., Inc., Reading, Massachusetts.

Values: the core of the culture
T. Deal and A. Kennedy

Allen Kennedy is president of a microcomputer software company in Boston, having spent 12 years as a consultant with McKinsey and Co. Terrence Deal is a professor at Vanderbilt University, where he specializes in the study of organizations. Deal and Kennedy's book, *Corporate Cultures*, was published in 1982 and was received with great enthusiasm by managers and researchers alike.

The book argues that companies need to focus on the soft areas as well as the conventional strategy aspects of administration. Management ought to put into place values that are 'relevant to Monday morning', say the authors in the chapter that follows. In order to maintain a relevant value system, management continually fine tunes and communicates its values to all members of the organization. And in order to be accepted by the organization, values should stand for something important to people.

Values are the bedrock of any corporate culture.* As the essence of a company's philosophy for achieving success, values provide a sense of common direction for all employees and guidelines for their day to day behavior. These formulas for success determine (and occasionally arise from) the types of corporate heroes, and the myths, rituals and ceremonies of the culture. In fact, we think that often companies succeed because their employees can identify, embrace and act on the values of the organization.

These values may be grand in scope ('Progress is our most important product'), or narrowly focused ('Underwriting excellence'). They can capture the imagination ('The first Irish multinational'). They can tell people how to work together ('It takes two to Tandem'). Or they can simply drive ('15 per cent period-to-period sales and earnings growth'). If they are strong, they command everyone's attention: 'What people really care about around here is quality.' If they are weak, they may often be ignored: 'It's not the same company since the old man stepped down. Nowadays everyone around here is just more or less doing his own thing.'

'Rational' managers rarely pay much attention to the value system of an organization. Values are not 'hard', like organizational structures, policies and procedures, strategies, or budgets. Often they are not even written down. And when someone does try to set them down in a formal statement of corporate philosophy, the product often bears an uncomfortable resemblance to the biblical beatitudes – good and true and broadly constructive, but not all that relevant to Monday morning.

We think that society today suffers from a pervasive uncertainty about values, a relativism that undermines leadership and commitment alike. After all, in this fast-paced world, who really *does* know what's right? On the philosophical level, we find ourselves without convincing responses. But the everyday business environment is quite different. Even if ultimate values are chimerical, particular values clearly make sense for specific organizations operating in specific economic circumstances. Perhaps because ultimate values seem so elusive, people respond positively to practical ones. Choices must be made, and values are an indispensable guide in making them.

Moreover, it is clear that organizations have, in fact, gained great strength from shared values – with emphasis on the 'shared'. If employees know what their company stands for, if they know what standards they are to uphold, then they are much more likely to make decisions that will support those standards. They are also more likely to feel as if they are an important part of the organization. They are motivated because life in the company has meaning for them.

Since organizational values can powerfully influence what people actually do, we think that values ought to be a matter of great concern to managers. In fact, shaping and enhancing values can become the most important job a manager can

* Much of the original work on the ideas expressed in this chapter was done by McKinsey consultant Julien Phillips.

do. In our work and study, we have found that successful companies place a great deal of emphasis on values. In general, these companies shared three characteristics.

- They stand for something – that is, they have a clear and explicit philosophy about how they aim to conduct their business.
- Management pays a great deal of attention to shaping and fine-tuning these values to conform to the economic and business environment of the company and to communicating them to the organization.
- These values are known and shared by all the people who work for the company – from the lowliest production worker right through to the ranks of senior management.

What are these values that hold a company and its workforce together? Where do they come from? And more important, how do they influence the successful operation of an organization?

The corporate character

For those who hold them, shared values define the fundamental character of their organization, the attitude that distinguishes it from all others. In this way, they create a sense of identity for those in the organization, making employees feel special. Moreover, values are a reality in the minds of most people throughout the company, not just the senior executives. It is this sense of pulling together that makes shared values so effective. Let's look at a few:

- *Caterpillar*: '24-hour parts service anywhere in the world' – symbolizing an extraordinary commitment to meeting customers' needs.
- *Leo Burnett Advertising Agency*: 'Make great ads' – commitment to a particular concept of excellence.
- *American Telephone & Telegraph*: 'Universal service' – a historical orientation toward standardized, highly reliable service to all possible users, now being reshaped into values more relevant to a newly competitive marketplace.
- *DuPont*: 'Better things for better living through chemistry' – a belief that product innovation, arising out of chemical engineering, is DuPont's most distinctive value.
- *Sears, Roebuck*: 'Quality at a good price' – the mass merchandiser for middle America.
- *Rouse Company*: 'Create the best environment for people' – a dominating concern to develop healthy and pleasant residential communities, not just to build subdivisions.
- *Continental Bank*: 'We'll find a way' (to meet customer needs).

- *Dana Corporation*: 'Productivity through people' – enlisting the ideas and commitment of employees at every level in support of Dana's strategy of competing largely on cost and dependability rather than product differentiation.
- *Chubb Insurance Company*: 'Underwriting excellence' – an overriding commitment to excellence in a critical function.
- *Price Waterhouse & Company*: 'Strive for technical perfection' (in accounting).

Most of these phrases sound utterly platitudinous to the outsider. Indeed, many of them are little more than slogans that might be (and often were) used in advertising campaigns. What makes them more than slogans is the degree to which these phrases capture something people in the organization deeply believe in. Within each of these corporations, these words take on rich and concrete meaning.

We call these phrases 'core values' because they become the essence of the organization's philosophy. These slogan-like themes are only the most visible parts of a complex system that includes a whole range of beliefs about how the organization should achieve success. These values and beliefs are closely linked to the basic concept of the business and provide guidelines for employees to follow in their work.

For example, if you are in the business of selling cars – as is Joe Girard, the world's most successful car salesman – and if your experience in the marketplace leads you to think that taking care of your customer is *the key way* to get them to come back again, then you will put this philosophy to work. Girard's core value is 'customer service'. From this basic concept, Girard has developed a number of beliefs – that you should studiously respond to all customer complaints, make sure their service problems are handled, even send them cards at Christmas and on their birthdays. In some months Girard sends out more than 13 000 cards to customers. He puts his values and beliefs into action, and he sells more automobiles every year than any single car salesman in the world.

In the case of one person, it is easy to see how one basic value backed by enormous energy can make for success. What is harder to understand is how this same principle applies in a larger corporation. Companies are, after all, only collections of individuals. If they all believe and behave as Joe Girard does, they will undoubtedly succeed at what they set out to do. And that is the real challenge for management: to make thousands and thousands of people Joe Girard-like figures who have a strongly ingrained sense of the company's value.

The Pepsi-Cola Company seems to have met this challenge by fostering the values of competition. As *Business Week* recently reported:

> Once the company was content in its No. 2 spot, offering Pepsi as a cheaper alternative to Coca-Cola. But today, a new employee at PepsiCo quickly learns that beating the competition, whether outside or inside the company, is the surest path to success . . . Because winning is the key value at Pepsi, losing has its penalties. Consistent runners-up find their

jobs gone. Employees know that they must win merely to stay in place – and must devastate the competition to get ahead.

Dana Corporation, on the other hand, has a very different, but still successful, set of values. As a competitor in the long established automobile parts manufacturing business, it has virtually doubled its productivity over the past seven years, a period when the overall growth of American productivity has been slowing. Dana did not accomplish this record with massive capital investment, with sophisticated industrial-engineering studies, or with management imposed speed-up measures. Instead, it relied on its people, right down to the shopfloor level. Management continually stressed the value of productivity to company success. It put this value into action by creating a multitude of task forces and other special activities; by giving its people practical opportunities to generate productivity; by listening to ideas and then implementing them; and by consistently, visibly and frequently rewarding success. 'Productivity through people' is no mere advertising phrase to the employees of Dana Corporation.

Procter & Gamble: forging a value system

Although a value system may be most visible in the few words that make up an advertising slogan, many successful companies have a very rich tradition of values, beliefs and themes that have developed over the years. Where do these values come from? They mostly come from experience, from testing what does and doesn't work in the economic environment. But individual people within an organization also have strong influence in shaping the standards and beliefs of the organization.

In Chapter 1 we looked briefly at the values of Tandem, a relatively new, fast growth company. Now let's look at a different kind of corporation, one that has been able to sustain its strong philosophy – and its success – over 150 years of growth.

By almost any measure, the Procter & Gamble Company of Cincinnati, Ohio, is one of the best models of persistent long term attention to building a strong culture company, particularly in its emphasis on values. First, let's look at a brief history:

In 1837, upon the suggestion of their father-in-law, William Procter and James Gamble joined forces in a partnership. The candle and soap industry they entered that year was a highly competitive one; there were 18 direct competitors in the Cincinnati market alone and many more across the burgeoning country. In P&G's early years, candles were the company's principal source of income, and the company enjoyed a modest success. By the 1870s, however, the growing popularity of oil lamps for illumination left Procter and Gamble justifiably worried about the future of their candle making business. To protect their future, they redoubled their efforts to become a leader in the soap market. In 1878, James N. Gamble, son of the founder and a chemist by education, perfected the formula for a new, white soap.

It was cousin Harley Procter's job to sell the soap. He sensed it could be a good product, so he spent weeks trying to come up with the right name. In church one Sunday it came to him while reciting Psalms 45:8 – 'All thy garments smell of myrrh and aloe, and cassia, out of the ivory palaces whereby they have made thee glad.' Ivory soap was born.

Realizing the opportunity this invention offered the company, Harley employed the creative use of the new medium of display advertising to turn Ivory into the first nationally branded soap product. The company's major growth had begun.

The initial success with Ivory soap was followed up some 33 years later by the introduction of Crisco shortening; as a substitute for lard, it was a radically new product at the time. Then came Camay (1923), Tide and Prell (1946), Joy (1949), Cheer (1950), then Crest and Comet (1956), Head & Shoulders (1960), Pampers (1961), Safeguard (1963), and, more recently, Downy, Mr Clean, and Top Job. As any consumer can attest, to this day these products are leaders in the market segments they serve.

What was it that made this company so strong in the field of consumer packaged goods? What is it about P&G that has allowed it to sustain its enviable track record so long and so consistently through good economic times and bad? Was it being first to the market with a new product? Perhaps true in the early days but certainly not relevant for products like Tide and Charmin. Was it an absence of competition in its main markets? Certainly never true in any of the markets P&G served. Was it a better strategy than Colgate or others? We doubt there are that many degrees of strategic freedom available to allow P&G to differentiate itself in all the diverse markets it serves.

We believe P&G's success can be traced most directly back to a very strong culture, founded on a set of beliefs and values. The first and most basic of these values is 'do what is right'. As William Cooper Procter said at the time he handed the reins of management to Richard R. Deupree, the first non-Procter or Gamble to run the company: 'Always try to do what's right. If you do that, nobody can really find fault'. This rule has lived to this day, being passed on to every head of P&G since Cooper – and every new employee as well.

Where did this and other beliefs and values come from? There was no visionary among the early Procters and Gambles to codify the value system and drum it into the heads of employees. Rather these values evolved over years and years of trial and error as many people worked to figure out just how such a business should be run. Let's see how a few of these key values evolved.

'The consumer is important'

From the earliest days of P&G, its founding fathers always had an eye clearly fixed on what might be important to customers. One morning in 1851, William Procter noticed that a wharfhand was painting black crosses on P&G's candle boxes. Asking why this was done, Procter learned that the crosses allowed illiterate wharfhands to distinguish the candle boxes from the soap boxes. Another artistic wharfhand soon changed the black cross to a circled star. Another replaced the single star with a cluster of stars. And then a quarter moon was added with a human profile. Finally, P&G painted the moon and stars emblem on all boxes of their candles.

At some later date, P&G decided that the 'man in the moon' was unnecessary so they dropped it from their boxes. Immediately P&G received a message from New Orleans that a jobber had refused delivery of an entire shipment of P&G candles. Since these boxes lacked the full 'moon and stars' design, the jobber thought they were imitations. P&G quickly recognized the value of the 'moon and stars' emblem and brought it back into use by registering it as a trademark. It was the beginning of brand name identification for P&G and the first of many times that P&G listened to its customers.

P&G paid attention to customers because over the years they learned that the more they did so, the greater the payback to the company. Certainly, the customers discovered and launched Ivory soap. Soon after it was introduced, P&G learned from its customers that Ivory floated. Initially, P&G managers were so surprised by this they assumed it was an accident in the mixing of the soap. So it was, but customers kept asking for the 'floating soap' so P&G incorporated the 'mistake' into their regular production.

P&G continued listening to customers, who helped them develop all of their major products. Their experience through the years has taught them step by step that such attention always pays off. P&G calls this mania 'consumerism: a response, after comprehensive market research, to what consumers need and want'. Over the company's history, consumerism has taken many forms, from testing kitchens for Crisco in 1912; to hiring housewives to provide consumer feedback on liquid dish detergents in 1922; to large scale, door to door sampling efforts for Camay in the 1920s. Today, P&G conducts over 1.5 million telephone interviews annually. That's the equivalent of 1000 Gallup polls each year.

In short, P&G is a culture that glories in listening and listening well to consumers. Furthermore, they have developed more ways to listen to customers than anyone else. And why wouldn't they, they've spent years learning how.

'Things don't just happen, you have to make them happen'

P&G is the largest consistent advertiser among the giant consumer products companies. For the last century, managers at P&G have believed that advertising works and they bet their company's future on it. How did they develop this trust in the media's efficacy? Again the answer did not come easily, but through years and years of hard work.

It all started with Harley Procter and his Ivory soap. For several years, Harley had been arguing with his relatives/colleagues in the company to convince them that media advertising could sell more soap. Finally, he convinced them to take the first step and allocate $11 000 to this new and unproven medium.

Harley decided to emphasize the purity of Ivory in his first advertising effort. To do this he hired a science consultant from New York who both defined purity and went on to determine that, given this definition, Ivory was 99.44 per cent pure. Armed with this statistic, Harley began advertising Ivory. The results of this brilliant innovation were twofold: booming sales for P&G and the birth of modern advertising. Like listening to consumers, it worked.

But getting hooked on advertising in a company like P&G does not mean standing still. When P&G begins to believe in something like advertising, given such bedrock cultural values as 'make it happen', they keep testing, keep trying new ideas, keep evolving the basic idea year by year. In 1923, P&G was first to capitalize on the use of what was then a brand new advertising medium – radio. Starting with informational radio spots, P&G went on to invent the daytime soap opera. Thirty years later, P&G did the same for television.

'We want to make employee interests our own'

Even as early as the late 1880s, and with a hot, new product in Ivory, William Cooper Procter had a problem: how to keep P&Gers not just productive but loyal, too, and how to express the company's sense of responsibility to its people.

In 1883, Procter started working for P&G at the lowest level of menial factory labor – loading the soap mixers, a job that wasn't just for show. At work, Procter lived the life of a laborer to its fullest, even eating lunch with the other workers while sitting on the factory floor. During this early work, Procter developed a first-hand understanding of the perspectives and concerns of the P&G workers. This understanding was to serve as a foundation for his insistence on improved labor relations.

In 1884, Procter finally persuaded his father and uncle to give workers

Saturday afternoons off without loss of pay, a radical proposal at the time. However, growing labor unrest across the country quickly proved Procter's plan to be grossly inadequate. He wrestled with this problem for two years, then suggested that profit sharing might develop greater loyalty and respect among P&G workers. Again failure – Procter's profit sharing plan realized no gains in productivity and loyalty; workers simply viewed the payments they received as extra salary. Undaunted, he tinkered with it over several years, and in 1903 devised a scheme to couple profit sharing with the purchase of P&G stock – the company would add $1 for every $1 invested by a worker up to an amount equal to the worker's annual salary. Its success emboldened Procter to establish ongoing two-way communications between management and workers by instituting the Employee Conference Plan (1918) and creating one seat for a worker representative from each domestic plant on P&G's board of directors (1919). Then he shortened the workday from 10 to 8 hours. Still not content in his efforts to improve worker relations and realizing his action would benefit all involved, Procter singlehandedly abolished job uncertainty at P&G by guaranteeing employment for workers. To do this he took the enormous risk of developing direct distribution (in other words, a salesforce), thus bypassing the distributors who previously had created highly uneven demand. The risk succeeded and, even during the Depression, P&G was able to keep its workers on the payrolls.

So Procter & Gamble has a long history of working hard on the 'right' things: James Gamble perfecting his soap, Harley Procter forging a new field of advertising, and William Cooper Procter establishing the principle that the interests of the company and those of its employees were inseparable. All along, P&G paid scrupulous attention to its customers. These values were formed and refined by years of experience in the marketplace. They didn't just appear overnight. Although P&G is a highly successful company, it has had its share of problems; Rely tampons are only the most recent example. Still, its continuing experiences in the marketplace have evolved into a rich and varied culture that has sustained it through difficult times.

The evolution of a value structure like P&G's is the core element in all the strong culture companies we studied. The stronger the culture, the richer and more complex the value system, the longer the chain of evidence that these values really do produce results.

The influence of corporate values

As we've seen with P&G, a corporation's values will affect all aspects of the company – from what products get manufactured to how workers are treated. Companies that are guided by strong shared values tend to reflect those values in the design of their formal organization. The most readily recognizable case is the company that believes that the way to put its values to work is to control costs tightly. Generally, its financial vice-president and controller will be leading members of the top management group, and very frequently the divisional controllers will report directly to the corporate controller rather than to the division head. Almost always, its dominant management systems will be those for budget development and operation control, and even its longer range planning will be geared to the needs of financial control.

A company with values geared primarily to the external marketplace, like P&G, will probably have several very senior marketing vice-presidents in its top management structure, and it is likely to rely on some version of product managers or brand managers to handle product marketing. It will surely have rather elaborate systems for gathering and shifting data on customer tastes, customer response to its products, and initiatives by its competitors.

The values and beliefs of an organization indicate what matters are to be attended to most assiduously – for instance, current operations in one company, external relations in a second, longer term strategy in a third. They suggest what kind of information is taken most seriously for decision making purposes – experienced judgment of 'old hands' in one organization, detailed 'number crunching' in another. They define what kind of people are most respected – engineers versus marketing men versus financial types.

Values also play a very important role in determining how far one can rise within an organization. If product development is the company's overriding ethic, the best people will want to work in the company's research and development laboratories. If customer service is the important value, the go-getters won't want to be in finance but in a sales or field service function. The company will tend to reinforce the primacy of that value by promoting a disproportionate share of the people in these jobs.

Shared values and beliefs also play an important role in communicating to the outside world what to expect of a company. The philosophy at Sears, for instance, marks its corporate personality consistently to suppliers and customers alike: the Sears value – 'Quality at a good price' – encourages buyers to become crusaders in driving down the cost of products. Many companies depend on Sears for most of their business, yet these companies often live in fear of the giant retailer. 'That price isn't good enough,' Sears buyers will say. 'We want to sell a muffler for $19.95 and buy it from you for $9.95 and that's it.' The producer can argue that the steel costs $7.14 and that something in addition must be charged to manufacture the muffler, but then Sears will only threaten to take their business someplace else. After all, Sears sells more mufflers than anyone in the world. So the producer huffs and puffs and figures how to make a muffler for $9.95. That's the way Sears does its purchasing and it's infamous for it. Yet that's part of its image for its customers: Sears gets the lowest prices for quality products.

Delta Airlines' value as 'the people company' is expressed in its slogan, 'The

Delta Family Feeling'. As only a caring family would, Delta pays higher salaries than the industry average and thus attracts the best employees – people whom the company works very hard to get and to whom it gives significant responsibilities for delivering quality service. It was only natural, therefore, that when Delta braced itself for the last recession, senior management, in effect, told shareholders and the financial community:

> Now that times are tough, you'll have to pay. We're not going to earn what we could over the long term if we let go of people now; our people are very important to our long term performance; they're what makes this place work. So, shareholders, it's your time to give a pint of blood; until this recession is over, our earnings and maybe even our dividends are going to be down because we are not going to lay our people off.

Such a move was acceptable only because Delta had communicated the sanctity of this value of 'family' over a long period of time. Shared values are what has made Delta great.

In 1982, while other carriers made cutbacks of 15 000 workers, Delta held firm. As a result, the company gained considerable loyalty from its employees. In the past, non-unionized employees have carried luggage and handled the ticket counters to help the airline get through the slumps so that regular employees would not be laid off.

Delta points up the importance of a company's living by its values, even in a difficult situation. Yet the example also underlines the all or nothing stakes involved. Once a company tries to shape values, the company is often locked in – the actions of management must be consistent, because the inconsistencies will be noticed and magnified out of proportion. In creating values that will work, managers are forced to live life as they say they would . . . whatever the circumstances.

How do shared values affect organizational performance? In broad terms, they act as an informal control system that tells people what is expected of them. More specifically, shared values affect performance in three main ways:

- *Managers and others throughout the organization give extraordinary attention to whatever matters are stressed in the corporate value system* – and this in turn tends to produce extraordinary results. An oil company produces crude and petroleum products much more efficiently than others because efficient operation is what it values and what its managers concentrate on. One of this company's principal competitors values trading and financial management most highly. Accordingly, its managers worry less about production operations and concentrate instead on squeezing every cent of potential revenues from their sales.
- *Down-the-line managers make marginally better decisions, on average, because they are guided by their perception of the shared values.* When a manager at Dana is confronted by a close question – like making a particular investment in

increased productivity versus one in new product development – the manager is likely to opt for productivity.

- *People simply work a little harder because they are dedicated to the cause.* 'I'm sorry I'm so late getting home, but the customer had a problem and we never leave a customer with a problem.'

Risks and pitfalls of strong values

The power of values is that people care about them. This power can be a problem as well as a source of strength. If managers choose to build or reinforce the shared values of the group of people they work with, they had better recognize the risks they are assuming:

The risk of obsolescence

What if the environment changes? One of the most serious risks of a potent system of shared values is that economic circumstances can change while shared values continue to guide behavior in ways no longer helpful to the organization's success. When a company with strongly held values finds that it has lost marketplace or economic relevance, it generally has great difficulty adjusting successfully. Witness AT&T's current difficulty in adapting to a newly competitive marketplace.

'Universal Service' is AT&T's slogan, which Theodore Vail, a former chairman of the company, first articulated. For a long time, that label served AT&T well because it was, until recently, a regulated entity that only needed to make its regulators happy to receive rate increases. As elected or appointed officials, regulators were naturally influenced by their constituencies; given AT&T's phenomenally good strategy to get a phone to everyone who wanted it ('Universal Service'), the company could consistently ask governmental regulators for rate increases and get them. After all, the mass of voters were well served and treated equally, even if equality meant the inefficiency of installing one telephone at the dead end of a desolate country road. Wherever the unconnected in America wanted a telephone, a line would be installed shortly thereafter.

Yet in clinging to this value, AT&T has had tremendous difficulty in adapting to a newly competitive, deregulated environment. Week in, week out over the past several years, newspapers have announced yet another element of the proposed realignment of the company. In the business press, especially, there have been repeated stories about the Bell system's 'new marketing thrust'. A different reality is apparent, however, when a repairman who visited one of our homes spent two full hours regaling us with his version of the demise of the company. His diatribe concluded with a recommendation that we buy a non-Bell answering device. And indeed, while AT&T continues to struggle to adapt, companies like MCI and Rolm have started to move in on its market, particularly in switchboard systems especially tailored for use in small offices and commercial long distance phone calls.

With a monopoly franchise, a paramount goal of universal service made sense and worked. (The United States does have the best telephone system in the world, in case you hadn't noticed.) But it also fostered a preoccupation with total system integrity that has inhibited AT&T's ability to identify and meet the needs of particular market segments – a serious limitation now that competitors have been allowed to enter the marketplace. Senior management perceives the threat very clearly and understands what must be done, but the mentality and work practices of down-the-line employees are so strongly tied to the obsolete value system that it will take years for the company to adapt itself fully to the new circumstances.

The consequences of obsolescence are serious enough to give some managers pause in their pursuit of shared values. But they should look at the other side of the coin as well: would AT&T have been as successful in the past had it lacked such strongly held values? Almost certainly not.

The risk of resistance to change

Barring an environmental upheaval that forces everyone to adapt or perish, can an institution of true believers ever change? Look at Sears, Roebuck. It faced no fundamental transformation in its environment like that in telecommunications, but its management nonetheless saw an opportunity to become an up-scale merchandiser on the department store model. The market was large and growing rapidly, and margins were undoubtedly fatter.

Yet no sooner had Sears set out on this road than it faltered. Its army of loyal employees, who had cut their eyeteeth on delivering value to middle-American consumers, simply did not know how to run a Macy's-style operation. As a result, performance lagged, and the appealing strategy had to be abandoned.

Sears is by no means an isolated example. In a glamour growth company, one of the authors spent two years trying to help the CEO in a determined effort to cut out excessive overhead in the face of increasingly strong cost competition. Overall, fewer than 1000 overhead positions were eliminated, and many of those were soon added back. Because of the powerful growth mentality that persisted in the company, cost reduction simply would not fly.

The risk of inconsistency

What if managerial behavior contradicts professed values? In one company we know, the CEO speaks frequently and eloquently about the value of serving customers better. But when the year end approaches, he demands financial performance – the customer be hanged. Given the demonstrated primacy of clearly articulated financial objectives, it is no wonder that very few people in the organization buy into the customer service rhetoric.

In a second company, a large bank, top management talks constantly about the need to become more entrepreneurial in response to the changing regulatory and competitive environment. When budget time comes around, however, new ventures are held to the same targets of financial return and cost growth as established divisions. Not surprisingly, evidence of real entrepreneurship is very hard to find.

In order to build a strong culture top management must be convinced that it can adhere faithfully and visibly to the values it intends to promote. Any inconsistency in adhering to or failing to promote the company's enunciated values will begin to undermine the strength of the culture.

In Part II of the book, we discuss in more detail how companies can avoid the risks and pitfalls of strong values by constantly tuning them to the business environment. But the point we want to make here is that values do their share of day to day business. What brings values to life is the awareness of everyone in the organization about these values and why they are important. It's not just values, it is the extensive sharing of them that makes a difference.

How do values come to be shared in a company? Through the reinforcement provided by all the other elements of the company's culture, but primarily by the culture's lead players – its heroes.

Reproduced from Deal, T. and Kennedy, A. (1982). *Corporate Cultures*, Chapter 2 by permission of Addison-Wesley Publishing Co., Inc., Reading, Massachusetts.

Minerva's Owl: building a corporate value system
William L. Weiss

William Weiss is chairman and chief executive officer of Ameritech (American Information Technologies Corporation), the parent company of Bell Telephones in five US states, which came into existence in January 1984. He has been involved in developing a new corporate culture for the company. As such he is in an excellent position to discuss in this article the place of values within a company's culture and their adaptation to a new environment.

Weiss talks about building a corporate conscience, which must coincide with the employees' own individual values, and which sets the framework for decision making. Values are also related to purpose. The article outlines the values Weiss hopes to instill in his company, such as the dignity of the individual, or optimum standards of service, and how these values are shaping the development of the corporation.

I'm grateful for the opportunity to take part in this seminar on corporate ethics and values. This is not only a chance for me to benefit from your research and thoughtful consideration of important issues. It is also an opportunity for me to offer some ideas of my own. The theories generated in academia have significant long term influence on the business community. But it is also important for business people to join in the academic debate so we can help define these values. Just as business can benefit from academic concepts, academic concepts can benefit from the pragmatism born of business experience. A useful analogy comes from an article by Irving Kristol in the 16 July *Wall Street Journal*. Kristol writes, and I quote:

> The trouble with most economists is that, though they may teach the virtues of markets, they don't really believe in economics – in the truths established by a chain of rigorous reasoning that begins with hypothetical models and reaches to conclusions in the real world. To criticize an economic policy by saying that 'it might work in practice but not in theory', would be regarded as somewhat peculiar by most people. But not by economists, who are doing it all the time, as they blandly subordinate obvious economic realities to their sovereign economic analysis.

Substitute 'ethics' for 'economics'. Our task is to discuss and crystallize issues of a corporate value system – values that have meaning and are useful in reality, as well as in the forum that created them. In short, we should be able not just to *define* a value system – we must be able to *live* by it!

Ameritech – the corporation I head – is in an unusually favorable position to reflect on values. We are a new corporation, half a year old. We are in the process of building a corporate culture for ourselves. We want to build our value system thoughtfully – by re-examining the values we inherit from our past, and by establishing fresh values appropriate to our new circumstances. There is a saying attributed to Hegel that 'Minerva's Owl takes flight in the gathering dusk'. Minerva, as you know, is the goddess of wisdom, and so, I presume, of culture. In my opinion, old cultural values are becoming obsolete. A new environment will bring forth new values, on which we will build a new corporate culture.

The dusk is beginning to gather on many years of regulatory orders, court decisions, and arbitrary changes in our industry. The competitive marketplace is beginning to rule. Let us hope that the Owl of Wisdom can now take flight.

As a way to begin, I will discuss some principles that can serve as the framework for the corporate values I wish to bring into focus today.

First, there is a question – that of corporate conscience. Is there such a thing? Or is it only the individual who has a conscience? Conscience is a practical judgment about the morality of a concrete action or decision. Ultimately, this means that the corporation's leadership must determine its value system and lead the management team to behavior that conforms to it. I am not suggesting that individuals do not have their *individual* values – the ethical guidance system for their own lives. It is clear to me that I cannot check my own value system at the door when I arrive at the office. I should be as comfortable at work as I am at home. I translate my own behavior into being willing to look into the mirror in the morning. I suspect this is not unique to me. Cicero said, 'The best audience for the practice of virtue is the approval of one's own conscience.' (*Disputations*, II, 26). However, there does result a *corporate* culture which effectively creates a *corporate* conscience. Given sufficient time, this set of ethical standards does begin to have its own momentum.

So, a corporation *can* instill within its basic policy structure and patterns of behavior a corporate culture, a corporate conscience, that can prevail. Perhaps this is not 'conscience' in the strict sense. I don't mean to get into a technical discussion about terminology. Whatever you call it, I am saying that a corporation can create a moral *environment*, a distinct set of *values* and *standards*, to which it holds its people accountable. If a person's individual values are significantly different, he will soon find he is in the wrong place. It is a key responsibility of corporate leaderhip to set the pattern and tone of this 'conscience'. Ameritech wants to build a value system – a conscience – that will provide the momentum to prevail, and to endure. We want it to be a strong value system, one that insists that falling short of its standards will not be acceptable.

Second, reality is essentially ambiguous. Dilemmas arise not just between good and evil, but, most commonly, between the good and the good. We are, of course, dealing with *perceived* good and *perceived* evil. There is often good even in a perceived evil. The choice is most difficult when one must decide which is the lesser of two perceived evils and choose accordingly. This is why a manager must sometimes make a decision – one over which he has, perhaps, agonized – a decision that appears unethical to many. Let me cite an example.

Suppose there is a trend in business – as there has been – to offer financial incentives to encourage early retirement. A chief executive does not favor such a plan, and plainly says so to his employees. On the basis of his word, many employees take early retirement – employees who might have waited for the incentive to be offered, had the chief executive not expressed his views.

A year and a half later, the course of events in the business dictates that you must offer such incentives. What do you do? What comes first – the corporation's financial health, or your previously expressed views – which to the employee body were accepted as your given word?

You can walk down a whole list of such pragmatic questions and ask, 'What is the *reality* of this issue?' There are very few easy answers. The ideal exists only in the mind. The world itself is concrete, and human behavior is determined not only by principle but by circumstances. Now, I am not attempting to establish that the end justifies the means – or that changed circumstances necessarily change one's obligation to ethical consistency. Perhaps the least I can offer is that a corporate conscience at least forces one to weigh a decision – any decision – within that framework.

A third principle is that values are related to purpose, which is the governing value. Every decision, every action, is for a purpose. Society's purpose for business is to contribute to economic well-being by producing and distributing goods and services. Making a profit is required to stay in business.

The various constituencies of business have their own objectives: shareowners expect a return on their investment; employees look to it for a living; customers expect quality service and products at acceptable prices. These are not necessarily conflicting interests; nor is it appropriate to ask which takes precedence. They are all *interdependent* – it is *together* that they produce results and share the benefits of the enterprise.

My experience tells me that, in business, if you spend much time trying to deal with the issues of integrity and ethics, you realize that there is no way to define a standard that makes ethical behavior easy. But if you raise the level of consciousness about your responsibility, there is a good probability your decisions will tend to be more ethical – made within the integrity of the situation – than they would otherwise be.

That's poor solace for those who would opt for easy answers. But it *is* the reality. The complexity of our large corporations makes it almost impossible to anticipate all the ethical implications of a particular policy decision. What seems to be perfectly ethical at one level may be totally different at another – and it will so be evaluated by the people who eventually feel its effects.

It could not have been foreseen, for example, when the internal combustion engine was invented, that it would eventually cause a major problem by polluting the atmosphere. *Should* such an effect have been foreseen? *Could* it have been foreseen? I think not.

With those thoughts as background, let me now mention some of the values I would like to see develop in my own corporation's emerging culture. I say *some* of the values. Because we are still evolving our value system, still forming our identity, still thinking carefully about what we want to be. My list of values starts with these:
1 The dignity of the individual.
2 Openness to people and to ideas.
3 Optimum standards of service.
4 Entrepreneurship.
5 Synergism.
6 Leadership through competence.
7 Behavior based on values.
Let me comment briefly on each of these.

1 The dignity of the individual

It is important to treat people with dignity. This has been repeated so frequently that just the saying seems trite. But all current literature emphasizes that the truly successful corporations are those which have this as their dominant value. It means not just saying it – but living it. It means leading people to self-realization and giving them the freedom to achieve it. I need not elaborate on this one. So many of the other values stem directly from it.

2 Openness to people and to ideas

I would like to depart from the cultural norm that presupposes that each of us does the job better than anyone else. This attitude means that we can't openly accept the ideas of others which might allow us to do the job, not just well, but better.

When Japanese business people visit our country, what do they want to know? The answer is simple – anything you tell them. They'll take an idea home and, rather than dismiss it out of hand, they'll always be willing to try it. They want to be winners, and they don't care where the idea comes from.

It is said that the ancient Greeks and the Americans are originators. The ancient Romans and the Japanese are assimilators. It is good to be creative. But it is also good to be able to accept a good idea from wherever it comes.

3 Optimum standards of service

Ameritech comes from a culture in which service was a supreme value. This value is even more important to us now than it was before. Previously, people had nowhere else to go for our products and services. Today the telecommunications industry is increasingly competitive. Service is a value from our past that we must and will keep. We are determined to offer not just *good* service, not just *excellent* service, but the *best*. We owe this to our customers. We owe this to our shareowners, too. Because without being the best we will not earn the return shareowners expect from us, we will not achieve the purpose for which we are in business.

4 Entrepreneurship

To give top quality service, and to treat people with dignity, you must give them significant latitude to accomplish their responsibility.

Ameritech is the parent corporation of 18 companies. The word 'parent' implies leading those for whom it is responsible to a mature, constructive future. This is why we encourage initiative, why each of our companies is a distinct profit center. This is why we have chosen a decentralized rather than a centralized organizational structure, one that permits the subsidiary companies to operate within the fabric of a broad strategic plan. We are firmly convinced that if we give people the freedom and motivation to do things on their own, the collective effort will be greater than the sum of the parts.

5 Synergism

This value tells us to move away from insularity and provincialism, to recognize that the corporation is part of the environment, part of the Gestalt. It tells us to maximize the individual's contribution for the benefit of the whole corporation. It tells us that our corporation is part of a larger social environment. We recognize that any business exists at the pleasure of society. A successful business must, therefore, take society's expectations into account.

We further recognize that our corporation, and our industry, have a role in shaping the general environment. We are determined, therefore, actively to promote public policy which we judge necessary to keep that environment healthy and to improve it, whenever possible.

6 Leadership through competence

Ameritech intends to develop managers who assert their power through competence rather than coercion. We believe in offering the maximum freedom to our people. Institutions of higher learning treasure academic freedom. In business we should treasure the freedom to manage our jobs. Ameritech operates with a lean corporate staff. It does so because we are convinced that elaborate hierarchy is restrictive and debilitating and restrains creativity and initiative.

7 Behavior based on values.

If behavior contradicts our espoused values, this leads to what the psychologists call 'cognitive dissonance'. When a corporation enunciates a set of standards and does not abide by them . . . when we talk one way but *act* another – people are torn in two directions, become cynical, and cease to take the value system seriously. This undermines the drive to corporate identity and to excellence. It is important, therefore, to encourage behavior consonant with the corporation's values – even before the realization of attitude changes, which may require more time.

A few years ago, one company was visited by representatives of the Department of Labor and found to be out of compliance with the Affirmative Action agreement to which it was committed. Management had worked for a long time to change attitudes. Yet the company was out of compliance. So, top management decided to change *behavior* and to worry about attitudes later. Achieving Affirmation Action targets became a factor in management appraisal. The targets were met. Later, it is good to observe, attitude changes followed the behavior. The company now *behaves* in a way that is appropriate to its values.

Allow me a concluding remark.

Although my corporation comes from a definite heritage, it is young. We are in the process of building a new corporate culture. Corporate culture is largely a matter of shared values, which are the dominant ideas of the business. These values must be communicated; they must be *shared*. I am acutely aware that culture is shaped by a handful of people who are the guardians of the vision and the shapers of the corporate conscience. I know it is most especially the role of the chief executive officer to define the character of the business and to establish the corporate culture.

This is a responsibility I take seriously. And I am grateful for this opportunity to think through some of my ideas and attempt to articulate them. Ameritech's culture is still in the process of formation. There is still going to be a great deal of discussion about our values, an evolution of the culture itself.

I have three personal goals for my corporation.

I would like each person in the organization to have a sense of pride in everything he or she does. I want them all to have the feeling that what they do is important, and that they have done the best job that could possibly have been done.

I want everyone in Ameritech to have respect for one another, respect for their co-workers and for their ideas and aspirations . . . respect for our customers and their needs and expectations. Respect for others, in my book, is an essential characteristic. Without it, you cannot have self-respect.

Finally, I want us to *trust* ourselves and to trust one another, so that together we can achieve more than we ever thought possible.

It is to achieve these goals that I am working to lay the foundation of a set of corporate values. I have given you some of my thoughts today. I am looking forward to discussing them with you and know that your insights will help clarify my own thinking.

Reproduced from Weiss, William L. (1986). *Journal of Business Ethics*, 5, pp. 243–7 by permission of Kluwer Academic Publishers.

Helping men grow
Thomas J. Watson Jr

Thomas Watson Jr is the son of the founder of IBM, and has been working for the company since 1937. He has been chairman emeritus since 1981. He won a National Business Hall of Fame Award for Business Leadership in 1976. *A Business and its Beliefs* describes the ideas that shaped one of the world's most successful corporations.

This chapter discusses what Watson sees as IBM's most important value, respect for the individual, and how this stems from his father's beliefs. This principle leads to such policies as job security, the concept of the 'open door', and job enlargement.

The beliefs that mold great organizations frequently grow out of the character, the experiences, and the convictions of a single person. More than most companies, IBM is the reflection of one individual – my father, T. J. Watson.

Father joined the company at 40, a point at which most businessmen, thinking they were middle-aged, might not feel able to start a new career. He had, by that time, a firm grip on most of the beliefs he felt necessary to be successful in business. He held to them so strongly that he was sometimes exasperating. But the depth of his belief was directly related to the success of our company.

My father was the son of an upstate New York farmer. He grew up in an ordinary but happy home where the means, and perhaps the wants, were modest and the moral environment strict. The important values, as he learned them, were to do every job well, to treat all people with dignity and respect, to appear neatly dressed, to be clean and forthright, to be eternally optimistic, and above all, loyal.

There was nothing very unusual about this. It was a normal upbringing in rural nineteenth century America. Whereas most men took the lessons of childhood for granted, however, and either lived by them or quietly forgot them, my father had the compulsion to work hard at them all his life. As far as he was concerned, those values were the rules of life – to be preserved at all costs, to be commended to others, and to be followed conscientiously in one's business life.

These early lessons were later reinforced by John H. Patterson, then president and major owner of The National Cash Register Company. Patterson was an eccentric in many ways, but he was a remarkable modern business pioneer – really a social reformer – as well as the father of modern salesmanship. His personality, his methods, and his liberal employee policies had a great impact on T. J. Watson. And my father was not alone in this. Patterson trained a number of outstanding businessmen who went on to notable success. Among them were Charles Kettering, the great inventor; Alvan Macauley, longtime head of Packard; and R. H. Grant, former president of Delco Light, and Frigidaire, and later sales vice-president of General Motors.

IBM's philosophy is largely contained in three simple beliefs.

I want to begin with what I think is the most important: *our respect for the individual*. This is a simple concept, but in IBM it occupies a major portion of management time. We devote more effort to it than anything else.

This belief was bone deep in my father. Some people who start out in modest circumstances have a certain contempt for the average man when they are able to rise above him. Others, by the time they become leaders, have built up a unique respect and understanding for the average man and a sympathy for his problems. They recognize that in a modern industrial nation the less fortunate often are victims of forces not wholly within their own control. This attitude forms the basis for many of the decisions they make having to do with people. T. J. Watson was in the latter category. He had known hard times, hard work, and unemployment himself, and he always had understanding for the problems of the working man. Moreover, he recognized that the greatest of these problems was job security.

In 1914, having been fired as sales manager of National Cash following a series of clashes with Mr Patterson, my father was brought in to run the Computing-Tabulating-Recording Company (C-T-R), a loose alliance of three small companies. It was the organization that was to become IBM 10 years later.

C-T-R was a demoralized organization. Many of the people there resented the newcomer who had been brought into the organization and quarrelled among themselves. It was a situation that presented him with an early test of his belief in job security.

Despite the questionable condition of the company, no one was fired. T. J. Watson didn't move in and shake up the organization. Instead he set out to buff and polish the people who were already there and to make a success of what he had.

That decision in 1914 led to the IBM policy on job security which has meant a great deal to our employees. From it has come our policy to build from within. We go to great lengths to develop our people, to retrain them when job requirements change, and to give them another chance if we find them experiencing difficulties in the jobs they are in.

This does not mean that a job at IBM is a lifetime ticket or that we do not occasionally let people go – we do, but only after we have made a genuine effort to help them improve. Nor does it mean that people do not leave us – they do. But policies like these, we have found, help us to win the goodwill of most of our people.

Among plant people, where job security is ordinarily a matter of major concern, IBM's ability to avoid layoffs and work interruptions has encouraged our people to respond with loyalty and with diligence on the job. Over the years we have been willing to take chances and strain our resources rather than resort to layoffs. For almost a quarter of a century now, no one has lost an hour's time in layoffs from IBM, in spite of recessions and major product shifts.

Fortunately we have had a relatively steady market, which has helped make this record possible. But there have been times when we might have taken the easy way out to save payroll. During the Great Depression, for example, when nearly one-quarter of the civilian labor force was unemployed, IBM embarked on a program of expansion. Rather than resort to mass factory layoffs, IBM produced parts for inventory and stored them. It was a gamble that took nerve, especially for a company doing less than $17 million worth of business a year. Happily, the risk paid off in 1935, when Congress passed the Social Security Act and IBM, in competitive bidding, was selected to undertake one of the greatest bookkeeping operations of all time. Thanks to our stockpiling of parts, we were able to build the machines and begin delivery almost at once.

Today our frequent attitude surveys show that the importance we attach to job security is one of the principal reasons why people like to work for IBM.

Steady employment, however, is only one part of good human relations, an area where IBM inherited much from John Patterson. In many ways Patterson was a typical nineteenth century businessman. He deplored competition and went to great lengths to overcome it. On the other hand, while most business-men were fighting off the demands of their workers, Patterson made great strides in employee welfare. He was decades ahead of his time. Early in his career he had learned a hard lesson when indifferent workmen produced $50 000 worth of defective machines and almost ruined his company. Patterson's response was to build modern factories with improved facilities for his people. He provided showers on company premises and company time, dining rooms serving meals at cost, entertainment, schools, clubs, libraries and parks. Other businessmen were shocked at Patterson's notions. But he said they were investments which would pay off – and they did. T. J. Watson observed Patterson's practices carefully and carried many of them with him to IBM.

In the early days C-T-R was working so close to the line that there was no money available to duplicate Patterson's handsome factory buildings and his generous benefits programs. Father used showmanship instead. He staged band concerts and picnics and made scores of speeches. Almost every kind of fanfare was tried to create enthusiasm. The more substantial things – above-average wages and benefits – came later.

Along with wages and job security, we have always thought it equally important that the company respect the dignity of its employees. People, as I have said, occupy more IBM management time than our products. As businessmen we think in terms of profits, but people continue to rank first. Occasionally our actions have been harsh. Sometimes a fair amount of dignity has been stripped from individual managers who were being ineffective, but great efforts were then made to rebuild their pride so they could carry on with self-respect.

Our early emphasis on human relations was not motivated by altruism but by the simple belief that if we respected our people and helped them to respect themselves the company would make the most profit.

Our management also recognized that the individual has his own problems, ambitions, abilities, frustrations and goals. We wanted to be certain that no one got lost in the organization and, most of all, that no individual became a victim of any manager's unfairness or personal whim. In this regard, we developed what we call our 'open door' policy. This is a key element in our employee relations.

The open door grew out of T. J. Watson's close and frequent association with individuals in the plant and field offices. It became a natural thing for them to bring their problems to him and in time was established as a regular procedure. My father encouraged this in his visits. He spoke of it in his telephone broadcasts to offices and plants. If a man was not getting along, or if he thought he was being treated unfairly by his manager, he was told to go to the plant or branch manager. If that did not work, he was then invited to come and lay his case before my father.

Hundreds of employees literally did just that. Many would take the day off from our plant in Endicott, NY, and come to his office in New York City to talk about their problems. More often than not, he favored the complaining employee – sometimes, I'm sure, more than he should have. But he built up a lasting relationship with a great many employees and they helped him to keep in touch with what was going on in the company. At the time of his death in 1956, most of our then 57 000 employees thought of T. J. Watson as a friend they could count on.

The open door exists today as it did then. I'm sure that a policy of this kind makes many a traditional manager's blood run cold. He probably sees it as a challenge to his authority or, worse yet, as a sharp sword hanging over his head. But the fact remains that in IBM it has been remarkably effective, primarily because – by its mere existence – it exercises a moderating influence on management. Whenever a manager makes a decision affecting one of his people, he knows that he may be held accountable to higher management for the fairness of that decision.

From time to time we have had second thoughts on the practicality of this policy, especially now that IBM has grown to a company of over 80 000 people in the United States alone. Obviously, if everyone with a problem insisted on seeing the president or me, we would both have run out of time long ago.

The answer, in the future, may have to come in a shift downward in this court of appeal, possibly to the level of division president or general manager. But whatever the difficulties, we certainly have no intention of denying anyone the opportunity to talk to whomever he wishes to in this business. Whether they exercise it or not, our people are reassured by the fact that they have this right. And by its existence, I believe, it acts as a deterrent to the possible abuse of managerial power.

Our management has long believed that sharp contrast between the blue and the white collar people in a business is to be avoided. For many years IBM benefits were the same for all employees with a given amount of service, regardless of rank or position. Insurance and vacation programs to this day relate to service. Other benefits, such as medical care, are the same for all. In our retirement plan, however, we now recognize salary as well as length of service.

Years ago all piecework was eliminated in our plants. First-line managers in the plants did not keep data on the production of parts because we did not want their evaluation of workers directly related to units produced. The IBM employee was compensated on the basis of his manager's judgment of his overall contribution to the business.

Obviously some of these practices caused inefficiencies. Yet on the whole they contributed in a major way to the morale of the hourly rated man.

Naturally the key factor in the maintenance of good human relations is the individual manager, and when my father first went on the road for The National Cash Register Company, he learned a lesson in management that he made a permanent part of IBM. Right after he joined 'The Cash' as it was known, he spent several weeks calling on prospects without making a single sale. His manager had him on the carpet, and after treating him pretty roughly, he said: 'Young man, I'll go out with you when you call on your prospects, and if we fall down we'll fall down together.' They went out and together made several sales. After that, having learned a little more about how to sell and after having recaptured his confidence, T. J. Watson found the job a great deal easier. The episode made a tremendous impression on him.

Today this same approach is expected of all IBM managers. The manager must know how to work with his people, how to help them, and how to train them. For example, if a salesman is having difficulty, we insist that his branch manager or even his district manager make a number of calls with him to help him improve.

Another consideration in human relations that has meant a great deal is the continual opportunity for advancement. Because we have grown so rapidly, we have created a great many opportunities for promotion. No matter how great the temptation to go outside for managers, we have almost always filled these new jobs from within; no more than a small percentage of our people have come into the company other than at the lowest level in their specialty. We have hired a few top scientists, lawyers, and other specialists, but with those exceptions all our executives came up from the bottom. This has been a great factor in maintaining morale.

You cannot always make as many promotions in a plant as you can elsewhere, but we have found that there are other things you can do to keep morale high. One technique is job enlargement. People running a nearly automatic machine tool all day making hundreds of the same item may have very little feeling of personal accomplishment. In IBM we fight this problem whenever practical by teaching our people to do their own set-up work when they change from one operation to another. In some cases they make up unit assemblies. In others, they do their own inspecting. We try to rotate the very boring jobs to break monotony. This helps a person to keep his sense of dignity, accomplishment and involvement.

Cause and effect are often impossible to match up, but I have always been convinced that without our attitude toward human relations we would have fallen short of our business goals.

Some say that when an organization tries to get too close to its people and make a lot of the 'team' idea, the individual gets swallowed up, loses his identity, and becomes a carbon copy of his fellow employees. So far as I can see, this is not true to any serious degree in our large organizations today. Corporate people may not necessarily be more independent than others, but neither do I believe that they are any less.

I suspect we have our fair quota of security minded men who are careful never to rock the boat. At the same time I suspect there are some college professors who are absent minded, some scientists who are eccentric, and some military men who are martinets. But just as these stereotypes do not apply to the general run of people in those occupations, the stereotype of the 'organization man' does not apply to all forms of corporate life.

IBM has more than 125 000 employees. A substantial number of them, many of whom I could pick out by name, are highly individualistic men and women. They value their social and intellectual freedom, and I question whether they would surrender it at any price. Admittedly, they may like their jobs and the security and salaries that go along with them. But I know of few who would not put on their hats and slam the door if they felt the organization had intruded so heavily on them that they no longer owned themselves. Business may have its share of hypocrites, but I am sure that big business has no more than any other group.

Early in 1961, in talking to our salesforce, I attempted to size up the then new Kennedy Administration as I saw it. It was not a political talk. I urged no views on them. It was an optimistic assessment, nothing more. But at the close of the meeting, a number of salesmen came up front. They would listen to what I had to say about business, they said, but they didn't want to hear about the new administration in a company meeting.

On my return to New York, I found a few letters in the same vein. Lay off, they seemed to say, you're stepping on our toes in something that's none of your business.

At first I was a bit annoyed at having been misunderstood. But when I thought about it, I was pleased, for they had made it quite clear they wore no man's collar and they weren't at all hesitant to tell me so. From what I have read of organization men, that is not the way they are supposed to act.

It is interesting to contemplate the possible nature of individual achievement in the absence of large organizations. It probably would be of a different order.

The challenges in a large organization are great, and achievement, really, is the successful response to challenge. Men who have accomplished great deeds in large organizations might have done less if they had been challenged with less, and they would have realized less of their potential and their individuality.

In IBM we frequently refer to our need for 'wild ducks'. The moral is drawn from a story by the Danish philosopher, Soren Kierkegaard. He told of a man on the coast of Zealand who liked to watch the wild ducks fly south in great flocks each fall. Out of charity, he took to putting feed for them in a nearby pond. After a while some of the ducks no longer bothered to fly south; they wintered in Denmark on what he fed them.

In time they flew less and less. When the wild ducks returned, the others would circle up to greet them but then head back to their feeding grounds on the pond. After three or four years they grew so lazy and fat that they found difficulty in flying at all.

Kierkegaard drew his point – you can make wild ducks tame, but you can never make tame ducks wild again. One might also add that the duck who is tamed will never go anywhere any more.

We are convinced that any business needs its wild ducks. And in IBM we try not to tame them.

Reproduced from Watson, Thomas J. Jr (1963). *A Business and its Beliefs: The Ideas that Helped Build IBM*, Chapter 2 by permission of McGraw-Hill Publishing Co., New York.

Great companies make meaning
Richard Tanner Pascale and Anthony G. Athos

Anthony Athos teaches at the Graduate School of Business Administration at Harvard University and has had wide consulting experience as well. Richard Tanner Pascale is at the Graduate School of Business at Stanford University. Both have worked closely with McKinsey and Co on a number of projects and are well known and respected in the world of consulting as well as academia. The empirical basis for the book is six years of intensive study into the management of 34 firms. These include firms in banking (Wells Fargo Bank, Mitsubishi Bank), retailing (J. C. Penney and Shirokiya), conglomerates (ITT and Rockwell International), automotive (Ford Motor Co and Toyota) to name but a few.

The chapter we reproduce illustrates the main points that Athos and Pascale wish to make. The best companies provide more than just a living for their people. They have what Athos and Pascale have dubbed 'superordinate goals'. The authors refer frequently to the companies they have researched and provide evidence for the fact that what most organizations need is a 'non-deified, nonreligious spiritualism that enables a firm's superordinate goals to respond to the inner meanings that most people seek in their work'.

In management, as in music, there is a bass clef as well as a treble. The treble generally carries the melody in music, and melody's equivalent in management is the manager's style. A manager's style – the way he focuses his attention and interacts with people – sets the 'tune' for his subordinates and communicates at the *operational* level what his expectations are and how he wants business conducted. Beneath these messages is a deeper rhythm that communicates more fundamentally. The bass in music – whether hard rock or a classical symphony – often contains much of what moves the listener. So, too, the 'bass' of management conveys meanings at a deeper level and communicates what management *really* cares about. These messages can influence an organization profoundly. In Japanese organizations, a great deal of managerial attention is devoted to ensuring the continuity and consistency of these 'bass clef' messages.

In earlier chapters, we have variously referred to these 'bass' clef messages as an organization's 'significant meanings', 'shared values', and 'spiritual fabric'. For clarity, we will adopt one all inclusive term to describe these characterizations: *superordinate goals* – the goals above all others (see Mintzberg, 1973; Crozier, 1964; Peters, 1976; Selznick, 1949). They are the seventh element in our framework. Superordinate goals provide the glue that holds the other six – strategy, structure, systems, style, staff and skills – together. When all are fitted together, organizations tend to become more internally unified and self-sustaining over time.

Superordinate goals play a pragmatic role by influencing implementation at the operational level. Because an executive cannot be everywhere at once, many decisions are made without his knowledge. What superordinate goals do, in effect, is provide employees with a 'compass' and point their footsteps in the right direction.* For example, at IBM that translates into never sacrificing customer service; at Matsushita it means never cheating a customer by knowingly producing or selling defective merchandise. These values permit the CEOs to influence the actions of their employees, to help the employees make correct independent decisions. These value systems act as 'tie breakers' in close cases, those in which decisions otherwise might be made the wrong way.*

Year after year, decade after decade, Delta Air Lines has been the most consistent money maker in the airline industry. Undoubtedly, its route structure, concentrated in the fast growing South, has contributed to its success. But route structure alone cannot explain Delta's performance – for neither United Airlines (with its dominant position in America's busiest air terminal,

* This imagery was proposed by Alan Kennedy, partner, McKinsey & Company, Evian, France, 20 March 1980.

Chicago) nor American Airlines (with the lion's share of the market in fast growing Dallas/Fort Worth) has been able to match Delta's performance over the long term.

Delta considers its key to success in the highly competitive and largely undifferentiated airline industry to be *service*. (As we saw, for a time Carlson succeeded in inculcating this idea at United, where it worked equally well.) Delta considers service to be the direct result of a motivated and friendly workforce. Delta's approach, which includes virtually open door access for all of its 36 500 employees, has enabled the airline to maintain its *esprit de corps* and remain non-union in an industry plagued by labor–management strife. Delta's management *style* and strongly reinforced *superordinate goals* are largely responsible for this achievement (Guyon, 1980).

At the heart of Delta's philosophy is 'the Delta family feeling'. More than a slogan, it is what makes Delta different. This 'family' emphasis was introduced and nurtured by the airline's founder and has been carefully institutionalized. 'It's just a feeling of caring within the company,' says Delta's current chairman, W. Thomas Beebe (Guyon, 1980).

It's difficult to find workers with serious complaints at Delta. The firm promotes from within, pays better than most airlines and rarely lays off workers. These policies are what makes the 'family feeling' real. When other airlines were slashing employment during the 1973 oil embargo, Mr Beebe told senior management: 'Now the time has come for the stockholders to pay a little penalty for keeping the team together' (Guyon, 1980). Notice how the superordinate goal of preserving the 'family feeling' took precedence over near term profits and return on investment.

Like Matsushita, Delta pays attention to the socialization of new employees. It makes sure employees embrace the 'family' concept by emphasizing it in training programmes and at meetings. It also carefully screens job applicants. Stewardess candidates, for example, are culled from thousands of applicants, interviewed twice and then sent to Delta's psychologist, Dr Sidney Janus. 'I try to determine their sense of cooperativeness or sense of teamwork,' he says. At Delta, 'you don't just join a company, you join an objective' (Guyon, 1980).

The Delta example sheds light on several features of effective superordinate goals. First, they need to tie into higher order human values. Second, they need to be consistent with the other six Ss, especially the firm's *style* and *staffing* and *systems* practices. Third, management needs to be meticulous in respecting these values (even if it means sacrificing short term profits) or they will be seen as empty slogans.

Kinds of superordinate goals

Effective superordinate goals should be (1) significant, (2) durable, and (3) achievable. Most tend to fall into one or more of the following categories:

1 *The company as an entity*

Here the whole organization is reinforced as an entity one lives within and should identify with and belong to, and which is deserving of admiration and approval from employees and society (e.g. Delta's belief in the 'family feeling').

2 *The company's external markets*

Here the emphasis is on the value of the company's products or services to humanity, and on those factors important in maintaining this value – that is, quality, delivery, service and customers' needs (e.g. Matsushita's belief in advancing the standard of living in Japan by distributing reliable and affordable electrical products).

3 *The company's internal operations*

Here attention is focused on such things as efficiency, cost, productivity, inventiveness, problem solving and customer attention (e.g. Delta's emphasis on 'service' and Matsushita's dedication to first class production engineering).

4 *The company's employees*

Here attention is paid to the needs of groups of people in reference to their productive function, and to individual employees as valued human beings in a larger context – that is, human resource systems, growth and development, opportunity and rewards, individual attention and exceptions (e.g. Matsushita's commitment to developing employees not only for the firm's benefit but to contribute to each employee's personal growth over a lifetime).

5 *The company's relation to society and the state*

Here the values, expectations and legal requirements of the surrounding larger community are explicitly honored, such as beliefs in competition, meritocracy, the necessity of obeying the law or being sensitive to other nations' customs (e.g. Matsushita sees itself as a major contributor in restoring Japanese status and prestige).

6 *The company's relation to culture (including religion)*

Here the underlying beliefs about 'the good' in the culture are honored – beliefs in our own case largely derived from Judeo-Christian tradition, and including such things as honesty, and fairness (e.g. the strong influence of religion in shaping the Matsushita philosophy – which reinforces many Confucian and Buddhist values including harmony, solidarity, discipline and dedication).

IBM, then and now

IBM has for many years been one of our most successful and effective US corporations. It is known for its remarkable development of strategy, structure, systems, style, skill and staff, and the fit among them, *and* for its equally advanced development of superordinate goals.

In a 1940 *Fortune* article describing the company and its president (Thomas John Watson), the author's imagery is initially surprising. For example, he describes the young Mr Watson as having the appearance and behavior of a 'somewhat puzzled divinity student' who:

> began to confect the aphoristic rules of thumb that have since guided his life and policies. 'Ever onward,' he told himself. 'Aim high and think in big figures; serve and sell; he who stops being better stops being good' . . . Mr Watson caused the word THINK to be hung all over the factory and offices . . . Generally it is framed, sometimes graven on pediments in imperishable granite or marble, again embossed in brass, yet again lettered in gold on a purple banner, but always and everywhere it is there . . . Whether you particularly agree with [what Mr Watson is saying] you listen . . . Mr Watson's monumental simplicity compels you to do so . . . Let him discourse on the manifest destiny of IBM, and you are ready to join the company for life. Let him retail plain homilies on the value of Vision, and a complex and terrifying world becomes transparent and simple. Let him expound the necessity for giving religion the preference over everything else, and you *could not help falling to your knees* . . . Everybody in the organization is expected to find the ubiquitous THINK sign a constant source of inspiration, as the weary travelers of old found new strength in the wayside crucifixes (Burck, 1940).

That the author found such images useful to *his* purpose does not necessarily mean, of course, that such images captured an important truth about the company. They could have been useful mostly in capturing the writer's *reaction* to IBM and Mr Watson. But three senior executives quoted in the article add weight to the 'religious' impression. One said: 'Mr Watson has spread his benign influence over the earth, and everywhere it has touched, people have gained, mentally and morally, materially and spiritually' (Burck, 1940). Another remarked: 'I think that we do not always count our blessings. Every so often we should all of us stop and think of the many things that have been done for each member of this organization' (Burck, 1940). A third echoes a similar theme: 'Mr Watson gave me something I lacked – the vision and the foresight to carry on in this business, which from that day forward I have never had any thought of leaving' (Burck, 1940).

There is an implied reference to cultural values of gratitude, faith and commitment. There is repeated reference to the beneficial impact of Mr Watson on *individuals*. The tone is evangelical. In the 1930s society's acceptance of various absolutes was not yet much undermined by existential beliefs and moral relativism, and there was still widespread acceptance of the use in business of explicit, usually Christian, religious metaphors.

It was then not uncommon, and even recently not unheard of, for secular enterprises to express their organizational fervor in fundamentalist religious ways. The development of 'creeds' which employees were expected to hold, of 'cults' of membership differentiating employees from outsiders and identifying them with insiders, and of 'codes' of behavior that reduced uncertainty and prescribed right action and attitudes was an important part of the early years of some companies. The use of company songs, dress codes, sales meetings that Elmer Gantry might have staged, ubiquitous displays of 'the leader' in photographs, oils and bronze statues, slogans presented in expensive and long-lasting materials, an often referred to book of the leader's speeches and essays (Mr Watson's was *Men, Minutes and Money*), and a house organ to reinforce values and educate were all part of early IBM. The rah-rah sales orientation of that time reminds us of the zealous proselytizing of some churches, and the ways of reinforcing the developing creeds, cults, and codes also seem similar. (It is not accidental, we think, that pushing a new product line is often referred to as 'missionary work' by businessmen.)

But Mr Watson's role certainly was not confined to devising those methods. He also created superordinate goals based on the beliefs of his society. The average person's belief in the Horatio Alger story, and in the dream of 'getting ahead', probably accounted for the following remark from the same article.

> There is a careful selection of all employees, whether for the factory or the sales department. Mr Watson never hires an office boy, but always a potential leader, or at any rate a potential assistant. Everyone addresses every man as 'Mr'. The company publications never refer to any man without prefixing a 'Mr' to his name (Burck, 1940).

That attention to selecting employees, the respect expressed by the prefix 'Mr', the numerous employee programmes, as well as efforts to assist employees in growth and development, indicate that Mr Watson was aware of the power of honoring within his organization the values and beliefs of the surrounding society.

In addition, Mr Watson attended to the developing conflict in Europe by having PEACE join THINK all over the company; he also commissioned a symphony on an important company occasion to express the longing for international cooperation, and gave and reprinted speeches on that theme. IBM was aligned with the *world* situation in employees' minds. (War was dangerous to mankind, as it was to IBM's developing international business (Burck, 1940).)

The article includes far more than attention to what we call superordinate goals. It includes fascinating and detailed descriptions of all the Seven Ss. But for our purposes here, it is interesting to note how the great corporation IBM has become is related in part to conscious attention over time to superordinate goals as well as the other elements.

In the years since 1940, IBM's expression of its beliefs, and its ways of honouring them, has become what seems fair to call 'more sophisticated'. The approach is much more analogous to the best functioning of some of our established formal religions. There is less obvious conformity required, more subtlety in technique, more complexity acknowledged in goals, and thus more skills required to behave 'well'. Yet the more recent statements of IBM's superordinate goals, the basic beliefs reinforced within the present firm, can be seen as having evolved from the first Mr Watson's original efforts. And that IBM has been at it so long gives the present beliefs the enormous advantage of a successful and shared history. A recent statement of IBM's basic beliefs is as follows (IBM):

Basic beliefs

A sense of accomplishment and pride in our work often go hand in hand with a basic understanding of what we're all about, both as individuals and as a company. IBM is fortunate to have a timeless statement of its purpose – in its basic beliefs.

The underlying meaning of these beliefs was best expressed by Tom Watson Jr in his McKinsey Foundation Lectures at Columbia University in New York in 1962, when he said (Watson, 1963):

I firmly believe that any organization, in order to survive and achieve success, must have a sound set of beliefs on which it premises all its policies and actions.

Next, I believe that the most important factor in corporate success is faithful adherence to those beliefs.

And finally, I believe that if an organization is to meet the challenges of a changing world, it must be prepared to change everything about itself except those beliefs as it moves through corporate life.

In other words, the basic philosophy, spirit, and drive of an organization have far more to do with its relative achievements than do technological or economic resources, organizational structure, innovation, and timing. All these things weigh heavily in success. But they are, I think, transcended by how strongly the people in the organization believe in its basic precepts and how faithfully they carry them out.

What is this set of beliefs Watson was talking about? There are three:

- *Respect for the individual.* Respect for the dignity and the rights of each person in the organization.
- *Customer service.* To give the best customer service of any company in the world.
- *Excellence.* The conviction that an organization should pursue all tasks with the objective of accomplishing them in a superior way.

In addition to these basic beliefs, there is a set of fundamental principles which guide IBM management in the conduct of the business. They are:

- To give intelligent, responsible, and capable direction to the business.
- To serve our customers as efficiently and as effectively as we can.
- To advance our technology, improve our products and develop new ones.
- To enlarge the capabilities of our people through job development and give them the opportunity to find satisfaction in their tasks.
- To provide equal opportunity to all our people.
- To recognize our obligation to stockholders by providing adequate return on their investment.
- To do our part in furthering the well-being of those communities in which our facilities are located.
- To accept our responsibilities as a corporate citizen of the US and in all the countries in which we operate throughout the world.

Note that Mr Watson Jr says he believes that a corporation's survival and success are dependent upon beliefs, sound beliefs, from which it acts, and to which it is faithful. He says everything else may change, but not the beliefs. They remain 'absolutes'. Given that last observation, the basic beliefs are naturally stated at high levels of abstraction, and in 'high-minded' language. Respect for the dignity and rights of the individual; the best customer service in the world; accomplishing tasks in a superior way. The individual, the customer, the *ways* of working. At least the first and third are not likely ever to require altering, although the ways they are applied may well change.

Notice, too, the statements of fundamental principles, expressed at lower levels of abstraction, and in somewhat less high-minded language. They refer to:

- management competence
- customer service
- technical progress
- employee opportunity development
- stockholders' return
- community well-being
- national and international responsibilities

It will be clear immediately that, over time, the trade-offs and balance will require a lot of managerial skill applied constantly in order to confirm these principles and their modes of application in the minds of thousands of people. If one assumes, as we do, that IBM really works at living up to its basic beliefs and principles, and if one assumes, as we do, that such effort has a powerful effect on the company's success, then it beomes possible to set aside the skepticism often reserved for high-minded pronouncements of top executives. If it is *not* just fluff, then it is a powerful and positive force indeed. One signal that IBM has been practicing what it preaches is the criticism it has received in the past related to employee 'commitment and conformity'. Those white-shirted, polite, competent, hard-working employees of 20 years ago were often regarded as corporate 'fanatics', or even corporate 'fascists', because they appeared not to display in superficial ways their 'American individuality'. White shirts were mistaken for laundered minds. The shirts are now colored, but it appears that their wearers are still politely service oriented, highly competent, and hard working (everything may change but the beliefs). And in our culture, any evidence of a reduction in obvious 'individuality', which naturally accompanies increases in organizational commitment, will produce cricitism from those who *overvalue* individuality. We have a suspicion that IBM executives in the early 1960s recognized the criticism for what it was, and smiled politely on their way to the bank. In any event, it seems to us that IBM has long attended explicitly to its superordinate goals, and that they have played an important part in its being a remarkably successful, self-renewing, profitable company with a very strong internal culture.

Mr Matsushita may have been quick to grasp the value of strategy, structure and systems, but the Watsons were not naïve about the 'soft' Ss and 'the arts of Japanese management'. (In the 1930s, Mr Watson Sr visited Mr Matsushita in Japan and presumably was influenced by what he saw there.) In the 1940s IBM was functioning very much like Matsushita. From company songs to employee recreation, from careful selection and indoctrination to employee 'uniforms', from pictures of the CEO everywhere to slogans, the two companies seemed more alike than different. Each has continued to fashion its internal culture to reflect changes in the society outside, but both still pay a lot of attention to articulating and honoring superordinate goals.

Superordinate goals and changing employee values

As noted, superordinate goals tie the purposes of the firm (e.g. goods, services, profits) to human values. We believe that this linkage to human values is growing in importance. The vast majority of Americans who work today do not view their jobs as 'the only alternative'. Fifteen per cent of all people who work are in skilled blue collar occupations; 45 per cent are white collar. Sixty per cent are employed by firms with over 1000 employees, and 47 per cent work for organizations with over 10 000 employees (Kanter, 1977). What these statistics tell us is that most people who work today are highly skilled and/or white collar, and employed in relatively large institutions. In these kinds of environments, all sorts of factors cushion employees against the occupational hazards that plagued those employed only three or four decades ago. First, the job market itself, while never as hungry as we might wish, offers backup employment opportunities for most people with qualifications who wish to work. In addition, there are financial cushions of various kinds – unemployment insurance, a spouse's income, the opportunity to moonlight, and the capacity to save enough over a period of time to handle a transition between jobs.

These factors have moved us a long way from the circumstances that shaped employment attitudes in the nineteenth and the first half of the twentieth century. The implications of these changes are profound. The majority of people who work don't have to for economic *survival* in the short term. Increasingly, they seek, *in addition* to pay and career opportunities, other kinds of income from their jobs, including work they enjoy, colleagues they like working with, and *meaning*. Far too many generalizations are made about work on the basis of the automobile assembly-line stereotype. For the vast majority, work is a far different and far more fulfilling experience. For people in these new circumstances to be satisfied, it helps enormously if they can see the link between what they do and a higher purpose.

When the linkage between human values and a firm's objectives is unclear, employees often seek to create meanings of their own which reconcile what they do on the job to higher purposes. Curiously, we may have seen some evidence of this at ITT.

Geneen inculcated in his organization a belief in the importance of 'unshakeable facts' in the service of 'bottom-line results'. These narrowly envisioned meanings were reinforced constantly and few managers failed to internalize them. Yet there are indications that some of Geneen's executives were unwilling to view their endeavors exclusively in terms of such bottom-line results. Their comments suggest that they created larger meanings. They told us they took pride in being a part of such a demanding, fast moving, successful company, that they saw themselves as stimulated, accomplished, fast track executives, a kind of corporate pro ball team. In short, they created *a larger meaning* to give value and dignity to their work lives. They were the outstanding, hard-ball pros in an economic game, no quarter given or taken. Tough, lean, mean. A winning-is-the-only-thing, best-of-their-kind elite.

Like ITT, many western organizations pride themselves on having made a virtue of bottom-line results and other similar measures of 'efficiency'. If anything, the emphasis has intensified in recent years as companies have sought to produce profits during a period of slowed growth and world economic uncertainty. The problem with efficiency is that it is a little like white bread and refined sugar: taken in isolation, it becomes bland and vaguely unhealthful – all the life-supporting nutrients seem to get refined out. Obviously, organizations need to be somewhat efficient in order to accomplish their tasks. But the problem is that people can end up performing instrumental functions as if they were truly interchangeable parts in a great machine.

Superordinate goals focusing on employees

Earlier we listed six kinds of superordinate goals. One category, of particular interest, focuses on the firm's relations with its employees. Generally speaking, people want to identify with their organization; they want to trust and depend on those they work with and invest through their labor in the organization's success. But, as we have seen, the tendency of western organizations to deal at arm's length, to neglect coaching and mentoring of subordinates, to abruptly transfer (rather than carefully *transplant*) people from one job to the next, to reorganize by decree and provide brutally direct feedback without regard for the grace and pace necessary for successful change – all these things teach employees to be wary. Most American executives think only in macro-terms about 'morale'. They do indeed worry about massive layoffs or gross inequities in pay or major contradictions in policy. What the preceding chapters have argued is that many far more subtle things are equally important and commonly neglected.

Employment involves a psychological contract as well as a contract involving the exchange of labor for capital. In many western organizations, that psychological contract, while never explicit, often assumes little trust by either party in the other. If the only basis for the relation of company and employee is an instrumental one, it should not be surprising that many people in our organizations do what they must do to get their paycheck but little more. While there can be all kinds of superordinate goals, those that concern themselves with the development and well-being of employees can play a particularly important role in establishing the moral context for this psychological contract. If such superordinate values are consistently honored (as we saw at Delta during the 1973 oil embargo), then employees tend to identify more fully with the company. They see the firm's interest and their own as more congruent and tend to invest themselves more fully in the organization – including looking for ways to improve how they do their job.

Most consultants will confirm that they have been called in to solve a client's problem only to discover in the course of conducting interviews that someone in the client organization already had the solution. But because communication channels were blocked, or, more often, because the individual with the good idea was 'turned off' and convinced that the organization wouldn't listen, no initiative was taken. The potential initiator hesitated to invest himself, in the last analysis because trying is linked to caring and history had taught him that the firm was not worth caring that much about.

Without a doubt, the most significant outcome of the way Japanese organizations manage themselves is that to a far greater extent than in the United States they get everyone in the organization to be alert, to look for opportunities to do things better, and to strive by virtue of each small contribution to make the company succeed. It is like building a pyramid or watching a colony of ants: thousands of 'little people' doing 'little' things, *all with the same basic purpose*, can move mountains.

A recent study of product innovation in the scientific instruments and tool machinery industries indicates that 80 per cent of all product innovations are initiated by the customer (Hippel, 1978). The majority of ideas doesn't flow from R&D labs down but from the customers up. To be sure, customers don't do the actual inventing, but their inquiries and complaints plant the seeds for improvements. Given these statistics, it matters a lot whether a company's sales force and others operating out at the tentacles of its field system are vigilant. They need to be open to new ideas *and* willing to initiate within their organization. Here is a key to success of many Japanese companies. We saw this at Matsushita, where they rarely originated it but had an unerring ability to do it better. This formula is not inconsistent with most of the major corporate success stories in the United States. Careful scrutiny reveals that despite the exalted status of 'strategy' in the lexicon of American management, few great successes stem from one bold-stroke strategic thrust. More often, they result from one half-good idea that is improved upon incrementally. These improvements are invariably the result of a lot of 'little people' paying attention to the product, the customer, and the marketplace.

To be sure, the case for superordinate goals can be overstated. Innovative firms tend to have a *style* of management that is open to new ideas, ways of handling *staff* that encourage innovation, *systems* that are customer focused and which reward innovation, *skills* at translating ideas into action and so forth. But the ideas don't flow unless the employee *believes* in the corporation and identifies enough with its purposes to 'give up' his good ideas. Further, any of us who work in organizations knows how hard they are to move. One has to really believe an organization *cares* in order to invest the energy and effort needed to help it change. Such commitment derives from superordinate goals. And if we look at outstanding American firms that have a sustained track record of innovation, we see this to be the case. Texas Instruments, Procter & Gamble, 3M, and IBM, for example, all pay close attention to the customer and each has a highly developed value system that causes its employees to identify strongly with the firm (see for example Prestbo, 1980). Perhaps the intense loyalty that these firms inspire is just an interesting idiosyncrasy. But we believe, on the contrary, that this bond of shared values is fundamental to all of the rest. In our view, this is probably the most under-publicized 'secret weapon' of great companies.

As we noted with Matsushita, Japanese firms, despite their evident success in adopting western technology and their skill at devising aggressive strategies, innovative organizational structure and comprehensive systems, have not followed the west in de-emphasizing the 'soft' Ss. They do not trade off human relationships for impersonal efficiency. Almost all of the American employees of the twelve Japanese subsidiaries in the United States whom we interviewed in this study remarked on the personal concern of these companies toward employees (Pascale, 1978). This concern was manifested in two ways. First, invariably, the Japanese firms made a big deal about 'meaning'. Whether Toyota, Sony, or YKK (a manufacturer of zippers), the senior managers stressed the importance of developing their employees and the contribution of their product to society as a whole. These were not just 'ad slogan' values, but something that management deeply believed in.

We call attention to the Japanese companies' commitment to people. One Japanese manager said, 'Anyone who works for a company seeks approval for what he does and acceptance for who he is . . . Almost all firms give approval through the normal reward system, but providing acceptance of each individual as a unique person requires a lot more effort.' Japanese firms in the United States institutionalized 'acceptance' in two ways. One was by increasing the contact between boss and subordinate. Even on the shop floor, Japanese firms fostered twice as much contact between workers and their foremen as was usual elsewhere. (Fifteen employees reported to each first-line supervisor as compared to a 30:1 ratio at American firms (Pascale, 1978).) One manager said, 'If you're striving to give employees a sense of being recognized for their unique contributions, you have to have enough supervisors to listen.' Supervisors at Japanese managed firms more frequently worked alongside their subordinates, were more extensively engaged in personal counseling, and permitted more interaction among workers than those of the American companies did. In an effort to express their commitment to people, the Japanese subsidiaries also spent an average of nearly three times as much per employee on social and recreational programmes as did their American control companies ($58.49/

employee/year vs. $20.79 for American companies) (Pascale, 1978). All of these programmes were presumably symbolic; but that's not all they were. Employees often commented that the programs also fostered increased off-the-job contact among employees, had the effect of personalizing the firm, and reinforced the superordinate goal that 'people mattered'.

Western history and superordinate goals

By an accident of history, we in the west have evolved a culture that separates man's spiritual life from his institutional life. This turn of events has had a far-reaching impact on modern western organizations. Our companies freely lay claim to mind and muscle, but they are actually discouraged from intruding upon our personal lives and deeper beliefs.

The dilemma for modern western organizations is that, like it or not, they play a very central role in the lives of many who work for them. Employees in all ranks of the hierarchy not only 'work' at their jobs, but (1) derive much of their daily social contact there, and (2) often locate themselves in social relations outside the firm through their association with their company and occupation. (One of the first questions we are asked when we meet a person for the first time is: 'What do you do for a living?') Splitting man into separate 'personal' and 'productive' beings makes somewhat artificial parts of what is the whole of his character. When we do so, our cultural heritage not only too strictly enforces this artificial dichotomization, but deprives us of two rather important ingredients for building employee commitment. First, companies are denied access to higher order human values, which are among the best known mechanisms for reconciling one's working life with one's inner life. Second, the firm itself is denied a meaning-making role in society, and thus pays excessive attention to instrumental values, such as profit, market share, and technological innovation.

If we trace the history of goal setting in US organizations, we find that over the past 20 years management's understanding of goals has greatly expanded – from mere monetary goals (e.g. profit and return on investment) to stockholder and constituency goals (such as environmental objectives and minority hiring). The trend has been toward expanding the notion of corporate purpose. Nevertheless, recognition of an organization's role in serving higher order human values still awaits full-scale acceptance.

We recognize that some readers will resist the specter of a merger between 'the Church and the corporation'. But that is not what we are proposing. There is an important difference between religiosity and spiritualism. In the west, because of the Church's monopoly on the spiritual side of man, all spiritualism was religious. That is not so in Japan, and it need not be so in the west.

There are no strong imperatives in Japan for an individual to choose among religious beliefs. People there commonly have several religions – believing in Confucianism, Buddhism and Shintoism simultaneously. Likewise, Japanese firms can take a general spiritual position without seeming insincere or superficial. Such firms are able to work with each employee to help him flow with the ups and downs of a career and to find deeper meanings in his own development. In the west, many managers feel both the employee and the organization are culturally conditioned to an arm's-length relationship. This causes the firm to let the employee fend for himself in adversity and draw upon the problematic spiritual resources available to him from friends, family and religious affiliations.

What is needed in the west is a non-deified, non-religious 'spiritualism' that enables a firm's superordinate goals to respond truly to the inner meanings that many people seek in their work – or, alternatively, seek in their lives and could find at work if only that were more culturally acceptable.

Western institutions are, in fact, backing into this role. Two forces are at work: employees seeking more meaning from their jobs and demanding more concern from the corporation, and legislative pressures enforcing a broad range of personal services, including employee rights to counseling. In response to these forces, most major firms now describe these activities as 'Human Resource Management' instead of 'Personnel' – it is to be hoped, the first step in adopting a larger perspective. Most larger firms also provide assistance to employees dealing with chronic personal problems, such as divorce, alcoholism and stress. And, as noted earlier, some of our most outstanding companies have long acknowledged a larger role in the lives of their employees and foster greater interdependence among them. All are remarkably 'Japanese' when we look at them closely. Their success may have important implications for western organizations of the future.

Superordinate goals and diversification

One problem inherent in diversification is that it becomes more and more difficult to establish *one* set of superordinate goals that provides useful guidance within a particular industry, yet is general enough to be relevant across many industries. Conglomerates, in particular, face this dilemma. Most tend to conclude that it is unnecessary or impossible to fashion unifying meanings for multiproduct, multimarket portfolios. Their method of growth through acquisition tends to encourage this. They acquire successful companies and are dedicated to making them even more successful. But they often overlook the fact that a conglomerate's meanings (which are almost always largely limited to the impersonal and financial) undermine the older meanings that gave the acquired firm its former sense of purpose. Most conglomerates stress their desire to be supportive, to avoid interfering. But the absence of positive new meanings, or, at least, the impetus for continually reinterpreting existing meanings, inevitably results in atrophy and empty slogans. Subtly, the new financial control system, the corporate emphasis on profit, or ROI, visits by the controllers, and messages conveyed at quarterly review meetings (as we saw at ITT) erode the earlier 'faith'. Is it any wonder that vibrancy and sense of commitment frequently disappear from subsidiaries within a year or two after they are acquired? One thinks of the change at Avis. Once a spirited company that was 'Trying Harder', Avis today seems just another enterprise. The meanings lost through acquisition are rarely offset by gains through superior resources and more 'scientific' management.

Trade-offs

In any particular situation requiring a decision, it is entirely possible that an executive may have to choose to affirm one superordinate goal rather than others. Let's say a firm has effectively developed goals which include 'service', as well as one related to the 'professional development' of managers. If an important customer's need for delivery requires a particular manager to stay on the job when he has been scheduled for a lengthy outside executive program – to which he has been unable to go twice previously – a choice may have to be made between goals. In any particular situation, it may not be possible to honor all the important superordinate goals simultaneously. They may have to be met sequentially. There are days when we need to sin bravely and make trade-offs between one goal and the other. A 'separate and related' way of thinking about superordinate goals enables us to 'fire (or transfer) an employee on Thursday' in order to attain higher levels of service, successive phases in a dynamic cycle. The issue is the *balance over time* of such decisions. If delivery-installation *always* comes first, even when a specific situation may not support such primacy, then people will come to see the goals related to managerial development as mostly noise.

It seems true that top executives measure, or try to monitor, what they care about. No measurement equals no real caring in most companies, and most managers know that early in their careers. In short, effectively honoring superordinate goals requires not only managerial skill and appropriate system development but also CEO reinforcement through style. Too little skill, or inappropriate systems, or CEO indifference, leads rapidly to cynicism. And cynicism is the enemy of the trusting commitment most CEOs sincerely want from their employees. The moral: Don't claim you care about it unless you are prepared to act accordingly, for you don't get goodwill from subordinates by promising what you do not deliver, any more than they do from you.

Strategic eras and superordinate goals

An organization's superordinate goals emerge, in part, from leadership which instills values through clarity and obsessive focus. A firm's history also contributes to its enduring value system. Organizations tend to grow through stages, face and surmount crises, and along the way learn lessons and draw morals that shape values and future actions. Usually these developments influence assumptions and the way people behave. Often key episodes are recounted in 'war stories' that convey lessons about the firm's origins and transformations in dramatic form (Leach, 1978). Eventually, this lore provides a consistent background for action. New members are exposed to the common history and acquire insight into some of the subtle aspects of their company. Matsushita made a considerable effort to pass on his company's legacy to each new recruit.

Superordinate goals are immensely helpful at the beginning of a strategic era.* Setting out to build a fast-food empire, not only did McDonald's stress price, quality, profit and market share, but they believed they were performing a real service to Americans living on limited means. This 'social mission' gave a larger meaning to operational objectives. The cooks and order takers in McDonald's franchises found higher order goals helpful in accepting the company's rigorous quality control system. Strict standards could be met more readily when seen in the context of 'helping society'. As one manager put it, 'The lower down you go in an organization, the more difficult it is for employees to identify with the firm's business objectives. A firm's social and humanitarian objectives are far more tangible to a dishwasher or janitor than is its goal of market share.'†

Toward the end of a strategic era, a firm's past meanings can get in the way. In fact, this invisible force has undone late-in-an-era executives who sought to change things. Case studies of incumbents whose terms of office spanned the time periods when their organizations were moving from one era to another seem to indicate that they 'failed' more often than they 'succeeded'. Organizational meanings can be so deeply ingrained, so fundamental to what people think and feel, and so important to their beliefs about their jobs and themselves, that when initially these meanings are challenged, there is often resistance and later dismay and a great sense of loss.

---

* The term 'strategic era' was coined by Thomas J. Peters, consultant, McKinsey & Company. The notion that superordinate goals impede the shift from one strategic era to the next was first introduced by McKinsey director Lee Walton, Ventura, California, 5 December 1979.

† Interview with middle management, McDonald's, San José, California, 6 June 1974.

One recent example is the current transition at AT&T.* That company's deeper meanings were built on providing *reliable* and *inexpensive* telephone *service* to America. The firm's superordinate goal uniting managers, workers and even stockholders has been the 'social mission' of providing a reliable, low cost phone system to America. Bell Labs and Western Electric further enshrined AT&T's pride as the 'World's Best Telephone Company'. But in the early 1970s competitive data processing applications began to spill over into AT&T's traditional domain. It became increasingly clear that the telecommunications fields and computer fields were overlapping. The result: AT&T was increasingly facing competitors in the computer industry; it would have to broaden its focus, change its strategy and become more of a marketing oriented company in order to meet that competition. Ideally, its superordinate goal needed to shift to being a 'marketer and innovator in telecommunications'. In competing with firms like IBM, AT&T had to tailor its products and respond more rapidly to shifting market needs – in short, to make significant changes in all Seven Ss.

Two of AT&T's chief executive officers saw this happening and began to move to change the company's direction. Their names are not likely to be enshrined as 'great leaders' in AT&T's legends. They attempted to realign the strategy, but all of AT&T's systems were oriented toward tight operational controls – the sort that keep track of costs, operator errors and equipment reliability in the traditional phone service. They also encountered a staff of employees whose middle and senior managers had come up through the ranks as managers of telephone switching offices and repair facilities. With backgrounds in engineering and accounting, this management cadre lacked strong instincts for sales and marketing. In short, there were formidable barriers to change. Perhaps this helps us understand why the current chairman of AT&T believes that the shift to a true marketing orientation will require 20 years.

Transitional times are periods in which older meanings and behaviors are slowly and painfully relinquished, and leaders who anticipate future threat when things are still apparently going well make an important contribution that is not often widely recognized at the time or, for that matter, honored later. Not until this painful and difficult process has run its course will the readiness for new meanings permit a 'great leader' to articulate them convincingly. Strategic eras impose their own destiny on organizations and their leaders.

There are, to be sure, numerous tales of CEOs who have taken an ailing company, revitalized it, and achieved great success and recognition for doing so. The key word is 'ailing'. When a firm is widely seen as being in deep difficulty, as Memorex was in 1971, for example, there is an obvious imperative for change and a general recognition by employees of the need to alter older beliefs and ways of doing things. With Memorex at the brink of bankruptcy, its former

* This example is based upon Waterman, R. H., Peters, T. J. and Phillips, J. R. (1980). 'Structure is not Organization'. *Business Horizons*, (June) no. 80302, p. 23.

beliefs in 'rapid growth' and 'free form entrepreneurialism' were in disgrace.*
Not only was Bob Wilson free to move forcefully, the organiztion was ready to
receive him. The mourning for past meanings had already largely taken place.
Many of the entrepreneurial figures connected with the earlier era had already
departed. Dissatisfaction with the way things were, and fears for the future,
were strong. Wilson was thus in a position to build from the near ruins. In
contrast, his contemporaries at AT&T were having first to tear down
monuments still standing *before* problems were clearly evident to all concerned
and the costs of changing accepted.

Superordinate goals affect nations as profoundly as they do companies.
Without such goals, around which a nation can rally, each constituency is out
for itself and each citizen is more on his own. It appears as if the same late-in-
the-era malaise is currently at work in our country. We have gone through a
string of Presidents, each roundly criticized in his time, each dropping low in
the polls during his tenure, and each facing great difficulty in building a
consensus as to what America is all about, what it is for, where it is going, how it
can get there, and what its priorities should be. The heart of these difficulties,
we think, is not just the quality of leadership, but the angry resistance of a
nation that is still mourning the accumulating losses of more of its earlier beliefs
than it is prepared to relinquish. Perhaps a new President will be able to fashion
a compelling expression of an adjustment of our nation's superordinate goals
and begin anew.

Misuse of superordinate goals

Having made the case for the importance of superordinate goals in motivating
employees and sustaining an organization over time, we must note that a skillful
grasp of the use of all of our seven variables *can* be directed toward truly tragic
outcomes. The staggering horror of the Third Reich and the mass suicides in
Guyana come to mind. It is not hard to imagine an indoctrination of people into
some kind of corporate Hitler Youth Corps. Indeed, fascist imagery is often
used to express our unease with enterprises that succeed in fashioning intense
commitment, and our fear of the fanatical is certainly not paranoid. We have
seen enough of it in our western history to be wary. There is no reason to rest
assured that we are safe from pathology, madness or evil in leaders or social
systems at any level of enterprise, from small corporations to larger religious
movements to nation states.

Yet, if our fear of the totalitarian of either the right or the left keeps us from

* These comments on Memorex based on the trial transcript, *Memorex* v. *IBM*,
C-73-2239-SC, U.S. District Court, Northern District of California, 11 August 1978.

struggling to encourage meanings that are between those extremes, that move men's hearts and compel action within ranges acceptable to our society and culture, we risk creating the kind of corporate emptiness which invites the extremists to fill the void. We cannot protect ourselves against such threats, either nationally or in a corporate context, by preferring a kind of pseudo-innocence (which suggests that our ignorance or naiveté about such meanings is acceptable, since others are 'assigned' the function of dealing with extremists in our society). Rather, we must accept that owning up to our power to influence meanings imposes responsibilities to guard against the risks of its misuse. In this, we have some advantages built into our society. The still large separation of the state, the corporation and the church from one another, and of the media from all three, provides at least reasonable assurance that checks exist to achieve balance in the distribution of power and its uses. But, nonetheless, it needs to be said that increasing our understanding of executive manipulation of super-ordinate goals does not necessarily ensure benign outcomes. Indeed, as the power and responsibilities of businessmen continue to expand, it is appropriate that they be subjected to the kind of scrutiny and limitations that our constitution imposed on the leaders of the nation. And if they are wise, these businessmen will not complain too much at these constraints, for in the long run history suggests they are useful and even necessary, even if they seem a damned nuisance a lot of the time.

References

Burck, Gil (1940). 'International Business Machines'. *Fortune*, January, pp. 36–40.

Crozier, Michel (1964). *The Bureaucratic Phenomenon*. Chicago: University of Chicago Press.

Guyon, Janet (1980). 'Family Feeling at Delta Creates Loyal Workers, Emnity of Unions'. *Wall Street Journal*, 17 July, p. 13.

Hippel, Eric von (1978). 'Users as Innovators'. *Technology Review*, January, pp. 31–9.

IBM (undated). 'IBM's Basic Beliefs'. *IBM Orientation Booklet*, p. 11.

Kanter, Rosabeth Moss (1977). *Men and Women of the Corporation*. New York: Basic Books, pp. 15–16.

Leach, John J. (1978). 'The Organizational History'. Thirty-eighth Annual Academy of Management Proceedings. John J. Leach of the University of

Chicago was one of the first to investigate organizational history as a diagnostic tool in consulting.

Mintzberg, Henry (1973). *The Nature of Managerial Work*. New York: Harper & Row.

Pascale, Richard T. (1978). 'Personnel Practices and Employee Attitudes: A Study of Japanese and American Managed Firms in the United States'. *Human Relations*, vol. 31, no. 7, pp. 597–615.

Peters, Thomas J. (1976). 'The Case for Getting Things Done'. Unpublished paper, 5 May, pp. 16–21.

Prestbo, John A. (1980). 'At Procter and Gamble Success is Largely Due to Heeding Customers'. *Wall Street Journal*, 29 April, p. 1.

Selznick, Philip (1949). *TVA and the Grass Roots*. Berkeley: University of California Press.

Watson, Thomas Jr (1963). 'A Business and Its Beliefs'. *McKinsey Foundation Lecture*. New York: McGraw-Hill.

Reproduced from Pascale, Richard Tanner and Athos, Anthony G. (1981). *The Art of Japanese Management*, Chapter 7 by permission of Simon & Schuster Inc., New York.

Chapter 4

Mission and leadership

Most organizations that have a mission are deeply indebted to one or more of their leaders. History is replete with examples like Thomas Watson of IBM; Konosuke Matsushita of Matsushita Electric; Jan Carlsson of SAS. The list is long and packed with well known and loved personalities. Each of these leaders acted in different scenarios. Watson shaped IBM's beliefs and values and these are the same principles on which the company is still run. Matsushita Electric was founded by Konosuke Matsushita and he grooved a spiritual and almost religious mission for Matsushita people. SAS were in dire straits when Carlsson took over as CEO. He set about to reinforce just one or two basic values which he communicates at every opportunity. These have formed the SAS mission. So what is the overlap between leadership and a sense of mission?

All these leaders have one thing in common: they have recognized the fact that their people need a value system to follow which coincides with their own personal beliefs and principles. People in organizations also need a common sense of purpose or direction. Leadership plays a vital role in establishing these two important aspects of work life. The organization's value system is moulded through the creation of a philosophy by the leader. The leader feels a deep commitment to this philosophy and makes it come alive through values and beliefs. People in the organization identify with these values and gain a sense of fulfilment. The other duty of leadership, the creation of a common purpose, is achieved by conceiving of a vision which motivates and transcends the daily work life, imparting it with a meaning. People find themselves working toward the common good of the organization and themselves. They feel energized and committed. The shared values and the common purpose unite to create a sense of mission in the organization.

The organization's need for a philosophy and purpose is well documented in the literature on leadership. We shall, however, confine our selection to the fathers of leadership theory, C. I. Barnard and P. Selznick; a contemporary work by W. Bennis and B. Nanus; and a case study on a company called Securicor.

Barnard's book *The Functions of the Executive*, published in 1938, started people thinking about the non-economic motives, interests and processes that exist in organizations. According to Barnard, these motives affect the behaviour of people and determine their actions and attitudes within large formal corporations. This realization led Barnard to propound a theory of executive responsibility. Executive responsibility, quite apart from the normal functions of administration etc., includes the creation of a philosophy for the organization. This Barnard called the creation of a *morality*. The philosophy, or morality as Barnard calls it, refers to the way a leader inspires commitment from his or her people by creating 'faith in the ultimate satisfaction of personal motives, faith in the integrity of objective authority, faith in the superiority of common purpose as a personal aim of those who undertake it'.

The executive responsibility that is vested in a leader is also to do with the influence the organization has on its people's private codes of conduct. Barnard therefore believes that it is the leader's duty not only to conform to a complex code of morals but also to be involved in the creation of moral codes for others. This is 'the highest exemplification of responsibility'. Thus the process of executive leadership is not only intellectual but 'aesthetic and moral'. This is because all sane people are 'moral'. Organizations that recognize this psychological aspect of humans and ensure a moral dimension to their work lives through values and beliefs are creating a superior environment in which people thrive and generate extraordinary commitment.

About two decades later Philip Selznick wrote *Leadership in Administration*. In this work, Selznick advocates the creation of a religion for an organization and believes that it is a vital task for leadership. Selznick is the originator of the terms 'institutional leadership' and 'distinctive competences'. He uses institutional leadership to describe management which has been infused with commitment. This creates an integrity which must be nurtured and protected by the leader. He refers to the organization's character or culture as being the organization's 'distinctive competences'. And it is when an organization has acquired these distinctive competences that it becomes an institution: an organization with enduring values. Thus, 'we shall stress that the task of building special values and a distinctive competence into the organization is the prime function of leadership'.

Leaders, by W. Bennis and B. Nanus, is an account of different strategies for leadership. Amongst others, they note 'attention through vision' as being an important strategy for good leadership. Vision enables people in an organization to 'gain a sense of importance as they are transformed from robots blindly following instructions to human beings engaged in a creative and purposeful venture'. This sense of purpose helps employees to bring a greater enthusiasm to their work and secures a commitment to the organization's goals. 'Attention through vision helps the leader operate on the emotional and spiritual resources of the organization, on its values, commitments, and aspirations'. These are characteristics of an organization with what we have called a sense of mission. An organization needs a sense of purpose and direction to release the potential commitment from its people.

The case on Securicor demonstrates how company beliefs and principles help people to identify with the organization. We see leadership at large in the real world. The importance of living the values of the organization is summed up in Erskine's words, 'Business cannot be divorced from living, both should be nobly done.'

The nature of executive responsibility
Chester I. Barnard

Chester Barnard was president of the Rockefeller Foundation and also held the post of president of the New Jersey Bell Telephone Company. After a long career in industry he moved to Harvard where he wrote his book, *The Functions of the Executive*. It was published in 1938, and was among the first of its kind. The concepts were unconventional; people were not accustomed to the idea of the chief executive as being the creator of a 'morality' in the organization. This, in Barnard's view, was a vital responsibility of the leader in order to secure commitment from his or her people. The applicability of his then revolutionary ideas has gained momentum steadily over the 50 years or so since the book was published.

The book was written as an attempt to explain the forces at work in organizations. The non-economic motivation for organization behaviour lacked scholarly attention. Barnard recognized that the intuition on which people in organizations act is an important part of management.

Barnard divides his analysis into four parts. The first two parts provide the scientific rationale for cooperative behaviour. Barnard puts forward the hypothesis that the willingness of people to cooperate with each other in the formal system affects their performance at work. The last two parts analyse the functions of the executive. These include two types of task, those that simply maintain the organization in operation and those that provide people with a sense of fulfilment in their work. The former includes recruitment, the formulation of objectives and purpose, as well as the motivating of people to contribute to the organization. The latter, which he labelled 'executive responsibility', is to do with the manner in which leaders mould the private codes of employees. These codes provide people with a sense of fulfilment in their work and become the morality of their work lives. The creation of moral codes for others is part of leaders' duty to inspire their people. Barnard is emphatic in his consecration of morality: 'A low morality will not sustain leadership long, its influence quickly vanishes, it cannot produce its own succession.' We reproduce his chapter on executive responsibility which explains in detail how this morality can be created.

In many instances it has been unavoidable in this study to refer to the dependence of action in formal organizations upon personal choice, motives, value attitudes, appraisals of utility, norms of conduct, ideals. In Chapter II all these elements were aggregated with others in the conception of 'personal psychology' and taken as granted without inquiry as to their sources. In Chapter XI on the Economy of Incentives these elements were presented in summary in relation to inducements and incentives and to persuasion as the means of securing organization activities. In Chapter XII on the Theory of Authority the same elements were implicit in the discussion of the subjective aspects of authority. In Chapters XIII and XIV concerning the processes of decision the reference to what was in one place called the 'moral sector' was to these same elements. In Chapter XVI the conception of 'utility' in the relations of persons to organizations implied these same aspects of personality.

Nevertheless, the effort has heretofore been so far as possible to avoid the consideration of the moral aspects of cooperation in order that we might first have a common understanding of the principles of the structure and of the processes of organization. There has been in this approach necessarily some distortion. Close study of the structure of organization or of its dynamic processes may induce an overemphasis upon some one or several of the more technical aspects of cooperation. Usually, however, the obscurity of the structural features and the elusiveness of the operative elements drive one to take refuge in 'leadership' as the factor of chief significance in human cooperation. The limitations imposed by the physical environment and the biological constitution of human beings, the uncertainties of the outcome of cooperation, the difficulties of common understanding of purpose, the delicacy of the systems of communication essential to organization, the dispersive tendencies of individuals, the necessity of individual assent to establish the authority for coordination, the great role of persuasion in securing adherence to organization and submission to its requirements, the complexity and instability of motives, the never ending burden of decision – all these elements of organization, in which the moral factor finds its concrete expression, spell the necessity of leadership, the power of individuals to inspire cooperative personal decision by creating faith: faith in common understanding, faith in the probability of success, faith in the ultimate satisfaction of personal motives, faith in the integrity of objective authority, faith in the superiority of common purpose as a personal aim of those who partake in it.

Nevertheless, to suppose that leadership, that the moral elements, are the only important or significant general factor in organization is as erroneous as to suppose that structure and process of cooperation without leadership are sufficient. Either view is out of accord with reason and experience. Purposeful cooperation is possible only within certain limits of a structural character, and it arises from forces derived from *all* who contribute to it. The work of cooperation is not a work of leadership, but of organization as a whole. But these structures do not remain in existence, they usually do not come into being, the vitality is lacking, there is no enduring cooperation, without the creation of faith, the catalyst by which the living system of human efforts is enabled to continue its incessant interchange of energies and satisfactions. Cooperation, not leadership, is the creative process; but leadership is the indispensable fulminator of its forces.

Leadership has two aspects. One is local, individual, particular, ephemeral. It is the aspect of individual superiority – in physique, in skill, in technology, in perception, in knowledge, in memory, in imagination. This is the immediate aspect, highly variable through time and in place; subject to specific development by conditioning, training, education; significant chiefly in conjunction with specific conditions; relative; rather easily determinable; comparatively objective; essential to *positive* action; commanding admiration, emulation. This is the technical aspect of leadership. Important as it is, it has by implication been included at length in the preceding chapters.

Now we shall confine our thoughts to the second aspect of leadership – the more general; the more constant; the least subject to specific development; the more absolute; the subjective; that which reflects the attitudes and ideals of society and its general institutions. It is the aspect of individual superiority in determination, persistence, endurance, courage; that which determines the *quality* of action; which often is most inferred from what is *not* done, from abstention; which commands respect, reverence. It is the aspect of leadership we commonly imply in the word 'responsibility', the quality which gives dependability and determination to human conduct, and foresight and ideality to purpose.

In this chapter we are to consider the moral factor in organization, focused in its aspects of leadership and executive responsibility. With the exception of one important respect we shall avoid any inquiry into the general and ultimate sources of individual morality or psychology, whether physiological, or arising from the physical environment or from the social influences, although we cannot avoid some consideration of the nature of the internal processes of individuals in immediate situations. The one exception is the reaction of specific formal organizations upon the psychology or morality of individuals who have close and lasting connections with them. The *fact* of such reactions is a major principle of the processes of organization, and hence the executive functions and of leadership and executive responsibility.

The elements and processes of leadership are observed and abstracted with great difficulty. In the present attempt to elucidate the subject it is first necessary to consider what we mean by moral character of persons and the nature of personal responsibility. Thus we must briefly indulge in some speculative description of internal processes, which are only to be surmised – with the aid of subjective experience – from external phenomena, though the latter are matters of common experience. We shall then note certain characteristic differences in the morals, responsibility and moral status of individuals. This will lead to stating some significant differences between the moral positions of individuals as affected by the executive functions. Finally, we shall consider the executive function of 'moral creativeness' as the highest expression of responsibility.

I shall describe the concept implicit in 'moral factor', 'moral element', 'morals', for our purposes, by the following definition: morals are personal forces or propensities of a general and stable character in individuals which tend to inhibit, control, or modify inconsistent immediate specific desires, impulses, or interests, and to intensify those which are consistent with such propensities. This tendency to inhibit, control, or modify inconsistent and to reinforce consistent immediate desires, impulses, or interests is a matter of sentiment, feeling, emotion, internal compulsion, rather than one of rational processes or deliberation, although in many instances such tendencies are subject to rationalization and occasionally to logical processes. When the tendency is strong and stable there exists a condition of responsibility.

Morals arise from forces external to the individual as a person. Some of them are believed by many to be directly of supernatural origin; some of them derive from the social environment, including general, political, religious and economic environments; some of them arise from experience of the physical environment, and from biological properties and phylogenetic history; some from technological practice or habit. Many moral forces are inculcated in the individual by education and training; and many of them accrue through absorption, as it were, from the environment – by limitation or emulation, and perhaps also in the negative form of absence from concrete experience.*

It is convenient to conceive of these innate forces or general propensities as a private code of conduct consisting of positive and negative prescriptions. In this way these forces are more easily susceptible to verbalization, although by definition morals cannot be a code in an ordinary sense, but are an active resultant of accumulated influences on persons, evident only from action in concrete conditions. That is, they are to be inferred from conduct under actual conditions, and to some extent from the verbal reflections of sentiments.

What has just been said about the origin of morals suggests the convenience of postulating several sets of general propensities or codes in the same person, arising from different sources of influence and related to several quite diverse types of activities. It implies that all persons must have such private codes. This

---

* For example, one hesitates to do things of some kinds which are not done by others, or have never been done before, even when there is no apparent reason that they should not be done.

conforms to the commonly accepted view that all sane men are 'moral' beings. The present thought may be expressed by saying that the conduct of every man is in part governed by several private moral codes. What these are determines his moral status, which may be simple or complex, high or low, comprehensive or narrow.

Moral status and responsibility are not identical. Responsibility, as I define it for present purposes, is the power of a particular private code of morals to control the conduct of the individual in the presence of strong contrary desires or impulses. For instance, two men may have substantially identical codes as respects a given field of activity, but the code will be dominant as respects the conduct of one man under adverse immediate conditions, while it will not be dominant as respects the other under the same or similar conditions. With reference to that code, the first man is said to be responsible, or to possess responsibility, or to have the capacity of responsibility; the second man not.

Since all men possess several, if not many, private codes, it is possible that a man may be responsible with respect to some of them and not so with respect to others. I observe cases in which this appears to be true, considering only major or important codes. For example, persons may be very responsible as respects national or religious obligations generally (that is, what *they* feel to be obligations), and be quite irresponsible as respects ordinary business obligations (what *they* also feel to be obligations). But except as to minor or inconsequential codes, it appears usually true that men who are responsible in one major respect are so also in other respects; that is, they possess a general capacity under adverse conditions for conduct consistent with their stable sentiments and beliefs. The important point here is that persons of high moral status may be weakly controlled by their moral codes, and are then relatively irresponsible; and vice versa.

There are many persons who are responsible provided the issues by which they are confronted are simple conformance or non-comformance which particular codes. But if there exist several or many private codes governing the conduct of an individual, specific acts or concrete situations are likely to involve conflicts between codes; that is, a desire or impulse may be entirely consistent with one code but inconsistent with another. In fact, one code may intensify a desire or impulse, or justify it, when the reverse is true of another code. This is a frequent situation in conduct regarded by the individual as purely private, for which illustration will be given later.

When there are occasions under which conflicts of codes may arise it may be that one of the codes involved is a superior or dominant code. In this case there is usually no serious personal difficulty, and the actor is usually not aware of conflict. The dominant code is the one which governs as a matter of course; and the action may involve inconsistency only from the point of view of an observer. In such cases the personal problem at most is one of sincerity or of the possibility of apparent violation of consistency.

When, however, codes have substantially equal validity or power in the subject affected, conflict of codes is a serious personal issue. The results of such a conflict may be of three kinds: (1) either there is paralysis of action, accompanied by emotional tension, and ending in a sense of frustration, blockade, uncertainty, or in loss of decisiveness and lack of confidence; or (2) there is conformance to one code and violation of the other, resulting in a sense of guilt, discomfort, dissatisfaction, or a loss of self-respect, or (3) there is found some substitute action which satisfies immediate desire or impulse or interest, or the dictates of one code, and yet conforms to all other codes. When the second situation of non-conformance to one code is the resolution and it is repeated often, it will have the effect of destroying that code, unless it is very powerful and is kept alive by continuing external influences. When the resolution of the conflict is accomplished by substitution of a new action for that originally conceived, all the codes are strengthened by the experience; but such a solution frequently requires imaginative and constructive ability. The way has to be 'worked out' to meet all the requirements.

Some private codes of morals may be regarded as common to many persons, others are special or particular to individuals or relatively small numbers of persons. Only where the code is very common is it likely to be recognized as 'moral', that is, as a public code; and in the United States generally only that code or the codes which derive from or are inculcated by the Christian churches may be considered *the* moral code or codes. But there are other common codes of great importance which are not generally so recognized: for example, those relating to or governing what is called patriotic conduct – the sense of obligations or duties of the citizen. There are others relating to commercial conduct which are comprehended in the word 'integrity'. There are others that relate to manners, social conduct, etc. In many respects these codes coincide; for example, 'Thou shalt not steal' is Hebrew morals, Christian morals, governmental morals, commercial morals, and good social conduct. But in other respects these codes do not coincide and may even conflict. To illustrate, gambling is prohibited in governmental morals, but not in Christian morals, I believe, except it be by indirect interpretation; nor is it prohibited by the standards of social conduct generally observed.

Codes commonly regarded as important or dominant are those most professed publicly. The mere fact that they are publicly professed unquestionably has an effect upon conduct generally, although the conduct affected is not necessarily in harmony with such public codes. Moreover, it does not follow because such codes have important effects that they are dominant or the most important codes in a majority of individuals or even in any single individual. For example, occasionally a person may be observed who subscribes to the publicly professed Christian codes and the patriotic codes, and whose conduct is undoubtedly modified by that fact, but who nevertheless is governed, under many circumstances, primarily by a code derived from the organization to which he is most attached. In case of conflict that code will be dominant. Doing things the 'right' way is a dominant *moral* code in the specialized work of many fine mechanics, musicians, artists, accountants, engineers, for example. No other code on earth dominates their conduct in case of conflict; and the domination will be so complete that they will not be aware of the conflict until perhaps after the event. Even then they will recognize or admit nothing but an apparent inconsistency, perhaps embarrassing and difficult to justify. To regard such domination as merely an incidence to technical habits is to miss the point. In these cases it is not a matter of better or worse, of superior or inferior processes – a judgment rationally arrived at. It is a matter of *right* or *wrong* in a moral sense, of deep feeling, of innate conviction, not arguable; emotional, not intellectual, in character.

Current opinion puts into the realm of important moral codes those most publicly professed and believed most dominant socially, and rejects all others, assigning to them a variety of names – for example, attitude, influences, psychological characteristics, technological standards, politics – in this way concealing the fact that these others are of the same nature even if of different origin or effect. Hence, in a vague way, we are led to think of responsibility as existing only when there is a strong conformance to the public codes; and, if non-conformance to such codes is observed, to believe that this is evidence of lack of responsibility. Or, if codes not recognized by the *observer* as socially important, but his own private codes instead, are the criterion, he denies the quality of responsibility when he sees non-conformance of others to *his* codes. In this way judgment of desirability or broad notions of ethics govern the popular appraisal of responsibility. An appraisal of moral status is confused with capacity of responsibility.

In illustration: I know men whose morals as a whole I cannot help believe to be lower ethically than my own. But these men command my attention and sometimes my admiration because they adhere to their codes rigidly in the face of great difficulties; whereas I observe that many others who have a 'higher' morality do not adhere to their codes when it would apparently not be difficult to do so. Men of the first class have a higher sense of responsibility than those having, as I view them, the higher ethical standards. *The point is that responsibility is the property of an individual by which whatever morality exists in him becomes effective in conduct.*

Let us apply these definitions and observations in an illustration that may be recognized as typical of common experience. Mr A, a citizen of Massachusetts, a member of the Baptist Church, having a father and mother living, and a wife and two children, is an expert machinist employed at a pump station of an important water system. For simplicity's sake, we omit further description. We impute to him several moral codes: Christian ethics, the patriotic code of the citizen, a code of family obligations, a code as an expert machinist, a code derived from the organization engaged in the operation of the water system. He is not aware of these codes. These intellectual abstractions are a part of his 'system', ingrained in him by causes, forces, experiences, which he has either forgotten or on the whole never recognized. Just what they are, in fact, can at best only be approximately inferred by his actions, preferably under stress. He has no idea as to the order of importance of these codes, although, if pressed, what he might say probably would indicate that his religious code is first in importance, either because he has some intellectual comprehension of it, or because it is socially dominant. I shall hazard the guess, however, that their order of importance is as follows: his code as to the support and protection of his own children, his code of obligations to the water system, his code as a skilled artisan, his code with reference to his parents, his religious code, and his code as a citizen. For his children he will kill, steal, cheat the government, rob the church, leave the water plant at a critical time, botch a job by hurrying. If his children are not directly at stake, he will sacrifice money, health, time, comfort, convenience, jury duty, church obligations, in order to keep the water plant running; except for his children and the water plant, he cannot be induced to do a botch mechanical job – wouldn't know how; to take care of his parents, he will lie, steal, or do anything else contrary to his code as a citizen or his religious code; if his government legally orders him to violate his religious code, he will go to jail first. He is, however, a very responsible man. It not only takes extraordinary pressure to make him violate any of his codes, but when faced with such pressure he makes great effort to find some solution that is compatible with all of them; and because he makes that effort and is capable he has in the past succeeded. Since he is a very responsible man, knowing his codes you can be fairly sure of what he will do under a rather wide range of conditions.

Now if we introduce a single disturbing factor, the use of alcoholic beverages, we have a considerable change. Our 'case' becomes rather irresponsible. The use of alcohol does not violate any of his codes. Because of it, however, he neglects the children, he botches his work, he has been discharged from the water system as undependable, his parents are on public support, he steals for liquor, etc., etc. He is irresponsible; but for the present his codes remain still the same. He will even fight about them if challenged, though intoxicated. He is as moral now as before. He sincerely believes all his conduct has become reprehensible and is sick with genuine remorse when sober; but he is irresponsible, nevertheless.

It may seem to some readers an exaggeration to call devotion to a water system a moral code. Many persons appear unaware of the force of such codes derived from organization associations. But organizations depend greatly upon such moral codes. I recall a telephone operator on duty at a lonely place from which she could see in the distance the house in which her mother lay bedridden. Her life was spent in taking care of her mother and in maintaining that home for her. To do so, she chose employment in that particular position, against other inclinations. Yet she stayed at her switchboard while she watched the house burn down.* No code, public or organizational, that has any general validity

* The mother was rescued.

under such circumstances governed her conduct, and she certainly violated some such codes, as well as some of her own. Nevertheless, she showed extraordinary 'moral courage', we would say, in conforming to a code of her organization – the *moral* necessity of uninterrupted service. This was high responsibility as respects that code.

These illustrations suggest the usefulness of considering the relation of sanctions to codes and to responsibility. Some codes, being the accumulated effect of custom, general opinion, and similar 'states of mind' of society, and of *informal* organizations of large and small size, have usually no specific sanctions associated with them which support their moral power. Other codes arise from experience and contact with *formal* organizations. These often have specific sanctions related to some details of conduct pertinent to them. For example, the code of citizenship is somewhat reinforced by penalties for violations or failure to conform. The codes related to industrial organizations are partly reinforced by possibilities of discharge, etc. It may be said that these sanctions help to establish codes, but not responsibility. Thus where conformance is secured by fear of penalties, what is operating is not the moral factor in the sense of the term as used here, but merely negative inducements or incentives. In practice, it is often, perhaps usually, impossible to distinguish the reasons for compliance; but it is quite well understood that good citizenship, for example, is not obtainable by such specific inducements. Only the deep convictions that operate regardless of either specific penalties or specific rewards are the stuff of high responsibility.

The private code of morals which derives from a definite formal organization is one aspect of what we have previously referred to as the 'organization personality'. It is also an aspect of the 'zone of indifference'. Those who have a strong attachment to an organization, however it comes about, are likely to have a code or codes derived from it if their connection has existed long; but whether they appear responsible with respect to such codes depends upon the general capacity for responsibility and upon their place in the spectrum of personal codes.

Hence, the assent of an individual to an order or requirement of an organization, that is, the question of whether he will grant authority to it, is very complex. It depends upon the effect of the order or requirement as a positive or negative incentive, modified by the sanctions, if any, involved in denying authority to it; upon whether or not the individual has a code of morals derived from the organization; upon whether there is conflict of his codes in respect to the specific requirements; upon how important the organization code is as compared with others; upon his sense of responsibility; and so on. If the sense of responsibility is generally weak, conflict of codes is not important but specific incentives and sanctions are. If the sense of responsibility is strong, conflict of codes will result in denial of authority if the organization code is the less important, and specific incentives in that event will usually be unimportant influences.

Persons differ not only as to the quality and relative importance of their moral codes, or as to their sense of responsibility toward them, or with respect to the effect of incentives; but also because of wide variations in the *number* of codes which govern their conduct. There are many causes of such variations in number. For one example, persons who live in one place and work in another, or those who live in different places at different seasons, are likely to have more codes than those who are more fixed. But probably the principal cause of variation in number of codes is difference in the number of organizations to which persons are attached. Most persons living and working on farms are likely to have relatively few organization connections; but many town and city dwellers have several important connections and a number of others of minor importance, and some men have many such connections.

Differences in the number of moral codes of individuals are of great significance. Conflicts of code will increase, as a matter of probability, with increase in number of codes, and perhaps in something like geometric ratio. To take a comparatively trivial matter for illustration, conflicts as respects appointments, meetings, etc., alone introduce active decisions for responsible men as to relative obligations; and these conflicts increase more rapidly than the number of such obligations. They are occasionally quite serious and by no means a negligible strain, as many can testify.

It is probable that some persons, though possessing quite complex moralities, are seldom plagued with conflicts because they are inactive. This is probably true of retired persons, for example. Conflicts appear to be a product of moral complexity and physical and social activity.

The dilemmas which result from numerous conflicts imply in general at least one of the following consequences: either general moral deterioration, beginning in frustration and indecisiveness; or diminution of the general sense of responsibility, manifest in the tendency to let decisions hinge on chance, external and irrelevant determinants, incidental pressures; or a deliberate withdrawal to a less active condition, thereby reducing the occasions of conflict; or the development of an ability to avoid conflicts, known as 'keeping out of trouble', 'avoiding temptation', 'avoidance of responsibility'; or the development of the ability to construct alternative measures that satisfy immediate desires or requirements without violating any codes. When the last alternative is taken it undoubtedly increases the general sense of responsibility and perhaps usually the moral status of the individual; but it requires resourcefulness, energy, imagination, general ability.

In short, neither men of weak responsibility nor those of limited capability can endure or carry the burden of many simultaneous obligations of different types. If they are 'overloaded', either ability, responsibility or morality, or all three, will be destroyed. Conversely, a condition of complex morality, great activity and high responsibility cannot continue without commensurate ability. I do not hesitate to affirm that those whom I believe to be the better and more able executives regard it as a major malefaction to induce or push men of fine character and great sense of responsibility into active positions greatly exceeding their technical capacities. Unless the process can be reversed in time, the result is destruction. In the doubtful cases, which are quite frequent, the risk of such results, I think, is commonly regarded by such executives as among the most important hazards of their decisions.

Executive positions (a) imply a complex morality, and (b) require a high capacity of responsibility, (c) under conditions of activity, necessitating (d) commensurate general and specific technical abilities as a *moral* factor. These are implicit in the previous discussion; in addition there is required (e) the faculty of *creating* morals for others. It is pertinent now to restate what has already been said, and to amplify and apply it in relation to formal organizations and to the discharge of the executive functions.

(a) Every executive possesses, independently of the position he occupies, personal moral codes. When the individual is placed in an executive position there are immediately incumbent upon him, officially at least, several *additional* codes that are codes of his organization. Codes of the organization are themselves accruals largely of intangible forces, influences, habitual practice, which must be accepted as a whole. These codes are quite different among organizations, being affected by their status – supreme, as in the case of governments or churches – or subsidiary, subordinate, dependent; and by their purposes – educational, industrial, commercial, political party, fraternal, governmental, religious, etc; and by their technologies.

It will be sufficient for present purposes of illustration to take a hypothetical industrial organization, and to suppose the case of an executive head of an important department. The *organization* codes to which he should conform are: (1) the government code as applying to his company, that is, the laws, charter provisions, etc; (2) obedience to the general purpose and general methods, including the established systems of objective authority; (3) the general purpose of his department; (4) the general moral (ethical) standards of his subordinates; (5) the technical situation as a whole; (6) the code of the informal executive organization, that is, that official conduct shall be that of a gentleman as *its members* understand it, and that personal conduct shall be so likewise; (7) the code that is suggested in the phrase 'the good of the organization as a whole'; (8) the code of the informal organization of the department; (9) the technical requirements of the department as a whole. There will often be others, but these will serve for example.

It will be quite evident from this brief discussion without consideration of specific organizations that the executive, by virtue of his position, adopts a more complex morality than he would otherwise have. This complexity is not peculiar, however, to executives. Both executives and professional men differ as a class from non-executive or non-professional persons as a class in that the conditions of their positions impose upon them numerous additional codes.

These are chiefly non-personal in their significance; most official or professional activities can be carried out with no involvement of strictly private codes. Therefore, the complexity of the individual's moral situation is not perhaps increased in proportion to the additions arising from organization and professional functions. But inevitably, at times, some action or requirement does involve the whole gamut. Then we say that a man cannot divorce his official or professional conduct from his private morals. When such issues occur, the alternatives presented are either to violate one's personal morality or to fail in an official or professional obligation. Resignation or withdrawal is often a solution which circumstances 'legitimately' permit. Then the result is maintenance of personal integrity. When, however, resignation or withdrawal is itself highly immoral, as is sometimes the case, there is potential tragedy. The penalty for lack of ability to avoid or find substitute action in such cases is severe.

That which is unique to the executive functions, however, is that they also impose the necessity of *creating* moral codes. Thus, to the moral problem of individuals generally, organization adds in the case of the executive substantial increase of moral complexity, and of tests of responsibility, and the function of creating moral conditions. The latter is a distinguishing characteristic of executive work, to be discussed later.

(b) The capacity of responsibility is that of being firmly governed by moral codes – against inconsistent immediate impulses, desires, or interests, and in the direction of desires or interests that are consonant with such codes. Our common word for one aspect of this capacity is 'dependability', by which we mean that, knowing a man's codes – that is, being aware of his 'character' – we can reasonably foresee what he is likely to do or not to do, usually under a variety of circumstances.

Almost uniformly, in all types of organizations, persons of executive capacity are assigned initially to executive positions of low rank. The fact of sense of responsibility is there demonstrated. The conditions of these lower rank positions are those of relatively limited moral complexity and possibly somewhat lower states of activity. The chief difference between the lower and the higher ranks is not in the capacity of responsibility but in the condition of moral complexity. In other words, the higher positions impose more responsibilities, as is often correctly said, but do not require greater *sense* of responsibility in important degree.

(c) Generally the conditions of executive work are those of great activity. This is not obvious, because the word 'activity' too much suggests physical action. But it is clear that the higher the position the more exposed the incumbent to action imposed from numerous directions, calling for the activity of decision. The increase of this activity is in practice not proportional to the level of position because it is deliberately controlled. This is a necessity which was referred to in Chapter XIII, 'The Environment of Decision', where some of the methods by which breakdown is avoided are stated.

(d) The capacity of responsibility is in executive ranks rather a constant, and the tendency of activity to increase with scope of position is often controllable. The increase in complexity of moral conditions, however, is not controllable by the person affected, so that despite control of activities the burden increases from conflicts of morals as the scope of the executive position broadens. For example, since a preliminary proposal usually raises a conflict of codes, and since proposals for concrete decision in non-routine matters increase with position, an executive position is exposed to more and more moral conflicts the higher it is, and the process of decision becomes morally and often technically more and more complex.

Where there is high sense of responsibility, these conflicts can only be resolved by one of two methods: either to analyze further the pertinent environment with a view to a more accurate determination of the strategic factor of the situation, which may lead to the discovery of that 'correct' action which violates no codes; or to adopt a new detailed purpose consistent with general objectives, that is, the more general purposes. Both methods are tests of general ability, the first of ability in discrimination, analysis; the second of imagination, invention, innovation. Either process in an important aspect is an expression of that phase of responsibility which is known as 'determination'.

The moral complications of the executive functions, then, can only be endured by those possessing a commensurate ability. While, on one hand, the requisite ability without an adequate complex of moralities or without a high sense of responsibility leads to the hopeless confusion of inconsistent expediences so often described as 'incompetence', on the other hand, the requisite morality and sense of responsibility without commensurate abilities leads to fatal indecision or emotional and impulsive decisions, with personal breakdown and ultimate destruction of the sense of responsibility. The important distinctions of rank lie in the fact that the higher the grade the more complex the *moralities* involved, and the more necessary higher abilities to discharge the responsibilities, that is, to resolve the moral conflicts implicit in the positions.

It is apparent that executives frequently fail. This failure may be ascribed in most cases, I believe, to inadequate abilities as a first cause, usually resulting in the destruction of responsibility. But in many cases it may be inferred that the conditions impose a moral complexity and a moral conflict presumably not soluble. Some actions which may within reason appear to be dictated by the good of the organization as a whole will obviously be counter to nearly all other codes, personal or official.

For example, suppose a combination of circumstances such that an appearance of malfeasance will lie against a particular executive, which, if known, would seriously injure the prestige of his organization. Suppose it impossible to refute that appearance, although, in fact, the charge is not true. Suppose that the only available alternative is for the executive to falsify books or records in such a way as to direct an accusation against a fellow executive, this not to be attended with the same damage to the organization. The only code supporting such nefarious action is one which derives from a sense of the good of the organization as a whole – obviously a powerful influence, especially in military and religious organizations. The action proposed would violate several other codes, both 'official' and personal.

Such clear cut cases are rare in industrial organizations but undoubtedly have occurred not infrequently in political, governmental and religious organizations. They occasionally occur also in family organizations; an extreme illustration is suicide for benefit of family through life-insurance proceeds. These are cases where the code of the organization as a whole is completely dominant and there is very high sense of responsibility, such that the dominant end justifies any means, that is, the violation of all other conflicting codes.*

Rare though such cases may be, in practice they will range from these extremes through to those where 'every consideration' leads to supporting a particular action – an opposite extreme probably also rare. Between these limits are the great majority in which action first contemplated is consonant with some codes, violates others. Most frequently the conflict is between organization codes and not between organization and personal codes, but there are many cases of the latter type, nevertheless. The consequences of failure, where no organization action interposes, are either the destruction of the sense of responsibility or the destruction of codes, leading to a simpler moral status. The best solution in such case would often be resignation, demotion or discharge, which would reduce activity, moral complexity and the requirements of ability.

It seems probable that moral deterioration and loss of personal responsibility is more frequent among executives, especially in political organizations, than among other persons. The very complexity of the moral situation and the 'overloading' that is inescapable under many conditions make this credible. This is, I think, confirmed by current observation. Either moral bewilderment or loss of ability – for example, from ill health – can and does produce 'collapse of character'. It seems to me inevitable that the struggle to maintain cooperation among men should as surely destroy some men morally as battle destroys some physically. When considering cases of failure where there were enough facts available to warrant a judgment, it has seemed clear to me that in most of them the cause was promotion beyond capacity as respects ability, not initial lack of responsibility, or even inferior morality. The cases may most frequently be observed in the political field, where, as compared with educational or industrial fields, selection is made, *and is almost necessarily made*, to a relatively high degree on the basis of loyalty as the prime qualification with minimum regard to ability. Its inevitable result is 'double-crossing', etc. – not really due to personal perfidy, though its effect may be the same, but to inability to find 'honest' solutions. Reason and history suggest that this condition is pronounced in political organizations, especially party organizations.

(e) The distinguishing mark of the executive responsibility is that it requires

---

* I have no doubt that in some cases where there is a false or 'framed' victim, he is a voluntary sacrifice, that is, he is even more dominated by 'the good of the organization'.

not merely conformance to a complex code of morals but also the creation of moral codes for others. The most generally recognized aspect of this function is called securing, creating, inspiring of 'morale' in an organization. This is the process of inculcating points of view, fundamental attitudes, loyalties, to the organization or cooperative system, and to the system of objective authority, that will result in subordinating individual interest and the minor dictates of personal codes to the good of the cooperative whole. This includes (also important) the establishment of the morality of standards of workmanship.

The function of moral creativeness, though not ordinarily described in this way, is of long history. Some aspects of it, such as those related to organization enthusiasm, are well appreciated; and what has already been said in this study concerning the economy of incentives, and especially concerning the necessity of the method of persuasion in the recruiting of organization forces, makes it unnecessary to elaborate the matter at greater length here. There is enough experience of the subject to make it clear that failure with respect to moral creativeness arises from inadequate attention, lack of persistence in the face of the inertia of human reluctance, and lack of sincerity of purpose.

But there is another aspect of moral creativeness that is little understood, except in the field of jurisprudence. This is the inventing of a *moral* basis for the solution of moral conflicts – variously called 'handling the exceptional case', 'the appellate function', 'the judicial function'. This function is exercised in the cases that seem 'right' from one point of view, 'wrong' from another. The solution of such cases lies either in substituting a new action which avoids the conflict, or in providing a moral justification for exception or compromise. We are accustomed to call the first solution 'executive', the second 'judicial'. They are both executive functions in the broad sense used in this essay. Were it not for the separation of powers in American government, we should better recognize that the judicial process is a highly specialized executive process.

There is no escape from the judicial process in the exercise of executive functions. Conflicts of codes in organization are inevitable. Probably most of them are solved by substitute action, largely a matter of technological decision. But often the requirements of technology (in the narrow sense), of organization codes, and of personal codes, press in conflicting directions. Not to do something that is technologically 'necessary' because it conflicts with an organization code (as expressed for example in an economic interest) does great violence to the moral codes arising from technological fitness. Its manifest result is discouragement, lack of interest, disgust. To do something that is technologically 'sound' but is economic heresy similarly destroys the general sense of economic appropriateness. It implies disregard of the economy of the organization, and tends to its destruction. To do something that is required obviously for the good of organization but which conflicts with deep personal codes – such as the sense of what is honest – destroys personal probity; but not to do it destroys organization cohesiveness and efficiency. The codes governing individual relationships to organized effort are of wide variation, so that either action or failure to act in these cases does violence to individual moralities, though the alternatives will affect different persons in different ways.

The judicial process, from the executive point of view, is one of morally justifying a change or redefinition or new particularizing of purpose so that the sense of conformance to moral codes is secured. One final effect is the elaboration and refinement of morals – of codes of conduct. This is most easily seen in the judicial process as exemplified in the law cases. That it can degenerate into mere subtlety to avoid rather than to discharge obligations is apparent in all executive experience. The invention of the constructions and fictions necessary to secure the preservation of morale is a severe test of both responsibility and ability, for to be sound they must be 'just' in the view of the executive, that is, really consonant with the morality of the whole; as well as acceptable, that is, really consonant with the morality of the part, of the individual.

The creative aspect of executive responsibility is the highest exemplification of responsibility. As to the great proportion of organization decisions required of the executive, the conflict of morals is within organization codes, and personal codes are not directly involved. The 'organization personality' alone is concerned. The conflict may be treated with relative objectivity, as a 'problem'. In fact, probably most executive decisions appear in the guise of technical decisions, and their moral aspects are not consciously appreciated. An executive may make many important decisions without reference to any sense of personal interest or of morality. But where creative morality is concerned, the sense of personal responsibility – of sincerity and honesty, in other words – is acutely emphasized. Probably few persons are able to do such work objectively. Indeed, few can do it long except on the basis of personal conviction – not conviction that they are obligated as officials to do it, but conviction that what they do for the good of organization they *personally* believe to be right.

The creative function as a whole is the essence of leadership. It is the highest test of executive responsibility because it requires for successful accomplishment that element of 'conviction' that means identification of personal codes and organization codes in the view of the leader. This is the coalescence that carries 'conviction' to the personnel of organization, to that informal organization underlying all formal organization that senses nothing more quickly than insincerity. Without it, all organization is dying, because it is the indispensable element in creating that desire for adherence – for which no incentive is a substitute – on the part of those whose efforts willingly contributed constitute organization.

The most general strategic factor in human cooperation is executive capacity. In the nature of the physical world and of the social world as well, opportunity and ideals outrun the immediate motives and interest and the practical abilities that are required of leaders. The accumulation of capital, the invention of processes, the innovations of human relationships that effective and efficient cooperation need as a preliminary necessity, call for special abilities in the technologies of materials, physical forces, economic systems and organization arts. Though indispensable, these abilities will not be put forth, will not even be developed, without that sense of responsibility which makes the sacrifices involved a matter of course, and which elicits the initial faith in cooperation. These abilities and capacities are sufficient to bring into life many organizations of low quality and of inferior or anti-social purposes, and to maintain their vitality for a time. The short interest, the immediate purpose, the impulses of the moment, may be as well served by new combinations as by old, and the appeal to individual self-existence is often gratified best by change if only immediate and material needs are at stake. Organizations endure, however, in proportion to the breadth of the morality by which they are governed. This is only to say that foresight, long purposes, high ideals, are the basis for the persistence of cooperation.

Thus the endurance of organization depends upon the quality of leadership; and that quality derives from the breadth of the morality upon which it rests. High responsibility there must be even in the lowest, the most immoral, organizations; but if the morality to which the responsibility relates is low, the organizations are short lived. A low morality will not sustain leadership long, its influence quickly vanishes, it cannot produce its own succession.

Leadership, of course, often is wrong, and often fails. Perhaps frequently the leader believes his personal morality and that of his organization are identical when they are not. Perhaps he is ignorant of the codes in the organization that are necessary by reason of the environment, which he fails to see objectively. Perhaps he mistakes a purely personal motive for an organization purpose. In these cases, the facts destroy his responsibility, his leadership fails, he no longer can create, he is trapped between the incompatibility of purpose and environment, insincerity rots his influence. But until that happens – as perhaps it inevitably does in time to all leaders, since established organizations often seem to outgrow their leaders – until that happens, the creation of organization morality is the spirit that overcomes the centrifugal forces of individual interests or motives. Without leadership in this supreme sense the inherent difficulties often cannot be overcome even for short periods. Leadership does not annul the laws of nature, nor is it a substitute for the elements essential to cooperative effort; but it is the indispensable social essence that gives common meaning to common purpose, that creates the incentive that makes other incentives effective, that infuses the subjective aspect of countless decisions with consistency in a changing environment, that inspires the personal conviction that produces the vital cohesiveness without which cooperation is impossible.

Executive responsibility, then, is that capacity of leaders by which, reflecting attitudes, ideals, hopes, derived largely from without themselves, they are compelled to bind the wills of men to the accomplishment of purposes beyond their immediate ends, beyond their times. Even when these purposes are lowly and the time is short, the transitory efforts of men become a part of that organization of living forces that transcends man unaided by man; but when these purposes are high and the wills of many men of many generations are bound together they live boundlessly.

For the morality that underlies enduring cooperation is multi-dimensional. It comes from and may expand to all the world, it is rooted deeply in the past, it faces toward the endless future. As it expands, it must become more complex, its conflicts must be more numerous and deeper, its call for abilities must be higher, its failures of ideal attainment must be perhaps more tragic; but the quality of leadership, the persistence of its influence, the durability of its related organizations, the power of the coordination it incites, all express the height of moral aspirations, the breadth of moral foundations.

So among those who cooperate the things that are seen are moved by the things unseen. Out of the void comes the spirit that shapes the ends of men.

Reproduced from Barnard, Chester I. (1968). *The Functions of the Executive*, Chapter XVII by permission of Harvard University Press, Cambridge, Massachusetts.

The case for institutionalizing values
Philip Selznick

Philip Selznick, a Berkeley sociologist, published his book on leadership in 1957. It has recently been reprinted. Selznick roots his discussion of leadership in sociological studies. He regarded organizations as social institutions. An ordinary organization evolves into an institution when its members become attached to the organization. This attachment is in a personal capacity and not just a professional relationship. The organization then begins to symbolize certain values and aspirations of its people and therefore assumes an identity of its own.

Leadership of such an organization is 'institutional leadership' and the duty of such a leader is to promote and protect the values that the organization holds dear. In doing so the leader has a number of tasks. It is incumbent upon the leader to define the organization's mission and role and thus unearth the true commitments of the organization. He or she is the shaper of the character of the organization and in addition is responsible for maintaining its values and identity.

These functions are brought together in the introduction Selznick's, reprinted below, which goes a step further and describes how the leader can build institutions which embody enduring values. Institution building is a process of releasing energies and integrating the mission with the philosophy.

The nature and quality of leadership, in the sense of statesmanship, is an elusive but persistent theme in the history of ideas. Most writers have centered their attention on *political* statesmen, leaders of whole communities who sit in the high places where great issues are joined and settled. In our time, there is no abatement of the need to continue the great discussion, to learn how to reconcile idealism with expediency, freedom with organization.

But an additional emphasis is necessary. Ours is a pluralist society made up of many large, influential, relatively autonomous groups. The United States government itself consists of independently powerful agencies which do a great deal on their own initiative and are largely self-governing. These, and the institutions of industry, politics, education and other fields, often command large resources; their leaders are inevitably responsible for the material and psychological well-being of numerous constituents; and they have become increasingly *public* in nature, attached to such interests and dealing with such problems as affect the welfare of the entire community. In our society the need for statesmanship is widely diffused and beset by special problems. An understanding of leadership in both public and private organizations must have a high place on the agenda of social inquiry.

The scientific study of large organizations is certainly not neglected. Much has been learned in the fields of industrial management and public administration. Recent years have seen a lively interest in new approaches to scientific management and in the development of a 'theory of organization'. Among students of political science, sociology, economics, and business administration there is a steady search for fresh ways of looking at organization, for new 'models' to help us achieve a better use of human resources and a more adequate understanding of decision making.

Much of this interest has quite practical roots. The question most often asked or implied is: how can we make our organizations more *efficient?* How can we improve incentives, communication, and decision making so as to achieve a smoother-running operation? How can we do the job most surely and at the least cost? This is a necessary and reasonable quest, for there is no doubt that most organizations operate at levels well below their potential capacity.

But does a preoccupation with administrative efficiency lead us to the knottiest and most significant problems of leadership in large organizations? Should efficiency be the central concern of the president of a university or a large business, the head of a government agency or the director of a voluntary association? Are we getting at what is truly basic in the experience of institutional leaders? Are we helping to improve the self-knowledge – and thereby the competence – of men charged with leadership responsibilities? Are we able to link the development of managerial skills to the larger problems of policy? This essay is an attempt to deal with these questions by exploring the nature of critical decisions and of institutional leadership.

As we ascend the echelons of administration, the analysis of decision making becomes increasingly difficult, not simply because the decisions are more important or more complex, but because a new 'logic' emerges. The logic of efficiency applies most clearly to subordinate units, usually having rather clearly defined operating responsibilities, limited discretion, set communication channels, and a sure position in the command structure. At these lower levels we may expect to find effective use of rather simple devices for increasing efficiency and control; and it is here that scientific techniques of observation and experiment are likely to be most advanced and most successful.

The logic of efficiency loses force, however, as we approach the top of the pyramid. Problems at this level are more resistant to the ordinary approach of management experts. Mechanical metaphors – the organization as a 'smooth running machine' – suggest an overemphasis on neat organization and on efficient techniques of administration. It is probable that these emphases induce in the analyst a trained incapacity to observe the interrelation of policy and administration, with the result that the really critical experience of organizational leadership is largely overlooked. This may explain the coolness with which organizational studies are often received by leading administrators, particularly when these studies deal with top command and staff areas. Much of this coolness undoubtedly stems from a natural reaction against proposed changes which may threaten vested interests. Yet there is also a feeling among administrators that the studies offered are naïve and irrelevant, perhaps because they apply a logic which does not adequately reflect the real problems that the administrator himself must face.

The search for a fresh approach to administration has led to a considerable interest in 'human relations'. This interest has brought about a wider understanding of why people work and how they get along together, particularly in small scale group settings. The characteristics of small groups, especially the psychological aspects of communication and perception, have received much emphasis. There is no doubt that this work can and does tell us much about the human problems of participation in organizations. But the observer of large enterprises, if he tries to see them whole, is left with a sense of inadequacy. He feels a need to look beyond personal relations to the larger patterns of institutional development. Yet he knows also that no social process can be understood save as it is located in the behavior of individuals, and especially in their perceptions of themselves and each other. The problem is to link the larger view to the more limited one, to see how institutional change is produced by, and in turn shapes, the interaction of individuals in day to day situations. The closer we get to the areas of far-reaching decision, the greater is the need for this deeper and more comprehensive understanding of social organization.

The argument of this essay is quite simply stated: *the executive becomes a statesman as he makes the transition from administrative management to institutional leadership*. This shift entails a reassessment of his own tasks and of the needs of the enterprise. It is marked by a concern for the evolution of the organization as a whole, including its changing aims and capabilities. In a word, it means viewing the organization as an institution. To understand the nature of institutional leadership, we must have some notion of the meaning and significance of the term 'institution' itself.

Organizations and institutions

The most striking and obvious thing about an administrative organization is its formal system of rules and objectives. Here tasks, powers, and procedures are set out according to some officially approved pattern. This pattern purports to say how the work of the organization is to be carried on, whether it be producing steel, winning votes, teaching children, or saving souls. The organization thus designed is a technical instrument for mobilizing human energies and directing them toward set aims. We allocate tasks, delegate authority, channel communication and find some way of co-ordinating all that has been divided up and parcelled out. All this is conceived as an exercise in engineering; it is governed by the related ideals of rationality and discipline.

The term 'organization' thus suggests a certain bareness, a lean, no-nonsense system of consciously coordinated activities (Barnard, 1938). It refers to an *expendable tool*, a rational instrument engineered to do a job. An 'institution', on the other hand, is more nearly a natural product of social needs and pressures – a responsive, adaptive organism. This distinction is a matter of analysis, not of direct description. It does not mean that any given enterprise must be either one or the other. While an extreme case may closely approach either an 'ideal' organization or an 'ideal' institution, most living associations resist so easy a classification. They are complex mixtures of both designed and responsive behavior.

When we say that the Standard Oil Company or the Department of Agriculture is to be studied as an institution, we usually mean that we are going to pay some attention to its history and to the way it has been influenced by the social environment. Thus we may be interested in how its organization adapts itself to existing centers of power in the community, often in unconscious ways; from what strata of society its leadership is drawn and how this affects policy; how it justifies its existence ideologically. We may ask what underlying need in the larger community – not necessarily expressed or recognized by the people involved – is filled by the organization or by some of its practices. Thus, the phrase 'as a social institution' suggests an emphasis on problems and experiences that are not adequately accounted for within the narrower framework of administrative analysis.

Perhaps a classic example is the analysis of a political constitution as an institution. In such an inquiry the social and cultural conditions (class structure, traditional patterns of loyalty, educational level, etc.) that affect its viability are studied. We see how the formal charter is given life and meaning by the informal 'social constitution' in which it is imbedded. When the latter is absent, the constitution is likely to be weak and ineffective. Giving life to a constitution is partly a matter of achieving general consensus regarding proper ways of winning power and making laws. But much more is also involved. The working of the American constitutional order cannot readily be grasped without understanding the function of the party system in accommodating diverse interests, in blunting the edge of ideological conflicts, in winning for the community a progressive erasure of old issues as new ones arise. Proposals to change the parties into single minded ideological instruments strike at the institutional basis of the political order. These and similar problems have long been recognized. It is important, however, to make the transition from these great constitutional issues to the less dramatic problems of administration that also arise from the interplay of formal or legal systems and their social environments.

An awareness of the social setting of administrative activity goes beyond 'public relations'. The latter phrase suggests practices that leave the organization intact, essentially what it has always been, using routine devices for smoothing over difficulties with groups on whom it is dependent. Indeed, much is accomplished in this way. But when an enterprise begins to be more profoundly aware of dependence on outside forces, its very conception of itself may change, with consequences for recruitment, policy, and adminstrative organization at many levels. As a business, a college, or a government agency develops a distinctive clientele, the enterprise gains the stability that comes with a secure source of support, an easy channel of communication. At the same time, it loses flexibility. The process of institutionalization has set in.

The relation of an organization to the external environment is, however, only one source of institutional experience. There is also an internal social world to be considered. An organization is a group of living human beings. The formal or official design for living never completely accounts for what the participants do. It is always supplemented by what is called the 'informal structure', which arises as the individual brings into play his own personality, his special problems and interests. Formal relations coordinate roles or specialized activities, not persons. Rules apply to foremen and machinists, to clerks, sergeants and vice-presidents, yet no durable organization is able to hold human experience to these formally defined roles. In actual practice, men tend to interact as many-faceted persons, adjusting to the daily round in ways that spill over the neat boundaries set by their assigned roles.

The formal, technical system is therefore never more than a part of the living enterprise we deal with in action. The persons and groups who make it up are not content to be treated as manipulable or expendable. As human beings and not mere tools they have their own needs for self-protection and self-fulfillment – needs that may either sustain the formal system or undermine it. These human relations are a great reservoir of energy. They may be directed in constructive ways toward desired ends or they may become recalcitrant sources of frustration. One objective of sound management practice is to direct and control these internal social pressures.

The relations outlined on an organization chart provide a framework within which fuller and more spontaneous human behavior takes place. The formal system may draw upon that behavior for added strength; it will in its turn be subordinated to personal and group egotism. Every official and employee will try to use his position to satisfy his psychological needs. This may result in a gain for the organization if he accepts its goals and extends himself in its interests. But usually, even in the best circumstances, some price is paid in organizational rigidity.

Similarly, when a technically devised organizational unit becomes a social group – a unity of persons rather than of technicians – newly deployable energy is created; but this, too, has inherently divisive and frustrating potentialities. For the unity of persons breaks through the neat confines of rational organization and procedure; it creates new strivings, primarily for the protection of group integrity, that exert an unceasing influence on the formal pattern of delegation and control. This search for security and fulfillment is reflected in the struggle of individuals for place and preferment, in rivalry among units within the organization, and in commitment to ingrained ways of behaving. These are universal features of organizational life, and the problems they raise are perennial ones.

Of these problems, organizational rivalry may be the most important. Such rivalry mobilizes individual egotism while binding it to group goals. This may create a powerful force, threatening the unity of the larger enterprise. Hence it is that within every association there is the same basic constitutional problem, the same need for an accommodative balance between fragmentary group interests and the aims of the whole, as exists in any polity. The problem is aggravated in a special-purpose enterprise because the aims of the whole are more sharply defined, and therefore more vulnerable to divisive activity, than in the natural community.

Organizational rivalry has received a great deal of attention in connection with efforts to unify the United States military establishment. This case is especially instructive, because throughout the discussion the positive value of competition among military agencies has been emphasized. The rivalry in question here does not pertain primarily to combat or low-echelon units, but rather to 'headquarters' competition involving the struggle for funds and prestige among the services.

What arrangements, it is asked, will best protect legitimate competition among military services, yet maintain the needed integration of strategic and tactical planning? This broad question depends in turn on others: Who are the key participants in various kinds of organizational rivalry? Of what value is integrated training and should it take place at low levels or at high levels in the command structure? Do weak technical services need special protection against stronger rivals? What can this protection consist of? These and many similar 'constitutional' problems arise because of the natural tendency for parochial, self-protective interests of subordinate individuals and groups to be given an undue priority. As in all constitution making, the problem is to fit this spontaneously generated competition into a framework that will hold it to the interests of the whole.

Once we turn our attention to the emergence of natural social processes within a formal association, and the pressure of these on policy, we are quickly led to a wide range of interesting questions. Thus, the tendency for a group to develop fixed ways of perceiving itself and the world, often unconsciously, is of considerable importance. With this sort of problem in mind, a study of a military intelligence agency, for example, can go beyond the more routine aspects of administrative efficiency. The study should also consider whether any institutional factors affect the ability of the agency *to ask the right questions*. Are its questions related to a general outlook, a tacit image of itself and its task? Is this image tradition-bound? Is it conditioned by long established organizational practices? Is there a self-restricted outlook due to insecurities that motivate a safe (but narrow and compartmentalized) concept of military intelligence? A study of these problems would explore the conditions under which organizational self-protection induces *withdrawal* from rivalry rather than participation in it. More needs to be known about such pathological withdrawal for it, too – no less than excessive rivalry itself – may frustrate the rational development of organizations and programs.

The dynamics of organizational rivalry – not the mere documentation of its existence – has received very little systematic attention. This is a good example of an area of experience not adequately accounted for within the conceptual framework of administrative analysis. Organizational struggles are usually thought of as adventitious and subversive. This outlook inhibits the development of a body of knowledge *about* organizational rivalry, e.g. stating the conditions and consequences of factional victory, defeat and withdrawal, or indicating the way external pressures on an organization are reflected in internal controversy.

A similar sensitivity to internal social needs is assumed when we raise the issue in an even more delicate form: does the conventional organization of military services according to distinctive weapons result in the espousal of self-serving strategies? If there is an intimate relation between strategy and capability, then the strategically unguided development of weapons may create ultimately undesirable commitments to strategies that depend on these weapons. Is it not worth inquiring whether the ability to adapt military planning – including, especially, research and development – to politically significant goals is not inhibited by this organization of the services? The tendency to emphasize methods rather than goals is an important source of disorientation in all organizations. It has the value of stimulating full development of these methods, but it risks loss of adaptability and sometimes results in a radical substitution of means for ends. Leaders may feel more secure when they emphasize the exploitation of technical potentialities, but the difficult task of defining goals and adapting methods to them may be unfulfilled. This is so because the definition of goals requires an appraisal of many coordinate objectives – for example, political as well as military – whereas technical development can be more comfortably single minded.

Taking account of both internal and external social forces, institutional studies emphasize the *adaptive* change and evolution of organizational forms and practices. In these studies the story is told of new patterns emerging and old ones declining, not as a result of conscious design but as natural and largely unplanned adaptations to new situations. The most interesting and perceptive analyses of this type show the organization responding to a problem posed by its history, an adaptation significantly changing the role and character of the organization. Typically, institutional analysis sees legal or formal changes as recording and regularizing an evolution that has already been substantially completed informally.

Thus the emergence of the Operations Division as General Marshall's command post, eclipsing other sections of the General Staff, is an important theme in Cline's institutional history of that agency (Cline, 1951). In this work we see the contending forces, the changing problems of command, the informal accommodations of interest and power, all contributing to a developing pattern that was largely 'in the cards'. A similar study of the present Joint Chiefs of Staff organization would attempt to discern the direction of its evolution, keeping in mind as a hypothesis the potential emergence of a single chief for all the services. Such an analysis of a Research and Development Board would take account of the inherent instability of advisory bodies, the pressures for integration into the military command structure and for providing an immediate operational pay-off, as well as the possibilities of allaying these pressures without sacrificing the basic character of the agency.* Throughout, emphasis is on the group processes at work – how they generate new problems and force new adaptations.

This emphasis on adaptive change suggests that in attempting to understand large and relatively enduring organizations we must draw upon what we know about natural communities. In doing so we are led to consider such matters as the following:

---

* Although realistic studies of such organizations are not readily feasible (though not excluded) even at much lower echelons, historical analyses of similar but less 'sensitive' agencies can provide a more adequate basis for organization planning. A program of case studies, guided by theoretical sophistication and alertness to significant problems, can provide the data needed. An important beginning along these lines has been made by the Inter-University Case Program under the direction of Harold Stein. See his *Public Administration and Policy Development*, New York: Harcourt, Brace, 1952.

1 The development of administrative ideologies as conscious and unconscious devices of communication and self-defense. Just as doctrinal orthodoxies help natural communities to maintain social order, so, too, in administrative agencies, technical programs and procedures are often elaborated into official 'philosophies'. These help to build a homogeneous staff and ensure institutional continuity. Sometimes they are created and manipulated self-consciously, but most administrative ideologies emerge in spontaneous and unplanned ways, as natural aids to organizational security. A well formulated doctrine is remarkably handy for boosting internal morale, communicating the bases for decisions, and rebuffing outside claims and criticisms.

2 The creation and protection of elites. In the natural community elites play a vital role in the creation and protection of values. Similarly, in organizations, and especially those that have or strive for some special identity, the formation of elites is a practical problem of the first importance. Specialized academies, selective recruiting and many other devices help to build up the self-consciousness and the confidence of present and potential leaders. However, again as in the natural community, counter pressures work to break down the insulation of these elites and to warp their self-confidence. A problem of institutional leadership, as of statesmanship generally, is to see that elites do exist and function while inhibiting their tendency to become sealed off and to be more concerned with their own fate than with that of the enterprise as a whole. One answer, as in the Catholic Church, is to avoid selectivity in the *choice* of leaders while emphasizing intensive indoctrination in their *training*. The whole problem of leadership training, and more generally of forming and maintaining elites, should receive a high priority in scientific studies of organization and policy.

3 The emergence of contending interest groups, many of which bid for dominant influence in society. The simple protection of their identity, and the attempt to control the conditions of existence, stimulate the normal push and pull of these groups; and the bid for social dominance is reflected in the crises that signify underlying shifts in the distribution of power. The same natural processes go on within organizations, often stimulating the rivalry of formal administrative units, sometimes creating factions that cut across the official lines of communication and command. Here, too, there is normal day to day contention, and there is the attempt to become the dominant or 'senior' unit, as when a personnel department replaces an accounting division as the source from which general managers are recruited; or when a sales organization comes to dominate the manufacturing organization in product design. These changes cannot, however, be accounted for as simply the products of bureaucratic maneuver. The outcome of the contest is conditioned by a shift in the character and role of the enterprise. Many internal controversies, although stimulated by rather narrow impulses, provide the channels through which broader pressures on the organization are absorbed.

The natural tendencies cited here – the development of defensive ideologies, the dependence of institutional values on the formation and sustaining of elites, the existence of internal conflicts expressing group interests – only illustrate the many elements that combine to form the social structure of an organization. Despite their diversity, these forces have a unified effect. In their operation we see the way group values are formed, for together they define the commitments of the organization and give it a distinctive identity. In other words, to the extent that they are natural communities, organizations have a history; and this history is compounded of discernible and repetitive modes of responding to internal and external pressures. As these responses crystallize into definite patterns, a social structure emerges. The more fully developed its social structure, the more will the organization become valued for itself, not as a tool but as an institutional fulfillment of group integrity and aspiration.

Institutionalization is a *process*. It is something that happens to an organization over time, reflecting the organization's own distinctive history, the people who have been in it, the groups it embodies and the vested interests they have created, and the way it has adapted to its environment. For purposes of this essay, the following point is of special importance: The degree of institutionalization depends on how much leeway there is for personal and group interaction. The more precise an organization's goals, and the more specialized and technical its operations, the less opportunity will there be for social forces to affect its development. A university has more such leeway than most businesses, because its goals are less clearly defined and it can give more free play to internal forces and historical adaptation. But no organization of any duration is completely free of institutionalization. Later we shall argue that leadership is most needed among those organizations, and in those periods of organizational life, where there is most freedom from the determination of decisions by technical goals and methods.

In what is perhaps its most significant meaning, 'to institutionalize' is to *infuse with value* beyond the technical requirements of the task at hand. The prizing of social machinery beyond its technical role is largely a reflection of the unique way in which it fulfills personal or group needs. Whenever individuals become attached to an organization or a way of doing things as persons rather than as technicians, the result is a prizing of the device for its own sake. From the standpoint of the committed person, the organization is changed from an expendable tool into a valued source of personal satisfaction. Some manifestations of this process are quite obvious; others are less easily recognized. It is a commonplace that administrative changes are difficult when individuals have become habituated to and identified with long established procedures. For example, the shifting of personnel is inhibited when business relations become personal ones and there is resistance to any change that threatens rewarding ties. A great deal of energy in organizations is expended in a continuous effort to preserve the rational, technical, impersonal system against such counter pressures.

Less generally recognized is the effect of this personal involvement on the rational choice of methods and goals. We have already hinted at the importance of 'self-images' in, say, restricting the outlook of military intelligence and similar agencies. These self-images are natural products of organizational experience. They provide the individual with an ordered approach to his day to day problems, a way of responding to the world consistently yet involuntarily, in accordance with approved perspectives yet without continuous reference to explicit and formalized rules. This consistent outlook or orientation is indicated when organizational names are applied to individuals as labels for characteristic ways of thinking and working, as when we speak of a 'regular army' or a 'Foreign Service' man. By long habituation, sometimes also as a result of aggressive indoctrination, the individual absorbs a way of perceiving and evaluating his experience. This reduces his anxiety by lending the world of fact a familiar cast; and it helps assure an easy conformity with established practice.

As in the case of all institutionalization, the development and transmission of self-images is useful but potentially frustrating. To mold the minds of individuals according to a definite pattern create a homogeneous organization, and this is an enormous aid to communication. A broad context of 'understood' meanings ensures that in the performance of assigned tasks the spirit as well as the letter will be observed. Similarly, emotional identification with the organization creates resources of energy that may increase day to day effort and, especially, be summoned in times of crisis or threat. But these commitments are costly. They bind the organization to specific aims and procedures, often greatly limiting the freedom of the leadership to deploy its resources, and reducing the capacity of the organization to survive under new conditions.

The test of infusion with value is *expendability*. If an organization is merely an instrument, it will be readily altered or cast aside when a more efficient tool becomes available. Most organizations are thus expendable. When value infusion takes place, however, there is a resistance to change. People feel a sense of personal loss; the 'identity' of the group or community seems somehow to be violated; they bow to economic or technological considerations only reluctantly, with regret. A case in point is the perennial effort to save San Francisco's cable cars from replacement by more economical forms of transportation. The Marine Corps has this institutional halo, and it resists adminstrative measures that would submerge its identity. In 1950, President Truman became irritated with political pressure favoring Marine Corps membership on the Joint Chiefs of Staff. He wrote a letter calling the Marines the Navy's 'police force' and likening their 'propaganda machine' to Stalin's. This raised a storm of protest which ended with a presidential apology.

From the standpoint of social systems rather than persons, organizations become infused with value as they come to symbolize the community's aspirations, its sense of identity. Some organizations perform this function more readily and fully than others. An organization that does take on this symbolic meaning has some claim on the community to avoid liquidation or transformation on purely technical or economic grounds. The Marine Corps has this halo far more than other military units and is correspondingly less expendable.

All this is a relative matter and one of degree. With respect to the national community most of the many thousands of organizations in the country are not highly valued for themselves, although certain principles on which they are based, such as free speech or competition, may have deep cultural roots. On the other hand, special groups, such as college alumni, are often urged to keep some organization from dying for lack of support. For the group that participates directly in it, an organization may acquire much institutional value, yet in the eyes of the larger community the organization may be readily expendable.

Both personal and social commitments combine to weaken the purely technical significance of organizations. Beginning as a tool, the organization derives added meaning from the psychological and social functions it performs. In doing so it becomes valued for itself. To be sure, the personal and group bonds that make for institutionalization are not wholly separable. As the individual works out his special problems, seeking his own satisfactions, he helps to tie the organization into the community's institutional network. Personal incentives may spark this absorption, and provide the needed energy; but its character and direction will be shaped by values already existent in the community at large. Similarly, although organizational controversy may be directly motivated by narrow personal and group aims, the contending programs usually reflect ideological differences in the larger arena. In this way, the internal struggle for power becomes a channel through which external environmental forces make themselves felt. This is, indeed, a classic function of the American political party system; but less formal and recognized groupings within administrative organizations follow the same pattern. Organizations do not so much create values as embody them. As this occurs, the organization becomes increasingly institutionalized.

The transformation of expendable technical organizations into institutions is marked by a *concern for self-maintenance*. A living association blends technical aims and procedures with personal desires and group interests. As a result, various elements in the association have a stake in its continued existence. Moreover, the aims of the organization may require a certain permanence and stability. There is a need to accommodate internal interests and adapt to outside forces, in order to maintain the organization as a 'going concern', minimize risks, and achieve long run as well as short run objectives. An important sign of this development is that the leaders become security conscious and are often willing to sacrifice quick returns for the sake of stability. The history of the labour movement is replete with efforts to win union security through provisions for compulsory membership and automatic deduction of dues payments from wages. These objectives look to the long run maintenance of the union rather than to immediate gains for the members.

There is a close relation between 'infusion with value' and 'self-maintenance'. As an organization acquires a self, a distinctive identity, it becomes an institution. This involves the taking on of values, ways of acting and believing that are deemed important for their own sake. From then on self-maintenance becomes more than bare organizational survival; it becomes a struggle to preserve the uniqueness of the group in the face of new problems and altered circumstances.

To summarize: organizations are technical instruments, designed as means to definite goals. They are judged on engineering premises; they are expendable. Institutions, whether conceived as groups or practices, may be partly engineered, but they have also a 'natural' dimension. They are products of interaction and adaptation; they become the receptacles of group idealism; they are less readily expendable.

Some premises about leadership

Leadership is not a familiar, everyday idea, as readily available to common sense as to social science. It is a slippery phenomenon that eludes them both. What leaders do is hardly self-evident. And it likely that much failure of leadership results from an inadequate understanding of its true nature and tasks. Most of this essay will be devoted to identifying and analyzing the chief functions of institutional leadership. By way of introduction, however, it may be helpful to state a few simple guiding ideas here.

1 *Leadership is a kind of work done to meet the needs of a social situation.* Possibly there are some individuals more likely to be leaders than others, possessed of distinguishing personal traits or capacities.* Whether or not this is so, we shall here be concerned with leadership as a specialized form of activity, a kind of work or function. Identifying what leaders do certainly bears on (and is perhaps indispensable to) the discovery of requisite personal attributes; but the questions are of a different kind and may be treated separately.

   To know the nature of the work done by leaders, we must know something about the social situations they are called upon to handle. This immediately

---

* This problem has received considerable attention, with largely negative but still inconclusive results. See Stogdill, Ralph M. (1948). 'Personal Factors Associated with Leadership: A Survey of the Literature', *J. Psychology*, 25, 35–71; also Jenkins, William O. (1947). 'A Review of Leadership Studies with Particular Reference to Military Problems', *Psychological Bulletin*, 44: 54–77.

suggests that there must be a very wide variety of activities associated with leadership.* However, it does not follow that the *nature* of leadership varies with each social situation. If that were so, there would be nothing determinate about it; its study would be a scientific blind alley. In fact, of course, we must assume that significant leadership patterns are relatively few; and that these patterns are related to *types* of social situations. This means that certain very general activities of leaders – e.g. facilitating communication within the group – reflect equally general characteristics of all human groups; and that the functions of leadership will be understood only as we develop a better understanding of the main types of groups and the recurrent problems they face. In other words, a theory of leadership is dependent on a theory of social organization.

We shall not be concerned here with all leadership, but with leadership in large scale organizations. This will require some consideration of the nature of such enterprises, including the characteristic problems that arise within them. It will be necessary to understand the institutional aspects of large scale organizations, for the central argument will stress the close connection between these aspects and the key functions of leadership. Although institutional leadership must share the general characteristics of all leadership, we shall not deal with the latter problem directly.

2 *Leadership is not equivalent to office holding or high prestige or authority or decision making.* It is not helpful to identify leadership with whatever is done by people in high places. The activity we have in mind may or may not be engaged in by those who are formally in positions of authority. This is inescapable if we are to develop a theory that will be useful in diagnosing cases of inadequate leadership on the part of persons in authority. If this view is correct, it means that only some (and sometimes none) of the activities of decision makers are leadership activities. Here again, understanding leadership requires understanding of a broader social process. If some types of decisions are more closely related to leadership activities than others, we should learn what they are. To this end in this analysis let us make a

---

* Indeed, the current literature on this subject, in part as a reaction against the 'trait' approach, in part due to the influence of 'situational' or 'field' theory in social psychology, has made this a central conclusion. Thus Jenkins, op. cit., p. 75, finds: 'Leadership is specific to the particular situation under investigation. Who becomes the leader of a given group engaging in a particular activity and what the leadership characteristics are in the given case are a function of the specific situation, including the measuring instruments employed. There is a wide variation in the characteristics of individuals who became leaders in similar situations, and even greater divergence in leadership in different situations.' But note the following by Stogdill, op. cit., p. 65: 'The evidence suggest that leadership is a relation that exists between persons in a social situation, and that persons who are leaders in one situation may not necessarily be leaders in other situations. Must it then be assumed that leadership is entirely incidental, haphazard, and unpredictable? Not at all. The very studies which provide the strongest arguments for the situational nature of leadership also supply the strongest evidence indicating that leadership patterns as well as non-leadership patterns of behavior are persistent and relatively stable.'

distinction between 'routine' and 'critical' decision making.

3 *Leadership is dispensable.* The word 'leadership' has its own halo, easily inviting the tacit assumption that, being a good thing, it is always in order. It may indeed be that all human groups require at all times *some* leadership activities. But if leadership is anything determinate, we should know how to distinguish its presence from its absence; similarly, if there are some social situations that especially require leadership, we should know how to tell them apart from other social situations. The idea is developed in this essay that leadership is not equally necessary in all large scale organizations, or in any one at all times, and that it becomes dispensable as the natural processes of institutionalization become eliminated or controlled. This will provide some clues to the general conditions that call for leadership decisions.

These premises emphasize the futility of attempting to understand leadership apart from the broader organizational experience of which it is a phase. A theory of leadership will necessarily reflect the level of sophistication we have reached in the study of organization. We are dealing with an activity, with a function, with work done; we can make no more sense of it than is allowed by our understanding of the field within which that activity takes place.

The default of leadership

When institutional leadership fails, it is perhaps more often by default than by positive error or sin. Leadership is lacking when it is needed; and the institution drifts, exposed to vagrant pressures, readily influenced by short run opportunistic trends. This default is partly a failure of nerve, partly a failure of understanding. It takes nerve to hold a course; it takes understanding to recognize and deal with the basic sources of institutional vulnerability.

One type of default is the failure to set goals. Once an organization becomes a 'going concern', with many forces working to keep it alive, the people who run it can readily escape the risk of defining its purposes. This evasion stems partly from the hard intellectual labor involved, a labor that often seems but to increase the burden of already onerous daily operations. In part, also, there is the wish to avoid conflicts with those in and out of the organization who would be threatened by a sharp definition of purpose, with its'attendant claims and responsibilities. Even business firms find it easy to fall back on conventional phrases, such as that 'our goal is to make profit', phrases which offer little guidance in the formulation of policy.

A critique of leadership, we shall argue, must include this emphasis on the leader's responsibility to define the mission of the enterprise. This view is not new. It is important because so much of administrative analysis takes the goal of the organization as given, whereas in many crucial instances this is precisely what is problematic. We shall also suggest that the analysis of goals is itself dependent on an understanding of the organization's social structure. In other words, the purposes we have or can have depend on what we are or what we can be. In statesmanship no less than in the search for personal wisdom, the Socratic dictum – know thyself – provides the ultimate guide.

Another type of default occurs when goals, however neatly formulated, enjoy only a superficial acceptance and do not genuinely influence the total structure of the enterprise. Truly accepted values must infuse the organization at many levels, affecting the perspectives and attitudes of personnel, the relative importance of staff activities, the distribution of authority, relations with outside groups, and many other matters. Thus if a large corporation asserts a wish to change its role in the community from a narrow emphasis on profit-making to a larger social responsibility (even though the ultimate goal remains some combination of survival and profit making ability), it must explore the implications of such a change for decision making in a wide variety of organizational activities. We shall stress that the task of building special values and a distinctive competence into the organization is a prime function of leadership.

In this sense, the leader is an agent of institutionalization, offering a guiding hand to a process that would otherwise occur more haphazardly, more readily subject to the accidents of circumstance and history. This is not to say that the leader is free to do as he wishes, to mold the organization according to his heart's desire, restrained only by the quality of his imagination and the strength of his will. Self-knowledge means knowledge of limits as well as of potentialities.

The default of leadership shows itself in an acute form when *organizational* achievement or survival is confounded with *institutional* success. To be sure, no institutional leader can avoid concern for the minimum conditions of continued organizational existence. But he fails if he permits sheer organizational achievement, in resources, stability, or reputation, to become the criterion of his success. A university led by administrators without a clear sense of values to be achieved may fail dismally while steadily growing larger and more secure.

Finally, the role of the institutional leader should be clearly distinguished from that of the 'interpersonal' leader. The latter's task is to smooth the path of human interaction, ease communication, evoke personal devotion, and allay anxiety. His expertness has relatively little to do with content; he is more concerned with persons than with policies. His main contribution is to the efficiency of the enterprise. The institutional leader, on the other hand, *is primarily an expert in the promotion and protection of values*. The interpretation that follows takes this idea as a starting point, exploring its meaning and implications.

References

Barnard, C. I. (1938). *The Functions of the Executive*. Cambridge: Harvard University Press, p. 73.

Cline, Ray S. (1951). *Washington Command Post: The Operations Division*. Washington DC: Office of the Chief of Military History, Department of the Army.

Reproduced from Selznick, Philip (1957). *Leadership in Administration: A Sociological Interpretation* by permission of University of California Press.

Attention through vision
Warren Bennis and Burt Nanus

Warren Bennis is an internationally recognized scholar of organizational behaviour and has written prolifically in the area of change, leadership and organization development. He received his PhD in Social Sciences and Economics from the Massachussetts Institute of Technology in 1955. He is the Vice President for Academic Development, State University of New York at Buffalo. Burt Nanus has written on a number of subjects including general management. *Leaders* is a contemporary work based on interviews with 90 CEOs. The sample of companies included 45 from Fortune's top 200 list and the rest from smaller companies. Three basic questions were addressed during the interviews: 'What are your strengths and weaknesses?', 'Was there any particular experience or event in your life that influenced your management philosophy or style?' and 'What were the major decision points in your career and how do you feel about your choices now?'

As a result of these interviews, the authors arrived at four strategies for good leadership. These are 'attention through vision'; 'meaning through communication'; 'trust through positioning'; and 'the deployment of self through (1) positive self regard and (2) the Wallenda factor'.

Meaning through communication is about the communication of the company's identity to its people in a way that aligns people behind the organization's goals. Trust through positioning implies the maintenance of the organization's predictability in so far as its identity and goals are concerned. The fourth strategy, the deployment of self, concerns the personal involvement of the leader and his confidence in his skills and abilities to steer the organization. The Wallenda factor is the ability to respond to failure and benefit from it.

The chapter we have selected describes the first strategy defined by Bennis and Nanus, attention through vision. Attention through vision is the creation of a common purpose for people in the organization to live by. Vision helps to build a consensus within the organization and this helps in the decision making of the organization. People can be fired up to achieve the goals and objectives required by the organization to attain the vision.

Both Mr Durant and Mr Ford had unusual vision, courage, daring, imagination, and foresight. Both gambled everything on the future of the automobile at a time when fewer were made in a year than are now made in a couple of days . . . Both created great and lasting institutions.   Alfred P. Sloan Jr.

I have a dream.   Martin Luther King Jr.

When William Paley took over at CBS in 1928, at the age of 27, it had no stations of its own, was losing money, and was insignificant in an industry completely dominated by NBC. Within 10 years, CBS had 114 stations and was earning $27.7 million. More than 40 years later, with Paley still at the helm, CBS was a dominant force in the broadcasting industry. As David Halberstam (Halberstam, 1979) has described Paley's ability:

The critical years were the early ones. What he had from the start was a sense of vision, a sense of what might be. It was as if he could sit in New York in his tiny office with his almost bankrupt company and see not just his own desk, or the row of potential advertisers outside along Madison Avenue, but millions of the American people out in the hinterlands, so many of them out there, almost alone, many of them in homes as yet unconnected to electricity, people alone with almost no form of entertainment other than radio. It was his sense, his confidence that he could reach them, that he had something for them, that made him different. He could envision the audience at a time when there was in fact no audience. He not only had the vision, he knew how to harness it, he could see that the larger the audience, the greater the benefit to the network, because it would mean that many more advertisers would want to participate . . . The larger the audience, the more time he could sell. To achieve that goal, he had something to offer – indeed to give away – by making his programs available to affiliate stations.

Over and over again, the leaders we spoke to told us that they did the same things when they took charge of their organizations – they paid attention to what was going on, they determined what part of the events at hand would be important for the future of the organization, they set a new direction, and they concentrated the attention of everyone in the organization on it. We soon found that this was a universal principle of leadership, as true for orchestra conductors, army generals, football coaches and school superintendents as for corporate leaders. But if it all seems too easy, there is a catch. How do leaders know what is important for the future of their organizations, and how do they choose the new directions? That is what we must examine; but first we need to discuss why we think the principle works and why it is so fundamental to effective leadership.

Vision and organizations

To choose a direction, a leader must first have developed a mental image of a possible and desirable future state of the organization. This image, which we call a *vision*, may be as vague as a dream or as precise as a goal or mission statement. The critical point is that a vision articulates a view of a realistic, credible, attractive future for the organization, a condition that is better in some important ways than what now exists.

A vision is a target that beckons. When John Kennedy set a goal of putting a man on the moon by 1970 or Sanford Weill aimed to make American Express the world's leading investment banking company in five years, they were focusing attention on worthwhile and attainable achievements. Note also that a vision always refers to a *future* state, a condition that does not presently exist and never existed before. With a vision, the leader provides the all-important bridge from the present to the future of the organization.

To understand why vision is so central to leadership success, we only need reflect on why organizations are formed in the first place. An organization is a group of people engaged in a common enterprise. Individuals join the enterprise in the hope of receiving rewards for their participation. Depending upon the organization and the individuals involved, the rewards might be largely economic, or they might be dominated by psychosocial considerations – status, self-esteem, a sense of accomplishment, a meaningful existence. Just as the individual derives rewards from his or her role in the organization, so too does the organization derive its rewards from finding an appropriate niche in the larger society. The organization's rewards might also be economic (profits, growth, access to resources) and/or psychosocial (prestige, legitimacy, power, and recognition).

So, on the one hand, an organization seeks to maximize its rewards from its position in the external environment and, on the other hand, individuals in the organization seek to maximize their reward from their participation in the organization. When the organization has a clear sense of its purpose, direction, and desired future state and when this image is widely shared, individuals are able to find their own roles both in the organization and in the larger society of which they are a part. This empowers individuals and confers status upon them because they can see themselves as part of a worthwhile enterprise. They gain a sense of importance, as they are transformed from robots blindly following instructions to human beings engaged in a creative and purposeful venture. When individuals feel that they can make a difference and that they can improve the society in which they are living through their participation in an organization, then it is much more likely that they will bring vigor and enthusiasm to their tasks and that the results of their work will be mutually reinforcing. Under these conditions, the human energies of the organization are aligned toward a common end, and a major precondition for success has been satisfied.

Consultants often report that they can feel this energy almost from the first moment they enter a corporation. It was present at Polaroid when Edwin Land led that firm into a new age of photography, and at Sears, Roebuck and Co when the decision was made to become a financial services powerhouse. It takes the form of enthusiasm, commitment, pride, willingness to work hard and 'go the extra mile'. It is notably absent in some of the large conglomerates, where every month brings a new deal that proclaims to the employees that management is going into or out of a new business – or, more likely, isn't really sure where it is going.

A shared vision of the future also suggests measures of effectiveness for the organization and for all its parts. It helps individuals distinguish between what's good and what's bad for the organization, and what it's worthwhile to want to achieve. And most important, it makes it possible to distribute decision making widely. People can make difficult decisions without having to appeal to higher levels in the organization each time because they know what end results are desired. Thus, in a very real sense, individual behavior can be shaped, directed and coordinated by a shared and empowering vision of the future.

As John Young, head of Hewlett-Packard, said, 'successful companies have a consensus from top to bottom on a set of overall goals. The most brilliant management strategy will fail if that consensus is missing'. (Carr, 1984)

We have here one of the clearest distinctions between the leader and the manager. By focusing attention on a vision, the leader operates on the *emotional and spiritual resources* of the organization, on its values, commitment, and aspirations. The manager, by contrast, operates on the *physical resources* of the organization, on its capital, human skills, raw materials and technology. Any competent manager can make it possible for people in the organization to earn a living. An excellent manager can see to it that work is done productively and efficiently, on schedule, and with a high level of quality. It remains for the effective leader, however, to help people in the organization know pride and satisfaction in their work. Great leaders often inspire their followers to high levels of achievement by showing them how their work contributes to worthwhile ends. It is an emotional appeal to some of the most fundamental of human needs – the need to be important, to make a difference, to feel useful, to be a part of a successful and worthwhile enterprise.

With all of these benefits, one would think that organizations would take great care to develop a clear image of their desired future, but that doesn't seem to be the case. Instead, the visions of many organizations are out of focus and lack coherence. The reasons for this blurred focus are myriad.

- Within the past several decades, important new interpretations have been given to the role of the family, the quality of life, the work ethic, the social
- responsibility of business, the rights of minorities, and many other values and institutions that were once thought to be enduring and permanent.
- Telecommunications and rapid transportation have helped to make the world increasingly interdependent for products, ideas, jobs and resources.
- The quickening pace of innovation has led to the specialization of experts and massive problems of coordinating technical workers.
- The general willingness to experiment with new social forms and norms has fractured society into a diversity of life-styles, each with its own product preferences.
- Workers are seeking and receiving a much greater voice in decisions that were once the exclusive territory of management.

All these forces and more contribute to the massive and growing complexity we see in today's world. This, in turn, creates great uncertainty and an overabundance of conflicting images in many organizations. The larger the organization, the greater the number of images is likely to be, the greater their complexity of interaction, and the quicker their shift in emphasis over time.

All these things tend to cause organizational vertigo and lead to myopia. At the same time, they tend to make vision more imperative for the functional success of the organization, since without a coherent view of the future, these forces would conspire to shatter it in every direction. This explains, for example, why Thornton Bradshaw had to be hired away from ARCO to restore focus and a sense of purpose to the giant RCA corporation. Starting with a strong base in radio, television and communications, RCA had drifted into such diverse fields as auto rental and financial services under a succession of presidents, until it had become nearly paralyzed by conflicting images of where it should be headed. But where does the leader's vision come from?

Paying attention: the leader's search for vision

Historians tend to write about great leaders as if they possessed transcendent genius, as if they were capable of creating their visions and sense of destiny out of some mysterious inner resource. Perhaps some do, but upon closer examination it usually turns out that the vision did not originate with the leader personally but rather from others. For example, Harold Williams told us that when he arrived at UCLA to take his new position as dean of its Graduate

School of Management, 'it was really the faculty that brought together the concept of what it is we ought to do. They had the vision'. Other leaders looked elsewhere. John Kennedy spent a great deal of time reading history and studying the ideas of great thinkers. Martin Luther King Jr found many of his ideas in the study of religious and ethical ideologies as well as in the traditions of his own and other peoples. Lenin was greatly influenced by the scholarship of Karl Marx, in much the same way as many contemporary business leaders are influenced by the works of leading economists and management scholars. Alfred P.Sloan's visions for the future of General Motors were greatly shaped by the prevailing cultural paradigm – the 'American Dream' and the role of capitalism in it. Steve Jobs at Apple and Edwin Land at Polaroid were able to develop their visions from logical processes, mostly by seeking the technical limits of known technologies.

In all these cases, the leader may have been the one who chose the image from those available at the moment, articulated it, gave it form and legitimacy, and focused attention on it, but the leader only rarely was the one who conceived of the vision in the first place. Therefore, the leader must be a superb listener, particularly to those advocating new or different images of the emerging reality. Many leaders establish both formal and informal channels of communication to gain access to these ideas. Most leaders also spend a substantial portion of their time interacting with advisers, consultants, other leaders, scholars, planners, and a wide variety of other people both inside and outside their own organizations in this search. Successful leaders, we have found, are *great askers*, and they do pay attention.

Consider a typical example. Suppose you've been asked to take charge of a regional bank operating in the state of California. The board of directors has turned to you for leadership as a result of your success with a smaller bank in another state. How will you develop a sense of direction in your new circumstances? To whom will you pay attention, and how, to help you develop an appropriate vision of the future? Basically, there are three sources from which to seek guidance – the past, the present, and alternative images of future possibilities. We'll consider each of these in turn.

The past

One obvious way to start is to reflect on your own experiences with other banks to identify analogies and precedents that might apply to the new situation. Next, you'll talk to leaders at other banks to collect their experiences with different approaches. You will surely want to learn about the history of the bank you are joining so you'll be able to understand how it reached its current status and what qualities contributed to its past successes and failures. This you'll get by talking to a wide variety of your new colleagues up and down the organization.

As you do this, you'll be building a mental model of what worked and what didn't work for this and similar banks in the past. You will be identifying some long term trends – say, in deposits or loan experiences – that might be projected into the future as a first approximation of where the bank is heading if it continues as in the past. You'll collect thoughts about how the bank's performance has been linked to outside indicators – say, the state of the economy, interest rates or development of the local community. And, of course, you'll pay attention to all the historical data you can get your hands on to increase your understanding of what this particular bank has been trying to do in the past, how successful it has been, and why.

The present

There is a lot to learn about the future from looking all around you at what is happening right now. For example, if you think about the year 1995, most of the buildings, roads, cities, people, corporations, and government agencies that will exist then are already here. The present provides a first approximation of the human, organizational and material resources out of which the future will be formed. By studying these resources, it is possible to develop an understanding of the constraints and opportunities for their use and the conditions under which they may grow, decline, interact, or self-destruct. As a banker, you'll pay a lot of attention to your current managers and their potential for development, to your current customer mix and the opportunities for expanding the services offered to them, to the locations of your branches, to your existing loan portfolios, and to what your competitors are doing.

There are early warning signals of impending change all around you. Your market researchers, for example, should be able to identify growing markets at an early stage of development. The plans of politicians and business leaders are often widely reported. Public opinion polls document changing values and needs, and special surveys in your own field of financial services are often reported in the trade press. In fact, trend monitoring to provide early warning is a large and growing industry in the United States.

Finally, you can conduct small experiments in your own bank. Suppose you are considering a major refocusing of the bank's attention in the direction of, say, loans for small businesses, or the professions, or particular industries. You can set up one branch or a small division with instructions to devote all its energies to the chosen area for some period of time, just as a chemical company develops a pilot plant before making a major commitment. You have, in effect, created a laboratory in which to experiment with your new vision.

The future

Your vision for the bank, as we have pointed out, will have to be set in some future time, so you need to study the conditions that may prevail at that time. Actually, although no one can predict what these conditions will be, there are many clues. Some sources of information have already been discussed – long term trends, particularly in demography and resource usage; planning documents at the international, national, state and corporate levels; the intentions and visions of policymakers in all kinds of organizations; public opinion polls; and the leading edges of phenomena that are expected to increase greatly in the future. But there are a few more sources of information.

You could look for structural clues to the future. For example, you might conclude that unless the government reverses its recent deregulation decisions, strong new competitors will continue to enter the banking business and a major restructuring of the industry will occur. You could then look at the kinds of structural changes and commitments being made by some of these potential competitors – Sears, Roebuck and Co., American Express, Prudential, and so on – and develop a scenario of what the marketplace may look like if all these changes are made. You could then go on to examine the implications of such a scenario for specific customer groups, for the economy in general, for the investment community, and ultimately for the banking industry and your particular bank.

Beyond structural clues, you could obtain forecasts of all kinds to study: economic projections, demographic analyses, all kinds of industry forecasts, and the like. You could explore some of the intellectual ideas that may shape the future: philosophical works, science fiction novels, political party platforms, and books by leading sociologists, political scientists and futurists. There are harbingers of future technological developments in research and developmental laboratories, technical papers presented at professional meetings, and government reports.

Thus, far from being devoid of information, you are likely to be inundated with information about the future, though only a small part may provide useful benchmarks or signposts in developing your vision for the bank. It is in the *interpretation* of this information that the real art of leadership lies. Just as the historian attempts to take piles of information about the past and construct an interpretation of the forces that may have been at work, so does the leader select, organize, structure, and interpret information about the future in an attempt to construct a viable and credible vision. But the leader has one distinctive advantage over the historian in that much of the future can be invented or designed. By synthesizing an appropriate vision, the leader is influential in shaping the future itself.

Synthesizing vision: the leader's choice of direction

All of the leaders to whom we spoke seemed to have been masters at selecting, synthesizing and articulating an appropriate vision of the future. Later, we learned that this was a common quality of leaders down through the ages. Consider, for example, how a contemporary biographer of Napoleon, Louis Madelin, described him:

> He would deal with three or four alternatives at the same time and endeavor to conjure up every possible eventuality – preferably the worst. This foresight, the fruit of meditation, generally enabled him to be ready for any setback; nothing ever took him by surprise . . . His vision, as I have said, was capable of both breadth and depth. Perhaps the most astonishing characteristic of his intellect was the combination of idealism and realism which enabled him to face the most exalted visions at the same time as the most insignificant realities. And, indeed, he was in a sense a visionary, a dreamer of dreams. (Hutt, 1972)

The task of synthesizing an appropriate direction for the organization is complicated by the many dimensions of vision that may be required. Leaders require *foresight*, so that they can judge how the vision fits into the way the environment of the organization may evolve; *hindsight*, so that the vision does not violate the traditions and culture of the organization; *a world view*, within which to interpret the impact of possible new developments and trends; *depth perception*, so that the whole picture can be seen in appropriate detail and perspective; *peripheral vision*, so that the possible responses of competitors and other stakeholders to the new direction can be comprehended; and a process of *revision*, so that all visions previously synthesized are constantly reviewed as the environment changes. Beyond this, decisions must be made about the appropriate time horizon to address, the simplicity or complexity of the image, the extent to which it will represent continuity with the past as opposed to a radical transformation, the degree of optimism or pessimism it will contain, its realism and credibility, and its potential impact on the organization.

If there is a spark of genius in the leadership function at all, it must lie in this transcending ability, a kind of magic, to assemble – out of all the variety of images, signals, forecasts and alternatives – a clearly articulated vision of the future that is at once simple, easily understood, clearly desirable and energizing.

Let's return to our banker example to see what might be involved. To this point, we have suggested how, as a new leader, you might collect all kinds of information that provides the raw material for a new vision of the future. Since vision cannot be limitless and still be credible to people in the organization, you will need to draw some boundaries. The vision should be projected in time and space beyond the boundaries of ordinary planning activities in the bank, but it should not be so far distant as to be beyond the ability of incumbents in the organization to realize. Perhaps you will decide to focus on a 10-year goal, far enough away to permit really dramatic change and yet within the comprehension and career aspirations of much of the current workforce. Perhaps too, you will want to move beyond the boundaries of current operations to include major new fields of activity such as personal financial planning or international banking or to focus on a broad range of services to one or more specific target markets, such as high-technology industry.

The actual boundaries chosen will depend heavily on values as well. Your own values will determine which alternatives you seriously consider and the way they are evaluated. For example, Harold Williams now heads the J. Paul Getty Museum and Foundation, but his values were formed during a distinguished career in industry, academia and public service. Thus, it is not surprising that he is steering the Getty Foundation in the direction of preservation and scholarship and has promised not to allow the vast Getty fortune to be used to bid art prices up so high that other museums will be unable to acquire new works or serve their publics.

The values of the rest of the people in the bank, as reflected in the prevailing ideology, also suggest limits to the amount of change that might reasonably be expected. Values, for example, might dictate that whatever the new vision for the future of the bank is, it should emphasize quality and excellence of service rather than price or breadth of service.

With information and some boundary conditions in mind, you will try to understand the possible alternatives and weigh how attractive they are. Your most powerful tool for this purpose is the mental model you have built up over time of how the world works and how your bank operates in it. As a wise leader, you will have tested this mental model many times in discussions with key executives, consultants, and others who have also thought deeply about the future of the bank. If you have access to a computer modeling facility and if the occasion justifies the cost, then a more formal, quantitative model can also be built.

Much of this analysis will have to be a series of 'judgment calls', but it is possible to suggest some of the questions that should be addressed, including the following:

- What are the institutions that have a stake in the future of this bank, and what is it that they would like to see happen?
- What are the possible indicators of performance for the bank, and how can they be measured?
- What would happen to the bank if it continued on its present path without any major changes?
- What early warning signals might you detect if the external environment of the bank were in fact to change substantially?
- What could you do to alter the course of events, and what would the consequences of your actions be?

- What resources does your bank possess or can it obtain to act in the various futures that are possible?
- Of the alternative possible futures for the bank and its environments, which are more likely to be favorable to survival and success?

Through a series of questions such as these, patterns may appear that suggest viable alternative visions. You must then synthesize all this information into a single vision, and here is where the art form of leadership really comes into play. The synthesis of a vision involves a great degree of judgment and, not infrequently, considerable intuition and creativity as well. Let us assume that in the banking example, you have decided that the future of your bank, all things considered, would be most enhanced if it concentrated its attention on serving high-technology companies, particularly in newly emerging industries, with a wide range of financial services. It still remains to translate this vision into action.

Focusing attention: the leader's search for commitment

The leader may generate new views of the future and may be a genius at synthesizing and articulating them, but this makes a difference only when the vision has been successfully communicated throughout the organization and effectively institutionalized as a guiding principle. Leaders are only as powerful as the ideas they can communicate. The leader's basic philosophy must be: 'We have seen what this organization can be, we undertand the consequences of that vision, and now we must act to make it so.'

A vision cannot be established in an organization by edict, or by the exercise of power or coercion. It is more an act of persuasion, of creating an enthusiastic and dedicated commitment to a vision because it is right for the times, right for the organization, and right for the people who are working in it.

We have found in our discussions with leaders that visions can often be communicated best by metaphors, or models – as when a political leader promises 'a chicken in every pot' or a phone company asks you to 'reach out and touch someone'. Perhaps in our banking example, it might be something like 'innovative banking for innovative companies', or 'financial services at the leading edge'.

In any communication, some distortion takes place, but the great leader seems to be able to find just the right metaphor that clarifies the idea and minimizes distortion. In fact, the right metaphor often transcends verbal communication altogether; like a good poem or song, it is much more than mere words. It 'feels right', it appeals at the gut level, it resonates with the listener's own emotional needs, it somehow 'clicks'.

Another way the leader communicates a new vision is by consistently acting on it and personifying it. Perhaps that is why so many corporate leaders have lately sought to appear in their firms' commercials, where some, like Lee Iacocca, do an outstanding job of communicating a new spirit. Others, like Ross Perot and Ted Turner, have shown by their own personal daring and adventure how innovative and risk taking they expect their own firms (EDS and Turner Broadcasting) to be. When Linden H. Blue recently took over as president of Beech Aircraft, he initiated a new technical thrust. As if to personify the new energy, he started a vigorous personal exercise program, reported as follows:

> Mr Hedrick, whose girth grew with his years, played golf. Mr Blue jumps rope three mornings a week and works out on a Nautilus machine another three mornings at an employee fitness center he had built in an old hangar.
>
> Mr Blue also seems to have pumped new life into Beech managers. They're mostly the same men and women, says a Beech supplier. 'They just breathe harder. They're all trying to run at Linden's pace.' (Wessel, 1984)

A vision of the future is not offered once and for all by the leader and then allowed to fade away. It must be repeated time and again. It must be incorporated in the organization's culture and reinforced through the strategy and decision making process. It must be constantly evaluated for possible change in the light of new circumstances.

In the end, the leader may be the one who articulates the vision and gives it legitimacy, who expresses the vision in captivating rhetoric that fires the imagination and emotions of followers, who – through the vision – empowers others to make decisions that get things done. But if the organization is to be successful, the image must grow out of the needs of the entire organization and must be 'claimed' or 'owned' by all the important actors. In short, it must become part of a new social architecture in the organization, the subject to which we next turn our attention.

References

Carr, Jonathan (1984). 'Success as a State of Mind', *Financial Times*, 13 February.

Halberstam, David (1979). *The Powers That Be*. New York: Dell, p. 40.

Hutt, Maurice (ed) (1972). *Napoleon*. Englewood Cliffs, NJ: Prentice-Hall, p. 151.

Wessel, David (1984). 'Beech's President Gambles Firm's Future on a Radically Designed Business Airplane'. *Wall Street Journal*, 8 March.

Securicor

Derek F. Channon

Securicor Limited was the largest commercial security organization in the United Kingdom with a group turnover in 1978 of £121 million and pre-tax profits of £5.4 million (detailed financial statistics are given in Tables 4.1 and 4.2). In addition, the Securicor Group, of which Securicor Limited was a member, operated a range of security services throughout Europe and in Hong Kong and several African countries. The group also owned interests, engaged in office cleaning, specialist parcel deliveries and property. In the UK, Securicor was estimated to hold a market share of around 65 per cent in 1978. The strategy which had led to this dominant position is the subject of this case.

This case was prepared by Professor Derek Channon from corporate strategy reports by Mike Laner and Sharon Pipe as a basis for classroom discussion rather than to illustrate either effective or ineffective handling of an administrative situation.

The security industry

The security industry in Britain had experienced rapid and highly profitable growth since the end of the 1950s. The industry began to gain importance in the early 1960s when the police almost completely withdrew escort services for cash in transit. The termination of this service coincided with a sharp increase in attacks on money on the move and with greater insurance pressures upon management for higher levels of security. There was therefore a rapid expansion in private cash in transit services to fill the void left by the withdrawal of the police.

Comparable internal losses in industrial and commercial establishments to which the police had no prescriptive rights of entry except in exceptional circumstances led to a similar demand for guard services. This trend had continued as awareness of the need for better fire protection and security had increased.

Industrial and commercial organizations could set up their own security systems, but many recognized the advantages of using professional services, particularly as security technology became more sophisticated. Public sector enterprises, too, had found they needed supplementary, custom designed security services, and by 1978 the British Security Industry Association (BSIA) had over 800 members, although the Metropolitan Police estimated that there

Table 4.1 *Securicor profit and loss account 1971–78*

£000	1971	1972	1973	1974	1975	1976	1977	1978
Group turnover	30 072	35 250	40 659	46 730	61 554	81 806	100 828	121 080
Group profit before tax								
Hotel division	595	615	473	–	–	–	–	–
Security division	1112	1390	1719	1996	2095	2688	3541	4085
Finance division	–	–	–	632	660	738	979	1066
Associated company profits	–	–	–	–	–	–	–	265
	1707	2005	2192	2628	2755	3426	4520	5416
Taxation	717	859	1026	1553	1550	1209	1275	1618
Profit after taxation	990	1146	1166	1075	1205	2217	3245	3798
Outside shareholders interest	377	444	495	437	488	956	1424	1634
				638	717		1821	
Extraordinary items				140	10	–	20	187
Net profit available for distribution	613	702	671	498	707	1261	1801	2351
Dividends	190	191	144	146	155	165	182	356
Profit retained	423	511	527	352	552	1096	1629	1995

Source: Annual Reports

were some 2000 firms operating in the security industry.

Most of the security firms were very small and operated solely on a highly localized basis. Only about a dozen firms operated nationwide. The services most commonly provided were alarm system installation (47 per cent of companies), guard dogs (39 per cent), mobile guards (38 per cent) and static guards (32 per cent). Other services were offered much less frequently and a majority of firms (60 per cent) offered only one service.

A few large firms dominated the market with Securicor being by far the largest. Group 4 was Securicor's nearest competitor and was the British subsidiary of Securitas International, a Swedish company and the largest non-American security organization in the world. Group 4, with a turnover of around £22 million, held about 12 per cent of the UK market. Security Express, a subsidiary of Thomas de la Rue was active in the cash transit and guarding segments, but was much smaller than Securicor, while Brinks MAT, a subsidiary of the US Brinks Corporation, was an important competitor in the transport of bullion and other precious metals.

There were no legal barriers to entering the security industry, although the main participants were actively pressing the Home Office for the introduction of some form of licensing system. This was expected to help weed out the many small operators who it was felt did not possess the resources, ability and perhaps integrity required for security work. Moreover, with a licensing scheme in being, the security companies hoped to gain access to police records to assist in vetting potential employees. The other major difficulty faced by would-be competitors was the cost involved in establishing a nationwide system of communications and logistics to rival that of Securicor in particular.

At the end of the 1970s, crime rates were still increasing annually, as was the value of property lost by crime, fire or vandalism, as shown in Figure 4.1, and leading to a growing demand for security services. Some changes were also occurring in the technology of the industry, with a growing use of electronic surveillance systems and the introduction of new systems such as electronic fund transfer to reduce the amounts of cash transported. In the 1980s therefore it was expected that there would be some reduction in the use of labour, an increase in skill levels and greater dependence on electronic systems.

Table 4.2 *Securicor group consolidated balance sheet for year ended 30 September**

Year	1971 £000	1972	1973	1974	1975	1976	1977	1978
Fixed assets	9819	11 707	6513	7895	10 777	13 100	20 661	27 029
Development expenditure	368	631	565	989	1265	585	515	415
Subsidiary companies	1353	1381	1419	1327	1227	1254	1252	1232
Investments	71	156	162	31	574	1174	2008	–
Associated company								
	11 611	13 875	8659	10 242	13 854	16 113	24 436	28 988
Current assets								
investment	+	–	–	–	–	–	–	4402
Stocks	487	683	635	1218	1969	2402	3290	3669
Debtors	4690	5515	6831	8538	9412	8533	11 521	11 631
Bank and deposit balances	619	1095	6317	5313	4395	6358	4580	7193
	5796	7293	13 783	15 069	15 776	17 293	19 391	26 895
Current liabilities								
Trade and other creditors	4105	5186	5844	6689	7522	9672	13 425	15 407
Hire purchase creditors				354	1183	2005	4443	6708

Taxation	422	844	1826	2276	2280	2197	1815	1713
Bank overdraft and advances	215	274	2179	2447	3138	1118	2535	1311
Proposed dividends	113	148	107	89	95	103	115	223
	4855	6452	9956	11 855	14 218	15 095	22 333	25 362
Net current assets	941	841	3837	3214	1558	2198	(2942)	1533
Total net assets	12 552	14 716	12 486	13 456	15 412	18 311	21 494	30 521
Financed by share capital	3247	2275	2275	2275	3074	3074	3074	3257
Reserves	3774	4987	5573	5898	5623	7150	8750	11 408
Shareholders funds	6021	7262	7848	8173	8697	10 224	11 824	14 665
Outside shareholders' interests	3003	4004	559	3769	4178	5576	6627	10 343
Loans	2737	2970	3631	595	612	2302	2341	4546
Deferred taxation	791	480	448	919	1925	409	702	967
	12 552	14 716	12 486	13 456	15 412	18 311	21 494	30 521

* For 1 October 1971
Source: Annual Reports

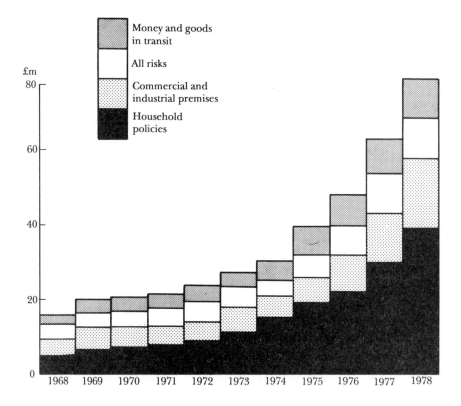

Figure 4.1   *Insurance losses through crime.*
Source: BIA 1979

Early history of Securicor

In 1935 a group of London householders, disturbed by the amount of theft and petty crime in their neighbourhood, clubbed together to form a small company called Night Watch Services Limited to protect their interests. The company provided uniformed guards to patrol (often on bicycle) private property such as flats and penthouses in Mayfair. In 1939 the Hampstead branch broke away and formed another company, Night Guards Limited, which provided similar services.

During the war, the companies all but disappeared and by 1945, Night Guards Limited consisted of just two guards. Then, in late 1945, Henry Tiarks and Lord Wallingdon (later Chairman of Securicor to 1966) revived Night Guards Limited, mainly as a means of providing work for ex-servicemen. Very soon after this the services offered were extended to cover commercial premises. The company thus formed became Securicor.

The security industry at that time consisted of Securicor and a few others (such as Factory Guards Limited, later Group 4), but no great growth occurred, with services essentially those of guarding premises. Then in 1955, a young man called Roy Winklemann, who had spent some time studying the more developed security industry in the US, returned to the UK and started the Armoured Car Company, based in West Drayton. This organization carried cash between banks and to and from bank customers in armoured vans. Winklemann imported many ideas from the US, such as American-style uniforms and helmets and the guards in the vans carried shotguns. The 'paramilitary' image did not endear the company to either the public or the press. However, as organized crime was on the increase in the UK, the idea quickly won support and soon Securicor had three of its own vans. Other firms such as Security Express (founded by Thomas de la Rue and Wells Fargo) also entered this new market and competition increased. In spite of the increase in business, Securicor's financial performance was not very good, and by 1956 the company looked as if it would fail.

One of Securicor's clients was the Allied Hotels – Kensington Palace Hotel Group, which was in the control of the Erskine family and run by Denys Erskine. Keith Erskine (Denys' younger brother) persuaded him to buy Securicor for the hotel group. At the time, Securicor was earning some £50 000 on a £450 000 turnover and the purchase price was £125 000. The Erskine family took little interest in the company and Securicor's fortunes continued to decline. It was not long before the company was losing money. As a result, Keith Erskine began to take a more definite interest in Securicor's activities. In 1960 a Securicor guard was seriously beaten up and, largely as a consequence of this, Keith Erskine literally moved into Securicor.

The Keith Erskine era

Keith Erskine's main work at the time was as senior partner of Hextall, Erskine and Company, the firm of solicitors he had founded and who acted as legal advisers to the hotel group and the Erskine family. In 1960 he pushed this work aside and set up his bed in the Securicor headquarters. He remained there for the next five years, going home only at weekends, in an attempt to put the firm back on its feet again. He followed a hard regimen for a man in his early fifties, rising at 5 a.m. every day and taking a swim in the Serpentine before starting his 18-hour working day! Members of his staff were often invited to join him on these early morning outings.

UK developments

Such determined action paid off and by 1963 Securicor was well established on an upward growth path. It was also in 1963 that Securicor purchased the Armoured Car Company where the effect of a series of criminal raids and a critical public inquiry had left the company in a perilous financial state. Keith Erskine could see a big future for the cash-carrying business in areas apart from banks. He examined in great detail the trends of organized crime in the UK and saw that as a result of the increase in the number of motorways and the generally improved road communications in Britain it was becoming very much easier for criminals based in London to do a job in a provincial town and make a quick getaway. In this manner major crime was extending into areas that had been relatively free hitherto. Also, because of the national operations of Securicor customers and prospects, Erskine saw the advantage of nationwide coverage from a competitive point of view. These trends, coupled with the introduction of the cash-carrying service, signalled the start (1960) of the construction programme to set up a widespread branch network which had reached 280 by the mid-1970s. The need for effective control and communications was seen as fundamental if the increase in the number of bank raids and other crime was to be contained. Therefore, the programme of expansion included the building of customized communications centres, of which there were nearly 60 by the mid-1970s, and the linking of all centres with sophisticated communications facilities including telex, radio and links into an on-line computer system.

In the early days the situation was somewhat different. Rather than wait for the business to come to Securicor, Erskine sent out almost raw recruits into the provinces to set up new branches. This was quite a risky business since Securicor had no real services to offer in the new areas and the 'branch' would often be set up in a vacant shop with just one chair, one table and a telephone! Security Express, which was the main competitor in the cash-carrying business, followed a different strategy and only built up branches in areas where business had first been found. The more positive approach of Securicor, combined with some shrewd property speculation by Keith Erskine, resulted in a complete national coverage for Securicor which was unrivalled by any competitor.

At a time of increasing levels of crime and growing interest in crime prevention, Securicor developed a nationwide position and a wide range of security services to meet market needs. As a result in the 14 years that Erskine was in control, profits multiplied 45 times on a turnover that increased nearly 85 times. Virtually all of the growth was achieved without recourse to acquisition, although in 1973 there was a slight diversification when a small firm of combined security guards and cleaning contractors was acquired, at a cost of £375 000.

The growth in the security side of the hotel group's business was such that by 1966 it had outstripped the parent as the major profit earner. In 1973 most of the hotel interests of the group were sold and the security services were reorganized into a new company. Keith Erskine, who had been chairman and managing director of the hotel group since his brother had died some years earlier, was now in control of Securicor Group Limited (formerly Associated Hotels Limited) which had a majority shareholding in Security Services Limited (formerly Kensington Palace Hotels Limited), of which Securicor was one of a number of UK and overseas subsidiaries. The shareholding structure of the group is shown in Figure 4.2.

Overseas expansion

From the early 1960s, Securicor followed a policy of expansion overseas. The first moves were into Australia where branches were established and in New Zealand, but because of a multitude of well established local operators, these ventures did not do well. Erskine's strategy was to try to avoid confrontation with entrenched competition and as a result the Australian branches were closed down in 1972. Securicor next entered the Far East in Singapore and Malaysia

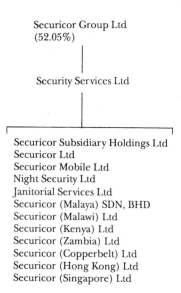

Securicor Group Ltd
(52.05%)

Security Services Ltd

Securicor Subsidiary Holdings Ltd
Securicor Ltd
Securicor Mobile Ltd
Night Security Ltd
Janitorial Services Ltd
Securicor (Malaya) SDN, BHD
Securicor (Malawi) Ltd
Securicor (Kenya) Ltd
Securicor (Zambia) Ltd
Securicor (Copperbelt) Ltd
Securicor (Hong Kong) Ltd
Securicor (Singapore) Ltd

* There are also minor operating subsidiaries in Norway, France, Germany, Holland, Belgium, Luxembourg and Cyprus.

Figure 4.2   *Securicor Group shareholding structure*

where the company was more successful and branches were operating satisfactorily by 1968.

Sir Derek Erskine, Keith's elder brother, had settled in Kenya and was chief whip in Jomo Kenyatta's African National Party. Securicor was therefore attracted to East Africa and three subsidiaries were set up in Kenya, Uganda and Malawi, and these still operated in the late 1970s, apart from the Ugandan subsidiary which was nationalized in 1973. By 1970, another subsidiary had been established, this time in Zambia.

Securicor had attempted to get a firm footing in Europe, but here again there were many other firms already well established and the business was of a different nature from that in Britain. The branches that had been established were small and were basically European depots for the Special Delivery Service. In the company report of 1973, Erskine outlined his strategy for growth in Europe which was to be through opening up new branches rather than by acquisition, as this was seen as a safer method and would save money in the long run. He had hoped to build up the European turnover to about £4 million over the next three years, at a cost of £2 million.

In establishing its overseas operations, Securicor had experienced some cultural problems in trying to introduce its 'mutual company' concept into countries where the local staff could not seem to grasp its significance, where money was more important and corruption a common occurrence. Nevertheless by 1973 turnover from overseas branches had reached £3.9 million and profits were £400K.

Keith Erskine – Chief Helper Securicor

The success of Securicor owed a great deal to the personality and philosophy of Mr Erskine. He came from a family with a tradition of public service, his father having been an MP. He was born in Scotland in 1908 and was a Kings Scholar at Westminster School. After qualifying as a solicitor in 1933 he saw war service in the Middle East, Italy and in the Eighth Army, attaining the rank of Captain in the Royal Artillery, having joined as a ranker. It was from his army experience that he said he learnt the importance of communications, an emphasis which later became apparent with Securicor's use of radio control and telex linkages between branches.

Keith Erskine was a founder of Hextall Erskine and Company, a firm of London solicitors. Due to his involvement with Securicor and other companies he ceased practising as a solicitor but he remained a senior partner in the firm until his death. It was while practising law that he got his first taste of management by being invited on to the boards of various companies for whom his firm worked.

Amongst his industrial appointments, Erskine was a director and past chairman of the London Advisory Board of the Norwich Union Insurance Company. This connection proved fruitful for a number of reasons. Firstly, for arranging mortgage finance and leaseback agreements for the acquisition of property in which to house the growth of Securicor. Secondly, it helped in the provision of insurance, an important point considering the high risk of either injury to a member of Securicor's workforce or of a substantial loss of clients' property. Thirdly, it introduced Erskine to the idea of a mutual company which he later adopted as part of Securicor's defence against nationalization.

Erskine was a highly active and energetic man who ate sparingly and did not smoke or drink. Fitness was almost an obsession and he brought this attitude to the operations of Securicor: 'In our job we have to keep fit. Frugality is our watchword, luxury is wasteful and weakening'. He was very self-disciplined and believed that this was a characteristic that should be developed in all Securicor's employees.

Erskine developed a very idealistic philosophy which became absolute in the case of Securicor and which, in the late 1960s and early 1970s, was used as part of a strategy to defend and develop the company.

Erskine quoted Drucker as saying that 'management should be by objective and self control.' He himself commented that 'People do not want to be managed, they want to be helped.' His own position in Securicor would conventionally have been referred to as that of managing director, but he was known within the company as chief helper. He encouraged all managers within Securicor to be referred to as helpers. The formal company hierarchy was removed ('There are no gradations, just people.') and so, too, were all the perks that traditionally went with advancement up the hierarchy. Erskine said 'I don't believe that one man can be worth £20 a week and another £30 000 a year. There are differences in what a man can do for a company but not such enormous differences.' It was partly because of this belief that Erskine pursued a policy of decentralization. He aimed to drive the level of decision making right down to the individual man, at the same time recognizing that this would lead to involvement and job enrichment. This was considered particularly crucial in a job such as that of a night watchman which was generally extremely boring and tedious. With such jobs, or where there was the high risk associated with handling large quantities of cash, the morale of the company's workforce was vitally important. To maintain morale Erskine felt it important that the top management team should 'get out into the field'. In line with this, he himself occasionally did a night watch or took part in a cash-in-transit run. In referring to this involvement, Erskine used military analogies, saying that all the best generals in history were never aloof from the battle and they were always in touch with the ordinary trooper.

Erskine did not believe in long term planning but was more concerned with actually getting things done. One of his mottos within Securicor was 'Get down to the *nitty gritty*, never mind the *airy fairy*, the *talkie talkie* must lead to the *doey doey*'.

Erskine's strategy for Securicor

Erskine displayed essentially an entrepreneurial style in his approach to Securicor. He considered that market research was a substitute for action. He said 'We must go in and do it and if it does not work we get out.' Erskine never moved into an area or service where there existed an established competitor. When he sent out people from London to establish branches throughout Britain there was no guarantee that there would be any business for the branch. Conversely, if there was any business, the branch could rely on being the market leader. In 1960 there were three branches; in April 1974 there were some 280 branches througout the UK.

The growth in Securicor brought with it the problem of property financing. This was solved by arranging leaseback agreements with the Norwich Union Assurance Society. However, Erskine also anticipated Securicor's growth and he set up a department to search for property bargains which could be bought out of the company's retained earnings and held until expansion required them to be used as a functional company building.

The property department within Securicor was originally responsible for devising conversions of suitable premises, but it came to supervise the construction of purpose-built security centres, of which there were eventually over 60 in the UK (by 1980). Erskine claimed that Securicor was the only security organization in Europe to have developed a specialized building programme on any scale.

Erskine also broadened the range of services that Securicor offered, usually by developing extensions to already existing services. Thus the Special Delivery Service, started in 1965 to carry computer tapes, was extended to carry goods less risk-prone than cash, and could deliver to anywhere in the UK within 24 hours.

Erskine produced a high morale within Securicor's workforce in a number of ways. By pursuing a policy of egalitarianism throughout the company he removed any perceived unfairness in the distribution of rewards for the job done. At the same time this policy had the sound business logic of cutting down overheads for such items as personal secretaries, large offices and plush furniture. He also encouraged the senior management to become involved in some of the company's actual operations.

The egalitarian ethic also promoted a process of decentralization. In the mid-1960s, Securicor was growing rapidly and had been based in a central office situated in London. With typical vigour and apparent lack of planning, Erskine decreed that the company should decentralize. Again this was a sound business move since he was able to cut the London office staff of Securicor by a half and profitably to sub-let one half of the 100 000 sq ft of office space that Securicor had on lease in London. The company operations became largely local in character but were based on an extensive branch network. With less centralization and the noted high risk nature of the industry, Securicor had to place even greater reliance on self-discipline. In order further to engender a spirit of commitment into the corporate culture, Erskine devised 'good housekeeping' meetings. These occurred weekly at each branch and involved all the workforce of that branch, except the night watchman who might nominate a representative. This meeting was charged with the management of the branch. Although Erskine believed in democracy, he only believed in what he termed 90 per cent industrial democracy. The missing 10 per cent was to be made up by 'wise guidance' which could provide leadership rather than driving force and could veto any stupid decisions. The question of who decided if a decision was stupid was left begging, but presumably the ultimate appeal would have been to Erskine himself as the chief helper on 'the continuous sitting National Good-housekeeping Department'. These measures had the effect of producing a commitment to the corporate culture. This aim was highlighted by another of Erskine's company mottos, 'not "I" but "*we*"'.

Erskine wrote of himself that 'being a Scotsman by origin, I sought to reconcile ethics with practical business'. As a result he formed Securicor into a mutual company in 1966. Overseas subsidiary companies did not become mutual companies because of the higher risks. Shareholders' profits were thus limited to no more than five per cent of turnover. By limiting shareholders in this way it was argued everything else would go to the benefit of the company's workers, the customers and the state.

The workers benefited through higher wages and merit awards given annually and the pay of guards rose by nearly double the national wages index over the period 1961 to 1971. There was also the additional effect that morale would improve since the workers no longer perceived that they were being exploited. Erskine said 'when profits are moderated, the workers know they are getting a fair deal'. The customers benefited because the price they paid for Securicor's services was not determined by demand but rather by a moderate fixed percentage of the turnover. The state benefited from the fact that the wealth which Securicor would have accrued had it charged more for its services could instead be invested in other industry. Thus Securicor could be seen to be assisting in reducing inflation.

These were the ethics of the mutual company but there were also practical advantages. Firstly, the growth in Securicor by the mid-1960s had given rise to suggestions by politicians that Securicor should be nationalized. By pointing to the fact that Securicor was not exploiting its virtual monopolistic position by making undue profits, Erskine had erected a defence against this suggestion. Secondly, by limiting its profits to five per cent of turnover, Securicor's pricing was extremely competitive. Erskine was quoted as saying 'like Henry Ford, I believe in big turnover and low margins'. In 1968 the profit limitation was reduced to 4.5 per cent and in the 1970s the profit had averaged out at four per cent.

Throughout their growth, Securicor and other security organizations had come under attack for being private armies. Keith Erskine was very sensitive to this and one of his strategies during the 1960s was to invite respected and distinguished men to be members of the board of the operating company. In 1970 he began a scheme to change the corporate image of Securicor so that it appeared to be less of a public threat. The slogan 'Securicor Cares' was developed and appeared on all Securicor vans and trucks. Company advertisements in the press appeared with the headline that 'Securicor Cares for Customers, Co-Workers and the Common Good.' Also stated were Securicor's aims in which Erskine's idealism was readily identifiable. The first aim was to observe the highest code of business conduct while the ninth and final aim was 'In sum, to seek Love, Truth and Justice'. Mr Erskine set out his views as follows:

> They say it is love that makes the world go round. Certainly, we could not take hate or fear as recipes for Securicor.
> Leaning on men more than machines, we have obeyed Pope's edict:

'The proper study of Mankind is Man'. Our answers have met with some success. Indeed we have figured in the Management Today list of the ten most successful companies.

Until I was pitchforked into Securicor, 13 years ago, as its head, I was a lawyer and much concerned with justice. I could not accept the present company law as adequate – so we formed the mutual company, both as a unilateral amendment and a reply to Karl Marx's prospect of dreary and eternal conflict.

Six years ago we declared that Securicor would not just serve the bosses, i.e. the shareholders, but also the employees, the customers and the State. We further limited the profits to 5% of turnover, as opposed to the 10% which was then regarded as a legitimate target for specialized transport, which is two-thirds of our business. As margins generally declined we have reduced this and in the last three years we have only averaged 4%. Bearing in mind that such limits are maxima, that ours is a risk business, that most companies have to compensate for the odd bad year and that, in fact, only one per cent is paid out in dividends, this is the very least that is needed to provide a financial basis for the stable employment of our members. If all the dividends went to them it would only add about 50p a week to their earnings – so much for worker shareholding!

As a result of this just and effective way of sharing profits, our men have done well and their wages have advanced much faster than the wages index. Our customers have also benefited. These have been the years when the mutual company has come into its own, when overheads have been slashed by higher efficiency and better planning; while the bandits have been contained.

The cycle clarifies: Profit restraint leads to better wages and a prices curb. These in turn lead to responsible workers, trained in skills, better service, happy customers, recommendation and growth.

In the last 13 years Securicor turnover has risen from £450 000 to £40 million; profits from £30 000 to £1 400 000; and branches from three to 300, including overseas.

Justice, our first pillar, has a cold ring. Care was the second and missing motive. Four years ago we proclaimed that 'Securicor Cares'. But how to demonstrate it?

1 We eliminated the conflict of interest by the mutual company. All profits over the safe minimum go to the workers and customers.
2 We respect the Dignity of Man.
3 We rebut prejudice, whether of race, class, religion, rank or sex.
4 We judge merit by character, rather than slickness.
5 We regard self-discipline as ennobling, enforced discipline as degrading.
6 We treat our men as educated and adult, capable, with a little help and guidance, of running their own show.

7 We lift motivation, whether for employers or employees, above the lowest common denominator of greed or necessity. Men, we have found, will join together in a 'common effort to a noble end'. So we have introduced the theme of Caring for the Common Good.

8 We have invented a new machinery of management and a new nomenclature. Each of our 250 UK branches is run by a weekly meeting of the Good-Housekeeping Team. The loose ends between branches are tied up by a sub-area aid team and anything else by a regional aid team. The aim is management in depth. Specialists exist but their job is mainly to teach our men to become all-rounders, batsmen and bowlers. In Caesar's 10th Legion each man carried the tools for fighting and for building roads. Our critics have said these are our old friends the Works Councils. Maybe, but they have teeth. They don't just debate the canteen food. Increasingly, they run the show. Decisions for the faint-hearts are refused; but not help or advice.

9 Men do not want to be managed – they want to be helped. But the need for leadership and for inspiration is as vital as before, only of a more quiet, patient and unselfish kind, giving credit to the men.

Human relations pose a challenge as exciting and rewarding as music, art or writing. They demand the same dedication.

As for names: Manager equals Helper, Management equals Guidance, Supervisor equals Carer-Trainer, Supervision (that stunting work which promotes 'them' and 'us') equals Caring/Training. Training, after initial schooling, is continuous by telephone or radio themes and visits (the sharing of skills is part of caring). If service is the central element in our lives we must care for those we serve.

Does it work? The proof of the pudding! Not all the time in all places, not without some inevitable reactions, but better than any of us dreamed. The success of the democracy depends on people being responsible. Our workers, like our voters, are basically responsible.

The third bulwark of all human endeavour is Truth. In Securicor, fighting dishonesty, honesty is our stock in trade. We have made it one of our aims to observe the highest code of ethics. But it is human to err; and we only claim to be striving towards the peak of integrity.

But if success is the result of these aims, it can be toppled by Pride. The temptations of the tycoon or boss to become pompous or to lose the common touch are understandable. So in Humility one finds the last and surest bulwark. All of us at the top in Securicor don uniform and work alongside the men, whether on night guarding or in armoured vans on the peak day, or at the Airports. There are no separate lavatories, canteens, close-covered carpets or luxury cars. We eschew ostentation. We avoid over-indulgence because in our job we have to keep fit. But democracy means equity not equality. We reward merit by higher salary, but not star salary, for none of us are stars. We are all in shirt-sleeves. We are all co-workers.

In Securicor, we have ceased to follow the false gods of doubt and division. We try in all modesty to follow the true gods of brotherhood and service.

As Emerson said: 'When the half gods go, the gods arrive.'

On 23 April 1974 the company was devastated by the news that Keith Erskine had been tragically killed in a car crash.

The Smith years

After the death of Keith Erskine, Peter Smith succeeded as head of Securicor. Also a solicitor, Smith had joined Hextall Erskine in 1951 and by 1966 was concentrating solely on Securicor. In 1968 he joined the board and was joint vice-chairman before becoming chairman in 1974.

Smith, although an admirer of many aspects of Keith Erskine's approach, believed that Securicor, with a turnover of £50 million and interests extending across Europe, was ready for a period of consolidation. He stated, 'It was my job to inject some conventional management.'

Under Smith's leadership, Securicor diversified further. Making use of the £6.5 million cash received from the sale of its hotel interests which had been placed on short term deposit, the company expanded in office cleaning and by 1975, 2000 people were employed in this activity. Smith also noted the falling growth rate in the cash in transit market. Although one of Securicor's major activities, this service operated on low margins yet was labour intensive and required expensive armoured vehicles.

Making use of the widespread branch and communications network, Securicor therefore embarked on a special parcel delivery service aimed at the gap between a normal parcels service and freight traffic. Offering guaranteed next-day delivery at a rate about double that charged by the Post Office, the service proved popular and was extended to Europe with daily trucking based in Brussels. Since 1975 the average growth rate for the parcels service had been around 35 per cent per annum and in 1978 via a rights issue, Securicor raised £3 million to finance an entry into a specialist freight service which permitted the carriage of items up to 100 kilos vs a 40 kilo maximum for the parcels service. The new freight service was carefully segregated from existing operations and 16 special depots were established, while in 1979 Securicor invested a further £2 million to build up its overnight parcels division by providing new vehicles and establishing 27 new depots.

Smith also reversed a previous decision not to enter the security equipment market. The new policy offered customers the best range of equipment available on the market rather than Securicor-developed systems. In addition, Securi-sound was established as a joint venture with electronics manufacturer, Sound Diffusion, to develop electronic systems to combat the growing number of attacks on security vehicles.

The traditional policy of financing investment from earnings had also been modified by Smith toward a more conventional approach, making use of new debt and equity funds. Thus, by 1978, leverage had reached 44 per cent and was more in line with the industry average. The company continued to invest heavily in custom developed property for the needs of the security division.

Group financial structure

The financial structure of the Securicor Group was somewhat unusual. The ultimate holding company, Securicor Group Limited, owned 52.05 per cent of Security Services Limited, an intermediate holding company which in turn held all the shares of 24 operating companies including Securicor Limited. The majority of both the voting and non-voting shares in Securicor Group were owned or controlled by the directors. In total they had control of 2.36 million enfranchised stock units out of a total of 2.83 issued shares. Mrs Denise Delaney, a member of the Erskine family, was the largest equity holder with 1.41 million shares or 48.99 per cent. Other directors collectively owned 0.46 per cent of the voting stock while other shares were held in trusts to which Securicor Group directors were trustees.

Mrs Delaney and other directors held only small holdings in Security Services Limited, but had control of this company and its subsidiaries via their control of Securicor Group. The Group had come in for criticism for its capital structure but there had been resistance to any change by Mrs Delaney and other members of the Securicor Group Board.

The Securicor range of services

Securicor offered a comprehensive range of nearly 40 specialized services covering most aspects of security. Further, the company claimed that if a client had a need for a service not in the current range, then within reason the company would initiate it. Indeed, many of Securicor's services had originated in this way. The main services offered by Securicor were guarding, money movement and Paypak, the parcel service, office cleaning and radio telephone services.

Guarding

The original foundation of Securicor, the guarding service, could be subdivided into two – internal guards and mobile, radio controlled operations.

The internal guards service was primarily concerned with providing adequate protection of invariably high value premises against break-ins, fire and flood, arson, terrorism and other acts of vandalism. Guards could work alone or as part of a team, in some cases using dogs. The team was supported by a network of control centres and monitoring by a team of night supervisors including telephone contacts at regular intervals. Each Securicor guard was carefully screened before acceptance and was also trained in fire prevention and as a doghandler.

Where the value of property or its contents did not justify the use of an internal guard, Securicor offered a mobile patrol service. This as regarded as a deterrent against vandals, thieves and fire and flood. Coverage could be tailored to the requirements of the user and included internal and external visits, round the clock coverage and immediate contact with the operations centre to ensure rapid alerts to the police and/or other public services.

Money movement and Paypak

The foundation of much of Securicor's growth in the 1960s, the cash in transit services covered every kind of cash movement. In addition, Securicor offered its Paypak service which involved breaking down bulk cash into wage packets for bulk delivery or individual distribution at a work site. Securicor took full responsibility for the cash and valuables it carried until the moment they were handed over to the user. All cargo was fully insured, and should the guards be attacked and the money stolen, Securicor undertook to replace the amount with the minimum of delay.

Special parcel service

A development of the cash in transit operations, Securicor offered a range of special parcel delivery services. Based on a network of around 300 branches in the UK, Securicor delivered between more than 18 000 collection and delivery points each day. With an emphasis on security and reliability, Securicor employed a national planning department to coordinate its fleet of some 2000 vans. A number of specialist supplementary services had evolved around the parcel service, including a contract parcel service for volume users, the Inner City Flier service emphasizing speed and maximum security, Securicor Data Services which specialized in carrying computer data, Air Cargo Service, Radiac, a service specializing in the carriage of radioactive materials, and the European Parcel Service.

Office cleaning

Securicor offered a general cleaning service using up-to-date equipment, some of which was specially designed to provide dust-free cleaning in computer centres, laboratories and other special case areas. The normal service included the cleaning and maintenance of both internal and external office and factory premises.

Radio telephone services

Centred upon its extensive communications network, Securicor had developed a wide range of radio telephone services for both business and private individuals. These services included Highway Link, aimed at the commercial haulage operator and designed to help combat the theft of high value loads; Linkline, a service coordinated with the Automobile Association for use by salesmen, business executives and the like to provide information on travel and weather conditions; and Maritime, a similar service for coastal waters and inland waterway users.

Securicor also offered a wide range of other security related services including store detectives; security hardware and alarm installation; security consultancy, ID card preparation and dog kennels and training.

Organization structure

Under Peter Smith the organization structure of Securicor had changed little from the personalized system created by Keith Erskine. With its emphasis upon industrial democracy there was no formal structure, although within each branch there were a number of permanent positions such as branch or business manager, cash in transit manager and security delivery services manager. Other positions within a branch might be allocated on a rota basis amongst the guards and patrolmen. This was facilitated by a union agreement to ensure no demarcation disputes.

Upon joining the company, each new recruit spent time at one of the training schools spread throughout the country to learn how the organization operated. Industrial democracy was developed through the weekly branch good house-keeping meeting. When first conceived these meetings had been permitted to make up their own agendas but this had later been replaced by the creation of the national good housekeeping department to provide 'wise guidance' for the democracy by drawing up a very precise and comprehensive agenda. In order to prevent these meetings being dominated by management, the internal nomen-clature was changed so that managers became 'helpers'. Decision making then rested with the branches with the helper there to provide guidance and advice, although he could impose a veto if he judged the meeting to have acted irresponsibly.

This system meant that each branch could be almost autonomous, a fact which gave rise to problems when there were customers whose service was covered by several branches. To overcome this Erskine formed 'aid teams'. These consisted of some 15 people drawn from a geographic sub-area which in turn was defined by a group of between four and six branches. The aid teams included men who had experience in all branches of Securicor, plus two or three women on the administrative side. Erskine defined the role of the aid team as follows: 'if there is a problem at one of their branches, the aid team can converge on it and give whatever help is required from first aid to a more lasting therapy'. The sub-area aid teams met fortnightly and were coordinated through regional aid teams, which in turn were run through a national aid team originally led by Erskine himself. The country was divided into 10 regions which were further divided into 50 sub-areas incorporating all the branches.

The branch and sub-area helpers were largely responsible for appointments and recommendations for the merit reward scheme. Promotion was based on merit only and this was judged in terms of integrity, industry and unselfishness. As Erskine had noted, 'We promote on character.' This was further enhanced by Erskine's dislike of using experts. Under Erskine Securicor had never employed a chartered accountant, although for a while it farmed out the preparation of the monthly accounts to a professional firm. Erskine was eventually advised to recruit a £15 000 a year finance man. In reply to this he dismissed the external accountants and persevered with a system of management accounts that he developed and which was maintained by a 'collection of girls'.

Thus Erskine had demonstrated his faith in the ability of Securicor's employees. With wise guidance there was no job that they could not tackle and it was not necessary to bring in an outside expert to solve internal problems.

The regional aid teams were known as CATs (Co-Workers Action Teams) and they provided much of the leadership and encouragement that was given by

Erskine in the days before decentralization. Erskine had still tried to visit each sub-area aid team once every eight weeks for a mixture of feedback and pep-talk. A similar function was provided at the weekly branch meetings through the appointment within the company of some 500 'professors'. These were older men within the organization who could provide wisdom and guidance through a half-hour lecture and a half-hour question period given before each good housekeeping meeting.

In line with the corporate image that Securicor 'cares', the company had also appointed some 400 night and day 'carers'. Erskine had defined their job as being to 'care for the men, to act as an elder brother, or perhaps in the case of the young 'uns as a father – to explain and to teach – to solve all their problems. Also to care for the customers, who prefer to get it from the horse's mouth than from a salesman however silver tongued.'

With operating control established at branch and regional level, there had been no need for large head office staff and no specialists. The chief helper had a small knot of 'assistants' and staff officers, some of whom performed reasonably well defined coordinating functions, while others were there to carry out any task that might be set them, such as developing a new line of business or checking up on the competition. Certain non-executive directors were occasionally called in to help with specific operations. Members of the board of the operating company had been chosen for the specific help they might be able to give in certain situations, as well as for their distinguished reputations and influential connections.

Aims of Securicor

Despite the death of Keith Erskine, his philosophy largely lived on and was reflected in the aims of the organization, which had remained unchanged from those established by Erskine, namely:

Aims of Securicor (a mutual company):
1 To observe the highest code of business conduct.
2 To devolve and involve; to enrich both jobs and lives; to combine private enterprise with social justice; to care for the individual.
3 To put principle before expediency and make sure our word is our bond.
4 Whilst not deviating from what is practical to enrol the idealism of youth.
5 To ignore class or race; to judge only by merit; to work in comradeship.
6 To divide more fairly the fruits of investment and work by means of the mutual company.

7 To combine what is best in public services, e.g. devotion to duty, with what is best in private endeavour, e.g. adaptability.
8 To express in the terms of guarding and watching Man's regard for his neighbour and wish to serve him.
9 In sum, to seek Love, Truth and Justice.

It is human to err. We in Securicor regret our errors; but slowly, painfully and persistently we are climbing to a peak of unimpeachable integrity where Service is an end, not just a means.

To the cynic we reply that these aims result in higher morale, goodwill and reward to our mutual company partners, i.e. the customers, co-workers, shareholders and the Nation. Business cannot be divorced from living, both should be nobly done.

Keith Erskine, Securicor Chairman's Review, September 29, 1972.

Reproduced from Channon, Derek F. (1979). Manchester Business School Case Number 382-030-1 by permission of the author.

Chapter 5

Mission and ethics

Politicians, business people and the general public are concerned about the moral impact of business on society. Does the profit motive corrupt individuals, causing them to behave immorally? Or, to put it another way, what are the ethics of business?

Examples of immoral and fraudulent behaviour abound – the Bhopal explosion, Ernest Saunders of Guinness, Ivan Boesky and many less famous examples litter the pages of the business press. Does this mean that business needs ethics?

Some believe it does. The Harvard Business School has been given a $30 million endowment to study and teach business ethics. Others believe that good ethics are the same as good values. Hence ethics becomes a subset of mission.

The following four pieces helped us to understand the relationship. In selecting these pieces we have avoided the narrow academics and technicians on the subject of ethics. We have chosen only the efforts of big thinkers, individuals who have the ability to see through the dust storm created by others to the essential issues. The first is by John Akers, chairman of IBM. He places business ethics in a broad societal context. The second is by Peter Drucker and is a polemical appeal to quash the concept of business ethics. Ethics is an individual issue according to Drucker. The third extract is by an ethics academic, Michael Hoffman, who addresses the problem of how a company can promote ethical behaviour. The final piece is by Robert Gunts, president of Whirlpool Trading. He tackles the practical problem of ethics across nationalities with different cultures and different ethical rules.

These four pieces do not begin to address the philosophical and moral issues posed by business decisions. Rather, they expose the dilemma that exists between those who believe that ethics is purely a matter of the personal responsibility of every individual, and those who believe that companies have a moral responsibility over and above that of the responsibilities of the individuals involved. If you support the latter view, as we do, mission and ethics are closely linked issues.

In 'Ethics and Competitiveness – Putting First Things First', John Akers gives a broad view of ethics as the moral common sense that we all ought to be taught as we grow up. Institutions from business to the boy scouts have a role to play in helping us build this common sense. Akers argues that this will only happen if we recognize that business is merely a means to an end. He quotes a famous sports manager to make the point that loyalty to religion and family should come before loyalty to business. By retaining this sense of priority, business people can avoid the ethical traps in business.

Peter Drucker, in 'What is Business Ethics?', attempts to demolish the moral responsibility of business. Morality, he argues, is an individual responsibility, not a collective one. Business people should not attempt to develop codes of business behavior that are any different to the codes of individual behavior required by each society. His argument attempts to deny the benefit and the moral justification of business codes of ethics.

Michael Hoffman argues the opposite case to that of Peter Drucker. Drawing heavily on the work of Peters and Waterman, he argues that companies have values. These values affect the behaviour of individuals in the organization. The company, therefore, should take responsibility for the values it espouses. Moral excellence, he argues, comes from having a set of values that are ethical. It is appropriate, in his view, for companies to develop codes of ethics.

Finally Robert Gunts gives a clear exposition of the morally self-righteous American business person. He asks the question, 'Should our ethical principles at home be transferred to the international business community?', and answers, 'Yes, I feel we can take them anywhere in the world.' Gunts is a missionary for Whirlpool's code of ethics.

As will have become clear to the reader by now, our view is closer to the Hoffman and Gunts views than it is to the position taken by Drucker. Organizations with a sense of mission will become missionary about their values. Because employees believe values are good in themselves, they are prepared to commit emotionally to the organization. It is not surprising, therefore, that they become salespeople for their values.

Ethics and competitiveness – putting first things first
John F. Akers

John Akers has been with the IBM Corporation since 1960, and its chairman since 1986. In this article he argues that business ethics should be considered from a worldwide standpoint, and that they are inseparable from competitiveness.

Akers gives three suggestions for maintaining a moral sense in society: reinforcing role models and professional standards; teaching ethics in schools, even to young children, and founded on a study of history and literature; and finally, recognizing that the good of society takes priority over the good of an individual business. He argues that following these steps will foster mutual trust and confidence and thereby improve the economic strength of society.

I should like to consider a subject central to international economic competitiveness: ethics. Let me urge at the outset that all of us in management look at both these words – ethics and competitiveness – with a wide angle of vision. When we think of competitiveness we should think not just as Americans, Europeans or Japanese seeking our own selfish beggar-thy-neighbor advantage, but as managers striving to succeed in an increasingly interdependent world, with the potential for improved living standards for all. And when we think of ethics, we should think not just as managers focusing on a narrow preserve labeled business ethics, but as citizens of a larger society.

Ethics and competitiveness are inseparable. We compete as a society. No society anywhere will compete very long or successfully with people stabbing each other in the back; with people trying to steal from each other; with everything requiring notarized confirmation because you can't trust the other fellow; with every little squabble ending in litigation; and with government writing reams of regulatory legislation, tying business hand and foot to keep it honest.

That is a recipe not only for headaches in running a company; it is a recipe for a nation to become wasteful, inefficient, and non-competitive. There is no escaping this fact: the greater the measure of mutual trust and confidence in the ethics of a society, the greater its economic strength.

I do not say the sky is falling here in the United States. I do not think we had a great ethical height in the good old days from which we've been tumbling downhill. We do face ethical and competitive problems, to be sure. We have all been reading about religious leaders who steal from their congregations, Wall Street brokers who profit from their insider status, assorted politicians and influence peddlers, law students who plagiarize, medical professors who falsify their research results, and Pentagon employees who sell classified information.

But most of us can agree with Thomas Jefferson that all human beings are endowed with a moral sense – that the average farmer behind a plow can decide a moral question as well as a university professor. Like Jefferson, we can have confidence in the man in the street, whether that street is in Armonk, San Francisco, or Cambridge – or in London, Paris or Tokyo.

That common moral sense, however, does not come out of nowhere or perpetuate itself automatically. Every generation must keep it alive and flourishing. All of us can think of means to this end. Here are three suggestions.

Ethical buttresses

First, we should fortify the practical ethical buttresses that help all of us – from childhood on – to know and understand and do exactly what is required of us. The simplest and most powerful buttress is the role model: parents and others who by precept and example set us straight on good and evil, right and wrong. Of all the role models in my own life, I think perhaps the most durable is my grandfather – a flinty New England headmaster whose portrait hangs in my home. To this day, whenever I go by it I check the knot in my tie and stiffen my backbone.

There are many other ethical buttresses. Some, despite condescending sophisticates, are simple credos: 'A Scout is trustworthy, loyal, helpful, friendly, courteous, kind, obedient, cheerful, thrifty, brave, clean, and reverent'; or 'a cadet will not lie, cheat or steal or tolerate those who do.' There are institutionalized buttresses like the honor system, by which college students police themselves – no plagiarism, no cheating on examinations. I find it ludicrous that even divinity schools and law schools and departments of philosophy – not to mention other parts of the university – have to pay proctors to pad up and down the aisles at examination time to make sure nobody is looking at crib notes or copying from a neighbor. A century and a half after Jefferson introduced the honor system at the University of Virginia, it is unfortunate that every college and university in America has not yet adopted it.

Finally there are professional standards and business codes of conduct, which spell out strict policies on such things as insider trading, gifts and entertainment, kickbacks and conflicts of interest.

It is naïve to believe these buttresses will solve all our problems. But it is equally naïve to expect ethical behavior to occur in the absence of clear requirements and consequences.

Can our schools teach ethics?

The time has come to take a hard look at ethical teaching in our schools – and I don't just mean graduate schools of business. We know John Shad is giving the Harvard Business School most of a $30 million endowment to be devoted to studying and teaching ethics. And we know that MIT Sloan School dean Lester Thurow and other educators have openly disagreed with this undertaking.

Let's begin by defining what we are talking about. Many businesspeople facing student audiences have been appalled by knee-jerk assertions that it is open-and-shut immorality to do business in South Africa, produce weapons for the military, to decide against setting up a day-care center, to run a nuclear power plant, or even to make a profit. An enormous amount of work needs to be done to help young people think clearly about complex questions like these, which defy pseudomoralistic answers. They require instead incisive definition and analysis, and a clear headed understanding of a company's sometimes conflicting responsibilities – to its employees, its stockholders, and its country. And these responsibilities often require some agonizingly difficult choices.

I wholeheartedly favor ethical instruction – in a business school or anywhere else in the university – that strengthens such analytical capabilities. I also favor ethical examination of workplace safety, consumer protection, environmental safeguards and the rights of the individual employee within the organization.

But recall what Samuel Johnson once said: if a person doesn't know the difference between good and evil, 'when he leaves our house, let us count our spoons'. If an MBA candidate doesn't know the difference between honesty and crime, between lying and telling the truth, then business school, in all probability, will not produce a born-again convert.

Elementary, grass-roots instruction on why it is bad to sneak, cheat, or steal – such instruction in a school of business administration is much too little, far too late. That's not the place to start. The place to start is kindergarten.

There are, to be sure, vexing constitutional and other problems over prayer in the classroom. But we need not wait for the debate to end – if it ever does – before we begin to reinvigorate ethical instruction in our schools. We can start now, in kindergarten through twelfth grade, and not by feeding our children some vague abstractions called 'values'. I mean we should start with a clear cut study of the past. Our ethical standards come out of the past – out of our inheritance as a people: religious, philosophical, historical. And the more we know of that past, the more surefootedly we can inculcate ethical conduct in the future.

If you want to know about Tammy Bakker, Senator Daniel Patrick Moynihan says, read Sinclair Lewis; if you want to know about insider trading, read Ida Tarbell. If you want to know what it is like to operate in a jungle where the individual predator profits as society suffers, read Thomas Hobbes and John

Locke. If you want to understand the conflict between the demands of the organization and the conscience of the individual, read Thoreau on civil disobedience and Sophocles's *Antigone*. If you want to know about civility, read the words of Confucius. And if you want to know about courage, temperance, truthfulness, and justice, read Aristotle or the Bible.

When I hear reports that American high school students know little or nothing about Chaucer or Walt Whitman or the Civil War or the Old Testament prophets, what bothers me most is not that they exhibit intellectual ignorance. What bothers me is that they have missed the humane lessons in individual ethical conduct that we find in the annals of world history, the biographies of great men and women, and the works of supreme imaginative literature.

A great classical writer once defined history as 'philosophy learned from example'. And a distinguished Brattle Street resident of Cambridge, Henry Wadsworth Longfellow, gave us this eloquent summary:

> Lives of great men all remind us
> We can make our lives sublime,
> And departing, leave behind us
> Footprints on the sands of time.

First things first

My third suggestion is this: let's keep our sense of order straight. Let's put first things first.

We have all heard shortsighted businesspeople attribute a quotation to Vince Lombardi: 'Winning is not the most important thing; it's the *only* thing'. That's a good quotation for firing up a team, but as a business philosophy it is sheer nonsense. There is another, much better Lombardi quotation. He once said he expected his players to have three kinds of loyalty: to God, to their families, and to the Green Bay Packers, 'in that order'.

He knew that some things count more than others. Businessmen and women can be unabashedly proud of their companies. But the good of an entire society transcends that of any single corporation. The moral order of the world transcends any single nation state. And one cannot be a good business leader – or a good doctor or lawyer or engineer – without understanding the place of business in the greater scheme of things.

There is an incandescent example of a group who understood this fact: who saw life steadily, saw it whole, and saw it in a hierarchy – the delegates who drafted the US Constitution in Philadelphia 200 years ago. What do we remember the oldest of them – Benjamin Franklin – for? Not for his vigorous advice on how to get up early in the morning, drive a business, make a profit, and win success in the marketplace, though he did all these things with gusto. We remember him and the others in Philadelphia – and those who signed the Declaration of Independence – because they did not see winning or self-advancement or even life itself as the *only* thing. To something greater than themselves – to a new nation 'conceived in liberty and dedicated to the proposition that all men are created equal' – to that concept they pledged all subordinate things – their lives, their fortunes and their sacred honor.

We should never forget their example.

So there are three suggestions:

• Fortify our ethical buttresses – role models, codes of conduct, the honor system.
• Reinvigorate our children's study of the past.
• Keep our priorities straight.

If we do these things, we shall go far toward discharging our responsibilities as managers and as human beings: contribute to our countries' strengths, heighten their capacity for leadership in an increasingly competitive and productive world, and keep them on the right track as we close out this century and enter the twenty-first.

Reproduced from Akers, John F. (1989). *Sloan Management Review*, Winter, pp. 69–71 by permission of Sloan Management Review Association.

What is 'business ethics'?
Peter F. Drucker

Peter Drucker is one of the leading contemporary writers on management, and has been Clarke Professor of Social Sciences at Claremont Graduate School in California since 1971. He has been an economic consultant to banks and insurance companies, and an advisor on business policy and management to several of America's largest corporations.

In this article Drucker argues that 'business ethics' cannot actually be ethics at all, since ethics is a code of individual behaviour. He claims that a concentration on business ethics is in fact more to do with business politics and fashion, '"ethical chic" rather than ethics'. However, Drucker stops short of saying that companies can have no moral responsibility, saying rather that they should espouse the normal ethical behaviour required of every individual, without creating separate organizational codes of ethics.

'Business ethics' is rapidly becoming the 'in' subject, replacing yesterday's 'social responsibilities'. 'Business ethics' is now being taught in departments of philosophy, business schools and theological seminaries. There are countless seminars on it, speeches, articles, conferences and books, not to mention the many earnest attempts to write 'business ethics' into the law. But what precisely is 'business ethics'? And what could, or should, it be? Is it just another fad, and only the latest round in the hoary American blood sport of business baiting? Is there more to 'business ethics' than the revivalist preacher's call to the sinner to repent? And if there is indeed something that one could call 'business ethics' and could take seriously, what could it be?

Ethics is, after all, not a recent discovery. Over the centuries philosophers in their struggle with human behavior have developed different approaches to ethics, each leading to different conclusions, indeed to conflicting rules of behavior. Where does 'business ethics' fit in – or does it fit in anywhere at all?

The confusion is so great – and the noise level even greater – that perhaps an attempt might be in order to sort out what 'business ethics' might be, and what it might not be, in the light of the major approaches which philosophers have taken throughout the ages (though my only qualification for making this attempt is that I once, many years before anybody even thought of 'business ethics', taught philosophy and religion, and then worked arduously on the tangled questions of 'political ethics').

Business ethics and the western tradition

To the moralist of the western tradition 'business ethics' would make no sense. Indeed, the very term would to him be most objectionable, and reeking of moral laxity. The authorities on ethics disagreed, of course, on what constitutes the grounds of morality – whether they be divine, human nature, or the needs of society. They equally disagreed on the specific rules of ethical behavior; that sternest of moral rules, the Ten Commandments, for instance, thunders 'Thou shalt not covet they neighbor's . . . maidservant.' But it says nothing about 'sexual harassment' of 'one's own' women employees, though it was surely just as common then as now.

All authorities of the western tradition – from the Old Testament prophets all the way to Spinoza in the seventeenth century, to Kant in the eighteenth century, Kierkegaard in the nineteenth century and, in this century, the Englishman F. H. Bradley (*Ethical Studies*) or the American Edmond Cahn (*The Moral Decision*) – are, however, in complete agreement on one point: there is only one ethics, one set of rules of morality, one code, that of *individual* behavior in which the same rules apply to everyone alike.

A pagan could say, 'Quod licet Jovi non licet bovi.' He could thus hold that different rules of behavior apply to Jupiter from those that apply to the ox. A Jew or a Christian would have to reject such differentiation in ethics – and precisely because all experience shows that it always leads to exempting the 'Jupiters', the great, powerful and rich, from the rules which 'the ox', the humble and poor, has to abide by.

The moralist of the western tradition accepts 'extenuating' and 'aggravating' circumstances. He accepts that the poor widow who steals bread to feed her starving children deserves clemency and that it is a more heinous offense for the bishop to have a concubine than for the poor curate in the village. But before there can be 'extenuating' or 'aggravating' circumstances, there has to be an offense. And the offense is the same for rich and poor, for high and low alike – theft is theft, concubinage is concubinage. The reason for this insistence on a code that considers only the individual and not his status in life or society, is precisely that otherwise the mighty, the powerful, the successful will gain exemption from the laws of ethics and morality.

The only differences between what is ethically right and ethically wrong behavior which traditional moralists, almost without exception, would accept – would indeed insist on – are differences grounded in social or cultural mores, and then only in respect to 'venial' offences. That is, the way things are done rather than the substance of behavior. Even in the most licentious society, fidelity to the marriage vow is meritorious, all moralists would agree; but the sexual license of an extremely 'permissive' society, say seventeenth century Restoration England or late twentieth century America, might be considered an 'extenuating circumstance' for the sexual transgressor. And even the sternest moralist has always insisted that, excepting only true 'matters of conscience', practices that are of questionable morality in one place and culture might be perfectly acceptable – and indeed might be quite ethical – in another cultural surrounding. Nepotism may be considered of dubious morality in one culture, in today's United States, for instance. In other cultures, a traditional Chinese one, for example, it may be the very essence of ethical behavior, both by satisfying the moral obligation to one's family and by making disinterested service to the public a little more likely.

But – and this is the crucial point – these are qualifications to the fundamental axiom on which the western tradition of ethics has always been based: there is only one code of ethics, that of individual behavior, for prince and pauper, for rich and poor, for the mighty and the meek alike. Ethics, in the Judaeo-Christian tradition, is the affirmation that all men and women are alike creatures – whether the creator be called God, nature, or society.

And this fundamental axiom 'business ethics' denies. Viewed from the mainstream of traditional ethics, 'business ethics' is not ethics at all, whatever else it may be. For it asserts that acts that are not immoral or illegal if done by ordinary folk become immoral or illegal if done by 'business'.

One blatant example is the treatment of extortion in the current discussions of 'business ethics'. No one ever has had a good word to say for extortion, or has advocated paying it. But if you and I are found to have paid extortion money under threat of physical or material harm, we are not considered to have behaved immorally or illegally. The extortioner is both immoral and a criminal. If a business submits to extortion, however, current 'business ethics' considers it to have acted unethically. There is no speech, article, book, or conference on 'business ethics', for instance, which does not point an accusing finger in great indignation at Lockheed for giving in to a Japanese airline company, which extorted money as a prerequisite to considering the purchase of Lockheed's faltering L-1011 jet plane. There was very little difference betwen Lockheed's paying the Japanese and the pedestrian in New York's Central Park handing his wallet over to a mugger. Yet no one would consider the pedestrian to have acted 'unethically'.

Similarly, in Senate confirmation hearings, one of President Reagan's cabinet appointees was accused of 'unethical practices' and investigated for weeks because his New Jersey construction company was alleged to have paid money to union goons under the threat of their beating up the employees, sabotaging the trucks, and vandalizing the building sites. The accusers were self-confessed labor racketeers; no one seemed to have worried about their 'ethics'.

One can argue that both Lockheed and the New Jersey builder were stupid to pay the holdup men. But as the old saying has it: 'Stupidity is not a court martial offense.' Under the new 'business ethics', it does become exactly that, however. And this is not compatible with what 'ethics' always were supposed to be.

The new 'business ethics' also denies to business the adaptation to cultural mores which has always been considered a moral duty in the traditional approach to ethics. It is now considered 'grossly unethical' – indeed it may even be a 'questionable practice' if not criminal offense – for an American business operating in Japan to retain as a 'counsellor' the distinguished civil servant who retires from his official position in the Japanese government. Yet the business that does not do this is considered in Japan to behave anti-socially and to violate its clear ethical duties. Business taking care of retired senior civil servants, the Japanese hold, makes possible two practices they consider essential to the public interest: that a civil servant past age 45 must retire as soon as he is out-ranked by anyone younger than he; and that governmental salaries and retirement pensions – and with them the burden of the bureaucracy on the taxpayer – be kept low, with the difference between what a first-rate man gets in government service and what he might earn in private employment made up after his retirement through his 'counsellor's fees'. The Japanese maintain that the expectation of later on being a 'counsellor' encourages a civil servant to remain incorruptible, impartial, and objective, and thus to serve only the public good; his counsellorships are obtained for him by his former ministry and its recommendation depends on his rating by his colleagues as a public servant. The Germans, who follow a somewhat similar practice – with senior civil servants expected to be 'taken care of' through appointment as industry-association executives – share this conviction. Yet, despite the fact that both the Japanese and the German systems seem to serve their respective societies well and indeed honorably, and even despite the fact that it is considered perfectly 'ethical' for American civil servants of equal rank and caliber to move into well paid executive jobs in business and foundations and into even more lucrative law practices, the American company in Japan that abides by a practice the Japanese consider the very essence of 'social responsibility', is pilloried in the present discussion of 'business ethics' as a horrible example of 'unethical practices'.

Surely 'business ethics' assumes that for some reason the ordinary rules of ethics do not apply to business. 'Business ethics', in other words, is not 'ethics' at all, as the term has commonly been used by western philosophers and western theologians. What is it then?

Casuistry: the ethics of social responsibility

'It's casuistry,' the history of western philosophy would answer. Casuistry asserted that rulers, because of their responsibility, have to strike a balance between the ordinary demands of ethics which apply to them as individuals and their 'social responsibility' to their subjects, their kingdom – or their company.

'Casuistry' was first propounded in Calvin's *Institutes*, then taken over by the Catholic theologians of the Counter-Reformation (Bellarmin, for instance, or St Charles Borromeus) and developed into a 'political ethics' by their Jesuit disciples in the seventeenth century.

'Casuistry' was the first attempt to think through 'social responsibility' and to embed it in a set of special ethics for those in power. In this respect, 'business ethics' tries to do exactly what the casuists did 300 years ago. And it must end the same way. If 'business ethics' continues to be 'casuistry' its speedy demise in a cloud of ill-repute can be confidently predicted.

To the casuist the 'social responsibility' inherent in being a 'ruler' – that is, someone whose actions have impact on others – is by itself an ethical imperative. As such, the ruler has a duty, as Calvin first laid down, to subordinate his individual behavior and his individual conscience to the demands of his social responsibility.

The *locus classicus* of casuistry is Henry VIII and his first marriage to Catherine of Aragon. A consummated marriage – and Catherine of Aragon had a daughter by Henry, the future 'Bloody Mary' – could not be dissolved except by death, both Catholic and Protestant theologians agreed. In casuistry, however, as both Catholics and Protestants agreed, Henry VIII had an ethical duty to seek annulment of the marriage. Until his father, well within living memory, had snatched the crown by force of arms, England had suffered a century of bloody and destructive civil war becuse of the lack of a legitimate male heir. Without annulment of his marriage, Henry VIII, in other words, exposed his country and its people to mortal danger, well beyond anything he could in conscience justify. The one point on which Protestants and Catholics disagreed was whether the Pope also had a social, and thereby an ethical, responsibility to grant Henry's request. By not granting it, he drove the King and his English subjects out of the Catholic Church. But had he granted the annulment, the Catholic casuists argued, the Pope would have driven Catherine's uncle, the Holy Roman Emperor, out of the Church and into the waiting arms of an emerging Protestanism; and that would have meant that instead of assigning a few million Englishmen to heresy, perdition and hell-fire, many times more souls – all the people in all the lands controlled by the Emperor, that is, in most of Europe – could have been consigned to everlasting perdition.

This may be considered a quaint example – but only because our time measures behavior in economic rather than theological absolutes. The example illustrates what is wrong with casuistry and indeed why it must fail as an approach to ethics. In the first place casuistry must end up becoming politicized, precisely because it considers social responsibility an ethical absolute. In giving primacy to political values and goals it subordinates ethics to politics. Clearly this is the approach 'business ethics' today is taking. Its very origin is in politics rather than in ethics. It expresses a belief that the responsibility which business and the business executive have, precisely because they have social impact, must determine ethics – and this is a political rather than an ethical imperative.

Equally important, the casuist inevitably becomes the apologist for the ruler, the powerful. Casuistry starts out with the insight that the behavior of 'rulers' affects more than themselves and their families. It thus starts out by making demands on the ruler – the starting point for both Calvin and his Catholic disciples in the Counter-Reformation 50 years later. It then concludes that 'rulers' must, therefore, in conscience and ethics, subordinate their interests, including their individual morality, to their social responsibility. But this implies that the rules which decide what is ethical for ordinary people do not apply equally, if at all, to those with social responsibility. Ethics for them is instead a cost-benefit calculation involving the demands of individual conscience and the demands of position – and that means that the 'rulers' are exempt from the demands of ethics, if only their behavior can be argued to confer benefits on other people. And this is precisely how 'business ethics' is going.

Indeed, under casuists' analysis the ethical violations which to most present proponents of 'business ethics' appear the most heinous crimes turn out to have been practically saintly.

Take Lockheed's bribe story for instance. Lockheed was led into paying extortion money to a Japanese airline by the collapse of the supplier of the engines for its wide-bodied L-1011 passenger jet, the English Rolls Royce Company. At that time Lockheed employed some 25 000 people making L-1011s, most of them in southern California which then, 1972–3, was suffering substantial unemployment from sharp cutbacks in defense orders in the aerospace industry. To safeguard the 25 000 jobs, Lockheed got a large government subsidy. But to be able to maintain these jobs, Lockheed needed at least one large L-1011 order from one major airline. The only one among the major airlines not then committed to a competitor's plane was All-Nippon Airways in Japan. The self-interest of Lockheed Corporation and of its stockholders would clearly have demanded speedy abandonment of the L-1011. It was certain that it would never make money – and it has not made a penny yet. Jettisoning the L-1011 would immediately have boosted Lockheed's earnings, maybe doubled them. It would have immediately boosted Lockheed's share price; stock market analysts and investment bankers pleaded with the firm to get rid of the albatross. If Lockheed had abandoned the L-1011, instead of paying extortion money to the Japanese for ordering a few planes and thus keeping the project alive, the company's earnings, its stock price, and the bonuses and stock options of top management, would immediately have risen sharply. Not to have paid extortion money to the Japanese would to a casuist, have been self-serving. To a casuist, paying the extortion money was a duty and social responsibility to which the self-interest of the company, its shareholders and its executives had to be subordinated. It was the discharge of social responsibility of the 'ruler' to keep alive the jobs of 25 000 people at a time when jobs in the aircraft industry in southern California were scarce indeed.

Similarly, the other great 'horror story' of 'business ethics' would, to the casuist, appear as an example of 'business virtue' if not of unselfish 'business martyrdom'. In the 'electrical apparatus conspiracy' of the late 1950s, several high ranking General Electric executives were sent to jail. They were found guilty of a criminal conspiracy in violation of antitrust because orders for heavy generating equipment, such as turbines, were parcelled out among the three electrical apparatus manufacturers in the US – General Electric, Westinghouse, and Allis Chalmers. But this 'criminal conspiracy' only served to reduce General Electric's sales, its profits, and the bonuses and stock options of the General Electric executives who took part in the conspiracy. Since the electric apparatus cartel was destroyed by the criminal prosecution of the General Electric executives, General Electric sales and profits in the heavy apparatus field have sharply increased, as has market penetration by the company, which now has what amounts to a near monopoly. The purpose of the cartel – which incidentally was started under federal government pressure in the Depression years to fight unemployment – was the protection of the weakest and most dependent of the companies, Allis Chalmers (which is located in Milwaukee, a depressed and declining old industrial area). As soon as government action destroyed the cartel, Allis Chalmers had to go out of the turbine business and had to lay off several thousand people. And while there is still abundant competition in the world market for heavy electric apparatus, General Electric now enjoys such market dominance in the home market that the United States, in case of war, would not have major alternative suppliers of so critical a product as turbines.

The casuist would agree that cartels are both illegal and considered immoral in the US – although not necessarily anywhere else in the world. But he would also argue that the General Electric executive who violated US law had an ethical duty to do so under the 'higher law' of social responsibility to safeguard both employment in the Milwaukee area and the defense production base of the United States.

The only thing that is surprising about these examples is that business has not yet used them to climb on the casuist bandwagon of 'business ethics'. For just as almost any behavior indulged in by the seventeenth century ruler could be shown to be an ethical duty by the seventeenth century disciples of Calvin, of Bellarmin and of Borromeus, so almost any behavior of the executive in organizations today – whether in a business, a hospital, a university, or a government agency – could be shown to be his ethical duty under the casuistic cost-benefit analysis between individual ethics and the demands of social responsibility. There are indeed signs aplenty that the most apolitical of 'rulers', the American business executive, is waking up to the political potential of 'business ethics'. Some of the advertisements which large companies – Mobil Oil, for example – are now running to counter the attacks made on them in the name of 'social responsibility' and 'business ethics', clearly use the casuist approach to defend business, and indeed to counter attack. But if 'business ethics' becomes a tool to defend as 'ethical' acts on the part of executives that would be condemned if committed by anyone else, the present proponents of 'business ethics', like their casuist predecessors 400 years ago, will have no one to blame but themselves.

Casuistry started out as high morality. In the end, its ethics came to be summed up in two well known pieces of cynicism: 'An ambassador is an honest man, lying abroad for the good of his country,' went a well known eighteenth century pun. And 100 years later, Bismarck said, 'What a scoundrel a minister would be if, in his own private life, he did half the things he has a duty to do to be true to his oath of office.'

Long before that, however, casuistry had been killed off by moral revulsion. Its most lasting memory perhaps are the reactions to it which re-established ethics in the west as a universal system, binding the individual regardless of station, function, or 'social responsibility': Spinoza's *Ethics*, and the *Provincial Letters* of his contemporary, Blaise Pascal. But also – and this is a lesson that might be pondered by today's proponents of 'business ethics', so many of whom are clergymen – it was their embracing casuistry that made the Jesuits hated and despised, made 'Jesuitical' a synonym of 'immoral', and led to the Jesuit order being suppressed by the Pope in the eighteenth century. And it is casuistry, more than anything else, that has caused the anti-clericalism of the intellectuals in Catholic Europe.

'Business ethics' undoubtedly is a close parallel to casuistry. Its origin is political, as was that of casuistry. Its basic thesis, that ethics for the ruler, and especially for the business executive, has to express 'social responsibility' is exactly the starting point of the casuist. But if 'business ethics' is casuistry, then it will not last long – and long before it dies, it will have become a tool of the business executive to justify what for other people would be unethical behavior, rather than a tool to restrain the business executive and to impose tight ethical limits on business.

The ethics of prudence and self-development

There is one other major tradition of ethics in the west, the ethics of prudence. It goes all the way back to Aristotle and his enthronement of prudence as a cardinal virtue. It continued for almost 2000 years in the popular literary tradition of the 'education of the Christian prince', which reached its ultimate triumph and its reduction to absurdity in Machiavelli's *Prince*. Its spirit can best be summed up by the advice which then-Senator Harry Truman gave to an army witness before his committee in the early years of World War Two: 'Generals should never do ãnything that needs to be explained to a Senate Committee – there is nothing one can explain to a Senate Committee.'

'Generals', whether the organization is an army, a corporation, or a university, are highly visible. They must expect their behaviour to be seen, scrutinized, analyzed, discussed and questioned. Prudence thus demands that they shun actions that cannot easily be understood, explained or justified. But 'generals', being visible, are also examples. They are 'leaders' by their very position and visibility. Their only choice is whether their example leads others to right action or to wrong action. Their only choice is between direction and misdirection, between leadership and misleadership. They thus have an ethical obligation to give the example of right behavior and to avoid giving the example of wrong behavior.

The ethics of prudence do not spell out what 'right' behavior is. They assume that what is wrong behavior is clear enough – and if there is any doubt, it is 'questionable' and to be avoided. Prudence makes it an ethical duty for the leader to exemplify the precepts of ethics in his own behavior.

And by following prudence, everyone regardless of status becomes a 'leader', a 'superior man' and will 'fulfill himself', to use the contemporary idiom. One becomes the 'superior man' by avoiding any act which would make one the kind of person one does not want to be, does not respect, does not accept as superior. 'If you don't want to see a pimp when you look in the shaving mirror in the morning, don't hire call girls the night before to entertain congressmen, customers or salesmen.' On any other basis, hiring call girls may be condemned as vulgar and tasteless, and may be shunned as something that fastidious people do not do. It may be frowned upon as uncouth. It may even be illegal. But only in prudence is it ethically relevant. This is what Kierkegaard, the sternest moralist of the nineteenth century, meant when he said that aesthetics is the true ethics.

The ethics of prudence can easily degenerate. Concern with what one can justify becomes, only too easily, concern with appearances – Machiavelli was by no means the first to point out that in a 'prince', that is, in someone in authority and high visibility, appearances may matter more than substance. The ethics of prudence thus easily decay into the hypocrisy of 'public relations'. Leadership through right example easily degenerates into the sham of 'charisma' and into a cloak for misdirection and misleadership – it is always the Hitlers and the Stalins who are the 'great charismatic leaders'. And fulfillment through self-development into a 'superior person' – what Kierkegaard called 'becoming a Christian' – may turn either into the smugness of the Pharisee who thanks God that he is not like other people, or into self-indulgence instead of self-discipline, moral sloth instead of self-respect, and into saying 'I like', rather than 'I know'.

Yet, despite these degenerative tendencies, the ethics of prudence is surely appropriate to a society of organizations. Of course, it will not be 'business ethics' – it makes absolutely no difference in the ethics of prudence whether the executive is a general in the army, a bureau chief in the Treasury Department in Washington, a senator, a judge, a senior vice-president in a bank, or a hospital administrator. But a 'society of organizations' is a society in which an extraordinarily large number of people are in positions of high visibility, if only within one organization. They enjoy this visibility not, like the 'Christian prince', by virtue of birth, nor by virtue of wealth – that is, not because they are 'personages'. They are 'functionaries' and important only through their responsibility to take right action. But this is exactly what the ethics of prudence are all about.

Similarly, executives set examples, whatever the organization. They 'set the tone', 'create the spirit', 'decide the values' for an organization and for the people in it. They lead or mislead, in other words. And they have no choice but to do one or the other. Above all, the ethics or aesthetics of self-development would seem to be tailor-made for the specific dilemma of the executive in the modern organization. By himself he is a nobody and indeed anonymous. A week after he has retired and has left that big corner office on the twenty-sixth floor of his company's skyscraper or the Secretary's six-room corner suite on Constitution Avenue, no one in the building even recognizes him anymore. And his neighbors in the pleasant suburb in which he lives in a comfortable middle class house – very different from anything one might call a 'palace' – only know that 'Joe works someplace on Park Avenue' or 'does something in the government'. Yet collectively these anonymous executives are the 'leaders' in a modern society. Their function demands the self-discipline and the self-respect of the 'superior man'. To live up to the performance expectations society makes upon them, they have to strive for self-fulfillment rather than be content with lackadaisical mediocrity. Yet at the pinnacle of their career and success, they are still cogs in an organization and easily replaceable. And this is exactly what self-fulfillment in ethics, the Kierkegaardian 'becoming a Christian', concerns itself with: how to become the 'superior man', important and autonomous, without being a 'big shot' let alone a 'prince'.

One would therefore expect the discussion of 'business ethics' to focus on the ethics of prudence. Some of the words, such as to 'fulfill oneself', indeed sound the same, though they mean something quite different. But by and large, the discussion of 'business ethics', even if more sensibly concerning itself with the 'ethics of organization', will have nothing to do with prudence.

The reason is clearly that the ethics of prudence are the ethics of authority. And while today's discussion of 'business ethics' (or of the ethics of university administration, of hospital administration, or of government) clamors for responsibility, it rejects out of hand any 'authority' and, of course, particularly any authority of the business executive. Authority is not 'legitimate'; it is 'elitism'. But there can be no responsibility where authority is denied. To deny it is not 'anarchism' nor 'radicalism', let alone 'socialism'. In a child, it is called a temper tantrum.

The ethics of interdependence

Casuistry was so thoroughly discredited that the only mention of it to be found in most textbooks on the history of philosophy is in connection with its ultimate adversaries – Spinoza and Pascal. Indeed, only 10 or 15 years ago, few if any philosophers would have thought it possible for anything like 'business ethics' to emerge. 'Particularist ethics', a set of ethics that postulates that this or that group is different in its ethical responsibilities from everyone else, would have been considered doomed forever by the failure of casuistry. Ethics, almost anyone in the west would have considered axiomatic, would surely always be ethics of the individual and independent of rank and station.

But there is another, non-western ethics that is situational. It is the most successful and most durable ethics of them all: the Confucian ethics of interdependence.

Confucian ethics elegantly sidesteps the trap into which the casuists fell; it is a universal ethics, in which the same rules and imperatives of behavior hold for every individual. There is no 'social responsibility' overriding individual conscience, no cost-benefit calculation, no greater good or higher measure than the individual and his behavior, and altogether no casuistry. In the Confucian ethics, the rules are the same for all. But there are different general rules, according to the five basic relationships of interdependence, which for the Confucian embrace the totality of individual interactions in civil society: superior and subordinate (or master and servant); father and child; husband and wife; oldest brother and sibling; friend and friend. Right behavior – what in the English translation of Confucian ethics is usually called 'sincerity'* – is that individual behavior which is truly appropriate to the specific relationship of mutual dependence because it optimizes benefits for both parties. Other behavior is 'insincere' and therefore wrong behavior and unethical. It creates dissonance instead of harmony, exploitation instead of benefits, manipulation instead of trust.

An example of the Confucian approach to the ethical problems discussed under the heading of 'business ethics' would be 'sexual harassment'. To the Confucian it is clearly unethical behavior because it injects power into a relationship that is based on function. This makes it exploitation. That this 'insincere' – that is, grossly unethical – behavior on the part of a superior takes place within a business or any other kind of organization, is basically irrelevant. The master/servant or superior/subordinate relationship is one between individuals. Hence, the Confucian would make no distinction between a general manager forcing his secretary into sexual intercourse and Mr Samuel Pepys, England's famous seventeenth century diarist, forcing his wife's maids to submit to his amorous advances. It would not even make much difference to the Confucian that today's secretary can, as a rule, quit without suffering more than inconvenience if she does not want to submit, whereas the poor wretches in Mrs Pepys' employ ended up as prostitutes, either because they did not submit and were fired and out on the street, or because they did submit and were fired when they got pregnant. Nor would the Confucian see much difference between a corporation vice-president engaging in 'sexual harassment' and a college professor seducing coeds with implied promises to raise their grades.

And finally, it would be immaterial to the Confucian that the particular 'insincerity' involves sexual relations. The superior would be equally guilty of grossly unethical behavior and violation of fundamental rules of conduct if, as a good many of the proponents of 'business ethics' ardently advocate, he were to set himself up as a mental therapist for his subordinates and help them to 'adjust.' No matter how benevolent his intentions, this is equally incompatible with the integrity of the superior/subordinate relationship. It equally abuses rank based on function and imposes power. It is therefore exploitation whether done because of lust for power or manipulation or done out of benevolence – either way it is unethical and destructive. Both sexual relations and the healer/patient relationship must be free of rank to be effective, harmonious, and ethically correct. They are constructive only as 'friend to friend' or as 'husband to wife' relations, in which differences in function confer no rank whatever.

This example makes it clear, I would say, that virtually all the concerns of

* No word has caused more misunderstanding in east/west relations than 'sincerity'. To a westerner, 'sincerity' means 'words that are true to conviction and feelings'; to an easterner, 'sincerity' means 'actions that are appropriate to a specific relationship and make it harmonious and of optimum mutual benefit'. For the westerner, 'sincerity' has to do with intentions, that is, with morality; to the easterner, 'sincerity' has to do with behavior, that is, with ethics.

'business ethics', indeed almost everything 'business ethics' considers a problem, have to do with relationship of interdependence, whether that between the organization and the employee, the manufacturer and the customer, the hospital and the patient, the university and the student, and so on.

Looking at the ethics of interdependence immediately resolves the conundrum which confounds the present discussion of 'business ethics': what difference does it make whether a certain act or behavior takes place in a 'business', in a 'non-profit organization', or outside any organization at all? The answer is clear: none at all. Indeed the questions that are so hotly debated in today's discussion of 'business ethics', such as whether changing a hospital from 'non-profit' to 'proprietary and for profit' will affect either its behavior or the ethics pertaining to it, the most cursory exposure to the ethics of interdependence reveals as sophistry and as non-questions.

The ethics of interdependence thus does address itself to the question that 'business ethics' tries to tackle. But today's discussion, explicitly or implicitly, denies the basic insight from which the ethics of interdependence starts and to which it owes its strength and durability: It denies *interdependence*.

The ethics of interdependence, as Confucian philosophers first codified it shortly after their master's death in 479 BC, considers illegitimate and unethical the injection of power into human relationships. It asserts that interdependence demands equality of obligations. Children owe obedience and respect to their parents. Parents, in turn, owe affection, sustenance and, yes, respect, to their children. For every paragon of filial piety in Confucian hagiology, such as the dutiful daughter, there is a paragon of parental sacrifice, such as the loving father who sacrificed his brilliant career at the court to the care of his five children and their demands on his time and attention. For every minister who risks his job, if not his life, by fearlessly correcting an Emperor guilty of violating harmony, there is an Emperor laying down his life rather than throw a loyal minister to the political wolves.

In the ethics of interdependence there are only 'obligations', and all obligations are mutual obligations. Harmony and trust – that is, interdependence – require that each side be obligated to provide what the other side needs to achieve its goals and to fulfill itself.

But in today's American – and European – discussion of 'business ethics', ethics means that one side has obligations and the other side has rights, if not 'entitlements'. This is not compatible with the ethics of interdependence and indeed with any ethics at all. It is the politics of power, and indeed the politics of naked exploitation and repression. And within the context of interdependence the 'exploiters' and 'oppressors' are not the 'bosses', but the ones who assert their 'rights' rather than accept mutual obligation, and with it, equality. To 'redress the balance' in a relationship of interdependence – or at least so the ethics of interdependence would insist – demands not pitting power against power or right against right, but matching obligation to obligation.

To illustrate: today's 'ethics of organization' debate pays great attention to the duty to be a 'whistle-blower' and to the protection of the 'whistle-blower' against retaliation or suppression by his boss or by his organization. This sounds high minded. Surely, the subordinate has a right, if not indeed a duty, to bring to public attention and remedial action his superior's misdeeds, let alone violation of the law on the part of a superior or of his employing organization. But in the context of the ethics of interdependence, 'whistle-blowing' is ethically quite ambiguous. To be sure, there are misdeeds of the superior or of the employing organization which so grossly violate propriety and laws that the subordinate (or the friend, or the child, or even the wife) cannot remain silent. This is, after all, what the word 'felony' implies; one become, a partner to a felony and criminally liable by not reporting, and thus 'compounding' it. But otherwise? It is not primarily that to encourage 'whistle-blowing' corrodes the bond of trust that ties the superior to the subordinate. Encouraging the 'whistle-blower' must make the subordinate lose his trust in the superior's willingness and ability to 'protect his people'. They simply are no longer 'his people' and become potential enemies or political pawns. And in the end, encouraging and indeed even permitting 'whistle-blowers' always makes the weaker one – that is, the subordinate – powerless against the unscrupulous superior, simply because the superior no longer can recognize or meet his obligation to the subordinate.

'Whistle-blowing', after all, is simply another word for 'informing'. And perhaps it is not quite irrelevant that the only societies in western history that encouraged informers were bloody and infamous tyrannies – Tiberius and Nero in Rome, the Inquisition in the Spain of Philip II, the French Terror, and Stalin. It may also be no accident that Mao, when he tried to establish dictatorship in China, organized 'whistle-blowing' on a massive scale. For under 'whistle-blowing', under the regime of the 'informer', no mutual trust, no interdependencies, and no ethics are possible. And Mao only followed history's first 'totalitarians', the 'legalists' of the third century BC, who suppressed Confucius and burned his books because he had taught ethics and had rejected the absolutism of political power.

The limits of mutual obligation are indeed a central and difficult issue in the ethics of interdependencies. But to start out, as the advocates of 'whistle-blowing' do, with the assumption that there are only rights on one side, makes any ethics impossible. And if the fundamental problem of ethics is the behaviour in relations of interdependence, then obligations have to be mutual and have to be equal for both sides. Indeed, in a relationship of interdependence it is the mutality of obligation that creates true equality, regardless of differences in rank, wealth, or power.

Today's discussion of 'business ethics' stridently denies this. It tends to assert that in relations of interdependence one side has all the duties and the other one all the rights. But this is the assertion of the legalist, the assertion of the totalitarians who shortly end up by denying all ethics. It must also mean that ethics becomes the tool of the powerful. If a set of ethics is one-sided, then the rules are written by those that have the position, the power, the wealth. If interdependence is not equality of obligations, it becomes domination.

Looking at 'business ethics' as an ethics of interdependence reveals an additional and equally serious problem – indeed a *more* serious problem.

Can an ethics of interdependence be anything more than ethics for individuals? The Confucians said 'no' – a main reason why Mao outlawed them. For the Confucian – but also for the philosopher of the western tradition – only *law* can handle the rights and objections of collectives. *Ethics* is always a matter of the person.

But is this adequate for a 'society of organizations' such as ours? This may be the central question for the philosopher of modern society, in which access to livelihood, career and achievement exist primarily in and through organizations – and especially for the highly educated person for whom opportunities outside the organization are very scarce indeed. In such a society, both the society and the individual increasingly depend on the performance, as well as the 'sincerity', of organizations.

But in today's discussion of 'business ethics' it is not even seen that there is a problem.

'Ethical chic' or ethics

'Business ethics', this discussion should have made clear, is to ethics what soft porn is to the Platonic Eros: soft porn too talks of something it calls 'love'. And in so far as 'business ethics' comes even close to ethics, it comes close to casuistry and will, predictably, end up as a fig leaf for the shameless and as special pleading for the powerful and the wealthy.

Clearly, one major element of the peculiar stew that goes by the name of 'business ethics' is plain old-fashioned hostility to business and to economic activity altogether – one of the oldest of American traditions and perhaps the only still-potent ingredient in the Puritan heritage. Otherwise, we would not even talk of 'business ethics'. There is no warrant in any ethics to consider one major sphere of activity as having its own ethical problems, let alone its own 'ethics'. 'Business' or 'economic activity' may have special political or legal dimensions as in 'business and government', to cite the title of a once-popular college course, or as in the anti-trust laws. And 'business ethics' may be good politics or good electioneering. But that is all. For ethics deals with the right actions of individuals. And then it surely makes no difference whether the setting is a community hospital, with the actors a nursing supervisor and the 'consumer' a patient, or whether the setting is National Universal General Corporation, the actors a quality control manager, and the consumer the buyer of a bicycle.

But one explanation for the popularity of 'business ethics' is surely also the human frailty of which Pascal accused the casuists of his day: the lust for power and prominence of a clerisy sworn to humility. 'Business ethics' is fashionable, and provides speeches at conferences, lecture fees, consulting assignments and lots of publicity. And surely 'business ethics', with its tales of wrongdoing in high places, caters also to the age-old enjoyment of 'society' gossip and to the prurience which – it was, I believe, Rabelais who said it – makes it fornication when a peasant has a toss in the hay and romance when the prince does it.

Altogether, 'business ethics' might well be called 'ethical chic' rather than ethics – and indeed might be considered more a media event than philosophy or morals.

But this discussion of the major approaches to ethics and of their concerns surely also shows that ethics has as much to say to the individual in our society of organizations as they ever had to say to the individual in earlier societies. They are just as important and just as needed nowadays. And they surely require hard and serious work.

A society of organizations is a society of interdependence. The specific relationship which the Confucian philosopher postulated as universal and basic may not be adequate, or even appropriate, to modern society and to the ethical problems within the modern organization and between the modern organization and its clients, customers, and constituents. But the fundamental concepts surely are. Indeed, if there ever is a viable 'ethics of organization', it will almost certainly have to adopt the key concepts which have made Confucian ethics both durable and effective:

- clear definition of the fundamental relationships
- universal and general rules of conduct – that is, rules that are binding on any one person or organization, according to its rules, function, and relationships
- focus on right behavior rather than on avoiding wrongdoing, and on behavior rather than on motives or intentions
- an effective organization ethic, indeed an organization ethic that deserves to be seriously considered as 'ethics', will have to define right behavior as the behavior which optimizes each party's benefits and thus makes the relationship harmonious, constructive, and mutually beneficial.

But a society of organizations is also a society in which a great many people are unimportant and indeed anonymous by themselves, yet are highly visible, and matter as 'leaders' in society. And thus it is a society that must stress the ethics of prudence and self-development. It must expect its managers, executives, and professionals to demand of themselves that they shun behavior they would not respect in others, and instead practice behavior appropriate to the sort of person they would want to see 'in the mirror in the morning'.

Reproduced from Drucker, Peter F. (1981). *The Public Interest*, Spring, by permission of the author.

What is necessary for corporate moral excellence?
W. Michael Hoffman

Michael Hoffman is director of the Center for Business Ethics and chair of the philosophy department at Bentley College, Massachusetts.

This article, in contrast to Peter Drucker, argues both that companies can be held morally responsible, and that individuals have independent moral responsibility within the company context. Companies can be morally good or bad according to the consequences of their actions; and individuals can commit good and bad acts within both good and bad companies. The culture of a company is defined by its values, and shapes the actions and attitudes of its employees. To Hoffman, 'The morally excellent coporation is one that discovers and makes operational the healthy reciprocity between its culture and the autonomy of its individuals'. He goes on to suggest guidelines for developing a corporate moral culture.

There are some who would argue that this question doesn't even make sense, not at least until explanation is given as to how we can predicate moral properties such as moral responsibility to the corporation. Here we seem to run head-on into the controversial topic often called corporate moral agency, the debate over which has come to almost dominate (unwisely, I think) business ethics studies, especially among philosophers. One side, in its strongest formulation, seems to want to identify, ethically at least, corporations and persons. Peter French, for example, 'accepts corporations as members of the moral community, of equal standing with the traditionally acknowledged residents – biological human beings' and as such 'they can have whatever privileges, rights, and duties as are, in the normal course of affairs, accorded to moral persons' (French, 1984). On the other side, it is argued that only human individuals can be moral agents and, as Manuel Velasquez so shockingly puts it, this is 'why corporations are not morally responsible for anything they do' (Velasquez, 1983). To make moral judgments of a corporation, then, is really only a shorthand way of speaking about certain individuals in the corporation.

Both of these positions go to what I see as mistaken extremes because of legitimate worries over where to place praise or blame when dealing with organized collectives. To say that only human individuals are morally responsible is to fail to recognize that collective entities like corporations, armies, nation states, faculties, committees do bring things about in ways that are not just reducible to or explainable by aggregates of individual actions. The whole of the collective entity is more than just the sum of its parts because the individuals who make up the collective (and whose actions are clearly necessary for the collective to act) are organized around cooperative purposes, goals, strategies, mission statements, policies, charters or whatever you call that which gives the collective its identity and spells out its function. People act on behalf of the collective purpose and according to collective directives. It is the collective relations that channel the actions of its individuals giving the collective itself a kind of causal efficacy. This is why it makes sense to hold a corporation, say Ford for the making of its Pinto gas tank (see Hoffman, 1984), not only legally but also morally responsible. Furthermore, to isolate just certain individuals within Ford as morally culpable, if that is even possible, seems to imply that by punishing or getting rid of those bad apples, the corporation will be fine in the future without any careful examination and change of the goals, strategies, and environment for decision making out of which the corporation operates. This is surely a cause for worry. Individuals should not be singled out as scapegoats for corporate systemic failure.

On the other hand, there is the worry that attributing moral responsibility to collectives like corporations blocks us from going inside the organization to get at praiseworthy or blameworthy individuals who in the most fundamental sense intentionally caused the action to come about. If individuals within Ford freely and knowingly produced an unsafe car, then they should not be allowed to escape legal or moral judgement by hiding behind a veil of corporate agency. Furthermore, to view the corporation as some sort of large scale moral organism with some kind of life of its own is not only anthropomorphism at its very worst, but also creates a situation where individual interest and autonomy can easily be submerged under what is perceived as the corporate good. Velasquez refers to this as organizational totalitarianism, and 'philosophers who subscribe to the theory that the corporation is a moral agent that is morally responsible for its wrongful acts are unwittingly allying themselves with this new form of totalitarianism' (Velasquez, 1983, p. 16). These, too, are legitimate concerns. Corporations should not be used to subordinate individual moral responsibility or individual autonomy.

My aim here is not to capture the richness and complexity of the corporate agency debate, nor will I take on the ambitious task of trying to resolve the issue. The literature is filled with such efforts to the extent that I suspect it is time for work in business ethics to move on to more fertile ground. This is not to say the debate has been unfruitful; on the contrary, the harvest has been rich, and we should carry with us the best of the fruits of our labors. In keeping with this I suggest there is insight to be gained from both sides of the debate as well as extremes to be avoided.

I see no need to further clutter our metaphysical landscape by granting a kind of personhood to collectives like corporations forcing us to search for something like a corporate mind. Nevertheless, we must recognize that the goals and strategies of an organization can lead to certain actions which are subject to moral judgement and that these actions are not, in many cases, attributable or distributable to individuals within the collective. Systems and structures can be morally good or bad, rather than just morally neutral, because they result in morally good or bad consequences when followed. There is surely some sense in which Lieutenant Calley was a victim of a system and that neither he nor any collection of individuals were alone responsible for the massacre at My Lai even though it was Calley who pulled the trigger. Therefore, although it may be tricky both conceptually and practically, corporations and other collectives can, must in fact, stand up to the demands of moral responsibility, even though their actions are carried out by individuals acting on their behalf. (Werhane, 1984) We should note that it is possible for there to be a complete change over in the membership of a corporation without changing the structure or character of the corporation itself. (French, 1982, pp. 271–78) The name 'Ford' or the 'US army' denotes something that is, in a very significant sense, indifferent to or independent of the particular constitution of its membership.

We must, however, recognize the importance of the individual, both ontologically and ethically, to and within the collective. While it is wrong, even dangerous, to say that corporations are not morally responsible for anything they do such that the only 'proper subject of a business ethic is the individual business person', (Velasquez, 1983, p. 1) it is, nevertheless, individuals who create corporations, constitute their membership, and carry out their functions. Although corporations are more than the sum of its members, without individuals there would be no corporations or any activities by corporations. We surely also want to recognize that individuals can be praiseworthy or blameworthy within both good and bad corporations and that it is certainly possible, although not necessary, for individuals to get swallowed up by the environments of corporations, thereby losing their autonomy.

Relating individual and corporate responsibility can happen in several ways. A corporation might be held morally responsible when no specific individual of the corporation is morally responsible, similar to Karl Marx's indictment of the capitalist system whose members are simply products and tools of it. A corporation can be morally responsible when certain individuals of the corporation are also morally responsible. To point a finger of blame at the policies and procedures of the US army should not necessarily absolve Lieutenant Calley of moral guilt, and perhaps Lee Iacocca and Henry Ford II should have been indicted along with Ford Motor Co. And a corporation might be morally responsible when each individual of the corporation is also morally responsible. Even while holding the Nazi regime morally responsible, Karl Jaspers proclaims that:'Every German is made to share the blame for the crimes committed in the name of the Reich . . . inasmuch as we let such a regime rise among us.' (Jaspers, 1971)

We must also make sure that, by granting moral status to organized collectives like corporations – a status which in many cases is distinct from the moral responsibility of its members, we don't turn the individual into just a pawn for the corporate purpose. Individuals should have the necessary room and knowledge to engage in critical reflection on the corporation for which they are acting out a particular role. It is possible for corporations in all sorts of ways to deny this to their individual members resulting in rational stagnation and moral blindness for the entire collective. (see Ewing, 1977) In fact, some feel this has become today's reality. We listen to William Scott and David Hart say that:

> In our time, the source of legitimacy for institutions is the organizational imperative, which requires individual obedience to it. What is more, such obedience is now a value in and of itself, supplanting the presumed ascendency of individuality. (Scott and Hart, 1979)

And we read in *Business Week* where 60 to 70 per cent of the managers of two major corporations feel pressure to sacrifice their own personal ethical integrity for corporate goals. (*Business Week*, 31 Jan 1977)

I believe these insights and concerns stemming out of both sides of the corporate agency debate help to point our way to what is necessary for corporate moral excellence. Talking about corporate moral excellence does make sense and not just by way of talking about individual moral excellence. We are referring here to what could be called the character or culture of the corporation which is formed by its goals and policies, its structure and strategies, which ultimately reflect its attitudes and values. It is the set of formalized relations among the individuals who make it up, and it may well outlast those individuals who originally created it. (see De George, 1983) This culture defines the corporation's way of doing business, and it is out of this culture that the actions and attitudes of corporate individuals are shepherded and shaped.

But it is individuals, of course, who create these goals, who nurture or change them, and who actively carry them out. Without individuals there would be no critical evaluation of corporate cultures and, therefore, no way for the corporation to move forward rationally and creatively. Here we are referring to what could be called the autonomy of the individual. A corporation is constituted both by its culture and by its individual members. The culture provides the relational framework of shared beliefs and values around which a collection of individuals is identified as a corporation. The morally excellent corporation is one that discovers and makes operational the healthy reciprocity between its culture and the autonomy of its individuals.

But this is no easy task. It is the age-old problem of the individual within a society. Social cultures formed around common goals give meaning and purpose to individuals, but at the same time they present the danger of robbing individuals of their autonomy. When individuals lose their autonomy, they cease to be individuals, yet to act without regard to the common goals of the society is to give up one's identity as a part of the culture and to fail to live up to one's duties as a part of the collective whole. In fact, John Dewey and James Tufts have observed that 'Apart from ties which bind [the individual] to others, [the individual] is nothing.' (Dewey and Tufts, 1980) Individualism and collectivism are both abstractions. Neither social cultures nor individuals can exist without the other. Their respective being and value are irrevocably interwoven. Referring again to Dewey and Tufts, 'no question can be reduced to the individual on one side and the social on the other'. (Dewey and Tufts, 1980, p. 314) And the question of what is necessary for corporate moral excellence is no exception. The trick is to find the proper weave.

For a corporation to be morally excellent, it must develop and act out of a moral corporate culture. Although Thomas Peters and Robert Waterman in their book *In Search of Excellence* do not focus on morality as such, there are, nevertheless, many moral lessons to be learned from America's excellent companies. And surely this concept of corporate culture is one of the most important:

> Every excellent company we studied is clear on what it stands for, and takes the process of value shaping seriously. In fact, we wonder whether it is possible to be an excellent company without clarity on values and without having the right sorts of values. (Peters and Waterman, 1982)

What we would want to add to this statement by Peters and Waterman is that morally excellent corporations must include ethical values in the shaping of their cultures. Or, better yet, their cultures must be shaped from a moral point of view.

Of course, there are those who argue that this whole tack is wrong. Corporations are amoral entities and by urging them to develop a conscience or a moral perspective is to turn them away from their legitimate function – namely, to be efficient machines for production and profit. The result, so it is argued, will be bad for business and thereby bad for the common social good. Morality for business ought to be externally established by the government and the courts and/or by the market, but not internally by the corporation itself. Enough arguments have already been put forward to defeat this position. And, I think, most of us, including corporations, are now sufficiently convinced that corporations can and must morally regulate themselves with the help of external forces. Society expects it and morality demands it. I might only add here that rather than being bad for business, the lessons learned from the best-run companies singled out by Peters and Waterman strengthen the belief many have in the connection between business excellence and a morally sensitive corporate culture.

But what steps must be taken in developing a morally sensitive corporate culture? What elements go into making up a moral point of view for corporate culture? I suggest that we follow Christopher Stone's advice and try to undersand what moral responsibility entails 'in the ordinary case of the responsible human being'. (Stone, 1975) After all, corporations are made up of human beings and act through human beings and are designed to ultimately serve the interests of human beings. Furthermore, I suggest that we can profit from Kenneth Goodpaster's 'projection' of the elements and steps involved in moral responsibility for the individual onto the corporation. Borrowing from W. K. Frankena, Goodpaster isolates two basic components of the moral point of view: rationality and respect. The former involves the objective and systematic reasoning out of one's purposes and the strategies for achieving them; the latter involves a concern for the intrinsic value of other human beings and a sensitivity toward their rights, needs, and interests. Using rationality and respect as moral guides, three steps can be identified in the moral decision-making process: perception, reflection, and action. (see Goodpaster, 1973)

First, one must be able to perceive or recognize an ethical issue as ethical and thereby deserving of moral attention. And what we see, in many cases, depends on what we are looking for – on how and why we gather and categorize our data. If we are not sensitive to or interested in finding something, then we may very well filter it out of our conscious awareness, becoming blind to it if you will. So it is with moral perception. If we are not wearing moral glasses, so to speak, we will not see or look for things from a moral viewpoint. In developing a moral culture a corporation must be on the watch for ethical situations.

Using moral glasses the corporation should cast its information net as wide as the effects of its activities on the quality of life. According to Ken Andrews, for the multinational corporation such a net would include the world within which it operates, the nation to which it belongs, the local community within which it is housed, the industry out of which it functions and the internal workings of the firm itself (Andrews, 1980). Moral awareness takes concentrated effort and a commitment of vision which eventually develops into an habitual way of seeing, gathering, interpreting, and processing data. Moral blindness does not excuse corporations from culpability. Corporations, like individuals, have the responsibility to pay attention to and seek out ethical facts.

Secondly, moral perception must then be synthesized through thinking. A moral point of view must bring rational principles and procedures to bear upon the moral data in order to arrive at a moral conclusion. In developing a moral culture a corporation must formulate clear ethical strategies and structures, taking into account opportunities and risks, resources and competencies, personal values and preferences, and economic and social responsibilities (Andrews, 1980, pp. 100, 101). Such a moral corporate thinking process might include ethical codification, management and worker ethical training programs, broad-based board representation, internal ethical audits, clear and open avenues for information flow to provide for ongoing communication and consultation at all levels, and the hiring and directing of top corporate officers to develop corporate ethical policies and management strategies for the carrying out of such policies. Moves such as these and others will enable the corporation to systematically reflect upon the moral data of which it becomes aware in an effort to arrive at a moral position for decision making.

But such moral reflection would be incomplete without coordinating moral demands with other demands, interests, and constraints. Just as one can be morally blind, one can also be morally foolish or quixotic. Surely morality doesn't demand that one plunge into a raging ocean to try vainly to save a life if one can't swim or give all of one's earnings to charity resulting in one's own destitution. Only when one sees one's total environment as consisting of many different and often conflicting demands, interests, and constraints will alternatives be sought. One might then throw out a life preserver to save the drowning victim and work for charity drives in order to procure more funds from a wider distribution.

Corporations are no different. They too face many conflicting demands, interests, and constraints. Corporations are designed for economic purposes and face pressures from laws and government regulations and from competitors in the market. I am reminded of a story told by George Cabot Lodge where a business went bankrupt by unilaterally pouring millions of dollars into pollution equipment. As a result the river was no cleaner and 400 people were put out of work (Cabot Lodge, 1977). I suggest that this was no action from a moral point of view because no rational effort at coordinating the intersecting pressures, needs, and goals was made. If such an effort had been made, then perhaps an alternative would have emerged such as bringing all the polluting companies together to discuss ways of cleaning up the river. Such coordination is frustrating, complex, and difficult to manage, especially in organizational structures; but it is the culmination of moral thinking and necessary to decision making from a moral point of view. Without thoughtful coordination of all its goals, corporations, like individuals, will lack in coherent functioning and character, resulting in failure of moral excellence.

Finally, through moral awareness and moral thinking moral decisions must be put into action. Good intentions and public relations statements are not enough for moral responsibility. To be morally excellent, corporations, like individuals, must demonstrate their characters through good deeds. For example, on the world level, the corporation might undertake partnership ventures with organizations of other countries rather than setting up operations with full controlling interests, and in other ways cooperate with governments of other countries to improve the dignity and quality of life for their people. On the national level, the corporation might demonstrate its ethical commitment through philanthropic contributions and use of its expertise and resources on our numerous social problems such as waste removal, health care, opportunities for women and the handicapped, minorities, education, housing, care of the elderly, crime, prison reform, care of our environment, etc.

In the communities within which the corporation does its business steps might be taken to minimize disruptive and harmful effects from pollution to pullouts and to maximize benefits and service to all its immediate neighbors. Within its own industry the corporation might initiate and cooperate in joint projects to further fair and healthy competition, to insure quality and safe products, and to avoid pollution and other effects of doing business which are injurious to the quality of life. And, within the firm itself, the corporation might act in any number of ways to implement its moral responsibilities: institutionalizing compliance steps for its ethical codes; hiring ombudspeople with responsibilities for ethical oversight; forming ethics committees within the board of directors; fostering ethical discussion and communication at all levels;

and providing positive incentives for employee pursuit of ethical goals such as affirmative action, worker health, product safety, environmental protection, truth in advertising, and community service. Obviously moral action at various levels is necessary for a corporation to be morally responsible, but only after it has perceived the moral situations within its environment and thought out its moral demands, coordinating those demands with its other demands, interests, and constraints. Moral action, without the other steps necessary for a fully mature moral point of view, would be implemented blindly and irrationally yielding ineffectual or perhaps even dangerous consequences.

Through the development of a moral point of view as outlined above, a moral corporate culture will begin to emerge. Definite ethical goals, structures, and strategies will be formally institutionalized and a moral framework of meaning and purpose will be created within which individuals of the corporation can develop ethical beliefs and attitudes and achieve a sense of ethical integrity. It is not necessary that everyone agree with all decisions and actions emanating from the corporate moral point of view for a corporation to be morally excellent. There might be disagreement from both inside and outside the corporation. Just as individuals can think and act out of moral points of view yet come to radically different ethical conclusions, so it is too with corporations. It is the structure and process of the moral point of view that is essential, and more often than not, the thought and action stemming from it will command our respect, if not also our agreement.

Furthermore, a corporate moral culture is not a fixed thing that once it is established it becomes complete. It is true that it consists of goals, structures, and strategies, but, as it is with individual moral character, it must be constantly nurtured and self-evaluated. This means that the corporate moral point of view, focusing on rationality and respect in each of its stages, must operate not only on new situations but on its own character as well. Only through such a moral dynamics, which requires the effort and commitment of all corporate members, will the corporation maintain a culture necessary for moral excellence.

For a corporation to be morally excellent it must allow for the moral autonomy of the individual within its culture. We find this theme throughout the pages of Peters and Waterman's *In Search of Excellence*:

> Virtually all of the excellent companies are driven by just a few key values, and then gives lots of space to employees to take initiatives in support of those values – finding their own paths, and so making the task and its outcome their own.
>
> There was hardly a more pervasive theme in the excellent companies than *respect for the individual*. That basic belief and assumption were omnipresent (Peters and Waterman, 1982, pp. 72–3, 238).

A corporation is made up of individuals and thinks and acts through them. For the corporation to deny those individuals the freedom to determine their own moral integrity within the company, to turn them into mere functionaries for the corporate purpose, is to fail to respect them as ends in themselves and to lose the ability to rationally evaluate its own moral character. In short, it would result in the abandonment of a moral point of view necessary for corporate moral excellence.

Can there be a corporate community that respects and fosters the development of individual autonomy? It might be argued that the work of the corporation can be carried out efficiently, smoothly, and quickly only if each member of the corporation accepts his or her assigned role on the team and pulls in unison toward the corporate goal. All the excellent corporations singled out by Peters and Waterman have strong corporate cultures providing a distinctive identity and shared meaning for the group. This clearly poses a threat to individual expression and is why some have commented that, while admiring the excellent companies, they wouldn't want to work for one. As the Delta psychologist states of his stewardess interviews: 'I try to determine their sense of cooperativeness or sense of team work. At Delta, you don't just join a company, you join an objective' (Peters and Waterman 1982, p. 245).

This surely calls forth images of William Whyte's organization man marching in step in his gray flannel suit singing company songs. Scott and Hart more recently observe that 'Obedience is the cornerstone of the organizational edifice because it's essential to the chains of command', and, according to them, it is occurring even more viciously today. Individuality is not being abolished through coercion but rather converted into an individual commitment to freely adopt the demands of the organizational imperative and to willingly substitute organizational values for personal values (Scott and Hart, 1979, see also Prakesh et al., 1984).

While the above corporate picture is surely possible, and even real in many cases, it is not inevitable. Having a strong corporate culture does not necessarily eliminate individual autonomy. Depending upon the nature of the culture, it can even enhance and encourage autonomy. Peters and Waterman find that their research of the excellent companies testifies to this:

> In the very same institutions in which culture is so dominant, the highest levels of true autonomy occur. The culture regulates rigorously the few variables that do count, and it provides meaning. But within those qualitative values (and in almost *all* other dimensions), people are encouraged to stick out, to innovate (Peters and Waterman, 1982, p. 105).

For example, Hewlett-Packard, having one of the strongest cultures, referred to as 'the HP Way', is proud of its people-oriented philosophy. The introduction to its revised corporate objective statement concludes:

> Hewlett-Packard [should not] have a tight, military-type organization but rather . . . give people the freedom to work toward [overall objectives] in ways they determine best for their own areas of responsibility (Peters and Waterman, 1982, p. 245).

It seems, then, that one of the essential features of the cultures of the excellent corporations is the respect that is given and the space that is allowed for personal expression and initiative. Rather than the culture snuffing out individual autonomy, the culture itself is actually built on and around such autonomy.

This happens in a number of ways in the excellent companies. No one in an organization can have a real sense of freedom and power if kept in the dark concerning one's environment. In the excellent companies, intense effort is made at open communication throughout by way of all sorts of informal devices – from omnipresent blackboards to daily coffee 'klatches' to 'town meetings' and 'open forums' to army mess tables in the company dining room. The excellent companies go to extreme lengths to avoid the problem of NETMA (Nobody Ever Tells Me Anything) even to GM's bringing financial information down to the shopfloor and Delta's top management open door policy to all employees.

Another feature important to autonomy inside an organization is having enough room and acceptance to try new projects and fail. The excellent companies not only provide room and encouragement for autonomy and entrepreneurship, but these policies work because they also provide a climate within which failure is allowed. They all seem to follow 3M's Fletcher Byrom's ninth commandment: 'Make sure you generate a reasonable number of mistakes'; some even treat failure with celebratory style.

Also, bigness can thwart individual freedom and lead to a feeling of impotence. The excellent companies handle this by breaking themselves up into smaller units – by decentralizing and divisionalizing. Blue Bell kept its manufacturing units down to 300 people, Dana reduced the layers in its organization from 11 to five, and Johnson and Johnson broke up its $5 billion dollar business into 150 divisions. 3M and HP 'hive off' new productive units when divisions grow too big and most of the excellent companies have some form of 'skunk works' teams of eight to 10 people initiating new projects.

Finally, although many other steps for insuring individual autonomy could be mentioned, people should feel that they are a meaningful part of the activities of the organization, that they matter. Out of respect for this, the excellent companies try hard not to rigidly follow a chain of command and to avoid overformalization. Rene McPherson at Dana discarded 22½ inches of policy manuals in favour of a one page statement of philosophy involving people. Sam Walton of Wal-Mart visits all 320 of his stores every year listening to his employees: 'It's terribly important for everyone to get involved. Our best ideas come from clerks and stockboys' (Peters and Waterman, 1982).

Although these lessons on individual autonomy from the excellent companies relayed to us by Peters and Waterman are directly connected to productivity gains, they are also lessons for understanding corporate moral excellence. Sufficient space should be given to every person in the corporation to initiate moral action within their own areas of responsibility, to make the corporate moral objectives their own. Failure to provide such space is failure to respect them as persons; the freedom to develop their moral integrity is essential to their humanity.

Avenues of communication concerning moral issues should be open to everyone and everyone should play a meaningful role in corporate ethical goal formation and decision making. After such goals are set and decisions made, they should be clearly explained to each and every individual and how they affect his or her own function area.

Room should be made for rational disagreement and protest, and every attempt should be made to allow individuals moral alternatives to such goals and decisions if they find it impossible to coordinate them with their own moral points of view. If this proves to be impossible, then support should be given to their withdrawal from the activities of the organization.

Corporate bureaucracy and chains of command should be kept to an absolute minimum and large corporations should divide into smaller independent units with responsibility for moral decision making within the guidelines of the overall moral corporate culture. Encouragement should be made not only to initiate moral action but understanding should be given when such action fails to achieve the moral objectives sought.

The morally excellent corporation must pursue the moral excellence of each of its individual members which demands a culture conducive to the pursuit of individual moral autonomy. In fact, it would seem impossible for the corporation to develop and maintain a moral culture independent of the moral autonomy of its members. The ideal of corporate moral excellence is that when the corporation is deserving of moral praise so too is each of its members because, in a very real and concrete way, they have freely made that which was morally praiseworthy their own. What else could be meant by taking moral pride in a society to which one belongs.

The weaving together of a moral culture and the moral autonomy of the individuals within it is the difficult challenge necessary for the attainment of corporate moral excellence. There is clearly an essential tension here as there is with the individual in any society. The culture of an organization can dominate the individual freedom and expression of its members. It can become a Dostoevskian 'Crystal Palace' destroying a human being's right and desire to assert his or her individuality, where life becomes like an oversized anthill with clearly fixed functions and duties, where no one stands out or makes one's self. On the other hand, culture does provide meaning, direction, security, and purpose for individuals. To stand out too much, outside the frameworks of social organizations, leads to separation, loneliness and isolation. The responsibility of societies and individuals is to avoid both extremes. We need to mold the above mentioned tension into a creative one rather than a destructive one.

Many of the best-run productive corporations have already taken giant steps toward the development of this creative tension – steps which are enlightening for the coming to be of the morally excellent corporation. In the words of Peters and Waterman:

> These companies provide the opportunity to stick out, yet combine it with a philosophy and system of beliefs . . . that provide the transcending meaning – a wonderful combination (Peters and Waterman, 1982, p. 81).

The nature of the moral corporate culture is the key. It must be created in such a way that definite ethical goals, structures, and strategies are clearly put forward to form a conceptual and operational framework for moral decision making. It must make clear to all its individual members that it values and will not tolerate any deviation from a moral point of view. But at the same time, this moral culture, which gives meaning, identity, and integrity to the whole corporate collective, must also value and encourage the moral autonomy of each of its individual members. To deny such moral autonomy is to cut off the possibility of rationally developing and examining the ethical principles of the culture itself and to fail to respect the persons making up the culture itself – both being violations of the moral point of view to which the moral culture is committed.

I am in total agreement with the following statement by Richard De George:

> Since human beings are social beings, they cannot be understood without understanding society. Since society is composed of human beings, it cannot be understood without understanding them. Both must be understood together, and to do this they must be understood in their relations (De George, 1983, p. 20).

For business ethics to focus on just corporate goals and structures or to focus on just individual moral responsibility results in dangerous abstractions. We might say moral culture provides the form and individual moral autonomy provides the content for the morally excellent corporation. Such is the necessary reciprocity for an evolving corporate collection of human beings working toward the actualization of moral excellence.

References

Andrews, Kenneth (1980). *The Concept of Corporate Strategy* rev. edn. Homewood, IL: Irwin, pp. 92–5.

Business Week, 1977, Jan 31, p. 107.

Cabot Lodge, George, (1977). '*The Connection Between Ethics and Ideology*', *Business Values and Social Justice: Proceedings of the First National Conference on Business Ethics*, Hoffman, W. Michael ed. Waltham, MA: The Center for Business Ethics at Bentley College, pp. 78–80.

Dewey, John, Tufts, James H. (1980). 'The Individual and the Social' in

Philosophy Now, 3rd ed., Struhl, Paul, Struhl, Karsten, (eds.) New York: Random House, p. 315.

Ewing, David. (1977). *Freedom Inside the Organization*, New York: McGraw-Hill; and (1983) *Do It My Way or You're Fired*, New York: Wiley.

French, Peter (1984). 'Corporate Moral Agency'. In *Business Ethics: Readings and Cases in Corporate Morality*, (Hoffman, W. Michael, Moore, Jennifer Mills, eds.) New York: McGraw-Hill, p. 163. French has also said that the corporation 'denotes an entity that is itself an individual, in fact, I think that in the relevant moral senses, it may be shown to be a person'. See 'Crowds and Corporations'. *American Philosophical Quarterly* 19, 3 (July 1982), p. 276.

De George, Richard, (1983). 'Social Reality and Social Relations', *Review of Metaphysics* 37, Sept, p. 8. Although De George doesn't refer to culture, much of what he develops along the lines of social institutions can be applied to my development of corporate culture.

Goodpaster, Kenneth, (1983). 'The Concept of Corporate Responsibility'. *Journal of Business Ethics* 2, 1 Feb, pp. 7–16. Goodpaster identifies four steps, namely (1) perception, (2) reasoning, (3) coordination, and (4) implementation. I have combined (2) and (3) under what I call 'reflection' since they are both really a part of moral thinking. However, my development of the moral decision-making process has been greatly influenced by Goodpaster's keen analysis.

Hoffman, W. Michael. 'The Ford Pinto'. In *Business Ethics: Readings and Cases in Corporate Morality*, pp. 412–20.

Jaspers, Karl (1971). 'Differentiation of German Guilt'. In *Guilt and Shame*, (H. Morris, ed.) Wadsworth, p. 40. For further development of these distinctions see Cooper, David, (1974) 'Responsibility and the System'. In *Individual and Collective Responsibility*, (French, Peter, ed.) Cambridge, MA: Schenkman, pp. 83–100.

Peters, Thomas, Waterman, Robert (1982). *In Search of Excellence: Lessons from America's Best-Run Companies*. New York: Harper & Row, p. 280.

Scott, William, Hart, David, (1979). *Organizational America*. Boston: Houghton Mifflin, p. 62.

Sethi, S. Prakash, Namiki, Nobuaki, Swanson, Carl (1984). *The False Promise of the Japanese Miracle*. Boston: Pitman.

Stone, Christopher (1975). *Where the Law Ends*. New York: Harper & Row, p. 111.

Velasquez, Manuel (1983). 'Why Corporations Are Not Morally Responsible for Anything They Do'. In *Business and Professional Ethics Journal* 2, 3, p. 1.

Werhane, Patricia (1984) calls such corporate actions 'secondary actions', see 'Corporations, Collective Action, and Institutional Moral Agency'. In *Corporate Governance and Institutionalizing Ethics: Proceedings of the Fifth National Conference on Business Ethics*. Moore, Jennifer Mills, Hoffman, W. Michael, Fedo, David A. (eds), Lexington, MA: Lexington Books. Larry May calls them 'vicarious actions', see 'Vicarious Agency and Corporate Responsibility'. *Philosophical Studies* 43 (1983), pp. 69—82.

Ethics as a way of life
Robert Gunts

At the time of writing this article, Robert Gunts was president of the Whirlpool Trading Company, a subsidiary of the Whirlpool Corporation, an American manufacturer of white goods and home appliances.

Gunts considers what should be ethical for a company in the international market. He raises the problem that there are differences in ethical and legal behaviour between countries, and even legal behaviour is sometimes unethical. However, at Whirlpool ethical behaviour is a fundamental part of the corporate culture, and this means that they will not compromise on such issues as payoffs, even if these are not illegal in the country concerned, and even if it results in lost business opportunities. A high code of ethics is an imperative for Gunts, and 'to accept less is a violation of a public trust'.

I have been asked to address a point of ethics from a somewhat unique point of view: what are the ethical considerations of a company that is looking to grow internationally? One of Whirlpool Corporation's most important business goals today is to become a larger, stronger international company with more sales and profits coming from foreign markets. So addressing this question is very timely for our company as well.

While we are not a big player in the *international* arena, we are one of the larger *American* companies with the resources to become a factor worldwide. We are a 75-year-old, $3 billion company that is a leading manufacturer of major home appliances for the United States market.

Internationally, to round out the Whirlpool picture, we export brand products to independently owned distributors in 39 countries and to United States military exchanges around the world. We license foreign manufacturers and own a substantial equity interest in three Brazilian companies which produce components and finished appliances for the Brazilian as well as export markets.

As further evidence of our new international thrust, last year we created the Whirlpool Trading Company of which I am president. International growth is essential if we are to meet our very ambitious corporate objectives. The United States appliance market, as strong as it is, does not offer the potential to meet our ambitious goals. Hence our need to look internationally.

Fortunately, our products serve common global needs. Everywhere in the world, people want appliances to store and cook food, clean clothes and clean their homes. In the industrialized countries, appliances mean more convenience, more freedom and enhanced lifestyle. In developing nations, expanding economies and improving infrastructures are making it possible for people to purchase their first major appliances for better health, nutrition and sanitation.

The potential for Whirlpool's growth and participation in this expanding world market is mind boggling. China and India's combined population of nearly two billion people is almost one-half of the world's populace. Both nations are virtually untapped as markets for home appliances. We plan to share in those market opportunities.

Even though our international business has been modest compared with some other United States corporations, we are by no means neophytes to world trade or to the economic and ethical pressures American companies must face in the world economy.

Prior to my current position, I was president of Whirlpool's subsidiary Thomas International Corporation, a builder and marketer of electronic organs and musical instruments. We also had an electronic subsidiary in Italy serving the European market and trading companies in Holland and England.

Our Thomas International manufacturing and assembly plant was near Los Angeles, while two of our feeder plants were located in Mexico. Shipments of our integrated circuit boards and other component parts moved continually across Mexican border points into the United States. As such, they were subject to Mexican inspections and demands for grease money if we did not want them delayed at the border.

Long before we established our plants in Mexico, we were advised by other businesses that our shipments would likely be delayed at border points if we did not meet demands for 'mordida'. To us, such demands were extortion, and we would have no part of it. The demands, always veiled, never outright, normally come from lower level border officials, many underpaid and living locally. Mexican officials at the state level were opposed to these payments and, in our meetings with them, they expressed their willingness and full cooperation to stamp out the practice. With that agreement, we established our two Mexican operations.

I wish I could say that our agreement solved the problem; but it did not. Shortly after we initiated our first shipments to Los Angeles, some Mexican border agents made it abundantly clear that payment of 'mordida' was necessary to guarantee swift passage of our trucks across the border. We refused, and our trucks were moved to the sidelines for time consuming and total, and I mean piece-by-piece, inspection. We immediately complained to higher level Mexican officials. True to their agreement, they demanded an explanation by border agents, and our shipments were processed without undue delay. I can say that we never, to my knowledge, succumbed to border extortion.

We were not alone in our effort. We worked closely with a number of other United States companies that faced similar harassment. As a group we brought pressure to bear on an intolerable situation. We could not have achieved this result without the full cooperation and aid of the Mexican government.

I'm not sure at this point if our Mexican experience is transferable elsewhere. But, unless my experience as a business executive has been totally misapplied, I believe that most business practices are fairly uniform around the world.

However, what is *legal* and what is *ethical* is *not* necessarily uniform worldwide. For example, in several countries payments of grease money to high level military officials to sell weaponry to their governments is not *illegal*. In fact, it is a common practice. But to *our* way of thinking, it is *unethical* as well as illegal. Payoffs like these feed on themselves, and there is no end in sight once the word is out that a company will barter on its principles.

At Whirlpool, we don't place a lot of ceremony on maintaining some lofty ethical standard. It is just part of our corporate culture. We expect our managers and employees to live by those standards and to perpetuate that culture to our future managers. As a corporate citizen, we believe our charter in the community demands of us the highest ethical standards and practices. In the final analysis, ethical behavior should be an integral part of the organization, a way of life that is deeply engrained in the collective corporate body.

If we cave in to demands for payoffs, we compromise our ethical standards. We have an analogous situation at the national level. Secretary of State George Shultz has affirmed our national policy that we will not yield to international blackmail or negotiate with terrorists for American hostages still in Lebanon. To do so, he said, would send a loud message to every terrorist organization around the world that the high principles for which America stands can be manipulated like some stringed puppet by amoral international thugs.

Let me say unequivocally here: Whirlpool will forego business opportunities if it takes unethical payments to acquire new business. We make that commitment with eyes wide open, knowing full well that we will lose some business opportunities, particularly when competing against business from nations that do not subscribe to our principles.

At Whirlpool we have a basic statement of ethics which places the ultimate responsibility for ethical behavior precisely where it belongs in any organization – on the shoulders of the person in charge. That statement reads:

> No employee of this company will ever be called upon to do anything in the line of duty that is morally, ethically or legally wrong. Furthermore, if in the operation of this complex enterprise, an employee should come upon circumstances of which he or she cannot be personally proud, it should be that person's duty to bring it to the attention of top management if unable to correct the matter in any other way.

That obligation applies to the chairman as well as the employee on the product line. Adherence to that basic philosophy has kept us in good stead throughout our company's history.

Back in the early 1900s, Lou Upton, co-founder of Upton Machine Company, our predecessor company, received a whopping order for 100 of his new-fangled electronic wringer-washers from a subsidiary of Commonwealth Edison in Chicago. When the washers were delivered, a cast iron gear in every single washer failed. This could have been the death knell for a company with only six employees, where neither Lou nor his brother Fred were receiving a salary and there was no cash on reserve. Rather than desert his customer, Lou and his people found a way to repair the defect and fixed all 100 units. There is another happy ending to the story: in the process, he gained an order for 100 more washers. Maintaining product quality is as much a matter of business ethics to consumers as any other issue. It is also a basic business fact that if a company offers a slipshod product or service its longevity is in serious doubt. We at Whirlpool firmly believe in this principle. Part of our corporate mission statement reads, and I quote, 'We promise to build, and sell only good quality, honest appliances designed to give you your money's worth, and we promise to stand behind them.'

A question for today is: should our ethical principles at home be transferred to the international business community? I believe the answer is 'yes'. I feel we can take them with us anywhere in the world. We may alter our actions or practices as local customs and law require, but we will never adopt business practices in violation of legal and moral principles.

Having said this, we are not naïve. There are no safeguards that Whirlpool employees will not act foolishly or out of greed, even in spite of our corporate guidelines. If a violation occurs, the parties will be acting for themselves, not on behalf of the company demands. But we will take corrective action to remedy the matter and to protect the good name of Whirlpool.

Just to let our employees know we mean business and that we will tolerate no breach of conduct, we employ some 15 internal auditors who, along with their other duties, have free reign to probe any aspect of our corporate life. To assure independence, the audit function reports to the chief financial officer. Our board of directors, of whom 10 of 13 are outsiders, also maintains an audit committee to investigate any company function.

There is another dimension to this matter of ethics not often discussed. Most laws are written to make *unethical* practices illegal. But occasionally the reverse occurs, and a law can make a normally *ethical* practice illegal. One of these United States laws is the Export Administration Act of 1979. In its present form, this law makes it extremely difficult for us to achieve our goals for international growth in the Middle East. Here is a little history.

In 1944, several Arab nations formed what is known as the Arab League. Its purpose was, and still is, essentially to identify and to boycott nations from the Arab world who also have trade relations with Israel. In the mid-50s, Whirlpool, to our utter surprise, was placed on the boycott list. It resulted from our former association with the RCA Corporation.

Back then, Whirlpool's tradename was not well known. To increase our name recognition, we reached a very important marketing agreement with RCA to create the RCA-Whirlpool brand name. However, the two companies were independent and, as some of you may know, the agreement no longer exists. At the time our agreement was in force, RCA began a record pressing business in Israel. Soon after, it was on the Arab boycott list. Because of our marketing association with RCA, Whirlpool's name was also added. Our products are still boycotted, even if unfairly so.

Passage of the Export Administration Act was, at least in part, United States retaliation to the Arab League boycott. Because of its 'eye-for-an-eye' mentality, it doesn't represent a high water mark in United States legislative history. The law places extremely controlled restrictions on how United States companies can petition the Arab Boycott League to remove their name from the list. Even minor unintentional infractions are punishable by imprisonment, fines or both.

Whirlpool will comply with the Export Administration Act. To do so takes an army of attorneys to study and advise our top management on how to comply with 69 pages of 'do's and 'don'ts' contained just in section 369 of the Act. This law makes no sense. Its moral and ethical justification is nothing more than an economic 'quid pro quo' which punishes United States firms for the Arab League's actions.

Companies like Whirlpool who are not a party to the Middle East political rift are being made economic captives for something beyond their control. I remind you, this law applies *only* to United States companies on the Arab League boycott list. The company down the street from you, which is *not* on the list, is not subject to the law. This law penalizes business actions that we feel are neither unethical nor immoral. We believe that it is high time to reassess the need and legitimacy of this law.

In these pages, I have highlighted what ethics means at Whirlpool. I have touched only the tip of the iceberg. In closing, I would compress my remarks into one sentence: ethics is nothing more than, in the words of one man, the obligations of morality. Business *must* subscribe to a high code of civil and ethical behavior. To accept less is a violation of a public trust.

Reproduced from Hoffman, W. Michael, Lange, Ann E. and Fedo, David A. (eds) (1986). *Ethics and the Multinational Enterprise* by permission of University Press of America, Lanham, MD.

Chapter 6

Mission and mission statements

The mission statement is a common management tool. Whether it is a small desktop reminder of 'our credo' or a more detailed policy and philosophy statement, it is the company's attempt to capture the principles and beliefs by which it wishes to run itself. In the final chapter, we explain what we believe should be in a mission statement. In this chapter we include the views of other researchers.

The following articles are all written by Americans. Two are by academics; one is by an organizational consultant; and one is by a lawyer and political scientist.

The article by Jack Pearce, 'The company mission as a strategic tool', published in the *Sloan Management Review* in 1982, was the leading contribution on the subject of mission. Before this article, managers and academics most frequently referred to Drucker when considering what to put in their mission statements. In *Management: Tasks, Responsibilities, and Practices*, published in 1973, Drucker states, 'Mission and philosophy is the key starting point in business'. He reinforces this message, adding, 'That business purpose and business mission are so rarely given adequate thought is perhaps the most important single cause of business frustration and failure.'

Drucker goes on to describe the questions that will help business people describe their mission and purpose. The most important question is 'What is our business?' 'Common vision, communal understanding and unity of direction and effort of the entire organization require definition of what our business is and what it should be.' Subsidiary to this question is a set of three questions that provide the key to business purpose – 'who is our customer?';

'where is our customer?'; and 'what is value to our customer?'. Clear answers to these questions will enable managers to define 'the basic concepts, values, policies and beliefs' of the organization.

Pearce's 1982 article was based on his long experience as an academic in strategic management and years of helping companies with strategic problems. He argues that a mission should contain the same fundamental elements that exist in the mind of a founder of a business at its outset. 'The company mission describes the firm's product, market and technology in a way that reflects the values and priorities of the strategic decision makers.'

He lists six components of a mission statement:

- product or service, market and technology
- goals for survival, growth and profitability
- company philosophy
- company self-concept
- public image
- responsibility to stakeholders

As will become apparent in the last chapter of this book, we do not fully agree with Pearce's list. We feel that he gives too little attention to corporate purpose and to behaviour standards. The best mission statements, we believe, describe some high ideal that rises above the interests of the claimants, giving a rationale for the energetic involvement of all stakeholders.

We also believe that mission statements should articulate some of the most important behaviour standards in the company. By doing so the statement becomes more practical and more relevant to managers.

One point in Pearce's article we disagree with is the importance he attaches to growth and profitability. He argues that a mission should explain how the company is going to secure growth in profits. In our view, a company needs only to be able to articulate its source of competitive advantage. If it has competitive advantage it will be able to grow.

Following the publication of his article, Pearce and another academic, Fred David, carried out some empirical work on mission statements. They surveyed the Fortune 500 firms and collected 61 mission statements. Using content analysis they examined the proportion of statements that included the main elements of Pearce's model and tested for differences between high performing organizations and low performing organizations. The results were mixed, but the study showed that many statements did in practice include the types of items suggested in Pearce's earlier article.

A similar piece of research was then carried out by Fred David on firms in the Business Week 1000. The research is described in the second article in this collection, 'How companies define their mission'. David's study added an extra item to the list of components of a mission – concern for employees. He also sought to compare the statements used by manufacturing firms with those used by service firms. Service firms, he concluded, seem to have less full missions with less attention given to describing the technology and the philosophy. He also tested for differences in performance between firms with statements and firms without statements. Little performance difference could be identified, implying that it is not the mere existence of a statement that counts.

The work by David and Pearce has been the most serious attempt to analyse mission statements, and to understand what they can contribute to business management. Although we have particular points of disagreement and differences of emphasis, we have learned a great deal from their work and see great similarity between our views and theirs.

The next article is by Dr Mark Frohman, an organization consultant, and Perry Pascarella, then editor of *Industry Week*. It is interesting because it addresses the management issues: what are the benefits of a mission and how to go about writing one. Their article even contains a discouragingly long list of questions that need positive answers before managers should consider writing a mission. We include this article because Frohman is a widely experienced consultant and because we can find little fault with the advice it gives.

The final article is included because it draws on a completely different body of knowledge, research into society's compliance with the law. Dr Steven Weller is a lawyer and political scientist turned academic. He has developed a number of hypotheses about the development of mission statements by referring to research done in the legal field. The article is aimed at codes of ethics, but has some useful insights for managers considering writing a mission.

Weller raises the issue of legitimacy. In decentralized organizations the traditional power of authority is diminished. Missions, therefore, must increasingly rely on rational authority created by involving managers in developing the mission.

Weller also points to the importance of having values in the mission that are congruent with the pre-existing values of employees. When this happens employees can identify with the mission, readily accepting it as their own.

Given the importance of mission in the strategic planning process and the high percentage of companies with mission statements, it is surprising how little literature there is on the subject. On the other hand, it is encouraging to find a high degree of unanimity about what should be in a statement.

The company mission as a strategic tool
John A. Pearce II

Jack Pearce is the Eakin Endowed Professor of Strategic Management at George Mason University. His views are based on experience working with companies on strategy problems and on research into mission statements. The latter he carried out with Fred David, the author of our next article.

This article uses examples to define the contents of a mission statement showing how each element helps the company think through its strategic problems. The article was recognized for a number of years as the leading contribution on the subject of mission statements.

When systematically and comprehensively developed, a firm's mission statement can serve as an invaluable tool in directing the formulation and implementation of strategy. A company achieves a heightened sense of purpose when its managers address the issues of: 'What business are we in?' 'What customer do we serve?' 'Why does this organization exist?' Yet managers can undermine the potential contribution of the company mission as a guide to company action when they accept platitudes or ambiguous generalizations in response to these questions. It is not enough to say that Lever Brothers is in the business of 'making anything that cleans anything', or that Polaroid is committed to businesses that deal with 'the interaction of light and matter'. Rather, a firm must clearly articulate its long term intentions so that its goals can serve as a basis for shared expectations, planning, and performance evaluation.

This article provides a practical framework that can be used in defining a meaningful company mission. The framework offers both recommendations for mission content and a process for melding the diverse and often conflicting demands placed on strategic direction. In particular, this framework is applied to the question of social responsibility and its impact on the mission statement.

What is a company mission?

In order to develop a new business or to reformulate the direction of an ongoing company, strategic decision makers must determine the basic goals, characteristics and philosophies that will shape the strategic posture of the firm. The outcome of this task, known as the *company mission*, provides the basis for a culture that will guide future executive action.

The company mission is a broadly defined but enduring statement of purpose that distinguishes a business from other firms of its type and identifies the scope of its operations in product and market terms. Not only does the company mission embody the strategic decision makers' business philosophy, but it also reveals the image the company seeks to project, reflects the firm's self-concept, and indicates the principal product or service areas and the primary customer needs the company will attempt to satisfy. In short, the company mission describe the firm's product, market and technology in a way that reflects the values and priorities of the strategic decision makers. For example, the Zale Corporation's mission statement (presented in Table 6.1) effectively incorporates these major features and provides the broad framework needed for strategic decision making.

Formulating the mission

The process of defining the mission for a specific business is perhaps best understood by thinking about a firm at its inception. The typical business organization begins with the beliefs, desires and aspirations of a single entrepreneur. The sense of mission for such an owner-manager is usually based on several fundamental elements:

- Belief that the company's product or service can provide benefits commensurate with its price;
- Belief that the product or service can satisfy a customer need currently not met adequately for specific market segments;
- Belief that the technology to be used in the production process will provide a product or service that is cost and quality competitive;
- Belief that with hard work and with the support of others, the business can do better than just survive; it can grow and be profitable;
- Belief that the management philosophy will result in a favourable public image and will provide financial and psychological rewards for those willing to invest their labour and money;
- Belief that the self-concept the entrepreneur has of the business can be communicated to and adopted by employees and stockholders of the company.

As the business grows, the need may arise to redefine the company mission, but, if and when it does, the revised mission statement will reflect the same set of elements as did the original. It will state: the basic type of product or service to be offered; the primary markets or customer groups whose needs will be served; the technology to be used in the production or delivery of the product or service; the fundamental concern for survival through growth and profitability; the managerial philosophy of the firm; the public image that is sought; and the firm's self-concept – that is, the image of the firm that should be held by those affiliated with it.

Table 6.1 *Zale Corporation: summary statement of the company mission*

Our business is specialty retailing. Retailing is a people-oriented business. We recognize that our business existence and continued success are dependent upon how well we meet our responsibilities to several critically important groups of people.

Our first responsibility is to our customers. Without them we would have no reason for being. We strive to appeal to a broad spectrum of consumers, catering in a professional manner to their needs. Our concept of value to the customer includes a wide selection of quality merchandise, competitively priced and delivered with courtesy and professionalism.

Our ultimate responsibility is to our shareholders. Our goal is to earn an optimum return on invested capital through steady profit growth and prudent, aggressive asset management. The attainment of this financial goal, coupled with a record of sound management, represents our approach toward influencing the value placed upon our common stock in the market.

We feel a deep, personal responsibility to our employees. As an equal opportunity employer, we seek to create and maintain an environment where every employee is provided the opportunity to develop to his or her maximum potential. We expect to reward employees commensurate with their contribution to the success of the company.

We are committed to honesty and integrity in all relationships with suppliers of goods and services. We are demanding but fair. We evaluate our suppliers on the basis of quality, price, and service.

We recognize community involvement as an important obligation and as a viable business objective. Support of worthwhile community projects in areas where we operate generally accrues to the health and well-being of the community. This makes the community a better place for our employees to live and a better place for us to operate.

We believe in the Free Enterprise System and in the American Democratic form of government under which this superior economic system has been permitted to flourish. We feel an incumbent responsibility to insure that our business operates at a reasonable profit. Profit provides opportunity for growth and job security. We believe growth is necessary to provide opportunities on an ever increasing scale for our people. Therefore, we are dedicated to profitable growth – growth as a company and growth as individuals.

This mission statement spells out the creed by which we live.

Components of the mission statement
Product or service, market, and technology

Three indispensable components of a mission statement are the company's basic product or service, the primary market, and the principal technology to be used in producing or delivering the product or service. In combination, these three components define the firm's present and potential business activity. A good example of these three mission components is found in the business plan of ITT Barton, a subsidiary of ITT. Under the heading of 'Business Mission and Area Served', the company presents the following information:

> The Unit's mission is to serve the industry and government with quality instruments used for the primary measurement, analysis, and local control of fluid flow, level, pressure, temperature, and fluid properties. This instrumentation includes flow meters, electronic readouts, indicators, recorders, switches, liquid level systems, analytical instruments such as titrators, integrators, controllers, transmitters, and various instruments for the measurement of fluid properties (density, viscosity, gravity) used for process variable sensing, data collection, control, and transmission. The Unit's mission includes fundamental 'loop-closing' control and display devices when economically justified, but excludes broadline central control room instrumentation, systems design, and turnkey responsibility.
>
> Markets served include instrumentation for oil and gas production, gas transportation, chemical and petrochemical processing, cryogenics, power generation, aerospace. Government and marine, as well as other instrument and equipment manufacturers.

This segment of the mission statement, accomplished in 129 words, clearly indicates to all readers – from company employees to casual observers – the firm's basic products, primary markets, and principal technologies.

Often a company's most referenced public statement of selected products and markets is presented in 'silver bullet' form in the mission statement. For example: 'Dayton-Hudson Corporation is a diversified retailing company whose business is to serve the American consumer through the retailing of fashion-oriented quality merchandise' (Ouchi, 1981). Such a statement serves as an abstract of company direction and is particularly helpful to outsiders who value condensed overviews.

Company goals: survival, growth and profitability

Three economic goals guide the strategic direction of almost every viable business organization. Although it is not always explicitly stated, a company mission reflects the firm's intention to secure its survival through sustained growth and profitability.

Unless a firm is able to survive, it will be incapable of satisfying any of its stakeholders' aims. Unfortunately, like growth and profitability, survival is such an assumed goal of the firm that it is often neglected as a principal criterion in strategic decision making. When this happens, the firm may focus on terminal aims at the expense of the long run. Concerns for expediency – a 'quick fix' or a 'bargain' – can displace the need for assessing long term impacts. Too often the result is near term economic failure, owing to a lack of resource synergy and sound business practice.

Profitability is the main goal of a business organization. No matter how it is measured or defined, profit over the long term is acccepted as the clearest indication of the firm's ability to satisfy the principal claims and desires of employees and stockholders. Clearly, the key phrase here is 'over the long term', since the use of short term profitability measures as a basis for strategic decision making would lead to a focus on terminal aims. For example, a firm might be misguided into overlooking the enduring concerns of customers, suppliers, creditors, ecologists and regulatory agents. Such a strategy could be profitable in the short run, but over time its financial consequences are likely to be seriously detrimental. The following excerpt from the Hewlett-Packard statement of corporate objectives (i.e. mission) ably expresses the importance of an orientation toward long term profit:

> *Objective: To achieve sufficient profit to finance our company growth and to provide the resources we need to achieve our other corporate objectives.*
> In our economic system, the profit we generate from our operations is the ultimate source of the funds we need to prosper and grow. It is the one absolutely essential measure of our corporate performance over the long term. Only if we continue to meet our profit objective can we achieve our other corporate objectives.

A firm's growth is inextricably tied to its survival and profitability. In this context, the meaning of growth must be broadly defined. While market share growth has been shown by the PIMS studies to be strongly correlated with firm profitability, there are other important forms of growth. For example, growth in the number of markets served, in the variety of products offered, and in the technologies used to provide goods or services frequently leads to improvements in the company's competitive ability. Growth means change, and proactive change is a necessity in the dynamic business environment. Hewlett-Packard's mission statement provides an excellent example of corporate regard for growth:

> *Objective: To let our growth be limited only by our profits and our ability to develop and produce technical products that satisfy real customer needs.*
> We do not believe that large size is important for its own sake; however, for at least two basic reasons, continuous growth is essential for us to achieve our other objectives.
>
> In the first place, we serve a rapidly growing and expanding segment of our technological society. To remain static would be to lose ground. We cannot maintain a position of strength and leadership in our field without growth.
>
> In the second place, growth is important in order to attract and hold high caliber people. These individuals will align their future only with a company that offers them considerable opportunity for personal progress. Opportunities are greater and more challenging in a growing company.

The issue of growth raises a concern about the definition of a company mission. How can a business specify sufficiently its intention in product, market, and technology terms to provide direction without delimiting its unanticipated strategic options? How can a company define its mission to permit consideration of opportunistic diversification without removing valuable parameters that the mission should incorporate to guide growth decisions? Perhaps, such questions are best addressed when a firm outlines within its mission statement the conditions under which it would consider departures from its ongoing stream of operations. Dayton-Hudson is one company that has pursued such an approach, as is disclosed in its growth philosophy:

> The stability and quality of the corporation's financial performance will be developed through the profitable execution of our existing businesses, as well as through the acquisition or development of new businesses. Our growth priorities, in order, are as follows:
> 1 Development of the profitable market preeminence of existing companies in existing markets through new store development or new strategies within existing stores;
> 2 Expansion of our companies to feasible new markets;
> 3 Acquisition of other retailing companies that are strategically and financially compatible with Dayton-Hudson;
> 4 Internal development of new retailing strategies.
> Capital allocations to fund the expansion of existing operations will be based on each company's return on investment, in relationship to its ROI objective and its consistency in earnings growth, and on its management capability to perform up to forecasts contained in capital requests.
>
> Expansion via acquisition or new venture will occur when the opportunity promises an acceptable rate of long-term growth and

profitability, acceptable degree of risk, and compatibility with the corporation's long-term strategy.

Company philosophy

The statement of a company's philosophy, or company creed as it is sometimes known, usually accompanies or appears as part of the mission. It reflects or explicitly states the basic beliefs, values, aspirations, and philosophical priorities that the strategic decision makers are committed to emphasize in their management of the firm. Fortunately, the topical content of company philosophies vary little from one firm to another. This means that business owners and managers implicitly accept a general, unwritten, yet pervasive, code of behavior by which actions in a business setting can be governed and largely self-regulated. Unfortunately, statements of philosophy display so great a degree of similarity among firms and are stated in such platitudinous ways as to look and read more like public relations promotions than like the commitments to values they are intended to be.

But despite the similarities among company philosophies, cynicism toward strategic managers' intentions in developing these philosophies is rarely justified. In almost all cases, managers attempt, and often succeed, to provide a distinctive and accurate picture of the firm's managerial outlook. One such valuable statement is that of Zale Corporation, whose company mission was presented earlier. As shown in Table 6.2, Zale has subdivided its statement of management's operating philosophy into four key areas: marketing and customer services, management tasks, human resources and finance and control. These subdivisions serve as a basis for even greater philosophical refinement than was provided through the mission statement itself. As a result, Zale has established especially clear directions for company decision making and action.

The mission statement of the Dayton-Hudson Corporation is at least equally specific in detailing the firm's management philosophy, as shown in Table 6.3. Perhaps the most noteworthy quality of the Dayton-Hudson statement is its delineation of responsibility at both the corporate and business levels. In many ways, it could serve as a prototype for the new three-tiered approach to strategic management, which argues that the mission statement needs to address strategic concerns at the corporate, business, and functional levels of the organization. To this end, Dayton-Hudson's management philosophy is a balance of operating autonomy and flexibility on the one hand, and corporate input and direction on the other hand.

Company self-concept

A major determinant of any company's continued success is the extent to which it can relate functionally to its external environment. Finding its 'place' in a competitive situation requires that the firm be able to evaluate realistically its own strengths and weaknesses as a competitor. This ideal – that the firm must know itself – is the essence of the company self-concept. The firm's ability to survive in a dynamic and highly competitive environment would be severely

Table 6.2 *Zale Corporation's operating philosophy*

I Marketing and Customer Services:

We require that the entire organization be continuously customer oriented. Our future success is dependent more on meeting the customers' needs better than on our competition.

We expect to maintain a marketing concept and distribution capability to identify changing trends and emerging markets and to promote effectively our products.

We strive to provide our customers with continuous offerings of quality merchandise that is competitively priced, stressing value and service.

We plan to constantly maintain our facilities as modern, attractive, clean, and orderly stores that are pleasing and exciting places for customers to shop.

II Management Tasks

We require profitable results from operations – activity does not necessarily equate with accomplishment. Results must be measurable.

We recognize there are always better ways to perform many functions. Continuous improvement in operating capability is a daily objective of the entire organization.

We expect all managers to demonstrate capabilities to plan objectives, delegate responsibilities, motivate people, control operations, and achieve results measured against planned objectives.

We must promote a spirit of teamwork. To succeed, a complex business such as ours requires good communication, clearly understood policies, effective controls, and, above all, a dedication to 'make things happen'.

We are highly competitive and dedicated to succeeding. However, as a human organization, we will make mistakes. We must openly acknowledge our mistakes, learn from them, and take corrective action.

III Human Resources

We must develop and maintain a competent, highly motivated, results-oriented organization.

We seek to attract, develop, and motivate people who demonstrate professional competence, courage, and integrity in performing their jobs.

We strive to identify individuals who are outstanding performers, to provide them with continuous challenges, and to search for new effective ways to compensate them by utilizing significant incentives.

Promotion from within is our goal. We must have the best talent available and, from time to time, will have to reach outside to meet our ever-improving standards. We heartily endorse and support development programs to prepare individuals for increased responsibility. In like manner, we must promptly advise those who are not geared to the pace, in order that they make the necessary adjustments without delay.

IV Finance and Control

We will maintain a sound financial plan that provides capital for growth of the business and provides optimum return for our stockholders.

We must develop and maintain a system of controls that highlights potential significant failures early for positive corrective action.

limited if it did not understand the impact that it has or could have on the environment, and vice versa.

A second look at the company mission of the Zale Corporation in Table 6.1 reveals much about this business's self-concept. The strategic decision makers see the firm as socially responsive, prudent, and fiercely independent. Characteristically, discussions of self-concept do not appear per se in company mission statements. Yet, strong impressions of a firm's self-image are often evident to readers of the company mission. For example, material from Intel Corporation, as seen in Table 6.4, provides a solid basis for such an understanding of the company's self-concept.

Public image

The issue of public image is an important one, particularly for a growing firm that is involved in redefining its company mission. Both present and potential customers attribute certain qualities to a particular business: Gerber and Johnson & Johnson make 'safe' products; Cross Pen makes 'professional'

Table 6.3   *Management philosophy of Dayton-Hudson Corporation*

I The corporation will:
Set standards for ROI and earnings growth;
Approve strategic plans;
Allocate capital;
Approve goals;
Monitor, measure, and audit results;
Reward performance;
Allocate management resources.

II The operating companies will be accorded the freedom and responsibility:
To manage their own business;
To develop strategic plans and goals that will optimize their growth;
To develop an organization that can assure consistency of results and optimum growth;
To operate their businesses consistent with the corporation's statement of philosophy.

III The corporate staff will provide only those services that are:
Essential to the protection of the corporation;
Needed for the growth of the corporation;
Wanted by operating companies and that provide a significant advantage in quality or cost.

IV The corporation will insist on:
Uniform accounting practices by type of business;
Prompt disclosure of operating results;
A systematic approach to training and developing people;
Adherence to appropriately high standards of business conduct and civic responsibility in accordance with the corporation's statement of philosophy.

---

writing instruments; Aigner makes 'stylish but affordable' leather products; Corvettes are 'power' machines; and Izod signifies the 'preppy' look. Thus, mission statements should reflect the anticipations of the public whenever the goals of the firm are likely to be achieved as a result. Gerber's mission should not open the possibility for diversification into pesticides, nor should Cross Pen's allow for the possibility of producing $.39 brandname disposables.

On the other hand, a negative public image often prompts firms to reemphasize the beneficial aspects of their character as reflected in their missions. For example, as a result of what Dow Chemical saw as a 'disturbing trend in public opinion', it undertook an aggressive promotional campaign to fortify its credibility, particularly among 'employees and those who live and work in [Dow's] plant communities'. Dow's approach was described in its 1980 annual report:

All around the world today, Dow people are speaking up. People who care deeply about their company, what it stands for, and how it is viewed by others. People who are immensely proud of their company's performance, yet realistic enough to realize it is the public's perception of that performance that counts in the long run.

Table 6.4 *Abstract of Intel's mission-related information*

I Management Style: Intel is a company of individuals, each with his or her own personality and characteristics.

Management is self-critical. The leaders must be capable of recognizing and accepting their mistakes and learning from them.

Open (constructive) confrontation is encouraged at all levels of the corporation and is viewed as a method of problem solving and conflict resolution.

Decision by consensus is the rule. Decisions once made are supported. Position in the organization is not the basis for quality of ideas.

A highly communicative/open management is part of the style.

A high degree of *organizational skills and discipline* are demanded.

Management must be ethical. Managing by telling the truth and treating all employees equitably have established credibility that is ethical.

II Work Ethic/Environment
It is a general objective of Intel to line up individual work assignments with career objectives.

We strive to provide an *opportunity for rapid development.*

Intel is a *results-oriented* company. The focus is on *substance* vs. form, *quality* vs. quantity.

We believe in the principle that *hard work, high productivity* is something to be proud of.

The concept of *assumed responsibility* is accepted. (If a task needs to be done, assume you have the responsibility to get it done.)

Commitments are long term: if career problems occur at some point, reassignment is a better alternative than termination.

We desire to have *all employees involved and participative* in their relationship with Intel.

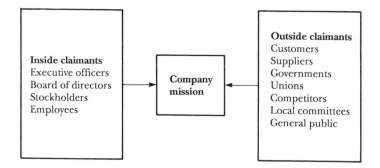

Figure 6.1   *Inputs to the company mission*

A firm's concern for its public image is seldom addressed in an intermittent fashion. While public agitation often stimulates a heightened corporate response, a corporation is concerned about its image even in the absence of expressed public concern. The following excerpt from the mission statement of Intel Corporation is exemplary of this attitude:

> We are sensitive to our *image with our customers and the business community*. Commitments to customers are considered sacred and we are upset with ourselves when we do not meet our commitments. We strive to demonstrate to the business world on a continuing basis that we are credible in describing the state of the corporation, and that we are well organized and in complete control of all things that determine the numbers.

The claimant approach to company responsibility

In defining or redefining the company mission, strategic managers must recognize and acknowledge the legitimate claims of other stakeholders of the firm. These stakeholders can be divided into two categories as indicated in Figure 6.1. 'Insiders' are individuals and groups who are stockholders or who are employed by the firm. 'Outsiders' are all other individuals and groups who are not insiders but who are affected by the actions of the firm as a producer and marketer of goods or services. Such outsiders commonly include customers, suppliers, governments, unions, competitors, local communities and the general public. Each of these interest groups has justifiable reasons to expect, and often to demand, that the company act in a responsible manner toward the satisfaction of its claims. In general, stockholders claim appropriate returns on their investments; employees seek broadly defined job satisfaction; customers want what they pay for; suppliers seek dependable buyers; governments want adherence to legislated regulations; unions seek benefits for members in proportion to their contributions to company success; competitors want fair competition; local communities want companies that are responsible 'citizens'; and the general public seeks some assurance that the quality of life will be improved as a result of the firm's existence.

However, when a specific business attempts to define its mission so as to incorporate the interests of these various claimant groups, such broad generalizations are insufficient. Four steps must be taken:

1 Identification of claimants.
2 Understanding claimants' specific demands vis-à-vis the company.
3 Reconciliation and prioritization of the claims.
4 Coordination of claims with other elements of the mission.

Identifying claimants

Every business faces a slightly different set of claimants who vary in number, size, influence and importance. In defining the company mission, strategic managers need to identify each claimant group and to weigh its relative ability to affect the firm's success.

Understanding claims

While the concerns of principal claimants tend to center on general issues such as those described above, it is important that strategic decision makers understand more specifically the demands that each group will make on the firm. By so doing, strategic managers will be better able to appreciate the concerns of claimants and to respond to them effectively.

The importance of identifying claimants and understanding their claims is nowhere better illustrated than in examining the issue of a firm's social responsibility. Broadly stated, outsiders often demand that the claims of insiders be subordinated to the greater good of the society – that is, to the greater good of the outsiders. This extremely large and often amorphous set of outsiders insists that the company be socially responsible. They believe that issues such as the elimination of solid and liquid wastes, the contamination of air and water, and the exhaustibility of natural resources should be principal considerations in the strategic decision making of the firm. On the other hand, insiders tend to believe that the competing claims of the outsiders should be balanced against each other in a way that protects the mission of the company. For example, the consumers' need for a product must be balanced against the water pollution resulting from its production if the company cannot totally afford to eliminate the pollution and remain profitable. Furthermore, some insiders argue that if society were sufficiently concerned about unwanted business by-products, such as water pollution, it could allocate tax monies to eliminate them.

Reconciling claims

Unfortunately, the concerns of various claimants are often in conflict. For example the claims of governments and the general public tend to limit profitability, which is the central concern of most creditors and stockholders. Such conflicting claims must be reconciled. In order for strategic managers to prepare a unifying approach for the company, they must be able to define a mission that has resolved the competing, conflicting, and contradictory claims placed on the company's direction by claimants and claimant groups. Internally consistent and precisely focused objectives and strategies require mission statements that display such a single-minded, though multidimensional, approach to business aims.

Claims on any business number in the hundreds, if not thousands – high wages, pure air, job security, product quality, community service, taxes, OSHA, EEO, product variety, wide markets, career opportunities, company growth, investment security, high ROI, etc. Although most, if not all, of these claims are desirable ends for the company, they cannot be pursued with equal emphasis. Claims must be prioritized in a way that reflects the relative attention the firm will give to each major claim. Such emphasis is shown by the criteria used in strategic decision making, by the company's allocation of human, financial, and physical resources, and by the long term objectives and strategies developed for the firm.

Coordinating mission components

Demands on a company for responsible action by claimant groups constitute only one set of inputs to the mission. Managerial operating philosophies and the determination of product-market segments are the other principal components that must be considered. These factors essentially pose a 'reality test' that the distilled set of accepted claims must pass in order to serve as a basis for a sound company mission. The key question to be addressed is: how can the company simultaneously satisfy claimants and optimize its success in the marketplace?

Again, the question of a firm's social responsibility illustrates the challenge that faces those who must coordinate the numerous components of the mission statement. In this realm, the issues are so complex and the problems so situational as to defy rigid rules of conduct. Thus, each business must decide on its own approach in trying to satisfy its perceived social responsibility. Different approaches will reflect differences in competitive positions, industries, countries, environmental and ecological pressures, and a host of other factors. In other words, they will reflect both situational factors and differing priorities in the companies' acknowledgments of claims.

Despite differences in their approaches, most American companies now take steps to assure outsiders of their efforts to conduct the business in a socially responsible manner. Many firms, including Abt Associates, Eastern Gas and Fuel Associates, and the Bank of America, have gone to the effort of conducting and publishing annual social audits. For example, the social audit of Eastern Gas and Fuel, as published in its 1981 annual report, provides numerical evidence of the firm's success on social responsibility topics including health and safety, charitable giving, minority employment, and employee pensions. Such social audits attempt to evaluate the business from a social responsibility perspective. They are often conducted for the firm by private consultants who offer minimally biased evaluations on what are inherently highly subjective issues. Many other firms periodically report to both insiders and outsiders on their progress to reach self-set social goals. Primarily through their annual reports, companies discuss their efforts and achievements in acting in a socially responsible fashion.

Conclusion

Undertaking the definition of a company mission is one of the most easily slighted tasks in the strategic management process. Emphasizing operational aspects of long-range management activities comes much more easily for most executives. But the critical role of the company mission as the basis of orchestrating managerial action is repeatedly demonstrated by failing firms whose short run actions are ultimately found to be counterproductive to their long-run purpose.

The principal value of a mission statement as a tool of strategic management is derived from its specification of the ultimate aims of the firm. It thus provides managers with a unity of direction that transcends individual, parochial and transitory needs. It promotes a sense of shared expectations among all levels and generations of employees. It consolidates values over time and across individuals and interest groups. It projects a sense of worth and intent that can be identified and assimilated by company outsiders, i.e. customers, suppliers, competitors, local committees, and the general public. Finally, it affirms the company's commitment to responsible action, which is symbiotic with its needs to preserve and protect the essential claims of insiders for sustained survival, growth, and profitability of the firm.

References

Ouchi, W. (1981). *Theory Z*. Reading, MA: Addison-Wesley. The author presents more complete mission statements of three of the companies discussed in this article; namely, Dayton-Hudson, Hewlett-Packard and Intel.

Reproduced from Pearce, John A. II (1982). *Sloan Management Review*, Spring, pp. 15–24 by permission of the Sloan Management Review Association.

How companies define their mission
Fred R. David

Fred David spent many years researching mission statements because he sees them as an essential building block in the strategic management process. David is an Associate Professor of Management at Auburn University, Alabama.

David's views are based on a careful and continually updated analysis of the academic literature. In addition, he carried out a survey of the top 1000 corporations in America. Of these who responded, 41 per cent had missions and from this sample David analysed 75 statements.

This article summarizes his research results. It does not add greatly to the previous article by Jack Pearce, David's colleague for some of his research. It is included in this book of readings mainly for its useful review of the literature.

The company mission: its nature and purpose

A business is not defined by its name, statutes, or articles of incorporation. It is defined by the business mission. Only a clear definition of the mission and purpose of the organization makes possible clear and realistic business objectives.

Peter Drucker, 1973

Current thought on mission statements is largely based on Peter Drucker's research and writings in the mid-1970s. Drucker said that asking the question, 'What is our Business?' is synonymous with asking the question, 'What is our Mission?'

Defined as an enduring statement of purpose that distinguishes one organization from other similar enterprises, a mission statement is a declaration of an organization's 'reason for being'. Considerable diversity exists among firms in the uses and composition of mission statement documents. Also, the perceived importance of a mission statement varies widely among senior executives and corporate planners. For example at General Mills, the mission statement is simple. It reads:

Our mission is to be a leader among corporations. We will strive to achieve excellence in any endeavors we undertake. To fulfill this mission, we must be both responsive and anticipatory as we serve our four major constituencies: consumers, employees, shareholders, and society.

In a recent speech, H. B. Atwater Jr, chairman and chief executive officer of General Mills, had this to say about the company's mission statement: 'I would agree that unless our mission statement is backed up with specific objectives and strategies, the words become meaningless, but I also believe that our objectives and strategies are far more likely to be acted upon when there exists a prior statement of belief from which specific plans and action flow.'

Sometimes called a creed statement, a statement of purpose, a statement of philosophy, a statement of beliefs, a statement of business principles, or a statement defining our business, a mission statement reveals the long term vision of an organization in terms of what it wants to be and who it wants to serve. All organizations have a reason for being, even if senior executives and corporate planners have not consciously put this in writing. A carefully prepared mission statement is widely recognized by managers and academics as the first step in strategic management, as illustrated in Figure 6.2.

The present study was designed to examine the mission statements of large manufacturing and service firms and to provide profiles and guidelines which may be useful to senior executives in developing a corporate mission statement document.

The literature

Pearce and David (1987) reported in the *Academy of Management Executive* that the mission statements of high performing *Fortune 500* firms more often include six of eight literature-derived components. The six components were: philosophy, self-concept, public image, location, technology, and concern for survival. These researchers found two other components, customer and product/service, to be more often included in the mission statements of low performing firms. Forty per cent of the responding *Fortune 500* firms indicated that their organization had no formal mission statement, while 60 per cent of the sample firms provided material considered to be a formal mission statement.

David and Cochran (1987) examined the mission statements of corporations and universities to determine the relative inclusion of eight components: customer, product or service, location, technology, concern for survival, philosophy, self-concept and public image. On average, the eight components

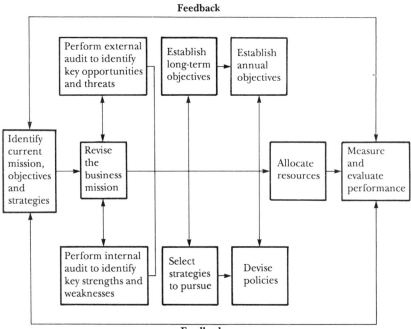

Figure 6.2 *The strategic management process*
Source: David, F. R. (1989). *Strategic Management*. Columbus, OH: Merrill Publishing Co.

were included in 65.64 per cent of the sample mission statements. Corporate mission statements were found to more clearly exhibit three dimensions (technology, concern for survival and public image), while university statements were superior on five dimensions (customer, product or service, location, philosophy and self-concept).

Want (1986) considered the primary components of a mission statement to be (1) purpose, (2) principal business aims, (3) corporate identity, (4) policies of the company and (5) values. 'Purpose' included the primary justification for the organization's existence, the primary lines of business for the company, the products and services provided, and the manner in which they are provided. 'Principal business aims' included market share, profitability or size, strategies for achieving growth and optimal productivity and impact on the competition. 'Corporate identity' included how the company wants to be recognized in the marketplace by its customers, competitors, communities, the larger business world and employees, so that they may develop a sense of identity and commitment with the company. 'Policies of the company' included the philosophy and style of leadership of senior management, the relationship beween top management and the company's board of directors, owners or shareholders, and the company's overall organizational decision making structure. Finally, 'values' included consideration for customers, competitors, employees, regulatory agencies and the general public.

According to McGinnis (1981), a mission statement (1) should define what the organization is and what the organization aspires to be, (2) should be limited enough to exclude some ventures and broad enough to allow for creative growth, (3) should distinguish a given organization from all others, (4) should serve as a framework for evaluating both current and prospective activities, and (5) should be stated in terms sufficiently clear to be widely understood throughout the organization.

King and Cleland (1979) recommend that organizations carefully develop a written mission statement for the following reasons:

1 To ensure unanimity of purpose within the organization.
2 To provide a basis, or standard, for allocating organizational resources.
3 To establish a general tone or organizational climate.
4 To serve as a focal point for individuals to identify with the organization's purpose and direction; and to deter those who cannot from participating further in the organization's activities.
5 To facilitate the translation of objectives into a work structure involving the assignment of tasks to responsible elements within the organization.
6 To specify organizational purposes and the translation of these purposes into objectives in such a way that cost, time, and performance parameters can be assessed and controlled p. 124).

The survey

A personal letter was mailed to the chief executive officers of all *Business Week* 1000 firms. The letter asked for a copy of the firm's mission statement. A mission statement was described in the letter as 'an enduring statement of purpose that reveals product and market information about a firm's operations'. The letter explained that a mission statement is sometimes called 'a creed statement, a statement of purpose, or a statement of general principles'.

The 1000 top service and manufacturing companies in the United States, ranked according to market value, comprise the *Business Week* 1000. Market value is determined by multiplying a firm's stock market price by its number of shares outstanding.

Market value is a composite measure of how large *and* healthy a firm is at a given point in time. *Business Week* uses market value annually to determine the top 1000 corporations in America.

A total of 181 responses were received, 75 firms providing a formal mission statement (41 per cent) and 106 chief executive officers indicating their firm had not developed a mission statement (59 per cent). Among the 75 organizations providing a formal document, there were 30 manufacturing firms and 45 service firms.

What components are included in company mission statements?

1 *Customers* – Who are the enterprise's customers?
2 *Products or services* – What are the firm's major products or services?
3 *Location* – Where does the firm compete?
4 *Technology* – What is the firm's basic technology?
5 *Concern for survival* – What is the firm's commitment to economic objectives?
6 *Philosophy* – What are the basic beliefs, values, aspirations and philosophical priorities of the firm?
7 *Self-concept* – What are the firm's major strengths and competitive advantages?
8 *Concern for public image* – What are the firm's public responsibilities and what image is desired?
9 *Concern for employees* – What is the firm's attitude towards its employees?

Excerpts from some sample mission statements are provided below to exemplify specifically how various companies included the particular components:

Customers

We believe our first responsibility is to the doctors, nurses, and patients, to mothers and all others who use our products and services. (Johnson & Johnson)

The purpose of Motorola is to honourably serve the needs of the community by providing products and services of superior quality at a fair price to our customers. (Motorola Inc.)

Products or services

AMAX's principal products are molybdenum, coal, iron ore, copper, lead, zinc, petroleum and natural gas, potash, phosphates, nickel, tungsten, silver, gold, and magnesium. (AMAX)

We provide our customers with retail banking, real estate finance, and corporate banking products which will meet their credit, investment, security and liquidity needs. (Carteret Savings and Loan Association)

Location

We are dedicated to the total success of Corning Glass Works as a worldwide competitor. (Corning Glass Works)

Sara Lee Corporation's mission is to be a leading consumer marketing company in the United States and internationally. (Sara Lee Corporation)

Technology

Control Data is in the business of applying micro-electronics and computer technology in two general areas: computer-related hardware; and computing-enhancing services, which include computation, information, education and finance. (Control Data)

Du Pont is a diversified chemical, energy and speciality products company with a strong tradition of discovery. Our global businesses are constantly evolving and continually searching for new and better ways to use our human, technological, and financial resources to improve the quality of life of people around the world. (Du Pont Chemical Corporation)

Concern for survival

To serve the worldwide need for knowledge at a fair profit by gathering, evaluating, producing and distributing valuable information in a way that benefits our customers, employees, authors, investors, and our society. (McGraw-Hill)

National City Corporation is a financial service organization committed to achieving and maintaining the highest attainable levels of performance and profitability, consistent with integrity, in order to provide shareholders with an above-average rate of total return on investment over the long term. (National City Corporation)

Philosophy

It's all part of the Mary Kay philosophy – a philosophy based on the golden rule. A spirit of sharing and caring where people give cheerfully of their time, knowledge, and experience. (Mary Kay Cosmetics)

We will realize this vision by dedicating our resources to achieving: 'Leadership in Serving People'. (Bank America Corporation)

Self-concept
Crown Zellerbach is committed to leapfrogging competition within 1000 days by unleashing the constructive and creative abilities and energies of each of its employees. (Crown Zellerbach)

The Corporation is committed to providing innovative engineering solutions to specialized problems where technology and close attention to customer service can differentiate it from commodity production or job-shop operations. (Harsco Corporation)

Concern for public image
To contribute to the economic strength of society and function as a good corporate citizen on a local, state, and national basis in all countries in which we do business. (Pfizer)

The company feels an obligation to be a good corporate citizen wherever it operates. (Eli Lilly and Company)

Concern for employees
To compensate its employees with remuneration and fringe benefits competitive with other employment opportunities in its geographical area and commensurate with their contributions toward efficient corporate operations. (Public Service Electric and Gas Company)

The mission specifically includes providing the best service for our customers, increasing earnings per share steadily, paying attractive dividends, avoiding dilution of equity, providing substantial protection for bondholders and other security holders, providing our employees with wages and benefits for a good standard of living, and participating in a meaningful way as a citizen in the communities we serve and the nation. (Arkla Inc.)

How do mission statements of manufacturing and service firms compare?

Service firms and manufacturing firms stress different variables for gaining competitive advantages in the marketplace. For example, manufacturing firms are often labour intensive and blue collar oriented, whereas service firms are generally more informative intensive and white collar oriented. The mission statements of service firms were thus expected to differ significantly from the mission statements of manufacturing firms.

Mission statements of manufacturing firms include two of nine components significantly more often than the documents of service firms, i.e. 'technology' (47 per cent) and 'philosophy' (37 per cent). This compares with service firms of which only 13 per cent include these dimensions. However, we also found that service firms generally have less comprehensive mission statements than manufacturing firms (see Appendix).

Less than 14 per cent of the mission statements of service firms include the 'location, technology, philosophy and self-concept' components. These are key elements in competitiveness, and communicating them to internal and external constituencies would be expected to enhance a firm's recognition in its industry. To illustrate how some service firms are able to communicate 'location, technology, philosophy and self-concept' in their mission statements, some excerpts from service firms' documents are provided below:

Location – Southeast Banking Corporation will be regarded as the leading financial services organization in the south-eastern United States. (Southeast Banking Corporation)

Technology – We will be a world leader using materials and technology to improve the way people work and live. (Norton Company)

Philosophy – The business of the Company shall be conducted in a legal and ethical manner guided by conservative principles, which include prudent stewardship of depositor funds. (Colorado National Bankshares Inc.)

Self-concept – Our most critical assets are the confidence and goodwill of our customers and investors, the knowledge, skills, ingenuity and dedication of our employees, and the basic economy in our electric service territory. (Ohio Edison and Penn Power)

Although manufacturing firms generally produced more comprehensive mission statements, three components were included in less then 45 per cent of their documents, i.e. 'location, philosophy and self-concept'. Some excerpts from sample manufacturing firms' mission statements are provided below to illustrate how these concepts were used:

Location – We seek to be the premier supplier of telecommunications products and services in our five-state operating area – but we will enter markets beyond our territory, and beyond our traditional business, which strengthens our capabilities in all the markets we serve. (Ameritech)

Self-concept – We must be calculated risk takers with a compulsive curiosity . . . the curiosity to seek the most innovative answers to the most complex problems . . . bringing better things for better living to the market place. (Du Pont)

Philosophy – The company is dedicated to the highest levels of ethics integrity, and excellence in research, manufacturing, marketing, and all other phases of its operations. (Eli Lilly and Company)

What is the nature of a mission statement?
A customer orientation

The results of this study provide a basis for describing the nature of corporate mission statement documents. Eighty-three per cent of manufacturing firms and 76 per cent of service firms include the 'concern for customers' component, and mission statements generally reflect the anticipations of customers. As Peter Drucker (1973, p. 61) expressed it:

> It is the customer who determines what a business is. It is the customer alone whose willingness to pay for a good or service converts economic resources into wealth and things into goods. What a business thinks it produces is not of first importance, especially not to the future of the business and to its success. What the customer thinks he/she is buying, what he/she considers value, is decisive – it determines what a business is, what it produces, and whether it will prosper. And what the customer buys and considers value is never a product. It is always utility, meaning what a product or services does for him. The customer is the foundation of a business and keeps it in existence.

A product/service statement

Eighty per cent of all firms included the 'product or service' component in their mission documents. Mission statements identify the value that a firm's products provide to customers. This is why AT & T's mission statement focuses on communication rather than telephones, Exxon's emphasis is on energy rather than oil and gas, Union Pacific speaks of transportation rather than railroads, and Universal Studios, is about entertainment rather than movies.

Social policy

Social policy embraces managerial philosophy and thinking at the highest levels of an organization. For this reason, social policy affects the development of a business mission statement. The mission statements of 83 per cent of manufacturing firms, and 67 per cent of service firms included 'concern for public image'. This refers to the firm's responsibilities to consumers, environmentalists, minorities, communities and other constituencies. Despite differences in approach, most companies try to assure outsiders that they conduct business in a socially responsible way. The mission statement is an effective instrument for conveying this message. The Norton Company, for example, concludes its mission statement by saying:

> In order to fulfill this mission, Norton will continue to demonstrate a sense of responsibility to the public interest and to earn the respect and loyalty of its customers, employees, shareholders, and suppliers, and the communities in which it does business.

Vagueness has its virtues

The mission statements received in this study were generally declarations of attitude and outlook rather than statements of specific programmes of action. There are important reasons for this. First, being broad in scope allows for the generation and consideration of a range of feasible alternative objectives and strategies without unduly stifling management creativity. Specific statements would limit the potential of creative growth for the organization. In addition, being broad in scope allows a mission statement to reconcile the differences among an organization's diverse stakeholders whose claims and concerns vary and often conflict. George Steiner (1979, p. 160) offers the following insight on the need for a mission statement to be broad in scope:

> Mission statements are not designed to express concrete ends, but rather to provide motivation, general direction, an image, a tone and a philosophy to guide the enterprise. An excess of detail could prove counterproductive since concrete specification could be the base for rallying opposition. Precision might stifle creativity in the formulation of an acceptable mission or purpose. Once an aim is cast in concrete it creates a rigidity in an organization and resists change. Vagueness leaves room for other managers to fill in the details, perhaps even to modify general patterns. Vagueness permits more flexibility in adapting to changing environments and internal operations. It facilitates flexibility in implementation.

Why do some firms have no mission statement?

In the study, 59 per cent of the responding chief executive officers indicated that their firm had not developed a formal mission statement. Why are many senior executives and corporate planners apparently reluctant to develop a statement of their business mission? There are undoubtedly many reasons, but one principal reason must be that the question 'What is our business?' can create controversy. Raising the question often reveals differences that need to be resolved among top managers in the organization. If considerable disagreement exists among top managers of an organization over the basic purpose and mission, this can cause trouble if it is not resolved. Managers who have worked together for a long time and who think that they know each other may realize in developing a mission statement that they are in fundamental disagreement.

Developing a corporate mission is always a choice between alternative strategies, each of which rests on different assumptions regarding the reality of the business environment. Drucker (1973) emphasizes that the mission decision is far too important to be made by acclamation, should never be made on plausibility alone, should never be made quickly, and should never be made painlessly. Developing a business mission is an important step in improving management effectiveness because disagreement on organizational direction may give rise to many conflicts on operational matters.

Another reason why firms may not have a mission statement is that some top managers spend almost all their time on administrative and tactical concerns. Developing a mission statement is often overlooked in these firms as managers rush too quickly to establish targets and implement strategies without spending sufficient time in clarifying their strategies. This problem is widespread even in large organizations.

When should a company develop a mission statement?

Developing and communicating a clear business mission is one of the most commonly neglected tasks in strategic management. Without a clear statement of mission, a firm's short term actions can be counter productive to long term interests. A mission statement should always be subject to revision, but will require changes infrequently if carefully prepared. Effective mission statements tend to stand the test of time.

A mission statement is sometimes developed only when an organization is in trouble. Of course it is needed then. Developing and communicating a clear mission during troubled times may have spectacular results and may help to reverse a decline. However, to wait until an organization is in trouble to develop a mission statement is a gamble that characterizes irresponsible management. As Drucker (1973, p. 88) states, the time to develop a mission statement is when a company has been successful:

> Success always obsoletes the very behaviour that achieved it, always creates new realities, and always creates new and different problems. Only

the fairy story ends 'They lived happily ever after'. It is never popular to argue with success or to rock the boat. The ancient Greeks knew that the penalty of success can be severe. The management that does not ask 'What is our mission?' when the company is successful is, in effect, smug, lazy and arrogant. It will not be long before success will turn into failure. Sooner or later, even the most successful answer to the question 'What is our business?' becomes obsolete.

An organization that fails to develop a comprehensive and inspiring mission statement loses the opportunity to present itself favourably to existing and potential constituencies. The mission statement is essentially a vehicle for communicating with important internal and external stakeholders, and its principal role is to clarify the ultimate aims of the firm.

Four examples. Four mission statements from different manufacturing and service organizations are presented in Table 6.5. These statements are then evaluated in Table 6.6 based on the nine components described above. Note in Table 6.6 that the PSE & G mission statement includes the most components (seven), while the Sunwest Bank document includes the fewest components (five).

Conclusion

Every organization has a unique purpose and reason for being. This uniqueness should be reflected in a statement of mission. An organization achieves a heightened sense of purpose when it develops and communicates a clear business mission. The nine basic components described in this article serve as a practical framework for evaluating and writing mission statements.

The importance of a mission statement as a motivating document is illustrated by a short story told by Porsche CEO Peter Schultz: 'Three people were at work on a construction site. All were doing the same job, but when each was asked what his job was, the answers varied. "Breaking rocks," replied the first. "Earning a living," answered the second. "Helping to build a cathedral." said the third.'

Few of us can build cathedrals. But to the extent we can see the cathedral in whatever cause we are following, the job seems more worthwhile. A clear mission helps us find those cathedrals in what otherwise could be dismal issues and empty causes. *Business Week* 14 September 1987, p. 120.

Table 6.5 *Four mission statements*

F. W. Woolworth Company
The mission of F. W. Woolworth Co. is to provide value to consumers in North America, Germany and Australia through distinctly individual but complementary retailing businesses. These businesses are being managed, on a decentralized basis, to generate levels of profit that reward investors, sustain long-term growth, provide competitive reward for employees, and benefit the communities in which they live and work.

Sunwest Bank
The purpose of Sunwest Bank is to provide financial and related services in a manner that: Maintains a level of earnings to support our growth and expansion, and sustains the confidence of those that invest in us. Anticipates and fulfills our customers' needs at a high level of product quality and staff performance. Provides a rewarding and challenging environment for our employees. Responds and contributes to the social and economic well being of the community and markets we serve.

Rockwell International
The leader in diverse markets, we are developing new technologies and applying them to products and systems in our four principal businesses – Aerospace, Electronics, Automotive and General Industries. Our 103 000 employees, more than 17 000 of them engineers and scientists, are dedicated to excellence in everything they do, from implementing new technologies, to managing complex systems, to making products of the highest quality. This effort is serving the needs and meeting the challenges of today's society. It also has given Rockwell International a momentum for continued outstanding financial performance.

Public Service Electric and Gas Company
Public Service Electric and Gas Company is an investor-owned, business-managed public utility, franchised by the State of New Jersey. Its primary purpose is to provide safe, reliable and economic electric and gas service to its customers at just and reasonable rates. In furtherance thereof, it is the aim of the corporation to afford its stockholders a return on their investment equivalent to that of other investments of similar risks, and to compensate its employees with remuneration and fringe benefits competitive with other employment opportunities in its geographical area and commensurate with their contributions toward efficient corporate operations.

Table 6.6   *An evaluation of the four mission statements*

Key components	F. W. Woolworth Co.	Sunwest	Rockwell	PSE & G
Customers	Yes	Yes	–	Yes
Products or services	Yes	Yes	Yes	Yes
Location	Yes	–	–	Yes
Technology	–	–	Yes	–
Concern for survival	Yes	Yes	Yes	Yes
Philosophy	–	–	Yes	Yes
Self-concept	–	–	–	Yes
Concern for public image	Yes	Yes	Yes	–
Concern for employees	Yes	Yes	Yes	Yes

Appendix: The research approach
Content analysis

Content analysis was used to evaluate each mission statement. This entailed selecting the written message, developing categories, and measuring the frequency of appearance of the categories using coding rules, applying an appropriate statistical test to the data collected, and then drawing conclusions.

Prior to reading and evaluating the sample mission statements, two raters studied the relevant literature and evaluated several mission statement documents, then, independently recorded whether or not each sample mission statement included each of nine components derived from the literature: concern for customers, product or service, location, technology, concern for survival, philosophy, self-concept, concern for public image and concern for employees.

Each mission statement was judged as including a particular component if both raters answered the respective component questions affirmatively. In this case, a value of '1' was assigned to the statement for that component. When a particular mission statement did not 'clearly' exhibit a given characteristic, a '0' was assigned to the statement for that component. The overall inter-judge reliability coefficient for the independent raters' evaluation of the sample mission statements was 0·833. The reliability coefficients for each of the components – customer, product or service, location, technology, concern for survival, philosophy, self-concept, public image and employees – were 0·75, 1·00, 1·00, 0·50, 0·75, 0·75, 1·00, 1·00 and 0·75 respectively. These coefficients indicate significant agreement between the independent raters' evaluations of the sample documents. The high reliability values also suggest that the literature-derived mission statement components have construct validity.

A comparison of firms that have a formal mission statement with firms that do not:

Variable	Firms that do have a mission statement (n = 75)	Firms that do not have a mission statement (n = 106)	t-value
Sales	$4283m	$5205m	0.57
Assets	$5444m	$8159m	1.70
Profits	$110m	$161m	0.71
1985 Earnings per share (EPS)	$2.66	$2.98	0.70
10-year average EPS	$12.09	$7.93	−1.64
1985 Return on investment (ROI)	$33.75	$22.99	−1.73
10-year average ROI	$16.76	$16.28	−0.25

Note: None of the t-values are statistically significant at the 0.05 level.

Profiles of the mission statements of manufacturing firms and service firms

Mission statement components	Mean for manufacturing firms[1] (n = 30)	Mean for service firms[2] (nn = 45)	t-value
Concern for customers	0.8333[3]		
Product or service	0.8000	0.8000	0.00
Technology	0.4667	0.1333	3.15[5]
Concern for survival	0.8667	0.8444	0.26
Philosophy	0.3667	0.1333	2.26[4]
Self-concept	0.2667	0.0889	1.92
Concern for public image	0.8333	0.6667	1.61
Concern for employees	0.8333	0.6667	1.61

[1] Manufacturing firms have an SIC Code of less than 40.
[2] Service firms have an SIC code of 40 or more.
[3] The mean values range from 0.0000 (no firms included this component in their mission statement) to 1.0000 (all firms included this component in their mission statement). The average inclusion rate for all firms is 54%.
[4] $p < 0.05$.
[5] $p < 0.01$.

Conclusion

It cannot be concluded from this or prior studies that a more comprehensive mission statement is related to higher performance. Many diverse factors impact organizational performance, such as oil prices, interest rates, deregulation and foreign competition. It would be inappropriate based on current knowledge of mission statements to level the literature-derived components as essential characteristics of mission statements. Rather, more theoretical and empirical research is needed before general conclusions can be made. It may be that a clear mission statement aids in selecting among alternative strategies, but does not particularly enhance environmental scanning or internal audit activities. The process of developing a formal mission statement may be of greater value and importance than the document itself.

Longitudinal research could especially improve management's understanding of mission statements. That is, monitoring how and why mission statements change over time in response to various environmental and strategy changes could provide further insight into the nature and appropriate uses of these documents under varying conditions. For optimal effectiveness, mission statements may need to be as distinctive as the relatively unique competitive environments in which organizations conduct their strategic planning.

References

Cochran, D., David, F. R. (1987). 'The communication effectiveness of organizational mission statements'. *Journal of Applied Communication Research*.

Drucker, P. F. (1973). *Management: Tasks, Responsibilities, and Practices*. New York: Harper & Row.

King, W. R. and Cleland, D. I. (1979). *Strategic Planning and Policy*. New York: Van Nostrand Reinhold, p. 124.

McGinnis, V. J. (1981). 'The mission statement: A key step in strategic planning'. *Business*, pp. 39–43, November/December.

Pearce, II J. A., David, F. R. (1987). 'Corporate mission statements: The bottom line'. *Academy of Management Executive*, 1 (2), 109–16.

Want, J. H. (1986). 'Corporate mission'. *Management Review*, pp. 46–50, August.

Further reading

Ackoff, R. (1985). 'Mission statements'. *Planning Review*, **15** (4), 30–2.

Bettinger, C. (1985). 'Behind the mission statement'. *ABA Banking Journal*, 154–60, October.

Byars, L. (1987). 'Organizational philosophy and mission statements'. *Planning Review*, **15** (4), 32–6.

Cochran, D., David, F. R., Gibson, K. (1985). 'A framework for developing an effective mission statement'. *Journal of Business Strategies*, **2** (2), 4.

David, F. R. (1989). 'Strategic Management' 2nd edn. Columbus, OH: Merrill Publishing Company.

Hunter J. C. (1985). 'Managers must know the mission: If it ain't broke don't fix it'. *Managerial Planning*, **33** (4), 18–22.

Pearce II, J. A. (1982). 'The company mission as a strategic tool'. *Sloan Management Review*, 15–24, Spring.

Peters, T. P. (1987). *Thriving in Chaos.* New York: Alfred A. Knopf.

Staples, W. A., Black, K. U. (1984). 'Defining your business mission: A strategic perspective'. *Journal of Business Strategies*, **1** (1), 33–9.

Waterman Jr, R. (1987). *The Renewal Factor: How the Best Get and Keep the Competitive Edge.* New York: Bantam Books Inc. Also, *Business Week*, 14 September 1987, 120.

Reproduced from David, Fred R. (1989). *Long Range Planning*, vol. 22, no. 1 by permission of Pergamon Press plc.

How to write a purpose statement
Mark Frohman and Perry Pascarella

Dr Mark Frohman is an experienced American organization consultant. He is president of a consulting company called Organizational Resources. He has written a book with Perry Pascarella on the 'purposeful organization'. Pascarella is editor-in-chief of the magazine *Industry Week*.

The purpose statements that Frohman and Pascarella refer to are the same in concept as our definition of mission statements. In the article they discuss the benefits of having a purpose statement, its contents and how to develop a statement. They also provide a questionnaire to test whether or not you should write a statement.

A purpose statement provides the basis for something that many organizations are missing today – the conviction that 'we know where we're going and how to get there.'

A purpose statement expresses business goals, values, and practices intended to win commitment and support for the organization over the long term.

Benefits

There are at least six benefits from a well developed purpose statement.

1 It provides *direction* and definition to the business. A purpose statement establishes what the organization wants to succeed in; it defines what the organization does and, in turn, what it does not do. As a result, it presents the parameters for strategic and annual planning, resource allocation, and the sort of opportunities for new or expanded business that should be considered in the planning process.

   The CEO of a large multinational firm says his company's purpose statement 'helps us keep on track when we wrestle with product-development proposals or acquisition opportunities'. His company's purpose statement reads in part: 'The company is in the business of developing, manufacturing, and marketing innovative equipment for the application of sealing coatings, adhesives, and other bonding agents under extreme pressure or temperatures.'

2 A well constructed purpose statement provides *focus for activities and consistency*. It distinguishes the organization from others by identifying its special and unique qualities and characteristics. It tells people how and where to channel their efforts to sustain company strengths and competitive advantages. It also provides a clear focus for responding to changes in the marketplace.

   A multibillion-dollar construction firm experienced substantial economic and competitive pressures in the early 1980s. Many members of the organization had been employed there for years and felt fairly treated and compensated. Top management, having never articulated a purpose, failed to provide a focus. As a result, the employees were paralyzed and felt that top management was losing control of the business. Many key employees left.

   When purpose is conceived and communicated, employees know what to work at and, as competitive pressures increase, where to put their emphasis.

3 All of us want to be more than a number at work. We want to work to provide *meaning* for us. A purpose statement gives each employee something greater to relate to than the job itself. The IBM cornerstone of 'customer service, excellence, and respect for the individual' is a classic example of how one organization has provided meaning and purposefulness to its employees for many years.

The purpose statement developed by a midwest designer and manufacturer of process-control system application packages lets its 2000 employees know that their work is to further the company by:

- establishing it as the quality leader and the most cost-effective supplier in each of its markets
- creating the opportunity for each employee to grow, participate and be recognized as a contributing member
- increasing aftertax earnings by an average of 18 per cent per year and working toward revenue growth of 14 per cent per year.

4 A purpose statement presents a *challenge*. It establishes goals and measures of achievement. It tells what characterizes success and prescribes how to achieve or maintain success.

People are goal oriented; they typically like a challenge. An effective purpose statement tells employees how to direct their efforts or the extra effort to meet the challenge. The victory is then an event that means success for the organization and satisfaction for the individuals.

5 Inherent in a well constructed purpose statement is a benefit that many proponents of individual freedom and creativity in organizations have ignored – outlining *policy*. Policy defines do's and dont's, the boundaries for the people associated with an organization. Statements of policy express the values of the organization; how the organization wants to be seen, both internally and externally; and how it wants to accomplish its goals. These value statements then are a 'stand' by the organization and a reference as to what is acceptable and what is not. A purpose statement, therefore, can simplify some decisions by prescribing what is 'in' and 'out'.

6 Perhaps the most important benefit is increased enthusiasm, commitment, and pride in one's organization – *passion*. A purpose statement supplies goals, prescribes methods and measures limits – in short, all the things people need to play the game and keep score. It also stimulates their commitment to win. The vice-president of operations of a small company observed after publishing a purpose statement: 'it did not say anything we'd not said before to our employees, many times. But it did give them in one statement our fundamentals. It not only reinforced and maybe clarified previous messages, it also got the employees excited.'

What makes it different

An effective purpose statement comes from asking the right people to describe, explain and anticipate the right things. It contains three basic ingredients that differentiate it from other statements.

First, a purpose statement contains a business mission that describes what business the organization is in or wants to be in. The description may draw upon the products, services, markets, customer needs, competitive advantages, and niches to define the business. The expression is both qualitative and quantitative. It provides performance measures such as aftertax earnings, market share, customer-satisfaction measures and revenue growth.

The second basic ingredient is an expression of values or beliefs about how the organization and its business should be conducted. This expresses the orientation toward the welfare and treatment of organization assets – technology, physical assets, financial assets and people.

Purpose statements of values regarding employee relations and practical business parameters may appear to be strange bedfellows. On the contrary, they make wonderful partners. Together they provide a coherent, integrated framework for people to understand the important whats, hows, and whys of the organization. In turn, people inside and outside the organization can more effectively and efficiently define their purposeful efforts.

The third basic characteristic of a purpose statement is a time horizon. It is not possible to offer a time horizon that fits every organization. Yet it is important to place some time line on the purpose statement so that its contributors can consider opportunities, investment, paybacks, trends, and the sustainability of strengths and resources over a prescribed period of time.

It takes time to develop, communicate, and gain commitment to the fulfillment of a purpose statement which provides the form for strategies and action plans that deal with the short term. A period of five to 10 years is a good place to start to develop a purpose statement with a lasting quality.

Whatever the time period, it is essential that the purpose statement be regularly reviewed to determine its relevance. As conditions change, an organization must re-examine itself in relation to its business, internal practices and relationships. Reviewing the purpose statement as part of an annual planning process is a sensible approach. In most instances, reaffirmation or clarification will be the likely outcome.

Six writing steps

There are six steps in the development of a purpose statement that can make its mark on the organization over the long term.

1 *Check for top-management* commitment to taking a stand in defining its current business, its vision of future business, and the management practices and values that should guide behavior.

   The top executive must decide if it's worth the investment to prepare an effective purpose statement. The statement and the process of developing it will be shaped by his or her views and values. In addition to appreciating the potential benefits, this person must assess whether the management team has something to say about the present and future scope and direction of the business.

2 *Make a preliminary outline* of the specific elements or contents of the purpose statement. Once the tentative contents are known, the data-collection methods to determine current conditions and practices should be spelled out. Then the methods to anticipate the future should be planned.

To identify the ingredients of the purpose statement the central question to be answered is,'What factors are important to our current and long-term success?' Several sets of people warrant an invitation to answer this question. First and foremost is the founder of the organization, if available. Second, previous leaders of the organization should be consulted. The current top manager and his or her staff should be polled too. A rich source of company history are longservice employees at all levels of the organization. They often can describe the flow of major events and important decisions that have led to the current circumstances.

Since success usually means 'meeting a need in the marketplace at a price the prospective customer is willing to pay', the customer or user certainly has relevant experience and views regarding the success factors. Opinions from the competition regarding organizational strengths and competitive advantages also may offer ideas for the contents of the purpose statement.

3 *Collect and interpret information* on the important internal success factors. Invariably, this generates opinions as to the current status of these factors. The people whose views were solicited earlier are not necessarily the best or only ones to comment on their current status or future role. Additional sources should be employed to get a broader reading.

Next, take stock inside the organization to determine the extent of the understanding of agreeing with, and committing to the internal practices and values. This is often an exciting part of the process since it can turn up discrepancies between prescriptions and practices.

This survey can take several forms: interviews, group discussions, or questionnaires. It can be conducted by internal staff or by persons outside the organization who may be perceived as more objective by the respondents.

The audit of current practices serves as a test of the success factors generated earlier. If the organization is successful and those factors are rated low in the audit, then something is missing which better explains current performance.

The survey may also point out inconsistencies between the business goals and other factors that top management wants in the purpose statement. The discrepancies are to be hammered out later in the development of the purpose statement.

Collect and interpret information on external success factors as perceived by customers and other outside groups. What needs is your organization meeting? (This is not the same as listing the features of your product or service. You are identifying 'why buys.') Then separate the customers into groups based on needs fulfilled.

Follow this with an analysis of major competitors in each customer-needs grouping. What does each competitor offer that leads customers to buy from that competitor rather than you?

You are now ready to consider your key success factors – competitive advantages – and define what the organization does for its customers that satisfies their needs better than the competition.

4 *Envision the future* by looking ahead five to ten years for external and internal trends and opportunitues. Although the best vision may not be totally accurate, the presence of such a vision prepares people to plan for and respond to future events in a coordinated and consistent manner.

Looking ahead to identify those things the organization wants to pursue to be successful brings us to the popular concept of 'vision'. Vision is, in part, a result of the hard work performed in steps one to three. It implies using the earlier work as a base to anticipate the relevant major trends and changes.

These questions are helpful in developing a picture of the future:

- What trends and assumptions should we consider in the world around us – political, regulatory, social, economic, technological?
- What trends or changes do we expect in our industry or marketplace?
- What trends or changes do we expect in the needs of our customers? This question should be asked for each 'need' group previously identified.
- What trends or changes will affect our customer base? What might happen that would reduce or increase the need for our product or service?
- What trends or changes do we expect in our competition? What do we expect our current competitors to do? Where might new competition come from?
- What specific trends or changes threaten our current competitive advantages?
- What opportunities to take greater advantage of current competitive strengths emerge from the anticipated trends and changes?
- What opportunities emerge from our 'vision' which, although not directly related to current strengths, appear to merit further assessment?

This work is not a substitute for a systematic planning process. Rather, it builds scenarios of how business conditions might change that can be used as the foundation for planning yet to be done.

The internal aspect of the vision also builds on earlier steps that provide a picture of 'what counts' in management beliefs and practices. These factors are subject to more control by management than those dealt with in the business-mission section. For example, the practice of teamwork can be enhanced by making team building programs available. Inventories can be better managed with information systems.

The internal vision is developed through careful response to these questions:

- What trends and changes do we expect in our financial and physical resources?
- What changes or trends do we anticipate with regard to our workforce (number, age, skills, and so on)?
- What management practices and values do we want to be known for in 10 years? Which ones must we sustain? Which ones must we develop?

5 *Write the purpose statement.* We have seen it successfully done five ways: by the top executive, the top management team, a task force, teams of specialists who each write specific parts, and external consultants. To be effective, however, the statement ultimately has to be thrashed out by the top management group because it is going to represent something that group is committed to.

Writing the purpose statement is when the 'rubber hits the road'. Now the original proposal for the current business-mission and management-practices statements are brought into the reality of how customers, employees and others see the organization. Putting the statement into final form means publicly taking a stand, deciding what is truly important and what does not warrant top priority.

The final form of the purpose statement expresses a commitment regarding how the organization will try to channel its business and its assets. It also defines how top management will channel its own time, energy, money and other resources.

Then the logical question is 'How do we know when we are done?' Essentially, that is determined by the level of satisfaction and commitment of the key participants. We suggest several test questions:

- Are you satisfied that you had your say and were listened to?
- Do you think the group was as creative as it could be in discussing opportunities, dangers, and management practices?
- Are you willing to walk out of this room, meet with your subordinates to present this purpose statement, and tell them you are personally committed to it?
- Are you confident that the mission and practices are realistic?

If the answers are affirmative, the statement is ready for the next step. If any of the answers are negative, the management team needs to discuss the reasons.

6 *Get a second opinion.* Before the purpose statement is formally unveiled, 'bounce it off' a few people inside and outside the organization who can judge its realism and worth. Ask them: 'is the expression of our business mission

clear and realistic? Is the portion on managerial practices and values clear and realistic? Does the purpose statement cover the things that are really important to our organization?

Extremely negative answers to any of the questions indicate that more work may be needed before unveiling the purpose statement.If there is affirmation by each of the groups, it is time to start communicating the purpose statement to the people who will use it.

Before you begin to write a purpose statement . . .

Unless you can answer 'yes' to all of these questions, you should weigh carefully whether proceeding to develop a purpose statement is the proper thing to do at this time.

1 Are we confident that the benefits of a purpose statement justify the time and effort required?
2 Do we really believe we have something to say about the mission of our business in the future that will make a difference now?
3 Do we really believe we have something to say about our management practices and values that is important to our success over the long term?
4 Can we afford to invest the time now to do the work necessary to prepare an effective purpose statement?
5 Are we willing to be objective in the examination of our management practices and relationships?
6 Are we willing to solicit and use feedback from our customers, competitors and others to help us understand the needs we satisfy and how our performance is perceived?
7 As a top management group, are we willing to take a stand about our business and values and commit ourselves to setting the example?
8 Do we think we can come up with a purpose that is general enough to guide the entire organization but specific enough to be meaningful for planning and decision-making?
9 Is there a champion for the development of a purpose statement who is in a position to drive it?

An ineffective purpose statement is:

1 A statement of performance goals only.
2 A statement of culture or employee-relations imperatives only.

3 A wish list from top management.
4 Not related to the marketplace.
5 Prepared using a bottom-up approach.
6 Too general.
7 Too specific.
8 Prepared hastily.
9 Treated as a 'one-shot' effort.
10 Not pushed by a champion.

Reproduced from Frohman, Mark and Pascarella, Perry (1987). *Industry Week*, 23 March by permission of Penton Publishing, Inc. Cleveland, Ohio.

The effectiveness of corporate codes of ethics
Steven Weller

Dr Steven Weller is an observer of the American court process and organizational behaviour. His background as a lawyer, his qualification as a PhD in political science and his experience as a teacher and consultant in law and in politics give him an unusual perspective on the issues of ethics statements and mission statements.

Although the article that follows addresses itself to codes of ethics, the points it makes are relevant to mission statements. Dr Weller refers to research done in compliance with the law and with court decisions to make some hypotheses about the content of codes of ethics and how they should be developed. He suggests that statements are most effective when they:

- specify priorities to be assigned to potentially conflicting desires
- define sanctions for non-compliance
- are congruent with the pre-existing values of employees
- are well communicated
- are perceived to have legitimacy resulting from authority, a track record of success or participative development.

There is a growing concern in society about business ethics and, in a larger sense, social control over business behavior. This concern is reflected in the popular press, in the writings of crusaders and scholars, and, increasingly, in the textbooks and curricula of schools of business and in the business world itself. It is rooted in a more general concern about the ethics of society's elite, both in the public and private sector, and a realization, at least since the Watergate era, that law alone does not, cannot and probably should not dictate all aspects of what a society might consider moral behavior. There have been dissenters, claiming that the only moral behavior of business is to make a legal profit, but they are in the minority.

One of the major aspects of this growing concern with ethical behavior has been the adoption by an increasing number of companies and industries of codes of ethics. These codes set up standards of behavior that, in many instances, make merely acting within the law not good enough. They cover a wide range of behavior, including dealings with competitors, the general public, customers, and peers and superiors within an organization. Some even attempt to cover activities in foreign countries.

This trend has been applauded as demonstrating a recognition on the part of business leaders that the social responsibility of business extends beyond the bottom line (Bowie, 1979). At the same time, the trend has been met with some skepticism. Critics believe that the codes are mere window dressing and a smokescreen to head off more stringent methods of social control (Bowie, 1979).

Both proponents and critics seem to accept the desirability of some form of self regulation of ethical standards by business. That desirability is based both on public conscience, the recognition that the law sets only minimum standards of behavior and the public expects a higher standard, and on self interest, the belief that government regulation is to be avoided and self regulation is a means of avoiding government regulation (Bowie, 1979).

One difference between the proponents and the critics has revolved around whether codes of ethics, as opposed to other forms of self regulation, are or even could be effective in controlling behavior. While it appears widely accepted that codes of ethics cannot provide a cure-all for all types of unethical behavior, there is disagreement on how much a code of ethics can do and on how best to set up and administer a code of ethics.

The scholarly literature on the subject to date shows little systematic thinking. It consists largely of opinion, backed up somewhat by economic theories of rational choice, and description of the individual experience of a few isolated companies and industries. (See, for example, Hoffman et al., 1984; and Beauchamp and Bowie, 1979.) With the importance of the issue and the stakes for the business world, we are, I believe, ready to embark on a more systematic investigation of the effectiveness of codes of ethics, based on carefully crafted hypotheses which can be tested by empirical data.

The purpose of this article is to begin that process by developing hypotheses concerning the potential effectiveness of codes of ethics. Although some commentary suggests that codes of ethics must be industry wide to be effective, I focus my discussion in this article on corporate codes of ethics. I have chosen that focus for two reasons. First, it is not clear yet that codes of ethics must be industry wide to be effective. Second, the individual corporation is more likely to be the starting place for the development of codes of ethics in that the corporation is a more manageable unit than an entire industry.

Given the paucity of empirical research on codes of ethics, the discussion that follows draws heavily from research on compliance with law and court decisions as a source of hypotheses concerning the efficacy of corporate codes of ethics. A great deal of research has been done on factors inhibiting or promoting compliance with law and with decisions of the United States Supreme Court. Codes of ethics are similar to laws in that both contain rules to guide future behavior. Our experience with law thus provides an analogy upon which to draw in analyzing the effectiveness of codes of ethics. That analogy provides the basis for the remainder of this article.

The discussion that follows is divided into three parts. First, hypotheses are developed based on the concept of legitimacy. Second, hypotheses are developed based on the content of the code, drawing from research on different types of laws. Finally, hypotheses are developed based on theories of individual behavior, drawing on models of rational choice.

The concept of legitimacy

People follow most laws most of the time even when they do not face any threat of immediate sanction for failure to obey. If this were not the case, there would be anarchy, for society cannot police all of the people all of the time. The most important force in bringing about compliance with the law is the belief that it is proper or morally right to obey the law. In turn, the extent to which people perceive that a law is proper depends in part on the degree to which those who produce the law possess authority that is perceived as legitimate.

For an understanding of legitimacy we are led to the work of Max Weber. (The following discussion is drawn from the summary of Weber's work in Dahl, 1970.) Weber describes three types of legitimacy:

1 Traditional
2 Charismatic
3 Rational/Legal

Any or all of the sources of legitimacy may be present in a given situation, so in the real world the categories are not mutually exclusive.

Traditional authority is authority arising from history or custom. In some societies, traditional authority is the dominant type of authority. Inherited authority such as that of a monarch is the most obvious example of traditional authority. Another example is the authority of a religious leader arising from the leader's position in the hierarchy of the religion, presumably stemming from a belief that the authority is granted by a higher being.

Charismatic authority is authority arising from the force of personality of a leader and the identification of the governed with the qualities exhibited by the leader. Qualities of bravery, wisdom, or fairness, among others, may give rise to charismatic authority. Authority from another source may be enhanced by charismatic authority.

Rational/legal authority is authority arising from the reasonableness of the rules or from the legality of the process through which the rules are produced. In a democracy, legal authority arises from grants of authority by the governed and the following of proper procedures for exercising that authority.

The importance of following procedures may be illustrated by what is or is not considered a 'law' in our society. Philosophers have struggled throughout history with the concept of law. While no single definition has ever gained ascendancy, some elements of law have been widely accepted. A law must emanate from the sovereign, contain a command and sanctions for failure to obey that command, and be coupled with mechanisms for enforcement and the application of sanctions.

Not all commands emanating from governmental authority, however, are given the effect of law. For example, a local district attorney may issue a decree to his staff not to accept any pleas to lesser offenses than the highest offense charged in drunk driving cases. While this decree will certainly affect people charged with drunk driving within his jurisdiction, the decree is not 'law'. A district attorney in another jurisdiction would not be bound by it, nor would a subsequent district attorney in the same jurisdiction. The decree is merely a statement of policy. Even the same district attorney would be free to change his mind at a later time and ignore his own decree.

The decree is not law because it was not promulgated according to proper proceedures, even though it did come from a governmental official. In our society, a law can be created only by a properly chosen legislative body following set rules, or through an executive or judicial body authorized by the legislature or the national or state constitution. This is the procedure required to create legal authority under our form of government.

While Weber's concepts have been applied primarily at the societal level, in terms of classifying political systems, they can apply to authority within organizations as well.

1 Traditional authority is the authority of the boss just because he/she is the boss. It is authority based on position.
2 Charismatic authority is authority based on success, particularly if success is obtained in the face of adversity.
3 Rational/legal authority is authority obtained through reason or obtained by involvement of subordinates in the process of developing rules.

For a code of ethics, the importance of legitimacy may be restated as a hypothesis:

Hypothesis: An ethical code will be more effective the greater the presence of one of the sources of legitimacy.

With regard to traditional authority, the structure of the organization will be important in determining which boss has authority. Organizations differ in their degree of centralization. In a highly centralized organization decision making comes primarily from the top, with little real authority delegated to lower level management. Usually even the resources to make decisions are possessed only by top management. In a highly decentralized organization, different parts of the organization are responsible for the majority of decisions concerning their scope of endeavor. Central management sets general policy and may exercise review functions or serve as a resource to resolve disputes. Each part of the organization possesses the resources to operate independently. The level of decentralization will determine the potential source of traditional authority.

> *Hypothesis*: In a decentralized organization, middle management will be a more effective source of authority for promoting a code of ethics than upper level management.

> *Hypothesis*: In a centralized organization, upper level management will be a more effective source of authority for promoting a code of ethics than middle level management.

> *Hypothesis*: A code of ethics that is supported by all levels of management will be more effective than a code that is supported by one level of management but not the other (i.e. there will be a clearer perception of what 'the boss' wants).

In a democratic society, rational/legal authority requires both that rules be produced by proper procedures, involving the participation, either directly or indirectly, of the governed, and that the rules be rational. The two requirements of participation and rationality give rise to several hypotheses.

> *Hypothesis*: The greater the participation of middle level management in the development of the code, the greater the effectiveness of the code.

> *Hypothesis*: The greater the participation of representatives of the rank and file employees in the development of the code, the greater the effectiveness of the code.

To be rational, the code must be produced by people who are informed and understand the circumstances in which the code will be applied. Too large a body may produce a code that is not rationally related to business needs and thus lack rational legitimacy.

> *Hypothesis*: A code produced by a large body, including many rank and file employees, will be less effective than a code produced by a small body, including a few representatives of the rank and file employees.

> *Hypothesis*: A code with unrealistic provisions will be less effective, even if produced with wide participation, than a code with realistic provisions, even if produced by a small body not including representatives of the rank and file.

The content of the code

A code of ethics is a statement of rules to guide present and future action. In this sense it is a set of policies. The explanation of the success or failure of a code of ethics, then, should be similar to the explanation for the success or failure of any policy.

It is important first to understand the difference between policy and action. The word 'policy' is defined by *Webster's New Collegiate Dictionary* as follows:

> . . . 2a: a definite course or method of action selected from among alternatives and in light of given conditions to guide and determine present and future decisions. b: a high-level overall plan embracing the general goals and acceptable procedures esp. of a governmental body.

Actions may thus be the results of policies but are not policies themselves. Policies may be inferred from actions, but actions are not always taken pursuant to policy.

It is important to separate policy from action, for it is crucial to our understanding of any system of social control, governmental, business or otherwise, to know when things are being done pursuant to a collective policy and when things are not and to be able to explain the resulting differences in outcomes. A police officer, for example, may decide not to arrest a speeder. His actions may be purposive but still may not be done pursuant to law or to any policy of the police department. We need to separate the policy of the police department from the actions of the individual police officer, for it is important to know how one affects or fails to affect the other.

Separating policy from action brings into focus the instruments of policy: rules, regulations, statutes, constitutions and court opinions. For all of these types of policies, a distinction can be made in terms of two roughly dichotomous categories which I call *agenda setting policy* and *priority setting policy*. The difference between the two is in the presence or absence of clear priorities to guide the application of general standards of behavior in specific situations.

Agenda setting policy sets the agenda and the issues which are to be considered in taking action but does not specify the priorities to be assigned to each consideration. This type of policy usually takes one of two forms: (1) a statement of some broad general goal which, more often than not, involves the application of conflicting subgoals and values; or (2) a list of concerns which the decision maker is expected to consider in deciding what action to take.

Priority setting policy not only sets out issues to be considered but specifies the priorities to be assigned to potentially conflicting concerns. This type of policy specifies a clear purpose or a statement of intent as to the desired outcome of the policy, often with standards to judge the ultimate performance of those acting under the policy.

The distinction between agenda setting policy and priority setting policy is more than simply a distinction between the general and the specific. It is possible to set out specific and highly detailed courses of action without specifying how the choice (the priority) between two conflicting courses of action is to be determined. It is also possible to set out very general goals while still clearly specifying which goal is to have priority. The presence or absence of guidelines to determine the choice between conflicting goals is the important classifying variable, not the detail with which possible courses of action are described.

Let us return briefly to our definition of policy. Policy is a set of rules to govern present and future action. The absence of policy, then, is the absence of rules to guide action. In a situation where there are no rules to guide action, individual actors will act in accord with their own individual desires and interests. The result will be determined by the relative values, powers and resources of those actors in interaction with each other. In other words, the ultimate outcome will be determined by the politics of the situation. The absence of policy, then, is politics.

The relationship between policy control and politics may be stated as a thesis which I call the policy control thesis: the importance of politics in determining action is inversely related to the degree of policy control. Stated in another way, 'Lack of definite standards creates a void into which attempts to influence are bound to rush' (Friendly, 1962). As priority setting policy provides greater policy control than agenda setting policy, the policy control thesis leads to a second thesis: the importance of politics in determining action will be greater for agenda setting policies than for priority setting policies. In another study I have shown how the policy control thesis helps explain differences in the implementation of different sections of The National Environmental Policy Act of 1969 by the US Army Corps of Engineers (Weller, S. 1979).

With regard to business codes of ethics, the policy control thesis may be stated as a hypothesis:

Hypothesis: A code of ethics that makes its priorities clear will be more effective than a code of ethics which merely adds ethical rules to the existing agenda.

It is thus important to understand what the existing agenda of the business person is, and to undertand this we must look at the organizational setting within which the business person operates.

All organizations are influenced by an insider perspective, determined by the need of the organization to survive (Sax, 1970). The insider perspective of an administrative agency is determined by its legislatively defined mission (Sax, 1970). The insider perspective of a business organization is largely determined by the need to make a profit. To be effective, then, a code of ethics must indicate to what extent ethical behavior is to have priority over profits (Bowie, 1979).

To the extent that a code of ethics fails to set priorities, individual actors will respond more to the politics of each situation in which they find themselves. Political pressures could include the need to please a superior, a customer or important segments of a locality. These pressures could override ethics. Further, as the pressure can vary from one situation to another, depending on the locality and the individuals involved, they can bring about behavior that is both variable and unpredictable.

We are thus led to several further hypotheses concerning the effectiveness of priority setting codes of ethics as opposed to agenda setting codes of ethics. With regard to the importance of management support, the following hypotheses may be proposed:

Hypothesis: The effectiveness of an agenda setting code of ethics will be more dependent on the support of middle level management than will the effectiveness of a priority setting code.

Hypothesis: The effectiveness of an agenda setting code will vary more with changes in middle level management than will the effectiveness of a priority setting code.

With regard to the need to obtain and please customers, the following hypotheses may be proposed:

Hypothesis: The effectiveness of an agenda setting code will be affected more by differences in the needs and wishes of customers than will the effectiveness of a priority setting code.

Hypothesis: The effectiveness of an agenda setting code will be affected more by changes in the business fortunes of the organization than will the effectiveness of a priority setting code.

Another potentially important aspect of the content of a code of ethics that is suggested by analogy from research on compliance with law is the threat of sanctions for non-compliance and the availability of a mechanism for enforcing those sanctions. Studies have shown that the enforceability of law and court decisions increases as the threat of sanctions for non-compliance increases (Krislov, 1965). This should be true for codes of ethics as well.

Hypothesis: The greater the provision of sanctions in a code of ethics for non-compliance, the greater the effectiveness of the code.

Hypothesis: The greater the perceived threat of imposition of sanctions for non-compliance, the greater the effectiveness of the code.

As to the reality of the threat of sanctions as a force in making a code self-executing, studies of compliance with court decisions have shown that the method of communication of a decision is important. Decisions that have unambiguous language and are communicated openly and repeatedly have a greater impact than those which are not so communicated (Wasby, 1970; and Bowie, 1979). This should also apply to codes of ethics.

Hypothesis: A code of ethics that specifies priorities clearly will carry a greater perceived threat of sanctions for non-compliance than a code which merely adds to the agenda of things to be considered prior to taking action.

Hypothesis: A code of ethics that is publicized and communicated to employees regularly through all levels of management will be more effective than one which is not so communicated.

There may be instances where there is pressure on a person not to comply with a code of ethics and a threat of sanctions for actually complying. An effective code of ethics may require mechanisms for protecting those wishing to comply or those who report instances of non-compliance on the part of peers or superiors (Bowie, 1979).

Hypothesis: A code of ethics that provides protection for compliance in contravention of the demands of an unethical superior will be more effective than a code which does not contain that protection.

Hypothesis: A code of ethics that provides a mechanism for reporting violations that protects the person reporting will be more effective than one which does not provide such a mechanism.

Again, the clarity of the code will affect the willingness of individual employees to follow it or report violations. An individual is at much greater risk in disobeying a superior if the code is ambiguous.

Hypothesis: Obedience to a priority setting code in the face of contrary demands of a superior will be greater than obedience to an agenda setting code in the face of such contrary demands.

Hypothesis: Reported violations will be greater for a priority setting code than for an agenda setting code.

Theories of individual behavior

Studies have shown that compliance with Supreme Court decisions is also affected by the values and needs of the individuals affected by the decision. The greater the congruence between the decision and the values and needs of the individuals to whom the decision is directed, the greater the compliance (Wasby, 1970).

Hypothesis: The greater the congruence of a code of ethics with the preexisting values of employees, the greater the effectiveness of the code.

Hypothesis: The greater the perceived personal advantages of employees in complying with a code of ethics, the greater the effectiveness of the code.

This in turn leads to a variation of the need for participation of affected employees in the development of a code of ethics.

> *Hypothesis*: The greater the participation of affected employees in the development of a code of ethics, the greater the congruence of the code with the values and needs of the employees, and thus the greater the effectiveness of the code.

Finally, studies have shown, drawing on the theory of cognitive dissonance, that a law which provides little opportunity to avoid compliance can actually bring about a change in attitudes to make the attitudes more congruent with the law. That is, an individual faced with demands in conflict with his personal attitudes will tend to reduce the conflict. If the conflict cannot be reduced by resisting the demand, it may be reduced by a change in attitudes to bring attitudes more in line with what must be done (Wasby, 1970). This leads to a final hypothesis.

> *Hypothesis*: A priority setting code with a clear commitment to enforce it on the part of management will increase attitudes supportive of ethical behavior.

In other words, if people cannot avoid complying with the code, they will be more likely to come to believe that the code is right.

Conclusion

It appears clear that the concern of American society with the ethics of business is not a passing fancy but a long term concern that will grow in the years to come. I believe that it is also clear that much of the response to this concern must be in the form of self regulation by business, due to the inadequacy of law as a solution and to the advantages to business of self regulation over regulation imposed from the outside.

This article has suggested hypotheses concerning why a code of ethics may or may not be effective. The hypotheses have been drawn largely from theories and research concerning an analagous form of social control, the law. They draw credibility both from the quality of the research on which they are based and from the strength of the analogy between law and codes of ethics. Both law and ethics attempt to control future behavior by a set of rules to guide action, albeit in different ways.

This article is meant as a starting point in developing systematic thinking and research. The hypotheses here have been stated in terms of one independent variable at a time, and it is important that research begin in this way, with research designed as much as possible to isolate single variables. More variables and hypotheses will certainly be added to the list proposed here, as thinking in the field becomes more sophisticated and can draw more on direct experience rather than analogy.

As the effects of each variable become more understood, research must then move on to investigate interactions between variables. The real world is much more complex than is pictured by the hypotheses presented here. For example, once the independent effects of sources of legitimacy and the need to set priorities are understood, research must then look at how these interact. Is a priority setting code with low legitimacy more or less effective than an agenda setting code with high legitimacy? The potential questions and possibilities for research will expand as fast as knowledge expands. If this article starts us on that path, then its purpose will have been well served.

References

Beauchamp, T. L., Bowie, N. E. eds. (1979). *Ethical Theory and Business.* Englewood Cliffs, NJ: Prentice-Hall, Inc.

Bowie, N. E. (1979). 'Business Codes of Ethics: Window Dressing or Legitimate Alternative to Government Regulation?'. In *Ethical Theory and Business*, Beauchamp, T. L., Bowie, N. E. (eds). Englewood Cliffs, NJ: Prentice-Hall, Inc.

Dahl, R. A. (1970). *Modern Political Analysis*, 2nd edn. Englewood Cliffs, NJ: Prentice-Hall, Inc.

Friendly, H. J. (1962). *The Federal Administrative Agencies.* Cambridge, MA: Harvard University Press.

Hoffman, W. M., Moore, J. M., Fedo, D. A. eds. (1984). *Corporate Governance and Institutionalizing Ethics.* Lexington, MA: D. C. Heath.

Krislov, S. (1965). *The Supreme Court in the Political Process.* New York, NY: Macmillan.

Sax, J. (1970). *Defending the Environment.* New York, NY: Vintage.

Wasby, S. L. (1970). *The Impact of the United States Supreme Court: Some Perspectives.* Homewood, IL: Dorsey.

Weller, S. (1979). Politics as Law in Action: The Implementation of the National Environmental Policy Act of 1969 by the US Army Corps of Engineers. Unpublished PhD dissertation, Cornell University, Department of Government, Ithaca, NY.

Chapter 7

Do you have a good mission statement?

A division planning manager recently produced a nicely bound, 52-page document simply headed 'Our Mission'. It included an eight-page summary of the mission statement for the division and subsidiary statements for each function, including one for marketing, sales, export, production, technical, finance, personnel and planning. But it lacked liveliness and it gave few insights into the business.

The statements did not demonstrate that the company had a sound strategy. The functional statements did not fit easily together. The company values did not shine through giving a sense of pride in the company. Finally, there was no tangible guidance for behaviour. It would be difficult for an individual manager to know what day to day behaviour was expected.

The document had been put together with a considerable amount of effort involving all members of senior management. Each function had written its own section and the management committee had worked together on the overall statement. Yet each member of the management committee agreed with our judgement that as a whole it was not effective.

Each manager had his or her own criticisms, but the real problem was that the committee had no objective criteria against which to judge the quality of the document. The planner, who was administering the process, had no basis for saying that the quality was poor. All agreed that it was a first draft effort, and that if they repeated the exercise next year it would probably be better. But there was no agreement about what would constitute a better document.

The need to assess the quality of a mission document is a problem being faced by many management teams and consultants. Research we have carried out in

Britain suggests that almost half the large businesses in the country have a mission statement or something similar. In addition, we have found that mission statements are more evident at the division and business unit level in large companies, than at the corporate level.

Mission statements have become a tool of management. They now get regular attention in texts on strategic management and it is not unusual for managers on management development courses to be asked to develop a mission statement for their business. As a tool mission statements are believed to help clarify management thinking and improve communication with the organization.

The use of mission statements in Britain was a surprise to the research team. Many British managers still find the word distasteful, associating it with hype and insincerity. Yet, whether their statements are titled company philosophy, vision and values, company credo or a host of other names, the objective appears to be the same – to describe the essence of the company and its ambitions in a way that provides a rationale for it to exist.

Despite the large scale use of missions by managers, little guidance is available on what constitutes a high quality statement.

Our work has given us a definition of mission, and we have turned this understanding into a questionnaire titled 'Do you have a good mission statement?' (Table 7.1). The questionnaire is based on four elements of mission – purpose, strategy, values and behaviour standards.

Purpose

Why does the organization exist? For what end result is all the effort being expended? Purpose is the ultimate rationale for the organization. Purpose provides people in the organization with a justification for their work. It is something that lies behind specific objectives or goals. It deals with the philosophical question of what is the role of business in society.

We have defined two questions that should assist managers in deciding whether they have created a satisfactory purpose:

1 Does the statement describe an inspiring purpose that avoids playing to the selfish interests of the stakeholders – shareholders, customers, employees, suppliers?

All stakeholders – shareholders, customers, employees, suppliers and even the community – have a claim on the company. It is, therefore, a legitimate philosophical question to ask whether the company is in business to maximize the return to shareholders, to produce the highest quality products for customers or to provide the most rewarding jobs for employees. Which stakeholder has the greatest claim?

The most common answer is that the shareholders, as the owners of the business, have the greatest claim. Companies like Hanson, Britain's largest diversified conglomerate, have made this choice explicit. Lord Hanson says that 'The central tenet of my faith is that the shareholder is king.' In other such companies it is not uncommon to hear the chairman say 'Managers should realize that we are in business to make profits.'

But it is philosophically possible to build a purpose around each of the other stakeholders. A consumer cooperative would be unabashed about serving its consumer-members, and giving them the greatest claim; a farm cooperative views its owner-suppliers as having the greatest claim; and a professional partnership might legitimately argue that the working partners have the greatest claim on the business.

What our research has shown is that some companies have defined a purpose that rises above the interests of any one stakeholder – a higher ideal. These companies have defined a cause that all the stakeholders can feel proud of supporting. By refusing to identify one stakeholder as having the greatest claim on the business, these companies are able to play down self-interest and emphasize the greater good that all stakeholders are supporting. By creating a greater cause, these companies are able to argue that each stakeholder should take from the business only what is reasonable. Surpluses are then applied to furthering the cause. Matsushita, the world's largest producer of electrical products, has probably developed the most coherent philosophy based on a higher ideal. In the words of Mr Konosuke Matsushita, the company's 88-year-old founder:

> Happiness of man is built on mental stability and material affluence. To serve the foundation of happiness, through making man's life affluent with inexpensive and inexhaustible supply of necessities like water inflow, is the duty of the manufacturer. Profit comes in compensation for contribution to society. Profit is a yardstick with which to measure the degree of social contribution made by an enterprise. Thus profit is a result rather than a goal. An enterprise in the red will make all co-operating people poor, and ultimately the whole society poor. If the enterprise tries to earn a reasonable profit but fails to do so, the reason is because the degree of its social contribution is still insufficient.

Matsushita sees the purpose of his company as being to serve society. Profit is merely a by-product and provides the engine for making further contributions.

Noble statements like these may initially seem out of place in a European or British context. Yet some of Europe's most successful companies have purposes aimed at a high ideal. Sainsbury, Britain's most successful grocer, states that its primary objective is 'to discharge the responsibility as leaders in our trade by acting with complete integrity, by carrying out our work to the highest standards, and by contributing to the public good and to the quality of life in the community'. Sainsbury's final objective, intentionally placed last, is 'to generate sufficient profit to finance continual improvement and growth of the business whilst providing our shareholders with an excellent return on their investment'. Like Matsushita, the Sainsbury philosophy sees profit as an engine for growth rather than an end in itself.

Ciba-Geigy, a Swiss pharmaceutical and chemical company, also sees business in the context of society. Its mission statement states, 'Ciba-Geigy believes that business is not simply an end in itself and that it must serve people and society. Its economic success is, however, a prerequisite to the achievement of its aims.' Ciba-Geigy's philosophy is also aiming at some higher ideal. Yet its philosophy is subtly different to that of Matsushita. Ciba-Geigy believes that profit must come first: it is only when a business makes a profit that it will have the spare resources to focus on doing good in society. The Matsushita philosophy is more holistic. Matsushita sees profit as coming after service to society. It is only by serving society well that a business is able to earn a good profit. Matsushita sees doing business as being synonymous with serving society; whereas Ciba-Geigy appears to see the two as somewhat at odds.

Both companies, however, see a higher ideal for business. With this higher ideal the organization is able to gain the cooperation of all its stakeholders to the same cause. Rivalry between stakeholders is reduced and all can more readily bind around a common sense of mission.

2 Does the statement describe the company's responsibility to its stakeholders?

While a purpose statement should avoid legitimizing the selfish interests of stakeholders, it must clarify the company's responsibility to each stakeholder. The company defines a cause (a purpose) that is inspiring and worthy of the support of its stakeholders. The stakeholders join the cause by giving their loyalty to the company. In return the company needs to define what each stakeholder should expect to gain from the relationship. On the surface, defining the company's responsibility is a reasonably straightforward process. Shareholders will get better than average returns, employees will get better than average compensation and working conditions; customers will get superior products; and suppliers will get fair dealing and loyalty from the company.

But, at a deeper level, a company needs to think through what is the nature of its preferred relationship with each stakeholder. It wishes to gain the loyalty of each stakeholder, but it may not be in a position to buy that loyalty by offering better financial terms. It may not choose to pay top rates to employees or commit to long term relationships with suppliers or guarantee to provide continuous supply to customers. But it must think through what it can offer each of those groups that will retain their loyalty.

The uniqueness of every company will cause it to have a reasonably unique set of statements about its responsibilities to its stakeholders. Ciba-Geigy emphasizes responsibility, service and teamwork in its statements:

We will behave as a responsible corporate member to society and will do our best to cooperate in a responsible manner with the appropriate authorities, local and national . . . We will provide a high standard of customer service in our efforts to maintain customer satisfaction and cooperation with our Company . . . We will strive to create an atmosphere which is conducive at all levels to the effective teamwork which is of great importance for the success of the Company.

Sainsbury's emphasizes value for money, a good shopping environment and good remuneration in its statements:

To provide unrivalled value to our customers . . . to create as attractive and friendly a shopping environment as possible . . . to offer our staff outstanding opportunities in remuneration relative to other companies in the same market.

The best mission statements make these commitments clear so that each stakeholder knows what to expect from its relationship with the company.

Strategy

Strategy is the commercial rationale for how the business is going to achieve its purpose. The subject of strategy has been much analysed and written about. The classic works are Michael Porter's two books, *Competitive Strategy* and *Competitive Advantage*.

Good strategy is about finding a way to run the business that is better than the most immediate competitors. Good strategy is also about choosing a market that is attractive, where the other players such as customers and competitors will not force prices down too low or insist on cost levels that are uneconomic. Articulating a particular strategy can be difficult and will need a full description to capture the detailed reasons why a market is attractive or why a set of activities will lead to better performance than the competitors.

All of these details cannot be included in a mission statement. Yet the mission needs to describe the central elements of strategy. From examining companies' statements we have judged that two questions will help managers include the appropriate level of detail about strategy in the mission statement.

1 Does the statement define a business domain explaining why it is attractive?

A mission statement needs to make clear what business the company is in. Sainsbury's is in the business of grocery retailing and Ciba-Geigy is 'engaged primarily in the field of specialty chemicals and related products and services'.

In describing the nature of the business the statement should be as specific as possible. It should define not only a general industry, but also what part of the industry the company prefers to compete in and why. The statement should give its readers confidence that the company knows clearly the type of business environment in which it can perform well.

Sainsbury's statement does not give a clear definition of its business domain. The only reference to its business comes in the statement, 'to discharge the responsibility as leaders in *our trade*.' For most readers of this statement it is clear that Sainsbury is referring to the grocery trade. But even with this understanding it is still not a clear definition. The document could be strengthened if it included a paragraph such as, 'We are food retailers to the mass market providing unrivalled value in the quality of the goods we sell, in the competitiveness of our prices, and in the choice we offer. We compete in countries where the customers appreciate this value and where the industry structure makes it possible for large retailers to create economies of scale.' This paragraph explains that Sainsbury's business domain is quality food retailing to the mass market, and that this business is attractive because of the potential for economies of scale.

Dist Inc. is a company that has addressed the business domain question in its statement. Dist is involved in the distribution of white goods. It also distributes industrial controls, mostly in the USA. Dist's statement of mission says, 'Dist will operate businesses where there exists an opportunity to differentiate profitably based on customer service. We will choose segments of such markets where there is sufficient potential for high volume to build scale.' In this statement Dist explains that its business domain is service businesses with potential for scale. These businesses are attractive because companies can differentiate themselves and gain advantage from scale.

Another company that gives a clear answer to the business domain question is a Yorkshire based heavy textiles company called BBA. In a one-page document famous for its blunt phrasing, called 'BBA – A Company Philosophy', Dr John Whyte, the chief executive, has stated, 'We will concentrate on markets where the products are in a state of maturity or decline (sunset industries), the capital cost of market entry is high, and fragmentation of ownership on the supply side facilitates rapid earnings growth by acquisition of contribution flows'. The statements about high barriers to entry and fragmented ownership give a rationale as to why sunset industries of this type are attractive.

Both Dist and BBA have clearly stated the business domains they want to compete in and why these domains are likely to be attractive. Their mission statements have more credibility as a result. The users of the statement can be confident that management have thought through an important element of strategy.

2 Does the statement describe the strategic positioning that the company prefers in a way that helps to identify the sort of competitive advantage it will look for?

The strategic positioning of a company is the role it takes on relative to its competitors. Within the business domain of food retailing, some companies seek to gain advantage from cost leadership, offering a cash and carry service. Others, such as Sainsbury, aim to be a quality supplier gaining economies of scale through volume and through brand leadership. Others position themselves as specialist delicatessens, offering a limited range to a narrow customer segment. Others provide a convenience to their locality, often opening at unusual times. Each type of company has chosen a different positioning in the food retailing business.

In many mission statements the description of a company's strategic position is intermingled with its description of business domain. By defining the business domain, the mission statement will often make clear at the same time the positioning that the company prefers.

The Dist statement is an example. Dist apparently seeks to be the service leader in its industry. It also seeks to be the market leader, gaining an advantage over competitors through economies of scale ('potential for high volume to build scale'). These points are reinforced further in our principles where the company states, 'We will achieve our standards through quality of the service delivery . . . and through a high quality, professional management and employee group who understand and are committed to a common business philosophy, value system and corporate culture.'

Where the description of business domain does not address strategic positioning, a separate paragraph or sentence is needed in the statement. In 'BBA – A Corporate Philosophy,' Dr Whyte describes in a separate part of the document the position that the company prefers to take up – the largest competitor with the lowest cost. The document explains that BBA seeks 'market niches where we are somebody . . . where the scale of our presence . . . will allow price leadership'.

It also seeks cost leadership 'to increase profit margins by drastic cost reduction' and 'to become market dominant by outproducing the competition'. At one point the document states bluntly, 'the cheapest producer will win'.

By clarifying its preferred business domain a company will often also describe the strategic position that it seeks. Nevertheless, a good mission statement should explicitly address both questions making sure that both are adequately answered. In doing so it gives the users of the mission statement confidence that the basic elements of strategy have been addressed by management.

Values

Values are the beliefs of the organization that have a moral basis. They are the founding stones for the corporate religion. They are hard to articulate because they are the assumptions that lie behind many of the rules and behaviour standards in the company. Yet it is important that they are articulated.

A company's values are often built on the personal values of its senior management. Where these personal values happen to fit the organization's purpose and its strategy, all is well. This fit normally occurs when an organization is founded. The founding managers create natural fit between all three elements, rejecting strategies that do not blend easily with their values and defining a purpose that captures their deeply held beliefs.

But when the founders retire and professional managers take their place, the fit between the personal beliefs of the senior managers and the organization's values can be broken. Only by making the organization's values explicit can this potential mismatch be avoided.

Two questions help to ensure that the organization's values fit with strategy and purpose:

1 Does the statement identify values that link with the organization's purpose an act as beliefs that employees can feel proud of?

We have pointed out that the best mission statements describe a purpose that is a high ideal. The purpose also clarifies the responsibility of the organization to its stakeholders. Values must link with these purpose elements.

Sainsbury has a purpose of being a leader in its trade and of contributing to the quality of life. Quality is, therefore, one of its central values. This value applies to the products, the shopping environment and the high standards to which people throughout the organization work. It is a value everyone can feel proud of because it can be seen to be good, almost morally good in itself. To strive for the best quality is to do something worthwhile.

Matsushita is another company with an elevating purpose – happiness through material affluence. Mr Matsushita took great care to articulate the company's values, describing them as Matsushita's seven spiritual values:

- national service through industry
- fairness
- harmony and cooperation
- struggle for betterment
- courtesy and humility
- adjustment and assimilation
- gratitude

These are not values that are normally associated with hard driving companies fighting to win in the international marketplace. But they were very carefully selected by Mr Matsushita for their moral content as well as their business good sense. He wanted employees to feel morally nourished by their work. By working to principles that they could be proud of, he felt that they would find work more fulfilling.

These values also link well with the Matsushita purpose. Fairness, betterment and harmony are all values that fit well with thoughts of people's happiness.

Both Matsushita and Sainsbury have values that link well with their purposes. They also both have values that are uplifting. Employees can feel proud of living up to these values.

2 Do the values 'resonate' with and reinforce the organization's strategy?

For the best performance, strategy and values need to work together. If the strategy is cost driven, the value system needs to emphasize frugality. If the strategy is about coordination and teamwork, the value system should give high regard to helpfulness and harmony.

Defining an organization's values is not about making a long list of all the good things in business that have moral content. It is about setting priorities. It is about whether frugality is more important than helpfulness. Day to day, these two values frequently come into conflict: 'Should I be extra helpful and courier this document because I know the person wants it urgently? Or should I send it the cheapest way?' is a mundane issue, but one where the values are in conflict. It is possible to develop a rational answer to this dilemma. But, in the day to day rush, most of these decisions are made on the basis of the value system rather than on a careful weighing of the pros and cons. Choosing the values that have the highest priority is therefore an essential part of managing the organization.

As we pointed out in the previous section on strategy, Sainsbury's strategy is heavily dependent on quality – 'good food costs less at Sainsbury's' is their slogan. It makes admirable sense, therefore, that one of their central values is quality.

Matsushita's early strategy was built on effective coordination between different units focusing on different steps in the business. Retailing companies were independent of the distribution companies, and both were independent of the manufacturing companies. In addition, most of the components were manufactured by sub-contractors. To get the manufacturing companies and sub-contractors to understand the needs of consumers, retailers and distributors, Matsushita needed to create close working relationships up and down the chain. The values of harmony and assimilation fit well with this strategy.

Another plank of Matsushita's strategy was low cost manufacturing. The company aimed to find cheaper methods of production. The restless 'struggle for betterment' promoted by the company fitted well with a philosophy of continuous improvement in search of low cost. In Matsushita the link between strategy and values is strong.

BBA's mission provides a third example of a good link between values and strategy. BBA's strategy is based on cost leadership, in niche markets, in sunset industries. Its values support this strategy well. The mission statement explains that in BBA 'grit and gumption are preferable to inertia and intellect' and 'Victorian thrift is not an antique'. This is reinforced by 'our tactic is to use less money in total'.

For some managers these puritan values might not seem uplifting or practically moral. Their fit with strategy is clear, but their ability to make employees feel that work is worthwhile is less obvious. Fortunately, BBA operates from Yorkshire in the north of England. Many managers brought up in this part of the country understand and value frugality. To them waste of any kind is viewed as evil. For these managers BBA's values have moral content, giving their work an added rationale.

BBA, Matsushita and Sainsbury are all examples of companies with values that fit. In all three, the values guide day to day behaviour and act as an inspiration making work more fulfilling. In all these the values also link closely with strategy and with purpose.

Behaviour standards

A mission is only made real when it affects behaviour: when it guides people's actions helping them decide what to do and what not to do. Strategy and values both have behaviour messages. Strategy contains messages about what should be achieved, e.g. low cost production, highly excellent service. Values contain messages about how things should be done, e.g. frugally or harmoniously, or with quality.

When strategy and values support each other, the behaviour messages are doubly powerful. But the messages don't achieve anything until they are translated by managers into behaviour standards. These behaviour standards are the organization's rules of thumb: 'the way we do things around here'; or, in religious terms, the organization's ten commandments.

There are two questions that the mission writer should answer to be sure that the mission clarifies the behaviour standards:

1 Does the statement describe important behaviour standards that serve as beacons of the strategy and the value?

Companies with clear missions have a few behaviour standards that have come to symbolize the purpose, strategy and values. If you ask managers why they like working for the company, or what is important about the way the company does business, it is these behaviour standards that they will most often refer to. They may be seemingly insignificant management actions such as the holding of regular staff briefing meetings or a policy of open accounting so that employees and customers can look at the figures. The culture has identified them as beacons of the mission. We belive that good mission statements identify these behaviour standards, increasing their importance as a result.

Most mission statements describe behaviour in a loose way, wrapped up in a statement of values. Sainsbury, for example, states as one of its objectives, 'in our stores, to achieve the highest standards of cleanliness and hygiene, efficiency of operation, convenience and customer service, and thereby create as attractive and friendly a shopping environment as possible'. There are plenty of behaviour messages in this statement, but there are no clear behaviour standards.

A behaviour standard for Sainsbury might read, 'Store managers meet with their staff weekly to discuss cleanliness, efficiency and customer service. Junior staff and customers join in these standard-raising meetings.' Or it might be a more simple behaviour standard, such as, 'Every day store managers ask themselves, each other and staff, "What have you done for the customer today?"'

Most mission statements do not contain behaviour standards as explicit as these because managers feel awkward about being so prescriptive. They do not want to tell people exactly how to behave. They are right. As a general rule it is better to use the creativity of the individual to make the best of the situation.

But some behaviour standards have a special importance that far outweighs the disadvantage of being over prescriptive. Just like the ten commandments, these behaviours capture the essence of a company's religion. By making a few behaviour standards explicit, senior managers can attempt to control which behaviours become the beacons of their mission. In this way they create a tighter link between the mission statement and what is happening day to day in the company.

Insisting that these behaviours are described in the mission statement has other benefits. It demonstrates to the users that senior managers have thought about how they are going to translate the strategy and the values into action. It also gives a mandate to managers throughout the company to demand compliance with these behaviours.

The most famous examples of behaviour standards come from two of the world's best known companies – Hewlett-Packard and IBM. Hewlett-Packard (HP) coined a phrase that has come to be known as 'MBWA' – Management By Wandering Around'. This is a behaviour standard at HP. The rationale for it is clearly described in 'The HP Way':

To have a well managed operation it is essential that managers/superiors be aware of what is happening in their areas – not just at their immediate level, but also at several levels below that. Our people are our most important resource and the managers have direct responsibility for their training, their performance, and for their well-being. To do this, managers must get around to find out how their people feel about their jobs and what they feel will make their work more productive and more worthwhile.

HP's strategy is to focus on high value niches in the industrial electronics market and to gain advantage through innovation. Their strategy depends on attracting quality people and encouraging them to contribute to the organization.

Linking with the HP strategy is a value of supportiveness based on a belief that all employees will be doing their best. MBWA acts as a beacon both of the strategy of innovation and of the value of supportiveness. HP have found that managers who wander around are more likely to be supportive and encourage innovation. By insisting on MBWA, HP is helping to implement the mission.

IBM is famous for its open door policy. Thomas Watson Jr, in *A Business and its Beliefs*, describes this behaviour standard that encourages employees to appeal directly to a higher authority when they are dissatisfied: 'The Open Door grew out of T. J. Watson's close and frequent association with individuals in the plant and field offices. It became a natural thing for them to bring their problems to him and in time was established as a regular procedure.' The open door is now a deeply held belief in IBM. Managers feel that their doors should be open both physically and metaphorically to any employee wishing to talk to them.

The open door is a beacon of IBM's strategy and values. It reinforces IBM's value of respect for the individual. It also links to strategy. Like HP, IBM needs to attract high quality people to execute its service-led strategy. High quality people prefer a working environment where their concerns and contributions can be freely voiced. The open door policy is a demonstration of IBM's commitment to an open working environment.

IBM and HP have made their missions easier to manage by identifying these behaviour standards. Because the behaviours are explicit they can be referred to in training, they can be used in assessment discussions and promotion decisions, and managers who ignore them can be officially reprimanded.

2 Are the behaviour standards described in a way that enables individual employees to judge whether they have behaved correctly or not?

Where behaviour standards are included in a mission statement they are frequently too vague to be useful. A typical statement might read: 'Ensure rapid response to meet customers' needs.' It is hard for employees to know whether their actions are complying with this standard or not. The real benefit of a behaviour standard is that it gives clear guidance for behaviour.

The suggested standard for Sainsbury in the previous section is clear.

IBM's open door policy, when included with the explanation of what it means, is also clear and measurable. Even HP's intentionally vague standard of 'Management By Wandering Around', when it is explained in 'The HP way', meets the test of being able to judge correct behaviour. To reinforce this point, it is only necessary to consider the ten commandments in the Bible. Each of these is clear about the difference between good and bad behaviour.

One mission statement we collected provides a particularly good example of how to work from a broad statement of values to a clear statement of the behaviour standards. BUPA is the largest private health insurance company in Britain. It also runs hospitals and a number of other activities. The Health Insurance Division of BUPA identified 'caring' as one of its most important values. As might be expected, this value links well with BUPA's strategy of being the service leader. It is also an attractive value for the type of person that BUPA would like to have working for it.

The issue is about how to translate the service strategy and the caring value into behaviour standards. BUPA's solution was to set about defining what caring means at BUPA. The definitions they came up with are neither brilliantly insightful, nor do they score particularly highly against our criteria. But they illustrate the process of searching for behaviour standards that meet the two criteria in this section – that they should be beacons of strategy and values, and clear about good and bad behaviour.

Part of BUPA's mission statement reads:

Caring means: – delivering to the customer more than we promise
recognizing the contribution of each member of staff
treating all our suppliers as we would wish them to treat us
paying attention to the needs of the whole community.

BUPA's kind of caring is not an 'all you need is love' type of caring. It is a more commercially based kind of caring that links back to the company's purpose and its responsibility to its stakeholders.

Character

Our final advice to the writer of a mission statement is to make it readable. The examples we have collected vary from a straight talking, thumbnail sketch written by the chairman over a weekend to smooth, jargon filled, advertising copy prepared for the annual general meeting by communication consultants. We have examples of mission statements that contain as few as 200 words and others that amount to books of more than 10 000 words.

Two questions will help writers assess their work:

1 Does the statement give a portrait to the company capturing the culture of the organization?

We do not advise writers to construct their mission statements around the four sections we have defined as important – purpose, strategy, values and behaviour standards. In preparing to write the statement each of these areas needs to be considered, but the statement itself should be designed to fit the company style.

The statement is a work of art that should capture the essence of the company in its size, format and wording. If the company is a non-nonsense, frugal, cost-driven organization based in Yorkshire, then the mission statement should be a few gruff words on one side of one piece of paper, photocopied rather than printed. BBA's mission statement is an excellent example. Photocopied, neatly typed, on one page, the document 'BBA – A Corporate Philosophy' begins:

The inertia of history is a powerful influence on corporate philosophy. BBA in its 103 years of experience has strayed little from

- Yorkshire paternalism
- weaving of heavy textiles
- friction technology via woven pressed resin media.

The philosophy of BBA for the next few years will be to adapt rather than abandon the insert.

The rest of the document is divided into five headings – Management, Markets, Money, Monday and Maybe. Each section consists of five to 10 terse sentences such as, 'The long run belongs to Oscar Wilde, who is dead'; 'The cheapest producer will win'; 'Avoid the belief that dealing is preferable to working'; 'Three years, in the current environment, is the limit of man's comprehension of what may be'; 'Go home tired'.

It is clearly a document written by the chief executive, John Whyte, containing important messages for the people in BBA. In presentation, in style, in the language it uses and in its content, the statement captures BBA. It does not attempt to separate purpose, strategy, values and behaviour standards. They are all bound up together in phrases that touch on the most important issues in BBA.

For example, under Money, the statement says, 'Budgets are personal commitments made by management to their superiors, subordinates, shareholders and their self respect.' On the face of it this sentence is a behaviour standard – managers must meet budget. But it is also a value statement – in BBA we believe in doing what we say we are going to do; we believe in living up to our promises. And the statement also describes some of the detail of BBA's strategy – to manage its diverse business in a decentralized structure controlled through demanding profit targets.

Another example of a mission statement that fits the organization is 'The HP Way'. It is a well written, well published document on three pages. There are no glossy photographs or other communication props. It is just a well presented document with good copy. It reflects the serious and no-nonsense nature of the HP culture. Many of the phrases have been crafted by Bill Hewlett or David Packard and are, therefore, well worn within the company. One page is devoted to HP's two central behaviour standards – 'Management by Wandering Around and the Open Door Policy'; one page addresses four 'business related' objectives such as 'Pay As You Go – No Long Term Borrowing'; and the third page addresses 'people related' issues such as 'Emphasis on Working Together and Sharing Rewards (Teamwork and Partnership)'.

Like BBA the purpose, strategy, values and behaviour standards at HP are interwoven throughout the document. As a whole it answers all the questions, and it does so in a way that speaks to HP people. They can read it and smile to themselves and say 'Yep, that is my company.'

Yet many companies want to develop a neat, one page summary of their mission that can be framed and hung on the wall, enclosed in wallet sized plastic folders or etched into the cover of the company's annual report. We counsel against producing these summaries. First, the real mission statement should be regarded as a work of art, and management should realize that a cut down sketch will not have the same impact. If management want to tell shareholders or customers about the mission they should be prepared to give them the whole document so that they get the whole message.

The second reason we are against shortened versions is because they normally become sanitized versions. The slang is removed; the sentences are polished by communications experts; and the final version reads like advertising copy. In this form the statement loses its essence and can become pious platitudes.

2 Is the statement easy to read?

Many writers of missions believe that the statement should be short enough and important enough to be memorized. 'If you can't remember it, it can't be worth the paper it's written on', is a common piece of advice. The argument is that the mission should be a kind of corporate creed that can be intoned repeatedly as a form of management character building.

Our view is quite different. Some of the best mission statements are much too long to remember. IBM's mission statement is best described in Watson's book *A Business and its Beliefs*. Brevity is not essential. But easy reading is essential. Whether the statement is 200 words or 20 000, it must be a good read. The 200-word statement will include some day to day company slang to bring it alive and it will touch on some behaviours that managers would naturally describe when talking about the company.

The 20 000-word statement will include anecdotes and stories, particularly ones that the chairman or the founder used to tell. It will describe major decisions and turning points in the recent past, explaining how they have moved the company closer to its mission. It will read like a conversation with the founder.

Table 7.1 *Do you have a good mission statement?*

Answer each question	*0 = No*	*1 = To some degree*	*2 = Yes*

1 The purpose

a Does the statement describe an inspiring purpose that avoids playing to the selfish interests of the stakeholders – shareholders, customers, employees, suppliers?   0   1   2

b Does the statement describe the company's responsibility to its stakeholders?   0   1   2

2 Strategy

a Does the statement define a business domain explaining why it is attractive?   0   1   2

b Does the statement describe the strategic positioning that the company prefers in a way that helps to identify the sort of competitive advantage it will look for?   0   1   2

3 Values

a Does the statement identify values that link with the organization's purpose and act as beliefs that employees can feel proud of ?   0   1   2

b Do the values 'resonate' with and reinforce the organization's strategy?   0   1   2

4 Behaviour standards

a Does the statement describe important behaviour standards that serve as beacons of the strategy and the values?   0   1   2

b Are the behaviour standards described in a way that enables individual employees to judge whether they have behaved correctly or not?   0   1   2

5 Character

a Does the statement give a portrait to the company capturing the culture of the organization?   0   1   2

b Is the statement easy to read?   0   1   2

Maximum score 20; good score 15; poor score less than 10

Bibliography

Abegglen, James C. and Stalk, George Jr (1985). *Kaisha: The Japanese Corporation*. New York: Basic Books Inc.

Abell, D. F. (1980). *Defining the Business: The Starting Point for Strategic Planning*. Englewood Cliffs, NJ: Prentice-Hall.

Ackerman, Robert W. (1975). *The Social Challenge to Business*. Cambridge, Mass: Harvard University Press.

Ackerman, Laurence D. (1984). 'The Psychology of Corporation: How Identity Influences Business'. *Journal of Business Strategy*, vol. 5, no. 1, Summer, pp. 56–65.

Ackoff, Russel L. (1986). *Management in Small Doses*. New York: John Wiley & Sons.

Adler, Patricia A. and Adler, Peter (1988). 'Intense Loyalty in Organizations: A Case Study of College Athletics'. *Administrative Science Quarterly*, 33, pp. 401–17.

Alexis, M. and Wilson, C. (1967). *Organizational Decision Making*. Englewood Cliffs, NJ: Prentice-Hall.

Andersen, Dan (1987). 'Vision Management', *European Management Journal*, vol. 5, no. 1, pp. 24–8.

Andrews, Kenneth R. (1980). *The Concept of Corporate Strategy*, Homewood, Ill: Irwin.

Andrews, Kenneth R. (1989). 'Ethics in Practice'. *Harvard Business Review*, September–October, pp. 99–104.

Andrews, R. R. (1971). *The Concept of Corporate Strategy*. Dow Jones-Irwin.

Ansoff, Igor (1979). *Strategic Management*. Macmillan.

Argyris, C. (1964). *Integrating the Individual and the Organisation*. Wiley.

Arrow, Kenneth, J. (1974). *The Limits of Organization*. New York: Norton.

Badaracco, Joseph L. and Ellsworth, Richard R. (1989). *Leadership and the Quest for Integrity*. Boston, Mass: Harvard Business School Press.

Barley, Stephen R., Meyer, Gordon W. and Gash, Debra G. (1988). 'Cultures of Culture: Academics, Practitioners and the Pragmatics of Normative Control'. *Administrative Science Quarterly*, 33, pp. 24–60.

Barnard, Chester L. (1938). *The Functions of the Executive*. Cambridge, Mass: Harvard University Press.

Barry, Vincent (1979). *Moral Issues in Business*. Belmont, California: Wadsworth.

Beauchamp, Thomas (1983). *Case Studies in Business, Society and Ethics*. Englewood Cliffs, NJ: Prentice-Hall.

Beauchamp, Thomas and Bowie, Norman (1983). *Ethical Theory and Business*. Englewood Cliffs, NJ: Prentice-Hall.

Beer, Michael (1988). 'The Critical Path for Change: Keys to Success and Failure in Six Companies'. In *Corporate Transformation*, Jossey-Bass.

Behrman, Jack (1981). *Discourses on Ethics and Business*. Cambridge, Mass: Oelgeschlager, Gunn and Hain.

Bell, Daniel (1976). *The Cultural Contradictions of Capitalism*. New York: Basic Books.

Bennis, Warren and Nanus, Burt (1985). *Leaders: The Strategies for Taking Charge*. New York: Harper & Row.

Berger, Peter (1976). *Pyramids of Sacrifice*. Garden City, NY: Doubleday.

Bettinger, Cass (1985). 'Behind the mission statement'. *ABA Banking Journal*, vol. 77, no. 10, October, pp. 154–60.

Bettinger, Cass (1989). 'Use Corporate Culture to Trigger High Performance'. *The Journal of Business Strategy*, March/April, pp. 38–42.

Bettman, Ralph B. (1989). 'Manage the Change Reaction'. *Personnel Journal*, November, pp. 60–7.

Bok, Sissela (1978). *Lying: Moral Choice in Public and Private Life*. New York: Pantheon.

Boulding, Kenneth (1968). *Beyond Economics*. Ann Arbor, Michigan: University of Michigan Press.

Bower, Joseph (1972). *Managing the Resource Allocation Process*. Irwin.

Bowie, Norman (1982). *Business Ethics*. Englewood Cliffs, NJ: Prentice-Hall.

Bradley, P. and Baird, P. (1983). *Communication for Business and the Professions*. Dubuqy, Iowa: Wm C Brown Co.

Bradshaw, Thornton and Vogel, David (1981). *Corporations and their Critics*. New York: McGraw Hill.

Braybrooke, David (1983). *Ethics in the World of Business*. Rowman & Allanhead.

Brown, Lester R. (1972). *World without Borders*. New York: Random House.

Brozen, Y., Johnson, E. and Powers, C. (1978). *Can the Market Sustain an Ethic?*. Chicago, Ill: University of Chicago Press.

Bumstead, Dennis and Eckblad, John (1984). 'Developing organisational cultures'. *Leadership and Organisation Development Journal*. 5 no. 4.

Byars, Lloyd L. and Neil, Thomas C. (1987). 'Organizational Philosophy and Mission Statements'. *Planning Review*, July/August, pp. 32–5.

Campbell, Andrew, Devine, Marion and Young, David (1990). *A Sense of Mission*. Economist/Hutchinson.

Campbell, Andrew and Yeung, Sally (1990). *Do You Have a Mission Statement?* Economist Publications.

Carlsson, Jan (1987). *Moments of Truth*. Ballinger.

Carr, Albert (1968). 'Is Business Bluffing Ethical?'. *Harvard Business Review*, January/February.

Carroll, Archie B. (1977). *Managing Corporate Social Responsibility*. Boston, Mass: Little, Brown.

Carroll A. and Hoy, F. (1984). 'Integrating Corporate Social Policy into Strategic Management'. *Journal of Business Strategy*, Winter.

Chandler, Alfred D. (1962). *Strategy and Structure*. MIT Press.

Chandler, Alfred D. (1977). *The Visible Hand: The Managerial Revolution in American Business*. Cambridge, Mass: Harvard University Press.

Chapman, Elwood (1981). *Scrambling: Zig-Zagging Your Way to the Top*. Los Angeles, California: Tarcher.

Chewning, Richard C. (1984). *Business in a Changing Culture*. Reston, Va: Reston Publishing Company.

Chrisman, J. J. and Carroll, A. B. (1984). 'Corporate Responsibility: Reconciling Economic and Social Goals'. *Sloan Management Review*, Winter.

Ciulla, Joanne B. (1986). 'Note on the Corporation as a Moral Environment'. Harvard Business School Case No. 9-386-012, 3/86.

Clifford, D. and Cavanagh, R. (1985). *The Winning Performance: How America's High-Growth Midsize Companies Succeed*. Sidgwick & Jackson.

Clinard, M. and Yeager, P. (1980). *Corporate Crime*. New York: Free Press.

Collins, James C. and Porras, Jerry I. (1989). 'Making Impossible Dreams Come True'. *Stanford Business School Magazine*, July, pp. 12–19.

Commoner, Barry (1976). *The Poverty of Power*. New York: Knopf.

Cotter, John (1983). *Designing Organizations that Work: An Open Sociotechnical Systems Perspective*. John J. Cotter & Associates Inc.

Cyert, Richard M. and March, James G. (1963). *A Behavioral Theory of the Firm*. Englewood Cliffs, NJ: Prentice-Hall, Inc.

David, Fred R. (1987). *Concepts of Strategic Management*. Merrill.

David F. R., Cochran, D. and Gibson, K. (1985). 'A Framework for Developing an Effective Mission Statement'. *Journal of Business Strategy*, 2, no. 2, Fall.

David, F. R., Cochran, D., Pearce II, J. A. and Gibson, K. (1985). 'An Empirical Investigation of Mission Statements'. *Southern Management Association Proceedings*.

David, Keith, Frederick, William and Blomstrom, Robert (1980). *Business and Society: Concepts and Policy Issues*. New York: McGraw-Hill.

Deal T. and Kennedy, A. (1982). *Corporate Cultures*. Reading, Mass: Addison-Wesley.

DeGeorge, Richard (1982). *Business Ethics*. New York: Macmillan.

DeGeorge, R. T. and Pichler, J. A. (1978). *Ethics, Free Enterprise and Public Policy*. Oxford University Press.

Demb, Ada, Chouet, Danielle, Lossius, Tom and Neubauer, Fred (1989). 'Defining the Role of the Board'. *Long Range Planning*, vol. 22, no. 1, pp. 61–8.

Desjardins, J. and McCall, J. (1984). *Contemporary Issues in Business Ethics*. Belmont, Calif: Wadsworth.

Diamond, Michael A. (1988). 'Organizational Identity: A Psychoanalytical Exploration of Organizational Meaning'. *Administration & Society*, vol. 20, no. 2, August, pp. 166–90.

Donaldson, Gordon and Lorsch, Jay (1983). *Decision Making at the Top*. New York: Basic Books.

Donaldson, Thomas (1982). *Corporations and Morality*. Englewood-Cliffs, NJ: Prentice-Hall.

Donaldson, Thomas (1984). *Case Studies in Business Ethics*. Englewood Cliffs, NJ: Prentice-Hall.

Donnelly, R. M. (1984). 'The Interrelationship of Planning with Corporate Culture in the Creation of Shared Values'. *Managerial Planning*, 32, May/June. pp. 8–12.

Drucker, Peter F. (1968). *The Age of Discontinuity*. New York: Harper.

Drucker, Peter F. (1969). 'Management's new role'. *Harvard Business Review*, November–December.

Drucker, Peter F. (1973). *Management: Tasks, Responsibilities, Practices*. Heinemann.

Dyke, C. (1981). *Philosophy of Economics*. Englewood Cliffs, NJ: Prentice-Hall.

Ellul, Jacques (1964). *The Technological Society*. New York: Random House.

Epstein, Edwin M. (1989). 'Business Ethics, Corporate Good Citizenship and the Corporate Social Policy Process: A View from the United States'. *Journal of Business Ethics*, 8, pp. 583–95.

Estes, Ralph (1976). *Corporate Social Accounting*. New York: Wiley.

Etzioni, A. and Lehman, E. W. (1961). *A Sociological Reader on Complex Organizations*. Holt, Rinehart & Winston.

Evans, William A. (1981). *Management Ethics: An Intercultural Perspective*. Martinus Nijhoff.

Ewen, Stuart (1976). *Captains of Consciousness: Advertising and the Social Roots of the Consumer Culture*. New York: McGraw-Hill.

Ewing, David (1976). *Freedom inside the Organization: Bringing Civil Liberties to the Workplace*. New York: Dutton.

Ewing, David (1983). *Do it My Way or You're Fired!*. New York: Wiley.

Fisher, Kim (1989). 'Managing in the High-Commitment Workplace'. *Organizational Dynamics*, vol. 17, no. 3, Winter, pp. 31–50.

Freeman, Edward and Gilbert, Daniel (1988). *Corporate Strategy and the Search for Ethics*. Englewood Cliffs, NJ: Prentice-Hall.

French, Peter A. (1979). 'The Corporation as a Moral Person'. *American Philosophical Quarterly*, 3, pp. 207–15.

Friedman, Milton (1962). *Capitalism and Freedom*. Chicago, Ill: University of Chicago Press.

Frohman, Mark and Pascarella, Perry (1986). 'Creating the Purposeful Organization'. *Industry Week*, 9 June, pp. 44–5.

Frohman, Mark and Pascarella, Perry (1987). 'How to write a purpose statement'. *Industry Week*, 23 March, pp. 31–4.

Garrett, Thomas M. et al (1963). *Cases in Business Ethics*. Des Moines, Iowa: Meredith.

Garrett, Thomas M. (1966). *Business Ethics*. Englewood Cliffs, NJ: Prentice-Hall.

Glisson, Charles and Durick, Mark (1988). 'Predictors of Job Satisfaction and Organizational Commitment in Human Service Organizations'. *Administrative Quarterly*, 33, pp. 61–81.

Goddard, Robert W. (1988). 'Are you an ethical manager?'. *Personnel Journal*, March, pp. 38–47.

Goldsmith, W. and Clutterbuck, D. (1985). *The Winning Streak*. Penguin.

Goodpaster, Kenneth E. (1982). 'Some Avenues for Ethical Analysis in General Management'. Harvard Business School Case No. 383–007.

Goodpaster, Kenneth E. (1983). 'The Concept of Corporate Responsibility'. *Journal of Business Ethics*, 2, pp. 1–22.

Goodpaster, Kenneth, E. (1983). 'Should Sponsors Screen for Moral Values'. The Hastings Center Report, December.

Goodpaster, Kenneth E. (1984). 'Ethics in Management'. Harvard Business School Case No. 9-985-001.

Goodpaster, Kenneth E. (1986). 'The Moral Agenda of Corporate Leadership: Concepts & Research Techniques'. Paper for D. S. MacNaughton Symposium Proceedings.

Goodpaster, Kenneth E. (1988). 'Ethical Imperatives and Corporate Leadership'. Ruffin Lecture in Business Ethics, April.

Goodpaster, Kenneth E. and Matthews, John B. Jr (1982). 'Can a corporation have a conscience?'. *Harvard Business Review*, January–February, pp. 132–41.

Goodpaster, Kenneth E. and Sayre, K. (1979). *Ethics and Problems of the 21st Century*. Notre Dame, Ind: University of Notre Dame Press.

Goold, Michael and Campbell, Andrew (1987). *Strategies and Styles: The Role of the Centre in Managing Diversified Corporations*. Oxford: Basil Blackwell.

Goold, Michael with Quinn, John J. (1990). *Strategic Control: Milestones for Long Term Performance*. Economist/Hutchinson.

Gould, R. (1970). *The Matsushita Phenomenon*. Tokyo: Diamond Sha.

Guth, William D. and Tagiuri, Renato (1965). 'Personal Values and Corporate Strategy'. *Harvard Business Review*, Sept–Oct, pp. 123–32.

Hahn, Frank and Hollis, Martin (eds) (1979). *Philosophy and Economic Theory*. Oxford University Press.

Hamel, Gary and Pralahad, C. K. (1989). 'Strategic Intent'. *Harvard Business Review*, May–June.

Hampshire, S. (1978). *Public and Private Morality*. Cambridge University Press.

Handy, Charles B. (1979). *The Gods of Management*. Pan.

Handy, Charles B. (1986). *Understanding Organizations*. Penguin.

Harrison, Roger (1987). 'Harnessing Personal Energy: How Companies Can Inspire Employees'. *Organizational Dynamics*, vol. 16, no. 2, Autumn, pp. 5–20.

Heilbroner, Robert L. (1967) *The Worldly Philosophers*. New York: Simon & Schuster.

Heilbroner, Robert L. (1976). *Business Civilization in Decline*. New York: Norton.

Herzberg, Frederick (1966). *Work and the Nature of Man*. World Publishing Co.

Herzberg, Frederick (1968). 'One more time: How do you motivate employees?'. *Harvard Business Review*, January–February.

Herzberg, Frederick (1985). 'Where is the Passion . . . and the Other Elements of Innovation?'. *Industry Week*, 11 November, pp. 37–43.

Hessen, Robert (1979). *In Defense of the Corporation*. Stanford, Calif: Hoover Institution Press.

Hoffman, W. Michael and Moore, Jennifer (1983). *Business Ethics: Readings and Cases in Corporate Morality*. New York: McGraw-Hill.

Hoffman, W. Michael, Moore, Jennifer and Fedo, David (1984). *Corporate Governance and Institutionalizing Ethics*. Lexington, Mass: Lexington.

Hunt, John W. (1972). *The Restless Organisation*. Wiley.

Hunt, John W. (1981). *Managing People at Work: A Manager's Guide to Behaviour in Organizations*. McGraw-Hill.

Hunter, Jairy C. (1985). 'Managers must know the mission: "If it ain't broke don't fix it"'. *Managerial Planning*, January/February, pp. 18–22.

Jones, D. (ed) (1982). *Business, Religion and Ethics*. Cambridge, Mass: Oelgeschlager, Gunn and Hain.

Jones, D. (ed) (1982). *Doing Ethics in Business*. Cambridge, Mass: Oelgeschlager, Gunn and Hain.

Kanter, R. M. (1972). *Commitment & Community*. Harvard University Press.

Kobayashi S. (1971). *Creative Management*. American Management Association Inc.

Kotter, J. F. (1988). *The Leadership Factor*. The Free Press.

Kotter, John P. and Schlesinger, Leonard A. (1979). 'Choosing Strategies for Change'. *Harvard Business Review*, March–April.

Lawler, Edward E. (1986). *High Involvement Management: Participative Strategies for Improving Organizational Performance*. Jossey-Bass.

Lawrence, P. R. and Lorsch, J. W. (1967). *Organization and Environment.* Irwin.

Leavitt, Harold J. (1978). *Management Psychology.* University of Chicago Press.

Leavitt, Harold J. (1986). *Corporate Pathfinders: Building Vision and Values into Organizations.* Homewood, Illinois: Dow Jones-Irwin.

Lemaitre, Nadine (1984). *In Search of Belgian Excellence.* Brussels: Université Libre de Bruxelles.

Levering, Robert (1988). *A Great Place to Work.* New York: Random House.

Levinson, Harry (1971). *The Exceptional Executive.* Cambridge, Mass: Harvard University Press.

Levitt, T. (1960). 'Marketing Myopia'. *Harvard Business Review,* July–August, pp. 45–56.

Liedtka, Jeanne M. (1989). 'Value Congruence: The Interplay of Individual and Organizational Value Systems'. *Journal of Business Ethics,* 8, pp. 805–15.

Likert, Rensis (1967). *The Human Organization: Its Management and Value.* McGraw-Hill.

Litschert R. and Nicholson E. (1977). *The Corporate Role and Ethical Behavior: Concepts and Cases.* New York: Van Nostrand.

Lorsch, Jay (1986). 'Managing Culture: The Invisible Barrier to Strategy'. *California Management Review,* Winter.

Lundberg, Craig C. (1984). 'Zero-in: A Technique for Formulating Better Mission Statements'. *Business Horizons,* September–October, pp. 30–3.

Luthans, Fred, Hodgetts, Richard and Thompson, Kenneth (1976). *Social Issues in Business.* New York: Macmillan.

Lyons, N. (1976). *The Sony Vision.* New York: Crown Publishers Inc.

Maccoby, Michael (1981). *The Leader.* New York: Simon & Schuster.

McGinnis, Vern J. (1981). 'The Mission Statement: A Key Step in Strategic Planning'. *Business,* November–December, pp. 39–43.

McGregor, Douglas (1960). *The Human Side of Enterprise.* McGraw-Hill.

McKay, Gilly and Locke, Alison (1986). *The Body Shop: Franchising a Philosophy.* Penguin.

Mackie, K. A. (1983). 'Managing Change: How Dayton Hudson Meets the Challenge'. *Journal of Business Strategy,* 4, Summer, pp. 78–81.

McLelland, D. (1979). *Power: The Inner Experience.* Irvington.

March, J. G. and Simon, H. A. (1968). *Organizations.* Wiley.

Maslow, Abraham H. (1970). *Motivation and Personality.* New York: Harper & Row.

Matsushita, Konosuke (1984). *Not for Bread Alone: A Business Ethos, A Management Ethic.* Tokyo: PHP Institute Inc.

Matsushita, Konosuke (1989). *As I See It.* Tokyo: PHP Institute Inc.

Miles, Robert (1982). *Coffin Nails and Corporate Strategies.* Englewood Cliffs, NJ: Prentice-Hall.

Miller, Paul (1989). 'Managing corporate identity in the diversified business'. *Personnel Management,* March, pp. 36–9.

Milter, Danny and Friesen, Peter (1984). *Organizations*. Prentice-Hall.

Mintzberg, Henry (1979). *The Structuring of Organizations: A Synthesis of Research*. Prentice-Hall.

Mintzberg, Henry (1983). *Power in and Around Organizations*. Prentice-Hall.

Mishima, Kasuo (1988). *Corporate Identity Programs in Japan*. Unpublished doctoral thesis.

Missner, Marshall (1980). *Ethics of the Business System*. Sherman Oaks, Calif: Alfred.

Molander, Earl A. (1980). *Responsive Capitalism*. New York: McGraw-Hill.

Morita, Akio (1986). *Made in Japan*. New York: E. P. Dutton.

Naisbitt, John and Abundene, Patricia (1985). *Re-inventing the Corporation*. Warner Books.

Novak, Michael (1978). *The American Vision*. Washington, DC: American Enterprise Institute.

Novak, Michael (1982). *The Spirit of Democratic Capitalism*. New York: Simon & Schuster.

Ogbonna, Emmanuel and Wilkinon, Barry (1988). 'Corporate Strategy and Corporate Culture: The Management of Change in the UK Supermarket Industry'. *Personnel Review*, 17, 6, pp. 10–14.

Ohmann, O. A. (1970). 'Skyhooks'. *Harvard Business Review*, January–February.

O'Reilly, Charles (1989). 'Corporations, Culture and Commitment: Motivation and Social Control in Organisations'. *California Management Review*, Summer, pp. 9–25.

Ouchi, W. (1981). *Theory Z: How American Business can meet the Japanese Challenge*. Reading, Mass: Addison Wesley.

Partridge, Scott (1982). *Cases in Business and Society*. Englewood Cliffs, NJ: Prentice-Hall.

Pascale, R. and Athos, A. (1981). *The Art of Japanese Management*. New York: Simon & Schuster.

Pascarella, Perry (1986). 'Is your mission clear?'. *Industry Week*, 13 October, p. 65.

Pearce, John A. II (1982). 'The company mission as a strategic tool'. *Sloan Management Review*, Spring, pp. 15–24.

Pearce, John A. II and David, Fred (1987). 'Corporate Mission Statements: The Bottom Line'. *Academy of Management EXECUTIVE*, vol. 1, no. 2, pp. 109–16.

Pearce, John A. II and Robinson, Richard B. Jr (1985). *Strategic Management: Strategy Formulation and Implementation*. Homewood, Ill: Richard D. Irwin.

Pearce, John A. II and Roth, K. (1986). 'Multinationalization of the Company Mission'. *Sloan Management Review*.

Peters, Tom and Austin, Nancy (1985). *A Passion for Excellence*. New York: Random House.

Peters, Thomas J. and Waterman, Robert H. (1982). *In Search of Excellence: Lessons from America's Best Run Companies*. New York: Harper & Row.

Pettigrew, Andrew (1985). *The Awakening Giant: Continuity and Change in ICI*. Oxford: Basil Blackwell.

Phillips, J. and Kennedy, A. (1980). 'Shaping and managing shared values'. *McKinsey Staff Paper*, December.

Plant, Roger (1987). *Managing Change and Making It Stick*. Fontana.

Porter, Michael (1987). 'From competitive advantage to corporate strategy'. *Harvard Business Review*, May–June, pp. 43–59.

Posner, Barry Z., Kouzes, James M. and Schmidt, Warren H. (1985). 'Shared Values Makes a Difference: An Empirical Test of Corporate Culture'. *Human Resource Management*, Fall, vol. 24, no. 3, pp. 293–309.

Regan, Tom (ed) (1984). *Just Business: New Introductory Essays in Business Ethics*. New York: Random House.

Regan, Tom and VanDeVeer, Donald (eds) (1982). *And Justice for All*. Totowa, NJ: Roman and Littlefield.

Rehder, Robert, Smith, Marta and Burr, Katherine (1989). 'A Salute to the Sun: Crosscultural Organisational Adaptation and Change'. *Leadership & Organization Development Journal*, vol. 10, no. 4, pp. 17–27.

Robson, Mike (1986). *The Journey to Excellence*. Wiley.

Roche, William J. and MacKinnon, Neil L. (1970). 'Motivating people with meaningful work'. *Harvard Business Review*, May–June.

Rodgers, Buck (1986). *The IBM Way*. Perennial Library.

Sayre, K. M. (1977). *Values in the Electric Power Industry*. Notre Dame, Ind: University of Notre Dame Press.

Schein, Edgar H. (1980). *Organizational Psychology*. Englewood Cliffs, NJ: Prentice-Hall.

Schlegelmilch, B. B. and Houston, J. E. (1988). 'Corporate Codes of Ethics in Large UK Companies: An Empirical Investigation of Use, Content and Attitudes', Working Paper Series 88/16, Department of Business Studies, University of Edinburgh.

Schnyder, Klaus (1986). 'Ethical Values in Company Policy'. Paper for Pontifical Council for the Laity, Washington, 28 September.

Schumacher, E. F. (1973). *Small is Beautiful*. London: Sphere Books.

Schumacher, E. F. (1979). *Good Work*. New York: Harper & Row.

Seidler, L. (1975). *Social Accounting: Theory, Issues and Cases*. Melville.

Selekman, Benjamin (1959). *A Moral Philosophy for Management*. New York: McGraw-Hill.

Selznick, Philip (1957). *Leadership in Administration: A Sociological Interpretation*. Berkeley, Calif: University of California Press.

Sethi, S. P. (1977). *Up Against the Corporate Wall*. Englewood Cliffs, NJ: Prentice-Hall.

Sethi, S. P. and Votaw, Dow (1973). *The Corporate Dilemma*. Englewood Cliffs, NJ: Prentice-Hall.

Sherwood, John (1988). 'Creating Work Cultures with Competitive Advantage'. *Organizational Dynamics*, Fall.

Shockley-Zalabak, Pamela and Morley, Donald Dean (1989). 'Adhering to Organizational Culture: What does it mean? Why does it matter?'. *Group & Organisation Studies*, vol. 14, no. 4, December, pp. 483–500.

Sieff, Marcus (1987). *Don't Ask the Price*. George Weidenfeld & Nicolson Ltd.

Simon, Herbert A. 'On the Concept of Organizational Goal'. *Administrative Science Quarterly*, vol. 9, pp. 1–22.

Simon, Herbert A. (1976). *Adminstrative Behavior*. New York: Macmillan.

Skinner, B. F. (1984). *Beyond Freedom & Dignity*. Bantam.

Sloan, Alfred (1963). *My Years with General Motors*. Doubleday.

Sober, Cyril (1972). *Organizations in Theory and Practice*. Heinemann.

Staples, W. A. and Black, K. U. (1984). 'Defining your business mission: A strategic perspective'. *Journal of Business Strategy*, Spring.

Steckmest, F. W. (1982). *Corporate Performance*. New York: McGraw-Hill.

Stewart, Rosemary (1963). *The Reality of Management*. Heinemann.

Tanaka (1988). *Personality in Industry*. London: Pinter Publishers.

Tregoe, B. and Zimmerman, J. (1980). *Top Management Strategy*. John Martin.

Tushman, Michael L., Newman, William H. and Nadler, David A. (1988). 'Executive Leadership and Organizational Evolution: Managing Incremental and Discontinuous Change'. In *Corporate Transformation*. Jossey-Bass.

Uttal, B. (1983). 'The corporate culture vultures'. *Fortune*, 17 October.

Walton, Clarence (1969). *Ethos and the Executive*. Englewood Cliffs, NJ: Prentice-Hall.

Walton, Clarence (1977). *The Ethics of Corporate Conduct*. Englewood Cliffs, NJ: Prentice-Hall.

Walton, Richard E. (1985). 'From Control to Commitment in the Workplace'. *Harvard Business Review*, March–April.

Wart, Jerome (1986). 'Corporate Mission: The Intangible Contributor to Performance'. *Management Review*, August.

Waterman, Robert (1988). *The Renewal Factor*. Bantam Press.

Watson, Thomas J. Jr (1963). *A Business and Its Beliefs: The Ideas that Helped Build IBM*. New York: McGraw-Hill.

Watts, Reginald (1977). *Public Relations for Top Management*. New Malden, Surrey: Croner Publications Ltd.

Weber, Max (1930). *The Protestant Ethic and the Spirit of Capitalism*. Allen & Unwin.

Webley, Simon (1988). *Company Philosophies and Codes of Business Ethics: A guide to their drafting and use*. London: Institute of Business Ethics.

Weiss, William L. (1986). 'Minerva's Owl: Building a Corporate Value System'. *Journal of Business Ethics*, vol. 5.

Weller, Steven (1988). 'The effectiveness of corporate codes of ethics'. *Journal of Business Ethics*, 7, pp. 389–95.

White, Bernard J. and Montgomery, B. Ruth (1980). 'Corporate Codes of

Conduct'. *California Management Review*, Winter, vol. XXIII, no. 2, pp. 80–7.

Wickers, P. (1987). *The Road to Nissan*. Macmillan.

Wilkins, Alan L. and Bristow, Nigel J. (1987). 'For Successful Organization Culture, Honor Your Past'. *Academy of Management EXECUTIVE*, vol. 1, no. 3, pp. 221–9.

Wille, Edgar (1989). 'Ethics at the Heart of Business – An Integrative Approach'. Ashridge Management Research Group, Paper for Second European Business Ethics Conference, Barcelona, Spain, September.

Williams, O. and Houck, J. (1978). *Full Value*. New York: Harper & Row.

Williams, Oliver and Houck, John (eds) (1982). *The Judeo-Christian Vision and the Modern Corporation*. Notre Dame, Ind: University of Notre Dame Press.

Wright, J. Patrick (1979). *On a Clear Day You Can See General Motors*. New York: Avon.

'The Dilemmas of Developing and Communicating Strategy' (1986). Harvard Business School Case No. 9–387–044.

'Institutional Leadership' (1986). Harvard Business School Case No. 9–385–108.

Index